Intermediality
in French-Language
Comics and Graphic Novels

Intermediality
in French-Language
Comics and Graphic Novels

EDITED BY

JAN BAETENS   **HUGO FREY**   **FABRICE LEROY**

2022
UNIVERSITY OF LOUISIANA AT LAFAYETTE PRESS

http://ulpress.org
University of Louisiana at Lafayette Press
P.O. Box 43558
Lafayette, LA 70504-3558

Printed on acid-free paper in the United States
Library of Congress Cataloging-in-Publication Data

Names: Baetens, Jan, editor. | Frey, Hugo, editor. | Leroy, Fabrice, editor.
Title: Intermediality in French-language comics and graphic novels / edited by Jan Baetens, Hugo Frey, Fabrice Leroy.
Description: Lafayette, LA : University of Louisiana at Lafayette Press, 2022. | Includes bibliographical references.
Identifiers: LCCN 2022011153 | ISBN 9781946160898 (paperback ; acid-free paper)
Subjects: LCSH: Comic books, strips, etc.--France--History and criticism. | Intermediality. | LCGFT: Literary criticism. | Essays.
Classification: LCC PN6745 .I58 2022 | DDC 741.5/944--dc23/eng/20220327
LC record available at https://lccn.loc.gov/2022011153

Cover illustration: excerpt of *Dolorès* by Anne Baltus, Benoît Peeters, and François Schuiten (Casterman, 1991, p. 23). Reprinted with kind permission from Éditions Casterman and the authors.

About the Editors

JAN BAETENS is professor of cultural studies at the University of Leuven, Belgium. His work focuses on the theory and practice of contemporary French poetry, cultural theory, and visual narrative in popular print genres (novelization, comics, photonovels, and film photonovels). Some of his recent publications include *The Graphic Novel* (Cambridge University Press, 2014, coauthored with Hugo Frey), *Novelization: From Film to Novel* (trans. Mary Feeney, Ohio State University Press, 2018), *The Cambridge History of the Graphic Novel* (Cambridge University Press, 2018, coedited with Hugo Frey and Stephen E. Tabachnick), *The Film Photonovel: A Cultural History of Forgotten Adaptations* (University of Texas Press, 2019), and *Rebuilding Storyworlds: On the Obscure Cities by Schuiten and Peeters* (Rutgers University Press, 2020). He is also a published poet (in French) and the author of several collections of poetry, some in collaboration with visual artists such as Olivier Deprez and Milan Chlumsky.

HUGO FREY is professor of cultural and visual history and director of Arts and Humanities at the University of Chichester, UK. He is the author of monographs on *Louis Malle* (MUP, 2004) and *Nationalism and the Cinema in France* (Berghahn, 2014). With Jan Baetens, he coauthored *The Graphic Novel: An Introduction* (Cambridge University Press, 2014), and coedited, with Jan Baetens and Stephen Tabachnick, *The Cambridge History of the Graphic Novel* (Cambridge University Press, 2018). His articles have been published in, among others, *Art History*, *South Central Review*, and *Yale French Studies*. In 2019, he was a co-recipient of a British Council grant to support an oral history of folk theatre in Vietnam.

FABRICE LEROY is professor of French and francophone studies at the University of Louisiana at Lafayette. He has published numerous book chapters on French and Belgian Francophone literature and graphic novels, as well as articles in leading scholarly journals (*Image & Narrative, European Comic Art, Revue des Sciences Humaines, Neuvième Art 2.0, Contemporary French and Francophone Studies/Sites, The International Journal of Comic Art*, among others). He recently contributed entries to Thierry Groensteen's *Le Bouquin de la bande dessinée: Dictionnaire esthétique et thématique* (Robert Laffont, 2020). His most recent monographs devoted to comics are *Sfar So Far. Identity, History, Fantasy, and Mimesis in Joann Sfar's Graphic Novels* (Leuven University Press, 2014), and *Pierre La Police: Une esthétique de la malfaçon* (with Livio Belloï, Serious Publishing, 2019).

Table of Contents

Part Four: Comics, Cultural Capital, and the Artistic Tradition

Part Five: Comics and Music

Editors' Acknowledgments

This edited volume grew out of a thematic issue of the *Études Francophones* journal (vol. 32, Spring 2020) devoted to the concept of "Bande dessinée et intermédialité." In addition to selected essays from this project, this book has been enriched by five new chapters from established comics scholars. The editors wish to thank all the individual contributors to this volume: Maaheen Ahmed, Renée Altergott, Jan Baetens, Livio Belloï, Michelle Bumatay, Erwin Dejasse, Hugo Frey, Maxence Leconte, Fabrice Leroy, Mark McKinney, Ana Oancea, Tamara Tasevska, Fred Truyen, and Charlotte F. Werbe.

Because research in the visual arts is highly dependent upon the ability to cite images, we are also indebted to the kind artists and their publishers (Casterman, Futuropolis, L'Association, Sarbacane, Des Bulles dans l'Océan, Syllepse, Dargaud, La "S" Grand Atelier, Éditions Tartamudo, Maisonneuve & Larose, and Soleil Productions), who have graciously authorized the reproduction of their works in this volume. We would also like to thank the museums and libraries, as well as the photographers, who gave us permission to reprint their images, including Mémorial de la Shoah, the University of Chicago Library, SABAM Belgium, Fotini Christia, Christiane Gruber, Reza Deghati, Trink Hall Museum, the Charlotte Salomon Foundation, coll. Nishiawaji Kibou-no-ye (Osaka), and Benoît Majerus. A special thank you to Anne Baltus, Benoît Peeters, and François Schuiten for allowing us to use an illustration from their graphic novel *Dolores* on our front cover.

The editors would like to express their gratitude to several people at the University of Louisiana at Lafayette for their support and assistance: Jordan Kellman (Liberal Arts), Monica Wright (Modern Languages), Sarah Smith (Modern Languages), who helped format some of the chapters, and Shelly Miller Leroy (English), who assisted in copyediting the manuscript and reviewing the translations from French to English. Many thanks also to Devon Lord, Joshua Caffery, Mary Karnath Duhé, and the staff of UL Press. Support for this research project was provided by the Board of Regents Support Fund of the State of Louisiana.

Comics and Intermediality: An Introduction

Jan Baetens, Hugo Frey, and Fabrice Leroy

If one accepts, as we do, that comics, in the most general sense of the word, is not a *genre*—for a long time seen as a "paraliterary" one and recently upgraded to "literary" status, thanks to the success of the graphic novel—but a cultural form or *medium*, that is a conventionally articulated use of a certain channel, a certain type of signs, and a certain type of content (Baetens and Frey 2014, 1–23; Labarre 2020, 17–28), the very notion of intermediality in comics is as much a *stereotype* as a *problem*.

Intermediality is indeed accepted to be a key characteristic of comics, which combine (drawn) images and words (dialogues and thoughts, narrative captions, onomatopoeias, verbal signs as part of the fictional world, and paratextual information—even in the so-called "wordless" graphic novels, see Beronä 2008 and Postema 2018). However, this kind of intermediality does not refer to the merger of two separate, already existing media, as the prefix "inter" would imply in a concept such as "interdisciplinarity," or as one might expect to see it function in the specific case of the comics adaptation of a literary text, for instance. Yet this is precisely what the founder of modern comics, Rodolphe Töpffer (1799–1846), strongly rejected when emphasizing the unique and totally original character of what he called a new type of novel: "The drawings, without the text, would only have an obscure meaning; the text, without the drawings, would have no meaning at all" (qtd. in Groensteen 2014, 81; our translation). Instead, intermediality refers to the use of different signs or types of signs within a single medium. From that point of view, one easily understands why certain scholars tend to prefer other terms, such as hybridity, or poly- or multimodality (see for example Grennan 2017). Nevertheless, to the extent that "meaning is use," as Wittgenstein powerfully advocated, the usage of the concept of intermediality to study the combination of words and images (and in some cases even other sensory material, see Hague 2014) within comics is so widespread that it would be unwise to make a plea for terminological revisions at this point.

Willingly or not, comics scholars have to live with the concept of inter-mediality, which covers a wide range of meanings between *internal* intermedi-ality—the mix of signs either in the very formal aspects of the medium or in its perception as well as interpretation (Mitchell 2005)—and *external* inter-mediality—as demonstrated for example in the two practices of intertextual relationships (Rajewsky 2005) and adaptational or transmedia expansions (Baetens and Sánchez-Mesa 2015).

As shown by the landmark publication *Handbook of Intermediality* (Rippl 2015), comics studies are but a tiny part of the burgeoning field of intermedi-ality studies. Yet in spite of this relative marginality, comics studies have always played a pioneering role. Moreover, it is possible to distinguish in this body of work a certain number of general patterns that make comics studies a possi-ble model for intermediality research in other, related media. Intermediality in comics studies often manages to strike the right balance between theoretical speculation and case-study-based close reading, while at the same time keeping in mind the spatial as well as temporal diversity of the phenomena and mecha-nisms under scrutiny. On the one hand, comics studies generally acknowledge the analogies but also dissymmetry between its three major traditions (US com-ics, European *bande dessinée*, Japanese manga). On the other hand, they have also proven to be very open to discussing both the divergent origins and the historical transformations of the medium (Groensteen 2009; Smolderen 2014).

A general overview of the recent and ongoing research on comics and intermediality reveals a four-level structure that leads from the purely for-mal and material dimensions of the word and image elements (a), over the interpretation of their semantic (b) and enunciative as well as narrative (c) dimensions, to the reading of hybridity in comics in the wider mediascape of semiotically mixed cultural forms in print (d). In the following paragraphs, we will briefly sketch some general concepts and orientations on each of these levels, which in practice are of course always strongly intertwined.

The first level addresses the *semiotic materiality* of the signs and their actual place in the comics panels and pages. Verbal and visual signs are in-deed not completely different categories. Images can be the carrier of verbal and narrative meanings, and this is exactly how comics readers process them: both as purely visual items—that is, in the terminology of the Groupe Mu, as *plastic* signs (having a certain shape, occupying a certain position, obeying a certain rhythmic pattern) that escape lexical manifestation while being rele-vant for the meaning of the sign as a whole—and as visual items representing lexical and narrative items and values—that is as *iconic* signs (the visual counterpart of a lexical item). For the Groupe Mu, plastic and iconic signs do not belong to two different groups of visual signs; they are instead two aspects of the same visual sign (to the extent that each iconic sign necessarily relies on a plastic infrastructure, but not all plastic signs eventually translate into an iconic value, unless at a rather metaphorical level; this is what happens for instance when we give to a dripping on a Pollock canvas the meaning of "energy" or "spontaneity"). Conversely, textual units also function as visual data, regardless, at least partially, of their intrinsic linguistic meaning. Letters, typographical signs, words, lines, paragraphs, and page layouts are carriers of what Jean Gérard Lapacherie has called *grammatextual* or, if one prefers, verbo-visual elements (Lapacherie 1984; Harpold 2008). From a broader point of view, these possible exchanges between the verbal and the visual also take the form of various interactions between "telling" and "showing." In comics, telling is not only on the side of the text, whereas showing is not only on that of the image. Pictures tell stories too, and words are not only to be read but also to be seen.

The materiality of verbal and visual units is obviously linked with the use of a certain channel or host medium, which has changed a lot over time (a possible timeline of successive innovations would list: the pre-Töpfferian broadsheet, the album à la Töpffer, the magazine of the second half of the nineteenth century, the late-nineteenth-century newspaper, the comic book of the 1930s, the postwar European album, the 3D installation space since the late twentieth century, and finally today's computer or tablet screen). Each of these channel changes has had an impact on how to draw (words and images) as well as how to tell (with words as well as with images), although it would be a mistake to take a stance of technological determinism in this regard: Changes of the host medium or channel may indeed open new possibilities, among other elements of the medium mix, but they never automatically translate into real changes (see Baetens and Surdiacourt 2013).

The second level of the analysis is content-related and tackles the relationships between the information purveyed by the images and that of the words respectively. The leading principle of this approach is that the relationship between words and images should be equal (think of the abovementioned claim of Rodolphe Töpffer that neither the words nor the images can signify by themselves). Verbal and visual units are not supposed to illustrate each other, according to the logic of *anchorage* that Roland Barthes studied in a still influential essay on photographic captions ("The Photographic Message"), but to complement and mutually enrich each other, thus co-building a new meaning adhering to the logic of what Barthes, in the same article, called *relay*.

From a historical and theoretical point of view, the priority given to relay at the expense of anchorage is inspired by the fear of reducing the input of the image to a narrow and ancillary role of illustration, that is, of a merely decorative expansion of a previously existing text. In our culture, which, despite the visual shift, continues to give more cultural prestige to the text than to the image, there are good reasons for such an anxiety. After all, traditional comics are always first written and then drawn, often by artists who can only follow the precise instructions of the scriptwriter—exceptions notwithstanding, such as for instance the hybrid composition technique of Jack Kirby, whose work testifies to the simultaneous emergence of drawing and narrative (Hatfield 2011). In quite a few cases, the actual contribution of the image to the work is undoubtedly thin. Even a master of visual narrative such as Hergé has not always been capable of avoiding the structural downgrading of the image in certain instances. A good example of the unequal treatment of word and image can be found in the concluding section of *Land of Black Gold* (1972). Not only are the speech balloons on the last page of this album overwhelmingly present (they literally eat almost all the available space), but the role of the rare visual adjunctions is close to nonexistent.

In light of this fear, one also understands why so many graphic novelists are in favor of (almost) wordless works. The apparent absence of verbal items is thereby seen as both the proof and the assurance that it is possible to create a comic that protects the visual elements from any form of textual colonization. As shown by most works of Chris Ware, the explicit grammatextualization of captions and other linguistic elements can point in the same direction. And since great artists are always eager to accept major challenges, one should not be surprised to notice that Seth recently dared to publish a nearly 500-page long graphic novel (*Clyde Fans,* 2019) whose first hundred pages do exactly what "good" comics are kindly requested to avoid, namely telling a text-only story (and in this case perhaps even a kind of non-story by a non-hero) with apparently very little support or input from the visual part of the graphic novel. (Further reading of the work will help understand however the perfect relevance of the seemingly poor visual setting and background of the story).

The third level of intermediality studies is that of storytelling. For many years, at least in the francophone tradition, there has been a strong emphasis on this kind of comics analysis, often directly related to the long-standing success of classic French narratology, with a "translation" of Genette and Todorov in comics studies by authors such as Fresnault-Deruelle (see the anthology of French theoretical studies compiled by Miller and Beaty, 2014). In the Anglo-Saxon field, the interest in stories and storytelling appears in the slipstream of the so-called "post-classical" narratology, which emphasizes the creative and productive role of the reader from various points of view (cognitive, emotional, ideological, political). In this tradition, the study of words and images is frequently linked with the fascination of what is now seen, though not unproblematically, as one of the major characteristics of the language of comics, namely the *gutter*, seen as a "gap" between panels (McCloud 1993; Baetens 2020).

The most interesting and highly original contribution of comics studies to the field of narratology lies however in the renewed interest for the notion of *voice*: the actual production of the narrative discourse. In classical narratology, voice is approached in rather metaphorical terms, for the very act of storytelling is of course no longer physically present in the print form of the story (and works in print constitute the corpus of this line of narrative analysis). The modern storyteller, who communicates via texts, is light-years away from the traditional storyteller, physically co-present with her or his audience. Comics, however, as convincingly argued by Jared Gardner, keep traces of the material act and presence of the storyteller:

> In fact, alone of all of the narrative arts born at the end of the nineteenth century, the sequential comic has not effaced the line of the artist, the handprint of the storyteller. This fact is central to what makes the comics form unique, and also to what makes the line, the mark of the individual upon the page, such a unique challenge for narrative theory. We simply have no language—because we have no parallel in any other narrative form for describing its narrative work. In comics alone the promise of Benjamin's looked-for "moving script" continued to develop throughout the twentieth century. Here the act of inscription remains always visible, and the story of its making remains central to the narrative work. (Gardner 2011, 56–57)

However, the hybridity of comics is such that this physical presence does not only appear in the "hand" or style of the drawings. It is no less visible in the way in which the words and other linguistic units are chosen, organized, and eventually drawn (as already mentioned in the study of grammatextuality). In this regard, the notion of *graphiation* or visual enunciation as coined by Belgian narratologist Philippe Marion (1993) has proven vital to develop a medium-specific type of narratology in comics. For Marion, graphiation

> refers to the fact that the hand and the body—as well as the whole personality of an artist—is visible in the way he or she gives a visual

representation of a certain object, character, setting, or event. It allows for a wide range of possible styles, which can be placed on a sliding scale between two extreme positions: the highly subjective style in which the personal expression of the author takes all priority over the representation itself (what matters at the subjective pole is the personal way something is drawn, not the object of the representation), and the decidedly objective style (in which the object of the representation is the highest priority, at the expense of the personal expression of the author who wants to stay as neutral and invisible as possible). (Baetens and Frey 2014, 137)

As such, graphiation is a powerful tool that demonstrates the aptness of comics studies to help advance the study of narrative in general, more precisely in its struggle with semiotically hybrid corpora such as cinema and theater.

Comics are not the only medium that combines words and images. The history of comics shows its close relationships with other media, and this type of research constitutes the fourth level of intermediality in comics studies. The invention of the speech balloon, more precisely the renewed use of the speech balloon as an instrument no longer for character identification but for rendering direct speech, cannot be separated from the invention of the gramophone, for instance, and the first attempts to combine image and sound in the first silent cinema era (Smolderen 2014, 137–47). Other studies go even further and extend the intertextual reading of comics to larger cultural phenomena such as the rise of the leisure industry and its translation into themed entertainment (see Roeder 2014 on the connections between the work of Winsor McCay and the new fairground attractions at Coney Island).

The countless bridges between comics and other media have always raised serious problems in terms of definition and delimitation of the medium. Early comics studies often fell prey to wide overgeneralizations, not shying away from the temptation to include in their field other, more culturally legitimate practices, from hieroglyphs to medieval tapestries. Today, this maneuver of cultural upgrading is no longer necessary, yet comics studies still struggle with the issue of medium-specificity, often challenged by marked similarities with other media such as cartoons, photo novels, or illustrated children's books. Granted, in most cases it is perfectly possible to make a strong case for the position of comics. In the case of picture books, for instance, the word-and-image relations seem at first sight so close to what one can observe in comics that it is no longer clear why one should continue to distinguish between picture books and comics. Yet if the formal and semiotic differences between words and images in comics and words and images in picture books are to a large extent negligible, the same cannot be said of their reception and actual use, which take place in completely different frames and settings. Comics reading is solitary, hence the suspicion raised by what goes on outside any parental control or guidance. On the contrary, picture book reading is heavily accompanied and marshaled by all kinds of mediators (parents, teachers, librarians), who add their own words to the texts of the books.

Medium-specificity is never an absolute given, however, and comics studies should always be open to changing their view of what comics are and what they can do. Intermediality studies are a key player in this regard, certainly when they take into account the larger publication and communication context. A remarkable example of such research is Eddie Campbell's book (2018) on early twentieth-century Californian newspaper and sport cartoons, a carefully edited and thoroughly contextualized account of a type of word-and-image storytelling and reporting that sheds new light on the origins of American newspaper comics. Works such as Campbell's, which show these "not yet" comics in their original publication context, offer multiple opportunities to come back to other aspects of intermediality studies as well as to prioritize word and image issues in the reflection on comics as a medium.

*

This collection of essays is devoted to the study of intermediality in French-language comics and graphic novels. It explores the relations or interconnections between the modalities of expression and representation used in *bande dessinée* and that of other media. The thirteen chapters that follow this introduction study comics that transgress established boundaries between media or combine various vehicles or platforms of representation. These individual analyses discuss mixed-media uses of comic art and film, literature, reportage, painting, photography, religious iconography, history and memory studies, video games, and music. All chapters primarily focus on French-language works, although some comparative essays partially discuss graphic works in other languages.

The first section of the book consists of three chapters that examine the intersection and interplay between comics and cinema. In **Chapter One**, Livio Belloï offers a close reading of the traveling gaze at play in Greg Shaw's *Travelling Square District*, an album whose central device relies on a shifting point of view spanned over a vast cityscape, akin to a moving cinematic frame. Responding, in Oulipian fashion, to a series of self-imposed constraints around the pattern of the square (which presides over the panels' shape and composition, as well as the page layout), Shaw's attempt at replicating a traveling frame in comics creates a singular challenge in a medium defined by its use of still pictures. Belloï studies in detail the internal mechanics of Shaw's "tracking shots" in graphic form, such as the subtle correlations between image fragments, the creative use of panel borders, and the multiple strategies designed to convey visual continuity, sometimes in the opposite direction of the standard reading path of comics. In doing so, he explores convincing parallels between Shaw's album and classic or experimental films that probe the possibilities of an uninterrupted gaze gliding over a spatial referent, as well as the correlations between Shaw's work and pictorial arts (in particular, the paintings of Paul Klee). He also situates *Travelling Square District* within a corpus of graphic works deeply infused with cinema or in a productive dialogue therewith, such as Thomas Ott's *Cinema Panopticum* and Marc-Antoine Mathieu's *3 secondes*, to argue in conclusion in favor of a "para-history of cinema": "a field of inquiry that would encompass all graphic projects that are, in one way or another, permeated, possessed, or obsessed by cinema."

Chapter Two echoes this reflection on graphic works "permeated, possessed, or obsessed by cinema." In this essay, Fabrice Leroy explores the cinephilic and cine-mimetic drive that shapes Nadar and Julien Frey's *Avec Édouard Luntz, le cinéaste des âmes inquiètes*, which recounts Frey's attempt at unearthing the "lost" films of a French filmmaker from the New Wave generation. A quest narrative of sorts, Frey and Nadar's album includes, in key locations, redrawn images from the original footage, thus the trans-mediation of photograms into graphic signifiers. Beyond their drawn replication of the original filmic material, Nadar and Frey project themselves, both affectively and visually, inside Luntz's diegetic universe in order to repurpose or resignify the source material in a dialogue with their present inquiry and their emotional attachment to these images. Retrospectively grafting his own presence into Luntz's photograms, Frey not only creates a temporal amalgam between past and present, but also a hybrid semiosis fusing creation and reception. Leroy also examines the opposite dynamic in Frey and Nadar's treatment of Luntz's *Le Grabuge*, in which the fantasy of reconnection (temporal, affective, and intermedial) results in ultimate disconnection, whereby the excised filmic fragments become opaque or illegible, compromising bonding at all levels: fictional (the plot cohesion), affective (the fantasized kinship with the filmmaker), and intermedial (the productive reliance on comics to preserve, salvage, or recreate lost films).

In **Chapter Three**, Tamara Tasevska studies the reverse configuration: the recurrent references to the comic strip that strangely surface, seemingly unattached to any meta-interpretational frame, throughout Jean-Luc Godard's scope of work over more than five decades, often creating instability and disproportion within the form of the films. Such references include characters reading *Les Pieds Nickelés, Zig et Puce*, or *Bécassine* in *À bout de souffle, Pierrot le fou*, and *Masculin-Féminin*, as well as instances in which the whole of the film itself resembles the compositions and frames of the comic book (*Une femme est une femme, Made in U.S.A.*). Comic book figures also appear in some of Godard's most recent video essays (*Histoire(s) du cinéma, Le Livre d'image*). Tasevska shows that Godard not only uses the comic book in order to provoke *distanciation* effects (as meta-representational devices drawing attention to their cartoonish artificiality), but also suggests that comic book elements may point to provocative connections between aesthetics and politics. Borrowing from Gilles Deleuze's remarks on Godard's oeuvre in *L'Image-temps*, in which the philosopher argued that Godard, in his predilection for trenchant, disconnected images, extracted autonomous fragments from comic books and repurposed their vivid imagery—which matched his own aesthetic fondness for provocative and grotesque tones, as well as childhood representations—as a means of political and historical critique, Tasevska reflects on the filmmaker's intermedial collage of disparate elements and recirculation of previous images. Her analysis of Godard's references to Forton's anarchistic *Les Pieds Nickelés* in *Pierrot le fou*, and of the movie's comics-like aspects (such as images in primary colors, balloon-like narration, framing effects, and exclamation sounds interspersed with dialogues) points out the profound formal and archaeological correlation between the film and the comic book series, and rethinks Godard's film as a modern cinematic form that activates fictional imageries of the past (notably imperial conquest and colonial domination), while bringing into play an unrealistic comics gaze that mirrors the characters' madness and rejection of contemporary society. In sharp contrast, Tasevska discusses how Godard's more recent work *Histoire(s) du cinéma* superimposes elements of comic books in a rudimentary form; their remnants reshaped or transformed over other images form a heterogeneous cinematic and historical archive. In *Le Livre d'image*, Godard uses the Bécassine character as a figure of history, a witness of the mutations of France over the course of the twentieth century. Godard's use of the comic book as one of the spectacles transforming the power of images is thus complex and ambiguous, suggesting at once the bankrupt abyss of the serial image and the potentially deterritorializing power of the comic book.

The second thematic cluster of chapters in this book explores connections between drawn images and photography. In **Chapter Four**, Charlotte F. Werbe examines the complex dynamics of photographic visibility, historical erasure, and graphic testimony in Horst Rosenthal's fifteen-page comic booklet, *Mickey au camp de Gurs*, written in 1942, while the author was imprisoned at the Gurs internment camp in southern France. The narrative follows Mickey Mouse as he is arrested and sent to Gurs, where he encounters camp administrators, fellow prisoners, and the bureaucratic machinery of the camp. This work is not only notable for the extraordinary circumstances under which it was produced, but also for its formal innovations, including its multimodal juxtaposition of fictional drawings linked to the children's entertainment industry and a photograph. Indeed, most strikingly, amid the stylized drawn panels in color, a single black-and-white picture is inserted: a high oblique aerial photograph of the Gurs internment camp. Beyond conveying authenticity, and thereby positioning the text as testimony, the remediation of the aerial photograph stages a more general confrontation between the photorealistic (documentary) and the cartoonish (aesthetic). Drawing on the works of Hilary Chute and Georges Didi-Huberman, among others, Werbe reflects on the interaction between these two adjacent image regimes and their respective signifying modes. Paying special attention to the status of the aerial photograph and the testimonial properties of handmade drawings, she argues that it is not only the copresence of photography and cartoons in *Mickey au camp de Gurs* that stages the encounters that condition testimony, but also the quintessentially documentary properties of the aerial photograph and the quintessentially cartoonish properties of Mickey Mouse. Her analysis proposes that the meeting of media in *Mickey au camp de Gurs* spotlights the ways in which testimony mediates internal and external perspectives, each with their own set of demands and expectations. *Mickey* offers fruitful terrain for countering the unspeakable, the unrepresentable, and the unimaginable, through the mixing of media that illuminates how truth and fact come into being.

In **Chapter Five**, Jan Baetens and Fred Truyen investigate the intermedial nature of the photonovel medium, a post-World War II creation of the publishing industry that created a specific visual language through a new, fictional, and sequential use of still images, in a layout inspired by the format of comics. Appearing in Italy in the late 1940s, then soon popular in France, the photonovel targeted a specific niche of the reading population (the female working class) and was firmly anchored in popular culture imagery (comics, melodrama), which it reshaped in its new format. As a "print version of cinema," produced and sold cheaply, it granted wide and easy access to entertainment and celebrity culture, but also drew critical condescension (as a lowbrow form of art) and generated ideological debates across the political spectrum (for its portrayal of the American way of life and its depiction of gender roles, notably). In their essay, Baetens and Truyen reflect on the defining characteristics of the photographic image in the photonovel of the immediate postwar years, all seeking immediate legibility: its specific way of putting bodies on display and framing the shots, its types of sequential shots, its repertoire of stereotypical facial expressions. They also identify the distinctive features of the photonovel's visual language, which are intermedial in nature: In the photonovel, "photography is a second-degree language, that is a visual . . . language superposed onto other, already existing, visual languages." The format of the photonovel is indeed a case of remediation of the preexisting "drawn novel," whose features it initially copied, which explains the numerous similarities and overlaps between the two forms. Distinctions between the two can also be blurred by the practice of retouching and colorizing black-and-white photographs, which brought a drawn quality thereto. However, Baetens and Truyen, in speaking of "kitchen sink realism," remark that the photonovel, suffering from a paucity of production values and mirroring contemporary Italian Neo-Realism (with its focus on ordinary life and its nonglamorous aesthetics) had more limited means of expressing glamour, luxury, and beauty, in contrast with the more lavish and embellished images of the drawn novel. Their essay also considers other sections of a typical photonovel magazine issue, such as illustrated gossip, movie news, or photos of star culture. Examining how and why "visual forms and the collective consciousness that supports them circulate between fictional and nonfictional representations," they pay special attention to the intermedial dialogue between the narrative sections of the photonovel magazine and its advertisements, photographic or drawn, which are often connected to the fictional universe and the visual language of the stories.

The third section of the book brings together four chapters that deal with issues of graphic reportage or, more widely, the connections between image, reality, and memory. In **Chapter Six**, Michelle Bumatay provides a close reading of French cartoonist Hippolyte's *L'Afrique de papa* (2009), an album that belongs to the category of "BD reportage," which has become a well-established nonfiction genre since the early 1990s (with seminal works such as Joe Sacco's *Palestine* and the creation of publishers' collections and awards dedicated to this specific form of graphic storytelling). The album chronicles the cartoonist's trip to the Senegalese seaside enclave of Saly, where his father decided to retire. Contrasting the hedonistic industry of Western tourism with the harsh realities faced by the local population, Hippolyte's gaze reflects on the economic inequities of tourism and its neocolonial dynamic of exploitation. Bumatay investigates the various modalities of the artist's gaze in cognitive and representational devices that make full use of intermediality, through a juxtaposition of multiple iconic regimes (drawings, grayscale photography, and sketchbook reproductions) and narrative modes (weaving written travel journal entries into the diegesis). She also analyzes the cartoonist's awareness, reflection, and questioning of his own gaze—how he encodes his own position of graphic witness in the novel, as an agent of perception and visualization, but also how he ultimately reconsiders his own visual intrusion into the depicted universe and reflects on his responsibility in the production and consumption of images of otherness. As many other cartoonists of BD reportage, including Joe Sacco, Guy Delisle, or the authors of the groundbreaking album *Le Photographe* (Emmanuel Guibert, Didier Lefèvre, and Frédéric Lemercier), Hippolyte accounts for his subject-position as an outsider and provides traces of his process of research and reflection, thus foregrounding his unique gaze. Taking into consideration scholarly essays on the role of photography in nonfiction comics, graphic novels, and *bandes dessinées*, as well as previous commentaries on comics as travel writing, this chapter examines how Hippolyte, through a highly subjective lens, seeks to deliver a nuanced look beyond the exotic touristic view of Senegal, and investigates the transcolonial dimension of Hippolyte's own multimodal aesthetic, textual, and narrative practices (including framing and cropping, page layout, thematic color palettes, and crosscutting).

Chapter Seven pursues a similar reflection on graphic reportage and the mediation of memories, identities, and sociopolitical dynamics through comics. In his analysis of Alex Inker's *Panama Al-Brown ou l'énigme de la force* (2017), Maxence Leconte examines the particular significance of the French-language graphic novel as both an aesthetic and political medium capable of reconstructing and empowering the memory of marginalized identities. Leconte demonstrates how both the body of the text—or hypertext, combining images and words in symbiosis—and the body of its main character Alfonso Brown, an elusive black flyweight champion who turned Paris on its head and became Jean Cocteau's lover during the Roaring Twenties, offer new possibilities for the depiction and understanding of black lives, racism, and resistance in the cultural landscapes of France and the United States during the interwar period. The reportage format of the graphic novel (staging a journalist's quest to uncover biographical fragments from the boxer's tumultuous life and rescue them from historical erasure) renegotiates and rehabilitates Al-Brown's memory through medium-specific mechanics, including rhythm effects marking spatial and temporal shifts, as well as enunciative devices of memorial polyphony. Simultaneously admired and reviled, Al-Brown's duality displays the fundamental paradoxes and complexity of self-identification, acknowledged through the prism of the graphic novel. A study in contrasts, confronting the literary canon on the one hand and hegemonic social constructs on the other, this chapter calls attention to the value of nonlinear, fluid readings of both texts and identities, and concludes by suggesting that hybridity, by challenging the normative spaces of high literature and white-centered, heteronormative identity, functions as an apt platform for the renewed understanding and the subsequent teaching of memory and history.

Renée Altergott explores the paradox of "mediated martyrdom" in Marjane Satrapi's *Persepolis* in **Chapter Eight**. Depicting the inculcation of young children into the gendered cultural practices of martyrdom and martyr veneration in Iran, Satrapi uses the naïve cruelty of young Marji to convey the true horror and historical trauma of these practices. *Persepolis* remediates an important visual practice in Iran, where glorified images of martyrs appear across media of all kinds, and in the city of Tehran itself, which becomes an important media landscape of martyr worship. Satrapi includes photographic newspaper portraits labeled "Martyres du Jour" ("Martyrs of the Day"), scenes where Marji's parents discuss the renaming of various streets after recent victims, and propaganda murals in various panels, including one depicting a veiled woman holding the fallen body of an unknown martyr. According to Hillary Chute, the double possibility for consonance and dissonance between image and text constitutes the very structural condition that permits the *bande dessinée* to perform the ethical and aesthetic work of witnessing. Satrapi herself has referred to her work as having the "duty of witnessing." The etymological link between "martyr" and "witness" in Persian and Arabic further reinforces the relationship between form and content in *Persepolis*. Altergott examines such "mediated martyrdom" through the artistic contribution of Marji, particularly in an episode where the latter redraws a photograph of Michelangelo's sculpture, *La Pietà*, according to the Islamic codes of martyrdom iconography, producing a hybrid icon straddling Eastern and Western cultures. She notes that this episode is inscribed within a system of formal repetition, a network of interconnected and inter-braided images within the album showing the same Pietà pose. Further investigating the Pietà figure, Altergott links Satrapi's remediated artwork with Islamic propaganda symbolism, idealized martyr portraiture, and Iranian visual culture through the works of two contemporary Iranian artists: Kazem Chalipa and Hamid Qadiriyan. Furthermore, she discusses another form of remediation—how selected panels from *Persepolis* (including a Pietà-like vignette) were reordered, repurposed, and recaptioned by two Iranian authors (Payman and Sina) to commemorate Neda Agha-Soltan, a young woman who was killed during a protest against President Mahmoud Ahmadinejad's 2009 election, thereby perpetuating the cycle of propaganda and martyr iconography.

In **Chapter Nine**, Maaheen Ahmed proposes a new concept for considering intermediality in comics: "media memories." Combining cultural historian Aby Warburg's use of the montage for his incomplete *Mnemosyne Atlas* and philosopher John Sutton's concept of "porous memories," Ahmed uses the concept of "media memories" ("tropes, styles, and images that travel from medium to medium, adapting to fit each new habitat") to capture and better understand how media remember other media and how certain media and images persist, often tenaciously. A complex picture emerges in unpacking the media memories underlying the representation of children, childhood, and childishness in three contemporary French-language comics: the first three issues of David B.'s *L'Ascension du Haut Mal* (*Epileptic*), Dominique Goblet's *Faire semblant c'est mentir* (*Pretending Is Lying*) and the fourth volume of Manu Larcenet's *Combat ordinaire* (*Ordinary Victories*). Ahmed's analysis of this corpus focuses on the media memories channeled through childlike drawing styles and other indicators of children's worlds and childishness (such as games and toys) to show how they encapsulate nostalgizing and affective connotations. The children, their childishness, and the (streamlined) world of childhood they bring with them inevitably reflect on the issues of legitimation that haunt comics and graphic novels.

The fourth section of this edited collection comprises three chapters that focus on the relationship between comics, cultural capital, and the artistic tradition. In **Chapter Ten**, Erwin Dejasse ponders the "artistic sympathies" or correlations between alternative comics (particularly those published by L'Association since 1990) and Art Brut (or "Outsider Art," encompassing "works produced by persons unscathed by artistic culture"), as initially defined by Jean Dubuffet. Dejasse's survey of this field focuses more specifically on works by Jean-Christophe Menu, Pakito Bolino, Dominique Goblet (with her daughter Nikita Fossoul), and Olivier Josso Hamel, as well as other practitioners of outsider comics (Dominique Théate, Walter Coumou, Katsutoshi Kuroda, etc.). In addition to noting these comics creators' awareness of and interest in Art Brut, Dejasse highlights several points of convergence between these two sectors of artistic expression: a shared predilection for autobiography, autofiction, or self-representation in general, often motivated by an "inner necessity" for expression rooted in individual trauma and void of any commercial preoccupations or concerns about reception; a deviation from the artistic canons and "prototypical devices" of their respective media, eschewing dominant forms and usages in favor of experimental approaches; a disinterest in "finished" products exhibiting narrative linearity and coherence, or formal perfection, in favor of flawed, spontaneous, and often technically impoverished results; and a mix of styles and techniques that remains unconcerned with aesthetic canons. Dejasse links such inherent imperfections with the voluntarily unskilled or "deskilled" approach of Dada and punk rock, which similarly resulted in redefining artistic boundaries, and reflects on the importance of the retrospective inclusion of Art Brut creators such as Charlotte Salomon in the realm of comics, which he considers indicative of the role played by alternative comics in widening the Ninth Art's corpus.

In **Chapter Eleven**, Hugo Frey explores the remediation of images in a classic of French-language comic art, Hergé's *L'Affaire Tournesol*, often considered as the pinnacle of the Belgian cartoonist's art. Setting aside the matters of remediation and appropriation of Tintin images in other products (from legitimate artistic allusions to its highly recognizable visuals by other cartoonists and visual artists, to official merchandising ventures, and even counterfeit or parodic reinterpretations), Frey focuses his analysis on another aspect of the recirculation of images—that which takes place inside Tintin's graphic universe, particularly in a citation-prone album such as *L'Affaire Tournesol*, in which Frey identifies a complex and multifarious network of intertextual, inter-pictural, and intra-pictural resonances. He connects the album's imagery to mass media graphic design, insignia, militaria, and advertising iconography. Reworked references in Hergé's classic include staples of consumer culture, such as logos for existing brands or places, as well as magazine covers, but also the cartoonist's logos for products of his own invention, whose overall design coincides with the advertising codes of the era. By contrast, Frey shows that Hergé depicts the fictitious Eastern-bloc country of Borduria as replete with state-sanctioned symbols (such as the leader's circumflex-like mustache) and markers of totalitarian conformism. Reflecting on this binary East/West iconography, Frey discusses Hergé's ideological "neither/nor" position as a European attempt at negotiating an independent, middle role between capitalism and communism. Frey also considers the similarities between Hergé's approach and pop art's redrawing of advertising and mass media iconography, and comments on the reflexive nature of Hergé's recirculation of images from his own works, by which the author repeats panels and plot sequences from his previous albums. He argues that such a network of internal references (which culminates in the plotless and entirely self-referential *Les Bijoux de la Castafiore*) cultivates the series' own recognizability and timelessness. Finally, Frey examines Hergé's self-representation and his coded depiction of family, friends, lovers, and collaborators in this album, which suggest multiple possible readings of certain scenes.

In **Chapter Twelve**, Ana Oancea studies a case of remediation among three media (literature, *bande dessinée*, and video games) by examining the successive adaptations of Flaubert's historical novel *Salammbô* (1862), first in Philippe Druillet's *bande dessinée* version, published in *Métal Hurlant* (1980–1985), then in the remediation of the latter (and of Flaubert's original text) as an adventure video game, *Salammbô: Battle for Carthage*, released in 2003 by French production company Cryo Interactive, which transferred Druillet's characters and location illustrations into a new format. Oancea's chapter shows how, in this chain of intertextual and inter-pictural borrowing, each successive iteration relies on medium-specific elements from its predecessor yet assigns them different functions in the new context. It investigates the reinterpretation of Flaubert's cryptic and grandiose novel (which the author famously considered incompatible with any illustrations) in Druillet's science fiction work, which reimaged and reimagined its source material as a dystopian science fiction tale typical of the cartoonist's idiosyncratic, futuristic style, not only at the visual level, but also at the diegetic one. Indeed, Druillet appropriated Flaubert's character of Mâtho and recast him as his own recurrent hero Lone Sloane, in the midst of ambitious aesthetics featuring ambitious layouts, psychedelic colors, and full-page illustrations or two-page spreads that draw the reader into an exploration of Carthage. Text-image dynamics constitute an important component of Druillet's trans-mediation: In his BD, textual excerpts from the novel are treated as images. Displayed alone, they are encased in ornate frames and rendered in distinctive lettering, distinguishing them from the captions or speech balloons used elsewhere in the album. Like illustrations in a novel, the quotes from Flaubert are apposite to the visual exposition but are relegated to a nonnarrative function. The video game strives for a certain amount of visual fidelity to the BD not only by replicating the style of Druillet's drawings, but also by referencing comic book elements such as panels, borders, and page layouts in order to reproduce the "look" of its graphic source, although the layout of the images, using hard borders and regular shapes, diverges strongly from the album's sprawling illustrations. The game also reproduces some of the BD's text/image interplay. In the video game, the borders of the Flaubertian citations frame the screen during sections that do not involve gameplay. However, the solving of puzzles, like in many video games of this kind, drives the principal game mechanism, which endows the format with new, narrative meaning. Extending her analysis to other video games that attempt to replicate key aspects of the BD experience graphically and through gameplay, Oancea draws productive parallels with other games inspired by comics such as *Persona 5* and *XIII*.

Finally, the book concludes with an important discussion of configurations intersecting music and comics. In **Chapter Thirteen**, Mark McKinney provides a detailed and comprehensive examination of the manner in which a large number of cartoonists who depicted French colonialism in the Maghreb and postcolonial Maghrebi immigration to France created an intermedial dialogue with songs in their works. McKinney shows how albums openly or implicitly celebrating colonialism, or expressing colonial nostalgia, embedded lyrics from military marching songs as "relics" intended to commemorate and glorify a lost era. (As a complement to this reflection, he also studies albums that employed Algerian patriotic songs and matched their lyrics with a nationalistic counternarrative to French rule.) By contrast, the author shows how song lyrics and traditional comics elements are not always in accord in the works of cartoonists who make an ironic use of the juxtaposition between colonial violence and the bravado of pro-colonial anthems, as a critical device. McKinney engages in a subtle reading of the markers of irony in such mechanisms of semantic and ideological opposition: how the repurposed lyrics are positioned in the panel, how the images may contradict the song's meaning, and which correlations are drawn by the artists in such visual and textual dialogues. McKinney also reassesses the ambivalent role of songs, dance, and music in the perpetuation of Orientalist stereotypes and fantasies such as the traditional "belly dance" often depicted in many albums that reproduce an unproblematized exotic imagery, although the author also shows that some works perform a conscious reversal of such tropes. In this regard, this chapter takes into consideration a wide corpus of French-language comics that spans a long history of the medium, from comics stories published by conservative Catholic outlets in the 1950s, which treat colonialism in a moralistic, idealized, and hagiographic mode that often hides colonial violence, to more recent comics by French artists of Maghrebi background and North African cartoonists, who seek cultural autonomy and authenticity, as well as intercultural communication in a postcolonial context. (McKinney provides a compelling reading of the renegotiation of identity and marginality in such works, including an analysis of key scenes from Joann Sfar's *The Rabbi's Cat*.) The chapter concludes with an exploration of Franc'Arab songs, whose lyrics may often reflect colonial stereotypes, but can also serve as a vehicle for their contestation. McKinney discusses the possibilities afforded by *métissage*, bilingualism, and biculturalism in song lyrics for the depiction of multicultural identities in comics.

Works Cited

BAETENS, JAN. 2020. "Gap or Gag? On the Myth of the Gutter in Comics Scholarship." *Études francophones* 32 (Spring): 213–17.

BAETENS, JAN, AND HUGO FREY. 2014. *The Graphic Novel. An Introduction.* Cambridge: Cambridge University Press.

BAETENS, JAN, AND DOMINGO SÁNCHEZ-MESA. 2015. "Literature in the Expanded Field: Intermediality at the Crossroads of Literary Theory and Comparative Literature." *Interfaces* 36 (January): 289–304.

BAETENS, JAN, AND STEVEN SURDIACOURT. 2013. "European Graphic Narratives: Towards a Cultural and Mediological History." In *Theory and History of the Graphic Novel,* edited by Daniel Stein and Jan Thon, 347–62. Berlin: De Gruyter.

BARTHES, ROLAND. 1977. "The Photographic Message." In *Image, Music, Text,* edited and translated by Stephen Heath, 15–31. New York: Hill.

BERONÄ, DAVID. 2008. *Wordless Books: The Original Graphic Novels.* New York: Abrams.

CAMPBELL, EDDIE. 2018. *The Goat-Getters: Jack Johnson, the Fight of the Century, and How a Bunch of Raucous Cartoonists Reinvented Comics.* Columbus: The Ohio State University Press.

FRESNAULT-DERUELLE, PIERRE. 2014. "From Linear to Tabular." In *The French Comics Theory Reader,* edited by Ann Miller and Bart Beaty, 121–38. Leuven, Belgium: Leuven University Press.

GARDNER, JARED. 2011. "Storylines." *Substance* 40 (1): 53–69.

GRENNAN, SIMON. 2017. *A Theory of Narrative Drawing.* New York: Palgrave Macmillan US.

GROENSTEEN, THIERRY. 2009. *La Bande dessinée: son histoire et ses maîtres.* Paris: Skira-Flammarion.

———. 2014. *Mr Töpffer invente la bande dessinée.* Brussels: Les Impressions Nouvelles.

GROUPE MU. 1993. *Traité du signe visuel.* Paris: Seuil.

HAGUE, IAN. 2014. *Comics and the Senses: A Multisensory Approach to Comics and Graphic Novels.* London: Routledge.

HARPOLD, TERRY. 2008. *Ex-foliations: Reading Machines and the Upgrade Path.* Minneapolis: University of Minnesota Press.

HATFIELD, CHARLES. 2011. *Hand of Fire: The Comics Art of Jack Kirby.* Jackson: University of Mississippi Press.

HERGÉ. 1972. *Land of Black Gold,* translated by Leslie Lonsdale-Cooper and Michael Turner. London: Methuen.

LABARRE, NICOLAS. 2020. *Understanding Genres in Comics*. London: Palgrave Macmillan.

LAPACHERIE, JEAN GÉRARD. 1984. "De la grammatextualité." *Poétique* 59: 283–94.

MARION, PHILIPPE. 1993. *Traces en cases*. Louvain-la-Neuve, Belgium: Académia.

MCCLOUD, SCOTT. 1993. *Understanding Comics: The Invisible Art*. Toronto: Tundra.

MILLER, ANN AND BART BEATY, eds. 2014. *The French Comics Theory Reader*. Leuven, Belgium: Leuven University Press.

MITCHELL, WJT. 2005. "There Are No Visual Media." *Journal of Visual Culture* 4 (2): 257–66.

POSTEMA, BARBARA. 2018. "Long- Length Wordless Books: Frans Masereel, Milt Gross, Lynd Ward, and Beyond." In *The Cambridge History of the Graphic Novel*, edited by Jan Baetens, Hugo Frey, and Stephen Tabachnick, 59–74. Cambridge: Cambridge University Press.

RAJEWSKY, IRINA O. 2005. "Intermediality, Intertextuality, and Remediation: A Literary Perspective on Intermediality." *Intermédialités/ Intermedialities* 6 (Autumn): 43–64.

RIPPL, GABRIELE, ed. 2015. *Handbook of Intermediality. Literature–Image–Sound– Music*. Berlin: De Gruyter.

ROEDER, KATHERINE. 2014. *Wide Awake in Slumberland: Fantasy, Mass Culture, and Modernism in the Art of Winsor McCay*. Jackson: University Press of Missisissppi.

SETH. *Clyde Fans*. 2019. Montreal: Drawn and Quarterly.

SMOLDEREN, THIERRY. 2014. *The Origins of Comics: From William Hogarth to Winsor McCay*, translated by Bart Beaty and Nick Nguyen. Jackson: University Press of Mississippi.

PART ONE
Comics and Cinema

CHAPTER ONE:
Still Pictures, Moving Frame: Comics on the Edge of Cinema

Livio Belloï

Published in 2010 by Éditions Sarbacane (Paris), *Travelling Square District* by the young Belgian cartoonist Greg Shaw emerged as an oddity in the field of contemporary comics. Loosely inspired by the works of OuBaPo ("Ouvroir de Bande Dessinée Potentielle" ["Workshop of Potential Comic Book Art"]),[1] Shaw composed an album that appears singular in many regards. First, it is singular to the extent that it presents itself as a profound meditation on the figure of the square, which determines not only the format of the book itself, but also the architecture of each page and the shape of each panel. Moreover, it is singular insofar as the contents of the entire album fit on its front cover, an actual matrix that delimits a perimeter outside of which the point of view will never venture (Fig. 1). As many readers have noted, this urban panorama evokes New York, most notably because of the bridge depicted on the bottom left portion of the cover, which spontaneously and rather distinctly recalls the Brooklyn Bridge, and because of the imposing statue located in the forefront on the right, a carnivalesque version of the Statue of Liberty, represented as a naked and pregnant woman, proudly brandishing a cellular phone. However, with regards to his matrix-like album cover, Greg Shaw has indicated on more than

Figure 1: Cover of *Travelling Square District*. ©*Éditions Sarbacane.*

one occasion that he initially drew his inspiration from the city of Sydney.[2] From the starting point of this cover, which serves as its one and only backdrop, Shaw's opus unfolds according to a highly concerted bipolarity, alternating description and narration.

The pages with a descriptive intent employ the systematic design of 4 x 4 panels with identical dimensions. Wordless, they aim to actualize a spatial shift, a continuous setting in motion of the frame (this is the "travelling" to which the title of the work alludes), whose function is to span in detail the vast cityscape depicted on the album cover (skyscrapers, towers, metallic bridge, docks, and miscellaneous buildings), but also to interconnect the various sites where the plot—essentially a detective story—will gradually unfold.

Positioned facing each other, the pages with narrative intent are themselves structured as 2 x 2 squares of larger dimensions, with each frame occupying a surface equal to four smaller squares. Launched by a forward tracking shot or zoom on the last panel of the preceding descriptive page, such pages tend to favor, as a general rule, a wide and fixed framing. Their distinguishing feature is to encase the main characters, as expected "the husband, the wife, the cops, [and] the lover" (as they are listed on the back cover), among whom prominently features a certain Georg W. Ashry, an activist suspected of planning a bombing attack, but also, on a more personal level, a betrayed husband who decided to have his wife executed by a professional hitman. In a typically Oulipian approach, all the characters staged in the narrative pages of *Travelling Square District* are named on the basis of anagrams derived from the author's first and last names. Thereby, the name "Gregory Shaw" becomes respectively Roy Eggwhars (a police inspector), Gerry Wagosh (also an inspector), Georg W. Ashry (the presumed terrorist previously mentioned), Rosah Wygger (his unfaithful wife), Howy Beggars[3] (the latter's lover, but also Ashry's accomplice in his criminal plot), Roger HG Ways (a police captain), Yorg Schwager (the hitman), etc. This is the same kind of genuine verbal prowess that Marc-Antoine Mathieu recently displayed in his highly singular publishing project entitled *Le Livre des livres* (*The Book of Books*, 2017).[4]

"START"

The entire dynamic of *Travelling Square District* likewise resides in this systematic alternation between description and narration, between tracking and fixed shots, between muteness and speech, etc. Let us now consider more attentively the opening pages of this work. On the first page, the initial visual event is not a frame but a pictogram inscribed in the left margin; this particular figure consists of a black equilateral triangle standing on one of its angles and pointing on the right, toward the first panel of the page. This pictogram—the only sign of its kind on this first page—presents itself as the customary equivalent of an arrow and therefore takes on an essentially deictic function.

At this precise moment of the reading process, we have already encountered this singular form on two occasions and in two distinct fashions. Its first occurrence is visible on the cover of the volume itself, in the top left corner, near the title displayed in capital letters. In this particular instance, a transparent, square shape is adjoined to the opaque triangle, on its right side: a black frame encasing a portion of the sky striated by a cloud fragment. These constitute two extradiegetic forms affixed to the very surface of the cover and placed in a highly strategic location, in the immediate vicinity of the focal point that the album title usually represents. In terms of page layout, these two shapes conform to the same centering operation as that of the written text: In this case, it is as if the triangle and the square were somehow comprised or integrated within the title of the work itself, which grants them a certain amount of visibility despite their small size relative to the surface in which they are inlaid.

The double figure of the triangle and the square reappears on the inside cover of the volume, in the same area of the page (Fig. 2). The same urban panorama is again depicted here, this time shrouded in a veil of obscurity, as if filtered through a cinematic day-for-night effect. Only a tiny portion of this space eludes this overall darkening: It is precisely the sky fragment already framed on the cover, albeit highlighted. Indeed, the black frame around the square has disappeared, as it is no longer necessary due to the surrounding darkness. As far as the triangle itself is concerned, its color has changed from

Figure 2: The triangle and square pictogram on the inside cover (detail of page). ©*Éditions Sarbacane.*

black to beige in order to heighten its definition in contrast with its backdrop. Although the book title, as well as the mentions of its author and publisher, are no longer present, this does not mean that this intermediate page remains void of any textual element. In fact, just before the triangle and in the same color, the page displays a verb in the imperative form, typed in capital letters.

"START": Such a scriptural element does not belong to the categories of the speech balloon nor the narrative caption. Rather, it seems more like a direct address or injunction directed toward the reader, which designates the starting point of a process about to be undertaken. One should note that the redundancy between the word "START" and the triangular pictogram is only superficial. While the verbal element alludes to a beginning, or the engagement of a process, the pictogram associated therewith rather tends to signify the act of playing, according to audiovisual signage ("PLAY" rather than "START"). Yet a reader never really "plays" a comic book (in the same way as he or she would "play" a record or a DVD). From the onset, this sign alludes to the fact that Shaw's album will be the site of formal procedures and effects referring to specific practices associated with moving images (cinema, video). Furthermore, in such a context, the alliance between the triangle and the square has a potentially ironic implication, in that the square, according to the same system of signs, indeed designates the idea of stopping. What these two conjoined pictograms therefore invite us to conceptualize at once is the paradox of a process interrupted as soon as it is initiated, as if stymied from the onset.

Celestial Path

Responding to Greg Shaw's invitation, let us begin to play by examining more closely the first page of the volume. The terms of the challenge with which the author faced himself (and, consequently, his reader) seem clear from the beginning: How can one endeavor to represent a regular and continuous movement of the frame using fixed images? One recalls that this is the same question that Régis Franc previously addressed—albeit on a smaller scale—in *Intérieurs* (*Interiors*, 1979), a work based on an uninterrupted circular panorama (Groensteen 2011, 71). In this regard, besides, Shaw does not opt for an easy solution. In order to acquaint his reader with his moving frame device, the artist indeed chooses a purely arbitrary movement, a celestial tracking shot deprived of any anthropomorphic point of reference (Fig. 3). After the triangular pictogram (the sign of a process set in motion and the reminder of a forward reading path), the frame thereby enters into an ample and continuous movement, which will only be interrupted at first on the

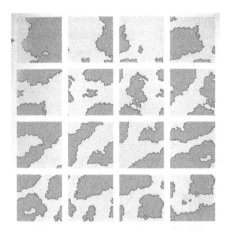

Figure 3: The opening celestial tracking shot of *Travelling Square District*. ©*Éditions Sarbacane*.

bottom of the third page. If the pictogram placed in the margin invites us to unfold a conventional reading from left to right, Shaw effectuates a striking deviation in the first strip by displaying a movement that actually spreads from right to left.

How does the author communicate such a contradictory movement, which produces an obvious interference with the standard reading path? The representational tactic that he employs here is as simple as it is efficient: Shaw ensures that each new panel retains a fragment of the preceding one (sky or cloud, blue or white zone). Between two frames, a repeated iconic fragment marks the transition and serves as a cue to the mobilization and orientation of the frame, both laterally and vertically. Thus, the second frame reveals and completes the cloud that, in the opening frame, was only partially visible, along the left edge of the frame.[5] In the third frame, while the whiteness of the cloud becomes dominant, the indication of continuity resides in a minuscule fragment of sky situated just above the lower edge of the frame, slowly gliding toward the right border. Finally, in the fourth frame, the relative apportionment of blue sky and clouds becomes more evenly balanced; the markers of continuity in this instance consist of sky segments carved by the boundaries of the frame (its two lateral borders and its bottom edge). Understandably, in this opening sequence, as in all pages of a descriptive nature, Shaw quite consciously plays with a powerful domino effect (Peeters 1998, 39); in this particular instance, he tends to give a literal meaning to the famous principle of "iconic solidarity" that, according to Thierry Groensteen, constitutes a "law" of the figurative language that is specific to comics (2011, 23–25).

In the transition between the fourth and the fifth frame, Shaw grapples with a new and rather thorny issue: how to negotiate, in such a configuration, the transition not between the frames this time, but between the strips. In this respect, the artist once again favors a radical solution that breaks with established conventions. As the reader's gaze naturally "falls" onto the fifth frame or descends upon the strip below, Shaw chooses to impart an upward trajectory to his framing, expressed through two graphic indicators of continuity (the fragmentation of the blue zone by its bottom edge and the emergence of a smaller blue zone, which trickles down along the edge of the left border). On all counts, the relationship between the fourth and fifth frames follows the overall articulation of the first strip; whether lateral or vertical, its first objective is to meet the reader's gaze against the grain.

Using the same figurative stratagem, the remainder of the page translates yet a new lateral movement from right to left (frames six, seven, eight, and nine), followed by a downward movement, this time unfolding in the same direction as the reading path (frames twelve, thirteen, fourteen, and fifteen), and a final descending movement (frame sixteen). In this first page, which undoubtedly has a programmatic importance, the four modalities of the tracking shot are therefore exemplified: the lateral movement toward the left or the right, and the vertical movement, either upward or downward—yet without any crossing of the two patterns, as any type of movement always remains in a straight line, for obvious reasons of legibility.[6] From the outset, this says everything about the vast, descriptive scrolling maneuver in which the point of view will engage from the beginning to the end of the volume.

The notion of spanning the celestial vault without visualizing any reference to the Earth below clearly alludes to cinema and, more specifically, to the experimental side of filmmaking. Faced with the opening page of *Travelling Square District*, one cannot refrain from thinking about certain sequences of *La Région centrale* (*The Central Region*, 1971), the monumental work of Canadian filmmaker Michael Snow. One may indeed recall that Snow's film presents itself as a systematic exploration of the almost infinite possibilities granted by the movement of the cinematographic frame, here deployed in all possible and imaginable directions (laterality, verticality, rotations, zooming effects, etc.).[7] Toward the eighteenth minute of the film, after having meticulously explored a vast mountainscape, deserted and ordinary, the remote-controlled camera that Snow blindly operates gains some altitude; it frees itself from the Earth's surface, detaches itself from any anchor, and, for more than ten minutes, fixates its mechanical and mobile eye on a blue sky scattered initially with thick clouds. Between Shaw and Snow, the area of convergence does not solely lie in the choice of a common motif; it also resides in the notion of a "celestial journey" made through a fluid, relatively slow and, above all, uninterrupted movement. Better yet, while the movement of the frame is evidently simulated in *Travelling Square District*—as opposed to the actual movement in *La Région centrale*—the clouds serve in both cases as the obvious indicators of this movement.[8]

Façades and Grids

Accommodating within its space a broken and rather complex trajectory, the first page of *Travelling Square District* announces the promise of a gradual descent toward Earth, in search of a material anchor after this initial feat, as well as more immediately legible points of reference; it also seeks the human figure, the main subject matter of the more narrative side of Shaw's work.

This is indeed what happens on the following page, on the surface of which the downward movements occupy ten of the sixteen panels. An architectural tracking shot now replaces its celestial counterpart. Within this second page, just as in the next one, Greg Shaw obviously remembers the broad camera movements, both independent and descriptive, by which many classic Hollywood films often begin. Most readers will undoubtedly have in mind the opening of *The Lost Weekend* (Billy Wilder, 1945) or the even better known and more striking beginning of *Psycho* (Alfred Hitchcock, 1960), in which the filmmaker starts with a wide-angled, panoramic shot of the city of Phoenix, then eventually manages, thanks to progressive tracking shots and subtle crossfades, to single out a building, then, within this building, a particular hotel room where Marion Crane (Janet Leigh) has just spent an intimate moment with her lover.[9] Moreover, it is worth noting that the reference to Hitchcock (the director of *Psycho*, but also, more appropriately, that of *Rear Window* [1954]) seems openly assumed by Shaw. Indeed, in a subsequent descriptive page of *Travelling Square District*, frames ten to fourteen depict a statue that unmistakably resembles the master of suspense.

Another clear reference is the repeated allusion to Georges Perec, in this instance in the form of a graffito. These are doubtless hints to the historical OuLiPo movement in general, and more specifically to Perec's own *La Vie mode d'emploi* (*Life: A User's Manual*, 1978), a "panoptic" description of everyday life in an apartment building, and a multifaceted and experimental novel that may have inspired *Travelling Square District* in one way or another.[10]

The third page of the album is entirely devoted—and this is a rather remarkable characteristic—to a downward tracking shot that spans the façade of a single building. The representational difficulty that such a setting may pose evidently resides in its strong uniformity, as opposed to the fantasy or the instability of the clouds previously depicted. In such an instance, how can a graphic artist give the illusion of a moving frame? To solve this particular problem, Shaw engages here in a rather subtle play on borders. Not only does he neutralize the lateral borders of these sixteen panels (so as to once again produce a straight-line trajectory), but he strives to resolutely activate the lower border of the panels. As the frame progressively moves over the surface of the building, new windows are thereby uncovered, most often in three phases: first, in a discreet and fragmentary fashion near the bottom border, then in a more straightforward manner, before appearing in full as the result of a progressive discovery—a process that is repeated several times. There again, the sheer literal principle of "iconic solidarity" prevails; should any one of these panels be missing, the very movement of the frame would fall into illegibility.

Segmenting the façade of the skyscraper in continuous fragments and thereby producing, in passing, various effects of *surcadrage* (a frame within frame) in repeated succession, this third page—like many others within the album—tends to make the original figurative material more abstract. In so doing, it sometimes evokes, in its very regularity, some of Paul Klee's works such as *Static-Dynamic Gradation* (1923) or *Ancient Sound, Abstract on Black* (1925), with the latter painting also adopting a square format, which perhaps is not an insignificant similarity. In its conformation, such a page is also reminiscent of the well-known grid structure, which Rosalind Krauss, in a notable essay, considered as "emblematic of the modernist ambition of visual arts" (1981, 167) and in which she sought to identify "the omnipresent form of [twentieth-century] art" (1981, 169).[11]

Spread over three pages and no fewer than forty-eight frames, the majestic framing movement with which *Travelling Square District* begins can only produce an intense effect of mystery or suspense: What is this continuous tracking shot seeking to find, what is it chasing exactly, and what will it capture in the end?

Flowing Down the River

In the final section of *Travelling Square District*, Yorg Schwager knocks out Georg W. Ashry, who had hired his services, before drowning him in his bathtub. Through this action, the hitman rids himself of an "inconvenient witness," in his own words ("un témoin gênant"). The last two narrative pages of the book show us, in a fixed and medium shot, the same character as he is finding refuge in what looks like a peep show building near the river.

Following this ultimate plot twist, Shaw's work ends like it started: with three strictly descriptive pages spanned by a moving point of view. Quite notably, the antepenultimate and penultimate pages of the volume enclose and concentrate compelling downward motions in their lower portions (panels twelve, thirteen, fourteen, fifteen, and sixteen on the first of these two pages, and panels eleven, twelve, thirteen, fourteen, fifteen, and sixteen on the second). As he reaches the end of his narrative, Shaw engages in a final

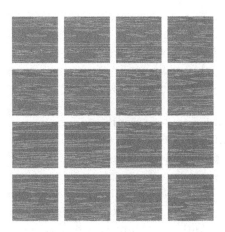

Figure 4: Spanning the flow of the river.
©*Éditions Sarbacane.*

reflection through images on the possibilities that a moving frame may offer to the language of comics. For this purpose, the author focuses his point of view on a site located, topographically speaking, at the antipode of the sky that was explored within the frame of the first page. Thanks to the aforementioned downward motions, he now directs his gaze onto the water in the river, with which the perspective aligns in the last frame of the penultimate page (Fig. 4).

Like the clouds on the opening page, the murky (grayish/greenish) water of the river presents itself as a relatively amorphous surface upon which the entire question of the mobile frame can acutely reformulate itself. In this instance, Shaw relies on the same device as in the opening of the volume; between two consecutive panels, he strives to maintain, in an overlapping fashion, a marker of graphic continuity that allows one to determine the direction followed by the frame. Yet this is not the main point. A more remarkable factor is that in this closing segment, Shaw sets out to constrict the movements of the frame by restricting them to two options: Either the tracking shot progresses from left to right (as in the first fifteen panels), or it proceeds from high to low (as in the last panel). In other words, nothing comes to hamper the wandering of the gaze on this final page. It removes any friction between the movements produced by the frame and the standard trajectory of the reading process. In such a composition, the reader's gaze only has to glide, to let itself be carried by the flow of the water until the last panel. This device functions as an implicit invitation to slide out of the narrative and to disengage from the relatively demanding design that presided over the structure of the work to that point.

For a Para-History of Cinema

From its title to the devices that it employs (horizontal or vertical tracking shots, zooms, long takes, but also, in some of the narrative episodes, flashbacks with subtle shifts from color to black and white), as well as in the various references that it evokes implicitly or explicitly (Vidor, Wilder,

Hitchcock, Snow, etc.), Shaw's album is evidently deeply infused, in the very heart of its apparatus, by cinema, either traditional or experimental. In a manner of speaking, *Travelling Square District* could be labeled as a "para-cinematographic" work, to the extent that this album applies its mechanics and reveals its actual stakes only in relation to or in proximity with cinema. In this regard, *Travelling Square District* benefits from a comparison with a work such as *Cinema Panopticum* (2008) by the Swiss graphic artist Thomas Ott, a completely wordless album in black and white that follows a little girl wandering in a fairground. Destitute, she ends up in a remote fairground stand, where she can view—thanks to slot machines that closely resemble the kinetoscope device invented by Thomas Edison in the 1890s—five different stories, one after the other (in chronological order: "The Hotel," "The Champion," "The Experiment," "The Prophet," and "The Girl"), which present themselves as various fantastic fictions filled with strange characters. In other words, this album derives its very substance from the moving pictures that unfurl in front of the little girl's gaze, sometimes intrigued and sometimes frightened, whose point of view the reader is led to share. Moreover, the relationship between Thomas Ott's work and cinema is not only a matter of narrative pretext. Indeed, it is worth noting that *Cinema Panopticum* became the subject of an actual art exhibit at the Bologna Film Archive in March of 2009—an initiative so rare that it deserves to be emphasized. Perhaps even more surprisingly, the work of the Swiss graphic artist also constitutes the visual subject matter of a kind of hybrid spectacle, a "comics-concert" conceived by the Skeleton Band, a folk-rock group from Montpellier that performs on stage while the frames from *Cinema Panopticum* are projected on a screen and organized in sequences, as a backdrop. Evidently, this is a rather singular display where the comics image turns into, not a filmic image per se, but at the very least an image traversed and transported by light.

One should also connect the present analysis to the radical experiment that is Marc-Antoine Mathieu's *3 secondes* (2011). This is a virtuosic album that responds to the ambitious challenge of detailing the scene of a crime in a single "playful zoom," which is dizzying, uninterrupted, and particularly rich in plot twists and visual rebounds of all kinds. Additionally, it is a hybrid work, as it also exists in digital version, between comics and video.[12] After having typed a password available on the inside cover of the hard copy of the book, the reader/spectator is put in control of the zoom around which the work is organized. He or she is invited to use a cursor in order to "bend time (toward the right in order to speed it up, the center to slow it down, and the left to reverse it)"—all temporal manipulations in which cinema engaged from its beginning,[13] and which later left their marks in films by directors as diverse as René Clair (*Entr'acte*, 1924, on a script by Francis Picabia), Jean Epstein (*The Fall of the House of Usher*, 1928), or Dziga Vertov (*Kino-Glaz*, 1924; *Man with a Movie Camera*, 1929), to cite only works from the 1920s.

Anecdotally—although this connection seems particularly revealing—one of the pages of *3 secondes* mentions, as an almost subliminal detail (the spine of a book only fully visible in one frame) or a nod, the name of Greg Shaw himself, in the vicinity of other artists to whom Mathieu likes to refer and whom he counts among his acknowledged influences, such as Nikki de Saint-Phalle, M. C. Escher, Anish Kapoor, or Jeff Koons.[14]

At the very least, one can conclude that we are dealing here with graphic works that are genuinely haunted by cinema as a device and a mode of representation. At any rate, are such visual objects not positioned in the margins of the history of cinema? In such, do they not share the inherent characteristic of bringing the limits of this history into question? More radically even, do they not argue in favor of extending the perimeter that is generally allocated to it? One can at least wonder, quite simply, if works of this kind do not call for the development of a para-history of cinema, a field of inquiry that would encompass all graphic projects that are, in one way or another, permeated, possessed, or obsessed by cinema.

Translated from the French by Fabrice Leroy,
Shelly Miller Leroy, and Livio Belloï

Endnotes

1. OuBaPo is a comics movement with variable membership that was created in 2002 by Thierry Groensteen and Jean-Christophe Menu. It conceives itself as the graphic prolongation of the OuLiPo (*Ouvroir de Littérature Potentielle* [Workshop of Potential Literature]), the illustrious collective founded in 1960 by Raymond Queneau and François Le Lionnais. Like its literary predecessor, the OuBaPo promotes the idea of creation under predefined constraints. For an overview of these constraints (random consecution, overlaying, iconic restriction, textual iteration, etc.) and the formal plays that they may generate, see OuBaPo 2003. For a history and a general description of the movement, see Menu 2011.

2. On this issue, see for instance the interview that the author granted to the website Génération BD in 2010 (last consulted 22 September 2020): https://www.generationbd.com/interviews/20-interviews-ecrites/1242-interview-bd-qgreg-shawq-travelling-square-district-sarbacane.html. Last consulted 9 April 2022.

3. Although not a perfect anagram of "Gregory Shaw," "Howy Beggars" contains the letters that make up "Greg Shaw."

4. In this work outside of the norms, the first and last names of the author are used to designate, thanks to a similar anagrammatic play, the authors of various imaginary works, whose covers are incorporated in the body of the book itself. Thus, the full name "Marc-Antoine Mathieu" becomes, rather poetically, "Mathieu Mainraconte," "Maurice-Nathan Moite," "Maria Toutenmachine," etc. We will come back to the connections between Mathieu and Shaw in more detail, later in this chapter.

5. Not surprisingly, this first frame corresponds exactly to the portion of sky delineated by the square with black borders located on the upper left side of the book cover. As it were, this frame was already precarved in the matrix image of the album.

6. To be completely precise, Shaw refrains in principle from any form of zigzag. Therefore, a lateral movement made in a given direction cannot be immediately followed by another lateral movement in the opposite direction. In other words, every directional shift in a particular dimension (lateral or vertical) must be announced, and, in a sense, buffered by a change of direction in the other dimension. Here lies a supplementary constraint, more discreet, yet effective.

7. On the complex device that governs *La Région centrale* and on the multiple effects of movement that it allows, see de Loppinot 2010, 81–93.

8. At the end of the first sequence of *La Région centrale*, around the thirtieth minute of the film, the filming apparatus only captures an empty, cloudless blue sky, a pure monochrome surface whose contact seems to reduce the camera to an apparent immobility.

9. In an earlier period of film history, one can also think of the beginning of *The Crowd* (King Vidor, 1928), with its ample vertical tracking shot focusing on the façade of an imposing New York skyscraper.

10. The sentence by Paul Klee that Perec places as the epigraph of his preamble ("The eye follows the paths that have been managed for it in the work") certainly takes on a particular resonance for the reader of *Travelling Square District*. For a stimulating re-reading of *Life: A User's Manual*, more specifically on the subject of the relations that it weaves between the parts and the whole, see Joly 2013. In the realm of comics, Perec's "architectural" composition, with its transversal cuts into cityscapes and its inventories of objects, has most notably inspired Chris Ware's *Building Stories* project (2012).

11. This correlation appears even more interesting insofar as one of the narrative threads weaved by *Travelling Square District*, as previously noted, involves a bomb attack on a Museum of Abstract Art (a building located on the left middle side of the cover). Let us also recall that the double question of painting and abstraction constitutes a paramount notion in *Parcours Pictural* (*Pictural Itinerary*), an album that Greg Shaw published in 2005. For a more general and more recent perspective on the grid motif, see Higgins 2009.

12. The digital version of *3 secondes* is available at the following address (last consulted on March 16, 2022): https://youtu.be/00xwHWeifPE.

13. On the subject of early cinema, one thinks especially of a maneuver that some of the Lumière cameramen would perform upon the projected film. In this regard, see Félix Mesguich's testimony: "In Boston at the Grand Opera House, in front of a packed audience, I show a new film, *Baths at Milan, Italy*, which I have just received. For the first time, on a whim, I take the chance of having the divers come out of the water, by turning the crank backward. The room erupts in overwhelming applause, and it is such a resounding success that my wages are increased. This is a surprise that I was not expecting; it proves that sometimes one benefits from beginning with the end" (1933, 12). As we know, the same process of reversing the reel was often applied to another well-known Lumière film, namely *Demolition of a Wall*. With regards to a frantic acceleration of time, the most exemplary film of this period is of course *Onésime Horloger* (*Onésime, Clockmaker*, 1912) directed by Jean Durand.

14. Mathieu's homage to Shaw can also be explained by the fact that the author of *3 secondes* has himself favored, in this particular work, the form of the square, much like his predecessor (in the format of the album, and in page layouts consisting of 3 x 3 squares). Reciprocally, Shaw has made his admiration for Mathieu quite clear by stating unequivocally that "this is undoubtedly the author that has put me on the path of experimentation." (See the 2010 interview mentioned in Note 2.)

Works Cited

DE LOPPINOT, Stéfani. 2010. *La Région centrale de Michael Snow*. Crisnée, Belgium: Éditions Yellow Now.

GROENSTEEN, Thierry. 2011. *Système de la bande dessinée* Paris: PUF. First published in 1999. Citations refer to the 2011 edition.

HIGGINS, Hannah B. 2009. *The Grid Book*. Cambridge, MA: MIT Press.

JOLY, Jean-Luc. 2013. "Détail et totalité dans *La Vie mode d'emploi*." In *La Mécanique du détail. Approches transversales*, edited by Livio Belloï and Maud Hagelstein, 65–80. Lyon, France: ENS Éditions.

KRAUSS, Rosalind. 1981. "Grilles." *Communications* 34: 167–76.

MATHIEU, Marc-Antoine. 2011. *3 secondes*. Paris: Delcourt.

———. 2017. *Le Livre des livres*. Paris: Delcourt.

MENU, Jean-Christophe. 2011. *La Bande dessinée et son double*. Paris: L'Association.

MESGUICH, Félix. 1933. *Tours de manivelle. Souvenirs d'un chasseur d'images*. Paris: Grasset.

OTT, Thomas. 2008. *Cinema panopticum*. Paris: L'Association.

OuBaPo. 2003. *OuPus 2*. Paris: L'Association.

PEETERS, Benoît. 1998. *Lire la bande dessinée*. Paris: Flammarion.

PEREC, Georges. 1978. *La Vie mode d'emploi*, "Le Livre de poche" edition. Paris: Hachette.

SHAW, Greg. 2010. *Travelling Square District*. Paris: Éditions Sarbacane.

CHAPTER TWO:

Ghosting the Film: Graphic Restitution and Intermediality in Nadar and Frey's *Avec Édouard Luntz, le cinéaste des âmes inquiètes*

Fabrice Leroy

Julien Frey and Nadar's graphic novel *Avec Édouard Luntz, le cinéaste des âmes inquiètes* (*With Édouard Luntz, the filmmaker of anxious souls*) published in 2018 by Futuropolis, presents itself as a double hermeneutic quest. First and foremost, the narrative recounts Julien Frey's laborious attempt at reassembling a cohesive portrait of a somewhat forgotten French filmmaker of the 1960s, the mercurial Édouard Luntz—an investigation into the past that involves the problematic exhuming of the creator's lost works. On a second level, Frey and Nadar's endeavor takes on a restorative or substitutive function: to compensate for the loss or inaccessibility of filmic images by redrawing them with graphic means, as transmedial equivalents. Although my analysis will necessarily focus on these two dimensions—the thematic attempt at biographical excavation and the intermedial dialogue between cinema and comics—I will devote most of my attention to the latter subject. It is important to note from the onset that the book's title has polysemic implications, to the extent that the opening preposition "avec" ("with") implies a relationship of complicity between the biographer and his subject, but also an artistic collaboration or hybridity of sorts, as if the hypotext of Luntz's films permeated the graphic representation itself.[1]

In a retrospective narrative, Frey recalls how he made the fortuitous acquaintance of Luntz and his films. Going back to his years as a young film student and budding filmmaker, Frey reveals how he once met the much older Luntz, who offered to produce one of his short films. The memory of this failed interaction provides the haunting impetus to repair a missed opportunity, as Frey, initially unimpressed by Luntz and even distrustful of the older man—who appeared on the decline both physically and economically and whose films he had not yet seen—was quick to dismiss him as a potential producer. Having subsequently discovered fragments of the great director's works, Frey begins an obsessive and sometimes comical quest to locate copies of his entire oeuvre in various archives, which proves far more difficult than he anticipated. Indeed, Luntz's films have either slipped through the gaps of a very imperfect preservation apparatus or have been purposefully disappeared by the filmmaker's enemies. None of them are currently available commercially and only a handful can be found here and there: in the makeshift VHS collection of the Sorbonne's Cinema Studies department, in the audiovisual collection of the Bibliothèque Nationale de France (BNF), and at the French Cinémathèque. One particular object of mystery is Luntz's *Le Grabuge* (*Mayhem*), a 1968 international production financed by Fox Studios. Frey eventually locates a reel of this movie at the Laboratoire Éclair, a film development agency, but the cost of printing a personal copy for his viewing is prohibitive. An archive in São Paulo, Brazil, lists the film among its holdings but has lost its only copy. Finally, Frey travels to the Library of Congress Film Library in Washington, DC, to secure a private viewing of this elusive work, only to be disappointed by it in the end for reasons that are worth discussing later.

The quest for this cinematic grail not only provides a linear plot structure filled with narrative tension, as Frey's investigation is repeatedly thwarted, but it is also the framework upon which Frey grafts a meta-filmic reflection, which centers on mechanisms of institutional production, legitimation, and conservation. As a "un film-fantôme" ("a ghost film") (Nadar and Frey 2018, 73), *Le Grabuge* embodies many of the paradoxes of the 1960s film industry. Frey struggles with the initial contradiction inherent to the relative anonymity[2] and invisibility of a prizewinning filmmaker who was a contemporary of more famous directors such as Jean-Luc Godard and Maurice Pialat, and whose films featured a soundtrack by Serge Gainsbourg,[3] as well as legendary actors of this generation, notably Jeanne Moreau and Michel Bouquet, with whom Frey stages an interview in this graphic novel. He also reminds his readers of the conflict between Luntz and American producer Darryl Zanuck over the final cut of *Le Grabuge*, which led to a lawsuit that Luntz won, but that ultimately resulted in Zanuck's retaliation by removing the movie from theaters and burying it in the vaults of Fox Studios. In the duel between these men, Frey draws a contrast between opposite figures: the entrepreneurial American studio producer, preoccupied with commercial imperatives[4] and exerting tyrannical control over creators, and the anti-establishment French filmmaker, self-destructive and unconcerned with market realities. Plagued with delays and difficulties caused by filming on location in Brazil in the tempestuous 1960s, tied to an ever-changing and often improvised script, bogged

down by the chaotic nature of an international cast and an international production, having incurred a massive budget overrun, and further mutilated by
Zanuck's ruthless cuts, which reduced the film's length from three hours to
a mere one hour and twenty minutes, the final version of *Le Grabuge* is an
imperfect object, which can only leave the viewer guessing at what it could
have been in the best of circumstances.

This is the other impetus for Frey's obsession with the film: Its flawed
nature and enigmatic incompleteness are invitations to reinvestigating its
voids. To this extent, the graphic novel celebrates the connecting power of
film and provides an opportunity to redeem the missed interaction of his
original encounter with a visibly damaged director, whose greatness he re-
grettably underestimated. Fascinated by the spectacle captured on film and
by the ontological reality of the filming itself, intrigued by the uniqueness
of Luntz's vision, and nostalgic for a lost era of French cinema, Frey seeks
metonymic contact with it through the testimonies of its actors and attempts
to reconstruct, fifty years after the filming of *Le Grabuge* in Brazil, a graphic
documentary on the "making of" this movie. Wishing to enter into vicarious
contact with the film, to be "with" it, as the title of the book suggests ("avec"),
he attempts to mediate his own proximity with the footage through people
who were once close to Luntz: his family and his actors. His son Thomas,
himself a scriptwriter for television, provides him with a digitized copy of
the films he has in his possession, and discusses the complications of making
them commercially available again (Nadar and Frey 2018, 110–15). Thomas
Luntz also draws an ambivalent portrait of his father, a notoriously difficult
man who struggled with addiction and depression.

Later, Frey meets two of the nonprofessional actors whom Luntz used
in his 1966 release *Les Cœurs verts* (*The Green Hearts*): Monique Prim, who
later became a film editor (Nadar and Frey 2018, 125–27), and Gérard
Zimmerman or Zim, also featured in *Le Grabuge* (128–35). The conversation with Zim centers on an iconic substitute, a black-and-white photograph
taken on the Brazilian set of *Le Grabuge*, showing the four male lead actors
riding horses (131). As a conversation piece, this visual artifact—itself of a
metonymic nature as it implies contact with its referent—negotiates a link
between past and present, representation and reality, presence and absence,
and, ultimately, Luntz and Frey. Furthermore, as a drawn replica,[5] an intermedial translation of another iconic sign, it belongs to the same realm created
by the intersection of photo-chemical arts (photography and cinema) and
graphic representation that I will discuss below. Zim also shares with Frey
another photograph—once again redrawn—of an actor and former juvenile

delinquent named Loulou, who is featured both in *Les Cœurs verts* and in a
Luntz documentary entitled *La Fête à Loulou* (*Loulou's Party*), showing his
release from prison (133).[6] In a reciprocal exchange, Frey gives Zim a copy of
all of Luntz's films in his possession, reconnecting the actor with his past work
(135). The most touching of Frey's encounters with Luntz's former collaborators is perhaps his visit with Michel Bouquet, a legend of French cinema and
theater, who at ninety years old is returning to the stage (143–53). Bouquet,
appearing frail and anxious, nevertheless draws a flattering portrait of Luntz,
a man of "immense talent" (146), who was a victim of his irritable temper
and unjustly missed the fame he deserved. After sharing some complicity with
his interviewer over his illustrious career and his most noted performances,
Bouquet leaves his interlocutor with a piece of advice: "Faites quelque chose
de grand!" ("Do something grand!")(153).

Over the course of Frey's investigation, it clearly appears that his captivation with Luntz's movies lies in their tangible sense of humanity. What
appeals to Frey is their closeness to people, their palpable intimacy, their manifest affection for people with existential difficulties: juvenile delinquents, the
disadvantaged youth on the fringes of society.[7] By employing and mentoring
nonprofessional actors who came from underprivileged backgrounds, the al-
truistic filmmaker infused his works with poetic realism and visible com-
passion (Fig. 1). Frey seeks to reciprocate this empathetic aspect of Luntz's
films not only by entering into contact with those who were involved in
making them, but also by *entering the films themselves* through his imaginative
self-projection, made possible by a series of graphic constructs.

This is accomplished by repurposing some of the filmic images within
a dialogue with Frey and his readers through various reflexive devices. The
section devoted to describing the making of *Le Grabuge*, for instance, redraws some photograms from the movie yet with a significant distanciation
effect, in that the graphic panel recedes from the actual frame to reveal how
it was produced by the act of filming (Nadar and Frey 2018, 62). A panel
showing the film crew is followed by other panels showing the camera lens,
the clapperboard with handwritten marks for editing purposes, and the filmmaker himself behind the camera. This return to the ontological moment of
filming also attempts to reactivate some realness within the simulacrum by
showing the actors not only exchanging small talk between takes, but also
commenting on the improbability of their situation, as young working-class
Parisians with little professional experience involved in the filming of a major
production in an exotic location (63). Breaking the fourth wall, the actors'
meta-commentary on their extraordinary situation places the reader within

Figure 1: Nadar redraws a scene from Luntz's documentary *Enfants des courants d'air*, featuring children from underprivileged backgrounds. ©*Futuropolis*.

the fabric of the film, in direct contact with its participants. A similar device is at play in another passage where Nadar[8] inserts Frey's gaze between the filmmaker and his actors. This sequence is displayed symmetrically, as a double-page unit devoted to an overview of *Les Cœurs verts*, Luntz's best known film (78–79). It shows, on the left page, Luntz looking directly at the reader to explain his creative objectives, and, on the right, his actors recalling the circumstances of their involvement with this semi-documentary project. From the testimonial perspective of Frey's investigation, this sequence is a pure visual construct, as it presents the film participants, drawn in relation to their appearance in 1966, communicating with present-day readers. Based on interviews with Luntz[9] and his protagonists reworked in graphic form, this segment probes the representational principle at play in *Les Cœurs verts*, between the authenticity of *cinéma-vérité* (albeit a label with which Luntz refused to be associated) and the anti-establishment worldview of the Nouvelle Vague and its fascination with adolescent revolt. Between the left section outlining the filmmaker's artistic intent and the right section focusing on the actors' fortuitous involvement in cinema, Nadar inserts two frames showing Frey's own creative and professional difficulties, as he is shown pitching script ideas for an animation series to a production company, without much enthusiasm for this venture. This graphic braiding (Groensteen 1999, 173–86) of two separate narrative lines and timeframes not only intertwines Luntz's biography with that of his own biographer, drawing a parallel between both, but it also projects Frey inside Luntz's artistic process. A close-up panel zooming in on his face, with his gaze pointed downward at Luntz's actors below, displays his disengagement from his own reality and engrossment with—and projection into—another creator's filmic universe.

Frey's symbolic absorption into Luntz's movies relies on trans- or intermedial devices that hybridize film and comics in a manner that breaks the fourth wall in reverse, allowing the present-day cinephile to infiltrate the representational realm of the movies he admires. Page eighty-seven offers a semiosis of this kind: Divided into six panels of constant dimensions, it faithfully reproduces photograms from *Les Cœurs verts* with matching black-and-white aesthetics. The duplicated scene, one of the film's most iconic passages, shows a gang of young men, dressed in jeans and black leather jackets, sitting or standing on a metal scaffold, a setting that embodies the industrial wasteland of the *banlieue* (suburb) and the boredom of its youth. In addition to their translation of photograms into comics frames, Frey and Nadar graft external elements onto the replicated images. First, above the top two frames, they insert narrative captions describing Luntz's preference for nonprofessional

Figure 2: Nadar depicts Frey entering into Luntz's film. ©*Futuropolis*.

actors who can infuse the film with their own existential veracity. This metanar-rative commentary results in a detachment from the original diegetic meaning of the images, to the extent that it repurposes and re-signifies the source material as a didactic exposé intended to illustrate the filmmaker's aesthetic and sociological intent. The bottom of the same page performs a second graft that goes far beyond the addition of a secondary layer of text: Nadar depicts Frey climbing the scaffold, then sitting next to one of the leather-clad youngsters, inside the diegetic universe. Here again, the textual elements of these two panels speak of Frey's desire to com-municate[10] with the movie's participants—"J'ai envie de leur parler" ("I feel like talking to them")—but ends with the actors reestablishing some distance with the intrusive viewer, as the young delinquent warns Frey that he does not belong in his world and neither is he equipped to hang with such company ("Tu tiendrais pas dix minutes avec nous" ["You would not be able to last ten minutes with us"]), which deflates his fantasy of kinship (Fig. 2).

Similar devices are put to use in other parts of the graphic novel. A few pages later, when viewing *Les Cœurs verts* at home for the first time, Frey's wife remarks that Gainsbourg's soundtrack is an earlier version of his 1969 erotic anthem "Je t'aime moi non plus" ("I love you me neither"). As if he had heard her observation across the temporal and mimetic divide, the ac-tor Zim displayed on screen replies to her statement from inside the film: "Gainsbourg la réutilisera. Pour l'instant, c'est juste parfait pour emballer" ("Gainsbourg will reuse it. For the moment, it's perfect to seduce girls"), al-luding to the slow dance he performs on film with his female partner (Nadar and Frey 2018, 90). His meta-commentary reshapes the source material, in-sofar as it fuses Frey's awareness of Gainsbourg's future history with the actor's exposition of his character's motives. In a later sequence, Frey and Nadar reproduce again some photograms of *Les Cœurs verts* and insert Frey's effigy into the diegetic universe, as a bystander of the same dance scene, sitting on a chair in the background, a spectator embedded in the film (123). Another temporal amalgam—a caption superimposed on a redrawn photogram, as an addendum to the film—indicates that one of the dancers, Monique Prim, will later become a renowned film editor in her own right. On the following page, Moustique, a future film set photographer and one of the film's char-acters, replies directly to his commentary and notes that Monique is his wife (another addendum inserted, this time, in the shape of a speech balloon). To conclude this scene, one of the tough guys from the gang—an individual named Loulou, who would eventually be sentenced to jail and become the subject of a 1980 Maurice Pialat film—confronts him and tells him that he is sitting in his chair (124).

Although the redrawing of photograms from Luntz's œuvre (as well as from other films[11]) is a recurrent device in Nadar and Frey's graphic novel, it takes on a particular significance in the case of *Le Grabuge*, precisely because of the film's unavailability to present-day viewers. Although the source material that inspired the drawn replicas exists as a model, the very inaccessibility of the film imbues the hand-traced images with a particular function and meaning, as iconic substitutes of "ghost" images. Indeed, remediation has often been understood within a "progressist" logic of media replacement (Baetens 2014, 44), implying either improved technological means (McLuhan 1964) or more mimetic forms of representation, better adapted to modern consumption expectations and standards of realism (Bolter and Grusin 1999). However, the remediation proposed by Nadar and Frey, despite its obvious concern for aesthetic integrity, appears more regressive in nature—far from a technological upgrade or an exercise toward enhanced verisimilitude, their comics panels translate film frames into simpler and more organic images. This process of graphic restatement, although mimetic in itself (to the extent that the drawn images are necessarily constrained by their fidelity to their source material) relies on approximation and simplification to produce new signifiers. The resulting product of such remediation appears therefore to have retrogressed in relation to its model, both technologically and mimetically. By the very nature of the comics frames, what remains of the duplicated films can only be partial and selective. Unable to reproduce the full cinematic experience—in particular, the sequential continuity of moving images[12]—Nadar and Frey can only excise photograms as indexical fragments of the whole, in a panel-to-frame analogy. Likewise, they cannot attain the same level of realism as the photo-chemical imprint and must resort to stylistic devices inherent to the visual vocabulary of comics to achieve a corresponding effect: In this instance, Nadar combines photorealistic elements in the depiction of the scenery with a more minimalistic style akin to *ligne claire* in the rendition of characters. Although Nadar's black-and-white aesthetics are aligned with Luntz's sober and somber realism, the "schematic realism" of the *ligne claire* (Groensteen 2013, 3) translates the morphology of the actors into outlines that only preserve its most essential traits yet forfeits the components of the filmic signifier that are superfluous to its immediate legibility.

Nadar and Frey's frequent interventions in the redrawn footage indicate that, despite the reportage format of their narrative, their treatment of film fragments and film in general often tends to be more symbolic than purely descriptive or reiterative. One double-page spread appears quite metaphorical in this regard; it shows Frey still on the hunt for *Le Grabuge* and engaged in conversation with Pierre Boustouller, the director of Laboratoire Éclair's cultural heritage division (Nadar and Frey 2018, 138–39). Discussing film history and the subject of American studios' perfunctory sponsorship of 1960s French cinema, the two interlocutors are shown walking on an unwound spool of film whose shape uncoils across the double page in a zigzag pattern. Deviating from realism, this figurative display replaces the grid format of comics with another composition pattern that relies on the analogy between film frames and graphic panels, with the film strip serving as a vehicle for a sequential arrangement, albeit one that guides the reader's gaze in a different direction than the standard left-to-right and top-to-bottom path. The reader can infer another analogy in this visual construct, as the meandering course of the strip reflects Frey's convoluted quest. Yet, the correlation between the film strip and the comics grid entails another distanciation effect that draws attention to the limits of the intermedial analogy, insofar as the characters themselves are not contained within the individual frames, but are represented as three-dimensional figures detached from the flatness of the strip, as if they had escaped from the realm of representation—they are not in the film itself but above it.

Nevertheless, Nadar and Frey's cinephilic or "epistemophilic" drive—to borrow Christine Sprengler's befitting expression (2014, 67)—does not result in a mere impoverishment of the source images. By intervening inside the film excerpts to enter into a cross-temporal and transmedial dialogue with Luntz's vision, as I have shown above, the authors of the graphic novel also renegotiate our distance therewith. Although the present-day reader of *Avec Édouard Luntz* is twice removed from the original filmic material, to the extent that he or she can only access it through images of (lost) images, Nadar and Frey's affective investment partially mitigates this separation. Furthermore, their treatment of *Le Grabuge* attempts to capture more than isolated photograms and to provide a fuller equivalent of the viewing experience, particularly in the section of the graphic novel where the authors reconstruct the first showing of Luntz's three-hour cut to the film crew and a baffled Zanuck, in January of 1969 (Nadar and Frey 2018, 64–67). In order to render the experience of the film projection, the pages of this segment alternate between frames from the film and depictions of the viewers' reactions thereto, in a complex system of braiding that oscillates between two diametrically opposed gazes: that of the film shot itself, and, in a manner of a counter-shot, that of the spectator. Page sixty-three begins with the title frame of the movie, then shows the anticipative gaze of the French actors (Erick Penet and Gérard Zimmerman), smiling. The middle row of three panels reproduces three frames of the movie's

Figure 3: Recreating the viewing experience of the first cut of *Le Grabuge*.
©Futuropolis.

opening sequence: the church wedding of Patricia Gozzi and Zim, arm in arm; a close-up on Gozzi's face, relatively expressionless, with her wedding veil lifted; and Zim's sideways glance at her, in a proportional close-up. The three panels of the bottom row show Zanuck's sour facial expression, contrasting with the hopeful attitude of the actors, across the page's left-to-right diagonal axis; Luntz's attentive and seemingly confident gaze; and another scene from the movie, with actors dancing (Fig. 3).

The double unit of pages sixty-six and sixty-seven continue the same system of alternance and parallels, with the occasional braiding of a third element: a depiction of the projector itself, accompanied by sound onomatopoeia, or shown frontally as a ray of light emanating from a center, in the darkness of the theater. In this regard, these pages of the graphic novel showcase the three main components of cinematic interaction: what is shown, what is showing, and who is seeing. While, in the interspersed panels, Luntz's reaction remains more or less identical—albeit neutral—the various panels presenting Zanuck display a visible progression in frustration and anger. Ostensibly bored and disinterested, his younger girlfriend falls asleep next to him.

More importantly, perhaps, the redrawn frames of Le Grabuge, despite their indexical or synecdochal function, prevent the reader from attaining a comprehensive grasp of the movie's plot. Three panels (two displayed continuously, side by side, and a third disjoined from the first series by a panel showing the projector) present two passengers (presumably the Gozzi and Zim couple) in a rowboat on the ocean, moving slowly from left to right across the length of each panel (Nadar and Frey 2018, 66). Another two sets of conjoined panels show two characters performing a rather acrobatic dancing scene (bottom of page 66) (Fig. 4) and two naked individuals walking on the beach under umbrellas (bottom of page 67).

Allusive, evocative, atmospheric at best, such enigmatic images seem disconnected from any semantic intelligibility or narrative linearity. Frey's disappointment with Le Grabuge lies ultimately in the film's inherent opaqueness, whether it results from Luntz's oneiric approach, which deviates from his usual documentary style, or, subsequently, from Zanuck's excessive cuts. In this regard, this section of the graphic novel, in contrast with other passages affirming a symbolic reconnection with the filmic material, adequately translates the viewer's alienation from cryptic signifiers. At the end of the graphic novel, another four-page section returns to the experience of viewing Le Grabuge (Nadar and Frey 2018, 172–75). Having finally located a copy of the elusive film in the Library of Congress holdings and made the journey to Washington with the exclusive intent of seeing this work at last, Frey relates

Figure 4: Redrawn frames from *Le Grabuge*. ©*Futuropolis*.

(through Nadar's drawings) his impression of the film. A single-panel page shows him from behind, facing a small video projection screen (172). The following page incorporates six redrawn photograms from the movie. The first four appear sequential, although without a clear narrative content; they show Zim and Gozzi elegantly dressed in 1960s fashion, sitting on lounge chairs near a body of water, either on a seaside terrace or a boat deck. They appear to be in conversation, but their faces are void of any clear expression and the panels contain no speech balloons that would assist the reader in extracting meaning from this scene. In a non sequitur, the last two panels occupying the bottom row of the page show a couple making love, although Gozzi's partner in this scene is no longer Zim but Bahamian-American actor Calvin Lockhart, a substitution that vaguely suggests a romantic twist in the plot. In this lovemaking scene, Frey and Nadar insert a caption stating their evaluation of the film's aesthetic beauty ("Certaines séquences sont très belles" ["Some of the sequences are quite beautiful"]), but the next page reaffirms the ultimate opaqueness of the plot: "Mais l'histoire n'est pas toujours compré-hensible" ("But the plot is not always intelligible") (174) (Fig. 5).

The other photograms graphically recreated on pages 174 and 175 re-main equally enigmatic or indeterminate: two men grabbing a woman's arms, a group of young men and women on a beach, shots of Patricia Gozzi, a close-up on actress Julie Dassin's face followed by images of the same actress running on a beach. In other captions, Frey comments on the apparent edit-ing complications that this movie must have presented and concludes about his eventual estrangement, which Nadar's cluster of narratively unpurposed images also conveyed to the reader: "Cette fois, je ne suis pas *avec* les person-nages. Je ne voyage pas" ("This time, I am not *with* the characters. I do not travel"). In contrast with the affective reconnection and iconic investment at play in the graphic remediation of other movies by Luntz, the section of the graphic novel devoted to *Le Grabuge* repeats its images only to stage a form of responsive dissociation.

Haunted by ghost films and haunting them in return, Frey and Nadar attempt to bridge the temporal and representational gap that separates them from Luntz's works.[13] In this endeavor, they co-opt the imaging and nar-rative capabilities of the comics medium to blend cinematic material into drawn signifiers and panel arrangements, which involves various intermedial constructs. Although their bittersweet narrative tells the story of a failed in-teraction between a film (and its creator) and its viewer, they mediate, miti-gate, and renegotiate this failure through the power of graphic representation, which ultimately results in a success.[14]

Figure 5: Juxtaposed fragments from *Le Grabuge* are allusive but opaque.
©Futuropolis.

Endnotes

1. From their early days, comics have redrawn filmic images, real or fictional, or have presented themselves as films. In the classic Hergéan corpus, well-known examples include the early, pre-Tintin series *Totor C.P. des Hannetons* (1926), presented as "un grand film comique" ("a great comic movie"), and the episode of *Le Lotus Bleu* (*The Blue Lotus*, 1936) in which Tintin watches the very movie whose filming he unknowingly interrupted in the previous album, *Les Cigares du Pharaon* (*The Cigars of the Pharaoh*). There is also a long-standing tradition of comic book adaptations (or novelizations) of films, such as Jack Kirby and Dan Adkins's graphic take on Stanley Kubrick's *2001: A Space Odyssey* (Marvel Comics, 1976) or Bruce Jones's various *Star Wars* albums for the same publisher. The appropriation and repurposing of film images within graphic narratives—along with that of many other different types of images such as photographs, maps, or charts—adds to the multimodal and multi-semiotic nature of the comics medium and changes their original signification. As Nancy Pedri notes: "When images are borrowed or quoted in the visual track of comics, their original context (real or imagined), as well as their re-presentation in the new context of the comics cartoon universe, also factor into the visual interpretative process. The appropriated images are made to exist in a different version, taking on new meanings with their new configuration and within the new comics context" (2017, 4). On the subject of comics redrawing movies, see Gordon et al., *Film and Comic Books* (2007) and Baetens, *Adaptation et bande dessinée* (2020).

2. Historians of French cinema have often overlooked Luntz. René Prédal's reference volume *Le Cinéma français depuis 1945* only contains two brief mentions of Luntz's name and refers to the filmmaker's career as an example of rapid decline after a promising first film, *Les Cœurs verts* (Prédal 1992, 218–19).

3. Frey finds a copy of Gainsbourg's single for Luntz's film *Les Cœurs verts* at a flea market in Montpellier (2018, 8).

4. Frey suggests that Zanuck's callous treatment of Luntz not only originates in his commercial mindset, but also in profound disinterest for French New Wave cinema, which American studios only supported for tax benefits. Conversely, he also proposes, via the testimony of Luntz's son, that the French filmmaker projected his own negativity onto Zanuck, which mitigates the latter's responsibility in the decline of Luntz's career.

5. This photograph also echoes a previous panel showing the same three men riding horses on a Brazilian beach, during the filming of *Le Grabuge* (Nadar and Frey 2018, 56). In this instance, the same referent is the object of three iconic representations: Zim's actual photograph inspired the drawn panel used diegetically to tell the story of the actors' personal adventure in Brazil; it is used again, later in the narrative, as a testimonial object aiding Zim's reminiscence (181–82).

6. The following page (Nadar and Frey 2018, 134) mentions that Maurice Pialat's film *Loulou* (1980), starring Gérard Depardieu and Isabelle Huppert, is based on the same

individual, who also had an affair with the film's scriptwriter (Arlette Langmann), who was Pialat's girlfriend at the time.

7. The title of the graphic novel borrows the phrase "âmes inquiètes" ("anxious souls") from Henri Chapier's review of *Les Coeurs verts* in the newspaper *Combat*: "Imaginez un cinéaste dont la poésie rappellerait les plus belles pages de Jean Genet (celles de *Notre-Dame-des-Fleurs* ou de *Querelle de Brest*), et une intelligence des phénomènes sociaux proche d'un Edgar Morin, visité par le rêve et la grâce . . . Imaginez un ci-néaste qui rompt avec la sempiternelle tradition bourgeoise, qui va chercher plus loin que le bout de son nez, sans se piquer d'intellectualisme, sans se croire investi d'un œil de moraliste ou de père de patronage. Ce cinéaste qui sait camper, décrire et faire vivre des êtres qui ne sont pas tout d'une pièce, *des âmes inquiètes*, romantiques et amères, des corps qui ressentent simultanément une série de désirs contradictoires, s'appelle Édouard Luntz. . . . En un mot, *Les Cœurs verts* donne au jeune cinéma français une dimension qui lui manquait : celle du reportage poétique, à partir d'une réalité traitée jusqu'ici par des esprits plats, bien-pensants. Pour la première fois, on saisit ce que signifient la déroute et l'angoisse, et que la violence et la brutalité peuvent naître du désarroi." ("Imagine a filmmaker whose poetry would echo the most beau-tiful pages from Jean Genet [those of *Notre-Dame-des-Fleurs* or of *Querelle de Brest*], with an understanding of social phenomena close to that of an Edgar Morin, touched by dream and grace . . . Imagine a filmmaker who breaks away from the usual mid-dle-class tradition, who looks farther than the tip of his nose, without claiming any intellectualism, without believing himself to be bestowed with the eyes of a moralist or those of a mentor of unprivileged children. This filmmaker who knows how to characterize, describe, and bring to life individuals who are not monolithic, who are *anxious souls*, romantic and bitter, bodies that simultaneously experience a series of contradictory desires, is called Édouard Luntz. . . . In a word, *Les Cœurs verts* brings to young French cinema a dimension that it was lacking: that of poetic reportage, based on a reality that was previously treated by one-dimensional, conformist minds. For the first time, one grasps the meaning of failure and anxiety, and understands that violence and brutality can be born of confusion.") (Chapier 1966).

8. Nadar is the pseudonym of Spanish comics illustrator Pep Domingo (born in 1985). He also collaborated with Julien Frey on an album entitled *L'Œil du STO* (2020), set during the German occupation of France and the Vichy regime.

9. One notable interview of Luntz was broadcasted on France Culture in June 1966, as part of Philippe Esnault's program entitled "Connaître le cinéma." Luntz discusses his perspective on the disenfranchised youth of the *banlieues* and his interest in de-picting adolescent revolt against society to highlight rejection of social marginality and his empathy for his characters' troubles. This interview is available at https://www.youtube.com/watch?v=eUCK6Rssowk.

10. In an interview broadcasted on *France Culture* (https://www.franceculture.fr/emissions/les-petits-matins/les-petits-matins-10), Julien Frey posits that one of the recurrent characteristics of Luntz's films is their desire to mitigate the experience of loss and separation that the author experienced during World War II, when he was

separated from his Jewish parents and hidden away from Paris. For instance, his documentary *Enfants des courants d'air* (*Children of the Breeze*) features children from the slums of Aubervilliers left to play in construction sites and urban wastelands. This movie ends with a close-up of an abandoned child crying to his playmates "Attendez-moi!" ("Wait for me!"), a scene reproduced on page eighty-one of the graphic novel. To that extent, the attempt at repairing a feeling of separateness at play in Luntz's works, like in those of other French-Jewish artists such as Georges Perec, may be infused with a biographical element.

11. In addition to images from *Les Coeurs verts*, which I already discussed, the graphic novel contains drawn reproductions of John Ford's *The Grapes of Wrath* (1940) as an example of Zanuck's domineering personality and harsh treatment of Henry Fonda (Nadar and Frey 2018, 29–32), and graphic stills from Jean Eustache's 1973 New Wave film *La Maman et la Putain* (*The Mother and the Whore*) (11–12), included in a segment recalling Frey's film school days. Nadar also redraws various scenes from Luntz's 1972 film *L'Humeur vagabonde* (*The Vagabond Mood*) (84), starring Michel Bouquet in a multitude of roles, including a nun.

12. Indeed, Nadar and Frey are not only unable to reproduce the impression of motion inherent to the frame rate of film projection, but they also do not attempt to reuse film stills to construct a full narrative arc through a page layout akin to the spatial arrangement of frames in the film photonovel (see Baetens 2019, 80–94). Instead, they favor a "sampling" approach: Their drawn replicas of film images only reproduce either brief and partial segments of the original movies, or a single image excised from its narrative context and reinserted in the expository logic of the story of Frey's investigation.

13. One could link this retrospective approach with a recent trend of film documentaries returning to the "making" of previous movies, for instance Nicolas Philibert's *Retour en Normandie* (*Return to Normandy*), which revisits the filming of René Allio's *Moi, Pierre Rivière, ayant égorgé ma mère, ma sœur et mon frère* (*I, Pierre Rivière, Having Slaughtered My Mother, My Sister and My Brother*) thirty years later, through interviews with the nonprofessional actors involved in the original project.

14. The success of the reconnecting enterprise is also achieved through a fruitful interaction with Luntz's original actors. In this regard, the ending of the graphic novel appears quite touching. As Frey conveys his ultimate disappointment with *Le Grabuge* to Zim, the two men tend to the latter's garden and drink beers together. Their final conversation centers on another absence, around which both men share a moment of complicity: When Frey remarks that the film set photograph showing the young actors on horseback has no equivalent in the script nor in the final cut of the movie, Zim retorts that the scene was likely one of Luntz's many improvised additions to the script and recalls that the horses were probably from the Brazilian Mangalarga breed—a detail of memorial clarity that provides partial closure to this conclusion, as if fragments of intelligibility escaped the movie's overall erasure. Frey also reciprocates the generosity of Zim's testimony by gifting him the Gainsbourg record he acquired at the flea market and reconciling him with his past through this exchange.

Works Cited

BAETENS, Jan. 2014. "Le médium n'est pas soluble dans les médias de masse." *Revue Hermès* 3 (7): 40–45.

BAETENS, Jan. 2019. *The Film Photonovel*. Austin: University of Texas Press.

BAETENS, Jan. 2020. *Adaptation et bande dessinée. Éloge de la fidélité*. Brussels: Les Impressions Nouvelles.

BOLTER, Jay David and Richard GRUSIN. 1999. *Remediation*. Cambridge, MA: MIT University Press.

CHAPIER, Henri. 1966. "Review of *Les Cœurs verts*." *Combat*, December 2, 1966.

ESNAULT, Philippe. 1966. Interview with Édouard Luntz. "Connaître le cinéma," France Culture, June 1966, www.youtube.com/watch?v=eUCK6Rssowk.

GORDON, Ian, Mark JANCOVICH, and Matthew P. MCALLISTER. 2007. *Film and Comic Books*. Jackson: University Press of Mississippi.

GROENSTEEN, Thierry. 1999. *Système de la bande dessinée*. Paris: Presses Universitaires de France.

———. 2013. "Ligne Claire." *Dictionnaire esthétique et thématique de la bande dessinée*. Neuvième Art 2.0, neuviemeart.citebd.org/spip.php?article690.

HAKEM, Tewfik. 2018. Entretien avec Julien Frey. "Les petits matins," *France Culture*, May 11, 2018. www.franceculture.fr/emissions/les-petits-matins/les-petits-matins-10.

McLUHAN, Marshall. 1964. *Understanding Media*. Toronto: University of Toronto Press.

NADAR and Julien FREY. 2018. *Avec Édouard Luntz, le cinéaste des âmes inquiètes*. Paris: Futuropolis.

PEDRI, Nancy. 2017. "Mixing Visual Media in Comics." *ImageTexT: Interdisciplinary Comics Studies* 9 (2): https://imagetextjournal.com/category/volume-9-issue-2/.

PRÉDAL, René. 1991. *Le Cinéma français depuis 1945*. Paris: Nathan Université.

SPRENGLER, Christine. 2014. "Remediation and Intermediality: From Moving to (Film) Still." *Hitchcock and Contemporary Art*, 67–89. New York: Palgrave McMillan.

CHAPTER THREE:
Godard's Contra-Bande: Early Comic Heroes in *Pierrot le fou* and *Le Livre d'image*

Tamara Tasevska

Introduction

Throughout Jean-Luc Godard's scope of work spanning over more than six decades, references to the comic strip strangely surface, seemingly unattached to any interpretative frame, creating instability and disproportion within the form of the films. Specific images of characters reading and performing *Les Pieds Nickelés* (*The Nickel Plated Feet*) or *Zig et Puce* appear in his early films À Bout de souffle (*Breathless*, 1960), *Une femme est une femme* (*A Woman is a Woman*, 1961), and *Pierrot le fou* (*Pierrot the Madman*, 1965), whereas in *Une femme est une femme* (1961), *Alphaville* (1965), *Made in U.S.A* (1966), and *Tout va bien* (*All's Well*, 1972), the whole of the diegetic world resembles the compositions and frames of the comic strip. In Godard's later period, even though we witness an acute shift in register of the image, comic figures ostensibly continue to appear, drained of color, as if photocopied several times, floating free in a void of empty black space detached from any definitive meaning. Without doubt, the filmmaker uses the comic strip as Brechtian means in order to provoke *distanciation* effects (Sterritt 1999, 64), but I would also suggest that these instances put forward by the comic may also function to point to provocative connections between aesthetics and politics.[1]

Thinking of Godard's œuvre, in the chapter "Au-delà de l'image-mouvement" ("Beyond the Movement-Image") of *L'Image-temps* (*The Time-Image*), Gilles Deleuze remarks that the filmmaker drew inspiration from the comic strip at its most cruel and cutting, thus constructing a world according to "émouvantes" ("touching") and "terrible" images that reach a level of autonomy in and of themselves (1985, 18–19). From a list of works spanning over a few decades, inhabited according to him with trenchant disconnected images, Deleuze extracts the still-vivid cartoonish quality of Godard's compositions and frames and substitutes it with the notion of *series:* "Avec Godard, l'image 'désenchaînée' devient sérielle et atonale" ("With Godard, the 'unchained' image becomes serial and atonal") (238). Godard's serial image, for Deleuze, responds to the political conditions of the errant, of the nomadic subject of a globalized world, and therefore to a set of entirely new problems than those of the subject in the pre-World War II period (253–55).

In this chapter, I would like to seize on the serial (unchained, atonal) image that Deleuze presents in relation to Godard's work as a leaping off point to ask how we might think about cinematic spectacles in relation to the notion of the historical image. My inquiry will be driven by two extraordinarily different sets of examples from Godard's work, both of which feature highly spectacular comic book images. The first involves *Pierrot le fou*, which spotlights Ferdinand, a disenchanted bourgeois driven into a road trip extravaganza with a female companion named Marianne. While Ferdinand continuously reads and references *Les Pieds Nickelés,* comic book elements also appear to affect the formal aspect of the film, giving rise to images dominated in primary colors, balloon-like narration repeating speech and exclamations interspersed with dialogues. First published in 1908, *Les Pieds Nickelés* is an early form of French-language *bande dessinée,*[2] centering on a group of young slackers who often get into trouble. Recent accounts have analyzed the theme of imperial conquest and colonial past in *Les Pieds Nickelés* as well as in other comics from the pre-World War II period such as *Zig et Puce,* pointing to the different adventures centered around white male characters with no regional traits whatsoever (McKinney 2011, 132–39, 156–58). An analysis involving the strangeness of the French countryside landscapes as it appears in *Pierrot le fou* and the politically vexed situations into which Ferdinand gets himself can suggest the profound formal and archaeological parallels between the film and the comic series and help rethink Godard's film as a modern cinematic form that activates fictional imageries and narratives of the past.

In sharp contrast, Godard's more recent work *Le Livre d'image* (*The Image Book*, 2018) superimposes elements of comic books in a rudimentary form; their remnants reshaped or transformed over other images form a heterogeneous cinematic and historical archive. The power of the spectacles these images create springs from their failure to metamorphose completely. This effect is furthered by Godard's revealing of his own technique—his voice-over narrates the effects while what we see are images of the cinematic mechanism that brought them into being. Godard's use of the comic strip as one of the spectacles transforming the power of images is thus complex and ambiguous, suggesting at once the bankrupt abyss of the serial image and the potentially deterritorializing power of comics that this world has produced.

Playing Panels and Cinematic Collage

A defining characteristic of Godard's films is their collage construction. Collage, along with its homologues *décollage* (ungluing, detaching) or *recollage* (patching up, reassembling), is often understood by most film critics as a radicalization of montage, a superimposition of media elements as well as verbal and visual quotations, and the creation of meaning through juxtaposition rather than narrative continuity.[3] These qualities make it easy to see parallels between Godard's films and the composition of *bande dessinée*. For example, *bande dessinée* produces meaning out of the relationship, linear and nonlinear, between discontinuous units or panels separated by a gutter (also called "intericonic space" between panels), techniques comparable to Godard's use of disjointed montage and jump-cuts. *Bande dessinée* also relies on "iconicity" or sets of cultural items that govern an image (and the iconic forms that words are taking), and which cartoonists transform within the *mise-en-page* (page layout) in order to create effects (Groensteen 1999, 112–15; Baetens and Frey 2015, 167–71).[4] As it is well known, Godard's variable use of iconicity, through transformation of advertisements and art-historical quotations, has unmistakably attributed him the epithet "the master iconoclast" (Sontag 1969, 147). While critics often compare the flat tone of Godard's vividly colored landscapes and detached sounds with the effect rising from the mass-printed graphicity of the comic strip, they go no further than saying that specific comic strip references function as direct quotations and/ or an inspiration for the *mise-en-scène*.[5] And yet, the transgressive potential of specific quotations "from the past" is worth emphasizing because, in Georges Didi-Huberman's words, they allow the images to *comparaître*—"faire apparaître ce qui est cité, puis de se donner les moyens de prononcer un jugement historique, éthique et politique" ("to make appear what is cited, then to give oneself the means to pronounce a historical, ethical, and political judgment") (2015, 102). In quoting and making episodes from *Les Pieds Nickelés* reemerge, I argue that Godard engages in an explicitly historical, political, and ethical critique that comments on the norms of production, distribution, and circulation of images in artistic practices in the modern period.

This parallel invites us to consider Godard himself, as a filmmaker in the mid-1960s, conceiving his tenth feature—the third filmed in color—but it also exemplifies the multilayered function of quotation in *Pierrot le fou*. Godard's early works in color were strategically constructed to allude to a cartoonish style and effect, which in the filmmaker's development can be traced back to the beginning of his career as a film critic. During those years, Godard published a few articles in the journal *Les Cahiers du cinéma* in which he celebrated the cinematic use of "tons violents" ("violent tones"), "l'emploi délibéré et systématique des couleurs les plus criardes" ("the deliberate and systematic use of the most garish colors"), and "scènes à l'extrême limite de l'absurde, dans le féroce et loufoque univers de notre enfance" ("scenes at the utmost limit of the absurd, in the ferocious and zany universe of our child-hood") (1989, 70–86). His article from 1956, figuratively titled "Mirliflores et Bécassines" ("Biscuits and Bécassines"), praises Frank Tashlin's genius in directing grotesque comedies (with Jerry Lewis) and highlights the ways in which popular figures create imaginative cartographies and alter percep-tions of contemporary spaces.[6] Tashlin, who was considered to be a marginal Hollywood filmmaker (or at least in the margins of the classical pantheon for the rest of the *Cahiers* circle), was also an established cartoonist, and an auteur of comics and children's magazines. Godard was particularly inter-ested in Tashlin's elegant and graphic manipulation of vulgar "documentary" elements, suggesting that they manage to pierce the heart of the American society in order to reveal its profoundly mercantile structure.[7] This surely in-fluenced Godard's metonymical and digressive figurations of his early filmic experimentations, especially the ones in color, which reveal similar political overtones. Needless to say, Godard's use of colors, comparable to Tashlin's cartoonish aesthetics, exceeds the powers of figuration and symbolism, and serves as a means to diversify the various levels of his social and historical cri-tique. For instance, the ostensible use of blue, white, and red in *Pierrot le fou* does not merely serve to represent the French nation, but becomes a complex crossroad of cultural and art-historical allusions, linking modern film color (a product of commercial productions) to the colors of other non-cinematic art forms, such as the comic, reverberating with the temporal layers of the narra-tive. Space, time, and scale become unhinged from the linear grounding, and the characters become a sheer surface, a crossroad of allusions within a texture of reality, an imitation of a documentary, that does not truly belong to them.

In *Pierrot le fou*, the world of the film collides with that of *bande dessinée* and history. In the opening sequence, Ferdinand Griffon (Jean-Paul Belmondo) nicknamed Pierrot, meaning "sad clown" (in reference to the "Pierrot lunaire" character of the *commedia dell'arte*) is portrayed as a husband of a rich Italian *bourgeoise*, who at a cocktail party hosted at the "Expressos'" becomes increasingly embittered by the mundane men and women of his social circle. Reciting lines of advertising slogans and ready-made formulas to each other, as if through another medium, these modern men and women appear to buttress the ideology of postwar capitalist demand and modern-ization. Lost amidst the disparate snippets of conversation, Ferdinand makes an effort to find a sense of unity and meaning in a world dominated by mechanic, uniform text and visual: "J'ai l'impression," he confesses, "d'avoir des machines séparées, que ça ne tient pas ensemble: les yeux, la bouche, les oreilles," ("I have the impression of having separate machines, that all of this is not held together: the eyes, the mouth, the ears") (Godard 1965). This scene is filmed as a series of montages with red, green, white, yellow, and blue filters, whose organization posits a critique of the film camera as perpetuating the capitalist ideology of the spectacle, but also to the background coloring of comic panels, especially the ones of early twentieth-century comics. Along the way in this splash field, Ferdinand loses his senses and returns home to find his children's babysitter, Marianne Renoir (Anna Karina)—a name that symbolically combines the embodied figure of the French nation with the Impressionist painter Pierre-Auguste Renoir and his son, the filmmaker Jean Renoir—reading an album of the *Les Pieds Nickelés* series. After telling Marianne he would drive her home, the characters leave the scene, taking the album with them, an event that shifts the filmic narrative by projecting them, as they become the last romantic couple and adventurers, into a completely disintegrated, vivid, cartoonish, and suicidal society marked by a swarm of references to various media, fictions, and situations of recent historic events.

Godard not only borrows the *bande dessinée*, but he tacitly links the album to the colonial history of its narrative, and its aftermaths on a global scale. After the opening scene, the film's form increasingly begins to resemble the formal composition of the BD: its Eastman color and Techniscope format, shot by cinematographer Raoul Coutard, give stark nightmarish angles of vision and a garish color appropriate for the exaggerated situations and the hyperreal human relations the film depicts. The overall *mise-en-scène* of Marianne's half-furnished apartment is constructed with uniform artificial light, flatly illuminating the characters and the few brightly accented colored objects scattered throughout the frames: We see shiny green glasses, red and yellow pans, pop art posters (another of the film's sources), Marianne's blue bathrobe, but also the devastating presence of a male corpse covered in bright red blood amidst piles of guns and weapons.[8] The intense white walls recall the blank pages and gutters of comics. Covered with disparate posters containing references to the French-Algerian past, as well as contemporary (1965) references to world catastrophes—from events such as the Vietnam War, the colonial war in Angola, and the Congolese coup d'état, through which Marianne moves back and forth as if in a linear sequencing of panels—the walls invite the viewers to involve themselves and participate in the creative process. But this jarring anachronistic chaos of historical and current references becomes dizzyingly disorienting, as it is depicted with the same flat

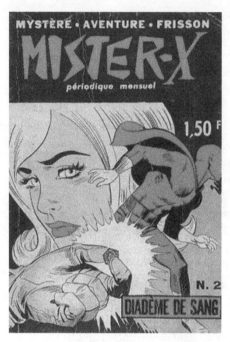

**Figure 1: The cover of *Mister X*
magazine featured in *Pierrot le fou***

cartoonish aesthetics as the other objects inside the frames. Godard thus complicates any attempt to metamorphose these figures or interpret the events in order to unmask an ideology. Consequently, he inserts even more fictional and visual references in addition to *Les Pieds Nickelés*: a close-up image of the covers of *Mister X* (a 1965 illustrated magazine of mystery stories adapted in French from Italian *fumetti*) [Fig. 1] and *Gérald Norton* (an early 1960s comics series written by Jerry Brondfield and drawn by Ken Bald, published in French translation by France-Soir, then in album format by Edi-Europe); reproductions of paintings by Renoir and Picasso; and a black-and-white poster of *Le Petit Soldat* (*The Little Soldier*), Godard's own fictional film from 1960 but censored until 1963 for depicting the conflicting political stances and torture scenes of the French-Algerian war. But, unlike all the other fictional references that slowly disintegrate into the aesthetic texture of the film, *Les Pieds Nickelés* ostensibly continues to follow the characters' trajectory, to the point of becoming their sole possession. By disseminating the album into the twisted filmic adventure that continues to develop through deserted landscapes while stealing cars and oil, setting fires and getting involved in accidents with murder, trafficking weapons in Algeria, and facing war devastations from the Vietnam War, Godard provocatively suggests that going mad in modern times is comparable to the actions of the famous trio of adventurers and criminals that Louis Forton depicts in his series.[9]

This album of *Les Pieds Nickelés* features the famous trio of French white men—Filochard, Ribouldingue, and Croquignol—who set off to pursue criminal adventures in non-European lands and casually interfere with the trans-African and trans-Asian expeditions that took place during the height of France's colonial empire. While the series occasionally mocked French colonial aspirations, it simultaneously "reproduced," as Mark McKinney has argued, "colonial structures of representation" (2011, 17). McKinney observes that the series drew inspiration from historically specific events such as the 1931 Exposition Coloniale in Paris, and the Croisière Noire,[10] as well as from real sites, typically the nexus of global culturalism (African, European, American, and Indigenous), the result of the transatlantic slave trade and colonialism, transforming them into fictionalized worlds of adventure. Re-inscribing these imaginative worlds of Western colonial narratives onto the colonized played a key role in bringing French imperialism and colonial ambitions to children, who constituted the predominant readership of the series (16–24).

Questions of imperialism and criminal adventure permeate *Pierrot le fou*. They formalize the film's unspoken sensations through a set of particularized historical and imaginary references, which chaotically and violently circulate through the film's scrambled speech and images. The ambivalent voice of the characters, intermittently enunciating and repeating phrases in the form of ephemeral and ineffectual dream or lived historical event—for instance, when Ferdinand says in a voice-over, "comme dans un mauvais rêve," ("like in a bad dream") followed by Marianne's voice-off, "comme pendant la guerre d'Algérie," ("like during the Algerian War") while the visualization appears as if captured from a wandering camera—exemplifies the dramatic circulation of this kind of speech that refuses to erect an authoritative voice. We find out that Marianne is associated with a crisis in the OAS[11] and wanted for murder. But the film does not offer us any framework to relate to her, as her crisis is mockingly featured through images of her browsing through *Les Pieds Nickelés* against a white wall onto which we see flashing "OASIS" (typographically broken into "OAS", written in sharp blue, and "IS" in bright red signaling Marianne's relation to OAS, but also a projection in the "oasis" of the two of them as the last romantic couple) while plotting with Ferdinand to knock out her suspicious "uncle" and OAS agent. Marianne's sudden transformation—which will repeat itself on two other occasions throughout the film: first, as she wears a U.S. Army jacket and second, as she morphs into a Vietnamese woman while dramatically performing a "Vietnam War scene" for American Marines and tourists, dressed in a traditional robe, her face painted yellow—clearly echoes the slackers' many disguises into officials and indigenous populations, in order to trick people and steal money. Thus, *Pierrot le fou* constantly lingers on the edge between one world and another, as more tropes alluding to the world of adventurers multiply and collide with associations of historical references.

In her essay "*Les Héritiers d'Hergé*: The Figure of the *Aventurier* in a Postcolonial Context," Ann Miller observes that the long-standing figure of the "adventurer," central to French-language comics, reaches back to the very first popular comics such as *Zig et Puce* and *Les Pieds Nickelés* (2004, 307). The readers of *Les Pieds Nickelés* have encountered adventures in distant places, which were "simply a pretext for a set of gags based on the hostile environment provided by the natives," which Miller contends were "depicted with unrestrained racism and no attempt to convey any effect of realism," unlike Hergé's *Tintin* and E.P. Jacobs's *Blake and Mortimer,* in which "realism became the paramount as the adventurer took on the role of *redresseur de torts*" ("righter of wrongs") (307; author's emphasis). Episodes in *Les Pieds Nickelés* do indeed present their readers with an onslaught of unrealistic, overly hyperbolic images, but I would argue that it is precisely these unrealistic comical appearances that reemerge hauntingly in *Pierrot le fou* as an undetermined, depersonalized hidden world, reclaiming to speak to us. In the film, Marianne and Ferdinand, unsure about who they are and how to act within the space of politics, are represented as two collective actors who have avidly consumed the adventures of *Les Pieds Nickelés.* The film's engagement with *Les Pieds Nickelés* is not without a reflection on the fetishization of the act of collecting and consuming the series, but also on the investment, fetishizing itself, in the actions that these adventurers pursue, which are significant to the shaping of the collective historical consciousness. The characters also represent the increasing disenchantment with the notions of *engagement* and classifications imposed by postwar modernization, a sphere which, as Godard shows us, is dominated by the media industry and exclusion. Throughout the film, most of the references to the Vietnam War are dispersed in a spectacularized form through radio and panels calling for protest, as well as documentary footage that Ferdinand briefly watches. While in contrast, the war in Algeria remerges as an affective collective image through fragmented voice-off narration from hazy figures related to Marianne's family (her "uncle," "brother," or "lover," and by extension France's), as well as through the film's dreamlike intertitles, verses, and typography written on the walls or enunciated. In short, the Algerian war reappears in the film as something haunting, which France has excluded or repressed.[12]

Through the film's characters, notably Ferdinand, Godard manages to provisionally express the grievances of the whole society, not in the form of images of recollections that belong to the character, nor through images of scenes as they happened, but as images suspended in the past and seen through the phantasmatic gaze of a child or a madman. This is nowhere more apparent than in a key scene in which direct elements from the comic become sites of fantasy. Midway through the film, Ferdinand (holding the album) and Marianne appear in a semi-rural countryside, framed against a Total gas pump, a visual element that represents a direct allusion to the Franco-Algerian economic cooperation assured by Algerian oil, resulting in the process of decolonialization and the ending of the war. Marianne has transformed herself by wearing a US military uniform, a reference that reflects the lingering dependence of France on foreign oil controlled by the American coalition during the war, and perhaps, the desire for the French to extricate themselves from this dependence through Saharan oil (a desire that Marianne perverts by decrying her will to flee to "Chicago" or "Las Vegas").[13] This scene slides from the referencing of the recent war to the broader historical colonial framework of the comic when Ferdinand, instead of speaking in a voice-off, begins to read a text from the episode *Les Pieds Nickelés voyagent* seemingly chosen at random (Fig. 2). The text reads:

> Après avoir bouffé pas mal de kilomètres, ils arrivèrent en vue du désert de Bahionda qu'ils devaient traverser avant d'atteindre Khartoum. Zut! Ça manque d'ombrage maugréaient les Pieds Nickelés … en s'aventurant dans cette plaine de sable, sous un soleil de feu. On serait bien mieux à l'ombre d'une demi-brune sans faux-col, et bien tassée.[14]

> (After having eaten many kilometers, they arrived in sight of the Bayuda desert, which they had to cross before reaching Khartoum. Heck! It lacks shade, the Pieds Nickelés would complain … as they ventured into this plain full of sand, under a burning sun. We would much prefer being in the shade of a glass of brown beer, filled to the brim and with no head.)

Figure 2: Anna Karina (Marianne) and Jean-Paul Belmondo (Ferdinand/Pierrot) reading *Les Pieds Nickelés* in *Pierrot le fou* (1965)

This is the only time that Godard explicitly has his actor read the text directly from the comic, instead of blending parts of its thematic and formal structure into his films' collage. After Ferdinand reads this decontextualized episode, he does not react nor respond to it, and the couple continues to pursue their adventure by stealing and burning cars for the rest of the film. The scene presents itself in a concealed phantasmatic form, occupying an impossible space outside of the film.

On the level of the comic action, the episode read in this sequence is apparently inspired by what McKinney calls the "colonial carnivalesque" (2011, 137) (or series of events related to the colonial-era expeditions from which cartoonists such as Forton borrowed in composing their comics) and depicts the slackers crossing the desert by trans-Saharan African camel caravans. In the comic, the text appears beneath the frame, describing what the image dramatically visualizes as an "exotic adventure" scene: the slacker's traversing Bahionda and Khartoum, a route that symbolically links France's North African colonies to their eastern counterparts. Read in the context of the film, this text is repeated and reversed by the movements of the filmic narrative. Simulating the original speech from the comic, this episode no longer reigns over the filmic narrative, since, as we are witnessing, the narrative breaks down and shatters into many possible and virtual trajectories. The comic's speech, thus depersonalized, would appear to be mocking the characters, or what at this point seems to us as their search for a unified narrative or meaning. Suspended in this way, at once within and outside of the filmic realm, this scene echoes a situation analogous to the first half of the film throughout which Ferdinand (carrying the album under his arms) enunciated in a voice-off: "Nous traversâmes la France . . . comme des apparences . . . comme un miroir," ("We crossed France . . . like ghosts . . . like a mirror") along with Marianne's reverberating voice-off, "Comme des apparences," while both were shown crossing a river, a forest, and deserted roads under the bright sun—indeed, "comme des apparences," with no sign whatsoever to indicate their location. Here, Godard anticipates the phantasmatic and redeeming appearance of Bécassine in *Le Livre d'image*: Disrupting and suspending the narrative continuity in this way, the film examines and eventually resists the truth-claiming narrative of the comic told from the perspective of an identifiable subject with a definite history corroborated by capitalist hegemony and its white imperialist ambitions. Instead, it mocks our expectations and demands us to think about the alternative potentialities of the single space that appears immediately in front of us.

Indeed, the last part of the film precisely dramatizes this movement of failure to ground an authoritative, identifiable narrative trajectory. Although

Ferdinand is increasingly becoming madder, toward the end of the film he attempts to get his life back on track by denouncing Marianne, after he has put himself at the mercy of her suspicious "brother," "qui fait du trafic . . . des trucs . . . en Afrique" ("who traffics . . . stuff . . . in Africa"), and the OAS agents who are after them. This scene is symbolically figured in an image of Ferdinand absorbed in contemplation in the middle of train tracks and deciding to get out of the frame at the right moment, when the train approaches him. When the hostile OAS agents use waterboarding—"le truc qu'on t'a appris au . . . " ("the thing they taught you in . . .") in order to torture him to confess about the money, the scene is dispersed with fragmented and suspended enunciation. Elliptically inflected, their dialogue, along with the speculative quasi-comical use of Marianne's bright dress for such a horrifying thing as torture ("Y a qu'à prendre la robe de la pute" ["Let's just take the whore's dress"]), produce a tone of unsettling familiarity with the past, creating an ambiguous distance from the enunciating voice. The visualization presents Ferdinand wearing a garish blue, red, and yellow shirt, as he struggles for air, his face covered with the poignantly red dress. Unrecognizable, he begins to sort through the verbal wreckage numbly, comically delivering: "ploom ploom tra la la. . ." This scene is a clear crossroad of further references to the practice of torture by OAS during the Algerian War. It closely resonates with another "fictional" scene from Godard's black-and-white film *Le Petit Soldat* in which FLN (Front de Libération Nationale) members are depicted torturing a French soldier, but it also stunningly resonates with documentation and photography from the Algerian War that circulated around France through clandestine anti-colonial materials. The traumatic images seem to float, impersonal, through the film's characters, who have become unrecognizable. Reconstructed with vivid colors, *Pierrot le fou*'s imagery can only affectively figure the unspeakable sensations of such scenes, with a poignant appeal to be seen. Ferdinand's grotesque transformation into a completely mad Pierrot, after preparing his own immolation and enunciating his final complaint in the form of a prolonged scream or cry and absurdly painting his face blue, is the ultimate commentary on this film's gesture.

In *Cinéma 2: L'image-temps*, Deleuze argues that modern (post-World War II) *auteur* cinema renders visible the affectively charged images, which are disconnected, serial and atonal as they circulate in a (cinematic) movement that proliferates them through various events and centers instead of organizing them around a single event. The camera begins to wander and move on its own, producing a sort of intensified free indirect discourse (or "free indirect vision," as Deleuze dubs it) in which transferable clichés become a primary matter of cinema (1985, 239). These are the deserts created with extremely saturated color in Michelangelo Antonioni's *Red Desert*, the homogenizing, empty, and symmetrical houses in Yasujirō Ozu's films, or Godard's cartoonish color schemes that secrete what the philosopher calls "deterritorialized" sociohistorical gestus: "ni réel ni imaginaire, ni quotidien ni cérémonial, mais à la frontière des deux, et qui renverra pour son compte à l'exercice d'un sens véritablement visionnaire ou hallucinatoire" ("neither real nor imaginary, neither mundane nor ceremonial, but at the border between the two, and that relates itself to the exercise of a truly visionary or hallucinatory sense") (252). Comical and tragic, the figure of the modern adventurer in *Pierrot le fou* is responding to the postwar ruins and to the loss of a center, denouncing the continuous illicit exercise of imperial power on a global scale. Incapable of organizing his narrative, nor mapping his place in a fragmented postmodern world, Ferdinand's mad struggle responds to the political conditions of a late-capitalist society, no longer centered around a grand Western narrative as in *Les Pieds Nickelés,* and can only lead us to reflect on how various individuals and collective actors might emerge to map their own respective places.

Bécassine's Gaze: Historicity and Untimeliness in Late Godard

In Godard's late films, we can read his demonstration of alternate narratives and historical practices—one that reemerges radically transformed—as an unprecedented experiment with the aesthetic possibilities of montage and digital technology. Along these lines, works that ought to be regarded as delivering a kind of archaeology of the medium of cinema and, simultaneously, an act of recalling the twentieth century, are Godard's latest experimental video essays: *Histoire(s) du cinema* (1988-1998), *Adieu au langage* (2014), and *Le Livre d'image* (2018). The latter is an 85-minute video project, an "objet cinématographique," as Godard's editor and collaborator Fabrice Aragno puts it, interweaving found footage, text, and still images in an attempt to reconstruct the space of accelerated circulation, dislocation, and degradation of images, and of a certain idea of cinema, which we may call "art cinema" in today's digital economy.[15] It is in this film that Godard amply returns to the popular figure of early comic art, Bécassine, a figure that affirms its own appearance, like *Les Pieds Nickelés,* laying claim to a new form of collective potential by reimagining the relations of the political.

Le Livre d'image opens with a close-up image solely of an index finger pointing upward toward the heavens, presumably borrowed from Leonardo da Vinci's final painting, *St. John the Baptist* (1513–1516). This image serves as an incongruous counterpoint to the following text that progressively appears written onto the black screen: "Les maîtres du monde devraient se méfier de Bécassine, précisément parce qu'elle se tait" ("The masters of the world should be wary of Bécassine, precisely because she does not speak"). This text, along with the painting of the index finger, reverberate with a new intensity as the filmic narrative unfolds, and images representing Bécassine, smiling enigmatically, index finger similarly pointing upward, appear floating free in a void of empty black space, detached from any grounding or meaning. Viewers of this experimental cinematic object will not take long to realize that it is far from *Pierrot le fou*'s material corporeality, calling upon us to think of the coexisting potentiality of modern film color in relation to other non-cinematic colors, notably that of comics. *Le Livre d'image*'s form insists on distancing itself from any material cinematic texture, including the most recent high-quality glossiness of contemporary cinema, again calling upon us to think about the material dimension of the film but from the perspective of the digital image, which is removed from any ontological ground or referent, enacting a temporality in a perpetual present tense.[16] This is what contributes to the overall mysterious tone of *Le Livre d'image*: its oscillation between images and sounds, as if sourced from a degraded VHS copy, seemingly without refinement or technical finesse, even though many of the images have been reworked through digital and other advanced technological means.

Along with this compilation of "second-or-third-generation of images,"[17] as Jonathan Crary puts it, through Godard's extraordinary use of montage, the figure of a pointing Bécassine appears as a divine incarnation of history, symbolically repeated three times: the first time in the form of a mysterious savior, then as an accusatory figure projected onto the catastrophes of the century she has witnessed, and finally, toward end of the film, as a prophetic icon who gives a final salute to the viewers and invites them to imagine a different life. Critics have noted that Godard identifies with the comic figure of this provincial maid, a claim that inevitably establishes a connection with Godard's previous works, in which iconic apparitions meta-cinematically draw a link with the figure of the filmmaker (Fletcher 2019, 60). Indeed, in his archaeological media project *Les Histoire(s) du cinéma*, we encounter the figure of the angel from Paul Klee's painting *Angelus Novus* dramatically superimposed upon that of Godard himself. Suggesting a process of critical recuperation of history, the angel of Klee's painting—which also metaphorically appears in the most celebrated passage of Walter Benjamin's essay "Theses on the Philosophy of History"—presents a divine spectator amid a hail of ruins who looks back on the past while being propelled into the future by a wind blowing from paradise (1969, 257–58). Godard strikingly revives this figure in *Le Livre d'image* through Bécassine, granting her angelic powers (Fig. 3). Initially she is superimposed onto Godard's image of himself, working meticulously on his montage table and contemplating the stock of images from historical archives, from films and other fictions anchored in collective memory. Close-up images of his hands dissolving into the film's celluloid track suggest the multiple planes of memory and the inevitable process of degradation. As the film unfolds, as if through Bécassine's vision commemorating all the miseries and injustices presented with Godard's montage, it leads us to this question: Does Bécassine's prophetic role, exemplified through the simple but cunning gesture of pointing with her finger, represent an act of redemption or an act of accusation? Or is she instructing us to remember past events interpenetrated with the present, warning of "un sens véritablement visionnaire ou hallucinatoire" ("a truly visionary or hallucinatory sense"), to reuse Gilles Deleuze's phrase (1985, 252)?

The provincial maid Bécassine, heroine of the popular French-language eponymous *bande dessinée* series, was created by Maurice Languereau and Jacqueline Rivière, illustrated by Joseph Porphyre Pinchon, and popularized since 1905, initially appearing in the pages of *La Semaine de la Suzette*. In her article "Strange Encounters During Wartime: *Bécassine chez les Turcs*," Annabelle Cone explains that Bécassine's arrival in the fictional and cultural sphere coincided with the demographic movements that occurred during the Third Republic and remain valuable to the French collective memory, notably the heavy migration of people from the provincial parts of the country to urban centers, mostly Paris, where many of the relocated citizens entered domestic service. The process of acculturation that hereto occurred was largely effected through massive public school education of rural children and their eventual migration to urban employment, a process that transformed this formerly provincial population into a more "nationalized" one (i.e., a homogenous citizenry) (Cone 2011, 183–84). Through a postcolonial lens, Kristin Ross observes that the folkloric, regionalist integration

Figure 3: Image of Bécassine in Godard's *Le Livre d'image* (2018)

into French national culture (a process that is represented in Bécassine's individual history), represents a form of "internal colonialism," which acquired new means as France was going through the homogenizing modernization and decolonization processes during the 1950s and 1960s, thus effectuating "the creation of a privatized and depoliticized broad middle strata: a 'national middle class'" (1996, 11). Highly personal, localized, and temporally specific, the Bécassine series provides an overarching articulation of the larger national and historical picture of France, from the beginning of the century until modernization, when the series ceased publication.[18] Analyzing the series's political implications, McKinney shows that even though Bécassine was a subject affected by "internal colonialism," the series, in general, complacently flattered French imperial ambitions. McKinney illustrates this argument by analyzing the pertinent use of specific visual and verbal tropes, ranging from advertisements featuring racist depictions of black women, to the "architecture exotique des pavillons étrangers et coloniaux" ("exotic architecture of foreign and colonial pavilions"), the discriminatory depictions of representative members of the colonized nations during the 1937 Paris exhibition, to the most hostile representations of Arabs as parasitic and lacking mastery of the French language in its later volumes (2011, 61–62).

In a different vein of inquiry, Annabelle Cone's article reevaluates the album *Bécassine chez les Turcs* (1919) to argue that this particular episode, produced at the historical juncture immediately after World War I, profoundly disturbs colonial stereotypes rather than confirming them. Cone agrees that Bécassine's position as an "infiltrator," a silent observer of the inner workings of the French haute bourgeoisie, means that she was already well situated to make visible a certain hierarchical, social order and its oppressive forces (2011, 185). However, Cone contends that the album, whose events take place during World War I, differs from the rest of the series to the extent that it attempts to give a representation of Bécassine's relationship to the global political situation and not merely the national.[19] Escaping her domestic environment, in this album, Bécassine gets to see the victory on the Eastern Front while befriending other culturally "subjugated" individuals, notably a young Arab. This event, Cone argues, enables the creation of a space of ideological contradiction that blurs national identities in favor of a more transnational one, eventually pointing to further ideological contradictions not entirely contained by the reassuring authority of the narrative (194–97).

Cone's critique is worth noting because it provides a rereading of Bécassine as a figure gaining historical consciousness in the immediate aftermath of a world catastrophe and reflecting on the global situation, but also as a figure that attempts to project her desire for a societal change into the future. Cone goes on to analyze the last scene of this album where the powerless maid overlooks the past at the gates of a ruined Constantinople, the bridge between the West and the Orient, gazing into an image that represents a reference to concentration camps, to suggest that Bécassine's vision transforms into a more prophetic one. The very last page of this album represents a strange utopian "memory-image" figuring together the various transnational characters Bécassine had encountered throughout the volume. This depiction is followed by Bécassine's isolated image, her index finger pointing to her head and then pointing upward as she confides to the readers her uncertainty for the future and her desire for social change. Cone highlights the importance of this unusual ending to the volume, as it offers an "alternative" to the common narrative with a colonial plot (Strange 194-195). Indeed, Cone's critique of *Bécassine chez les Turcs* situates the provincial maid into a figurative framework that intimately resonates with Godard's cinematic and historic project of finding new potentialities that exist at the juncture of history, haunting individuals and collectivities from a distance, and projecting a desire for a different life.

These potentialities are revealed in Godard's *Le Livre d'image* in the way that the filmmaker conflates Bécassine's prophecy with cinema's projecting powers, as well as with the history of the twentieth century, notably what has come to be regarded as its memory, marked by devastations of the two World Wars and the decolonization wars. Bécassine's contested representation as a silent observer echoes the beginnings of cinema as a silent medium, hinging on the interaction between moving images and image-texts or intertitles. In early cinema, Godard tells us, "parole" ("speech") was separated from "voix" ("voice"). This system, considered "primitive," offered stunning possibilities for the filmmaker, as it allowed for indefinite associations (or "rapprochements," to use his vocabulary)[20] between text and image. For Godard (and we can extend this concern to Gilles Deleuze, who shares with the filmmaker a similar understanding of the importance of the late 1910s and the early 1920s as crucial moments of potentiality for cinema and history), this revelatory possibility of the cinematic medium, comparable to that of comics, was never taken up after the invention of talkies, in which "parole" and "voix" became one and the same thing. It can be said that Godard laments cinema's unrealized potential in the history of moving images, which after the invention of talkies became (for the most part) an authoritative, ideologically charged sphere, or in the words of Deleuze, "liée à l'organisation de guerre, à la propagande d'État, au fascisme ordinaire, historiquement et essentiellement" ("linked to the organization of the war, to State propaganda, to ordinary fascism, historically and essentially") (1985, 214), instead of becoming a field in which thought itself (in his words "une forme qui pense" ["a form that thinks"]) would be reinvented.

Godard's Bécassine also appears critical of her own muteness in the face of history, as does "cinema" in his *Histoire(s) du cinéma*, for having excluded and repressed the catastrophes and experiences of the century, such as French colonialism in Algeria. In an episode that Cone analyzes, Bécassine leaves France's bourgeois décor and encounters the Orient, its everyday scenes, its diverse music, people, and voices. She finds herself fearful when, on a ship sailing to Yemen, the captain threatens to throw out at sea a young North African who was hiding in a box of garbage among the other passengers. Connecting Bécassine's individual history to the history of images and oppressive regimes, Godard's *Le Livre d'image* poignantly echoes this episode of Bécassine on the boat as well as at the gate of Constantinople, reviving her gaze. The film comprises images of Belle Époque Paris from Ophuls's film *Le Plaisir* (1952) along with images of nineteenth-century Russia in Maistre's *St. Petersburg Dialogues* (1821), countered with images of violence and brutality from western films such as Pasolini's *Salo* (1975) and Van Sant's *Elephant* (2003), as well as images from an ISIS video of people being thrown out to sea and Rossellini's *Paisan* (1946), in which people jump into the sea to signal the end of the war—an intricate assemblage of visual and sound quotations from infinite virtual sources. Godard's project includes a number of references from his own films, a gesture which can be viewed as an auto-critical inquiry of the problems encountered when filming outside of the "West," in particular for his collaboration with Jean-Pierre Gorin on their unfinished film project *Jusqu'à la victoire* (1970), about the Palestinian resistance movement in Jordan. The filmmaker is constantly interrogating whether he and Gorin failed to grasp the protest of the situation they sought to depict or unintentionally silenced the voices and cries of those that needed to be heard.

Alex Fletcher writes that the central problem raised in *Le Livre d'image* "is not simply the representation of violence, but the constitutive violence of representation itself" (2019, 65). The problem of violence of representation in the film, strongly echoing Edward Said's and Gayatry Spivak's works on the subject of Orientalism and Otherness, appears with piercing sensibility in Godard's redeeming of the figure of Bécassine. The gentle simplicity of her drawing, her sincere yet silenced mouth, her observing eyes, and the indexing act of her pointing finger remain secret and indescribable when we see them confronted to the dizzying cohort of images borrowed from Western and non-Western literary and cinematic cultural representations of the Orient, ranging from Dumas's nineteenth-century fictional travelogue, *L'Arabie heureuse*, to Pasolini's *Arabian Nights* (1974), and also including a number of images from Arab cinema, such as frames from Chahine's *Cairo Station* (1958) and *Jamila, the Algerian* (1958), Khemir's *Wanderers of the Desert* (1984), and Sissako's *Timbuktu* (2014). Mirroring Bécassine's image, Godard's voice-off further reverberates with intensity: "La demi-voix douce et faible disant de grandes choses" ("The low, soft, and weak voice saying big things"), while interspersed with high-definition and color saturated footage that depicts tranquil quotidian scenes and vast landscapes of the Tunisian coastal town La Marsa. These scenes are followed by another intertitle, "Sous les yeux de l'Occident," that superimposes Bécassine's ostensibly silent and reassuring image, pointing her finger upward while Godard's omnipresent voice-off goes on: "Une sorte de murmure en français infiniment pur" ("A sort of murmur in infinitely pure French"), inviting the spectators to further reflection. The intertitle "Les Arabes peuvent-ils parler?" ("Can the Arabs speak?") emerges in one sequence, recalling the title of Gayatri Spivak's famous essay "Can the Subaltern Speak?" (1985), ultimately resonating with the ethical and political irresolution in Godard's film. Although the political significance in some of these images of violence is greater than in others, Godard's radical act of removing all of them from their ontological ground demonstrates the filmmaker's concern with the single production power of the apparatus, a spectacular and quasi-divine space that yields with uncountable sources of memory of the century. Godard thus reweaves and suspends the strands of history and voices into a new strategic fiction, allowing us both to remember what cinema and Bécassine could have been and to project powers of the image that might invite us to reimagine them beyond the limits of their history.

Le Livre d'image, then, can be understood as extending the critique of the interaction of fiction, historical consciousness, and politics that Godard develops in *Pierrot le fou*. In both films, the filmmaker not only borrows from early comics, he also conducts a dialogue therewith and comments on their aesthetic and historical implications. If *Les Pieds Nickelés* ostensibly reemerges in *Pierrot le fou* as a kind of historical residue, as I have attempted to show, threatening to undo the integrity of the characters, it also opens up a space of inquiry in which imagining alternative relations to political consciousness is possible. Commenting on that gesture, the figure of Bécassine allows the filmmaker to take up the question of the political against its own materiality and representation, exploring new ways of imagining the history of the century. Godard's most recent film thus presents an extraordinary reflection on the circulation of seen, heard, imagined, feared, or dreamed images but also on their active, unrealized, and pressing demands.

Endnotes

1. Henceforth within the text, I will interchangeably use the terms "comic," "comic strip," and "comic book," as well as the French-language term "bande dessinée" (une "bédé or "bd"), which, as Mark McKinney explains, is translated literally as *a drawn strip* (or band) and "has an advantage over the English term, *comics*, insofar as it contains no suggestion that the material is comic or funny" (2008, xiii). For a more comparative analysis of this terminology, see McKinney's "French-Language Comics Terminology and Referencing" (2008, xiii–xv).

2. For earlier attempts at graphic storytelling, see recent works by theoreticians Thierry Smolderen, including *Naissances de la bande dessinée: de William Hogarth à Winsor McCay* (2009) and Benoît Peeters, particularly his 1994 collaboration with Thierry Groensteen, *Töpffer, l'invention de la bande dessinée.*

3. Already in 1965, the surrealist Louis Aragon, inspired by the European Cubist collage practices, used the term "collage cinématographique" to describe Godard's active appropriation of source materials with a view to an original project (1965, 126–27). For other uses of the term in relation to Godard's works, see, for example, Angela Della Vacche's 1995 essay, "Jean-Luc Godard's *Pierrot le fou*: Cinema as Collage against Painting," in *Literature/Film Quarterly* and Katherine Hoffman chapter, "Collage in the Twentieth Century: An Overview," in her book *Collage: Critical Views* (1989). Douglas Smith explains how Godard's avant-garde practice of "décollage" has a political function in his essay, "(Dé)collage Bazin, Godard, Aragon" (Conley and Kline 2014, 210–223). In a conversation with Marguerite Duras, Godard mentions "racolage" to describe his own craft. For comparative analysis of these terms, see Georges Didi-Huberman's *Passé Cités par JLG* (2015), especially pages 11–30.

4. For more on the semiotics of comics, see Baetens and Frey 2015, especially 103–187, and Groensteen 1999. Groensteen develops the notion of *solidarité iconique* (iconic solidarity) in graphic storytelling as "les images solidaires qui, participant d'une suite, présentent la double caractéristique d'être séparées (cette précision pour écarter les images uniques enfermant en leur sein une profusion de motifs et d'anecdotes) et d'être plastiquement et sémiotiquement surdéterminées par le fait même de leur coexistence *in praesentia*" ("interdependent images that, participating in a series, present the double characteristic of being separated—this specification dismisses unique enclosed images within a profusion of patterns and anecdotes—and which are plastically and semantically over-determined by the fact of their coexistence *in praesentia*"). For more on *solidarité iconique*, see Groensteen 1999, 21, 23–25, 133, 187.

5. See, for example, James Roy Macbean's analysis of Godard's comic strip iconography in *Made in USA* in relation to pop art and the "active painters" (Pollock, Poliakoff, Hoffman) in "Politics, Painting, and the Language of Signs in Godard's *Made in USA*," published in *Film Quarterly* (Spring 1969). In his essay, "Godard's Remote Control," John Hulsey explores Godard's appropriations of Jules Feiffer's comic in the film *Deux ou trois choses que je sais d'elle* (Conley and Kline 2014, 264–65). For

Godard's construction of the mise-en-scène in *Made in USA* as visual investigation of the notion of the "sign" in relation to the comic strip, see Drew Morton's "Godard's Comic Strip Mise-en-Scène" in *Senses of Cinema* 53 (2009), www.sensesofcinema. com/2009/feature-articles/godards-comic-strip-mise-en-scene/.

6. See Godard, "Hollywood ou Mourir: Frank Tashlin, Un vrai cinglé de cinéma" (Godard 1989, 108–10).

7. Reminding us of the basic filmic necessity, even as a fiction, of documentary elements, people, and places, Godard highlights Tashlin's interventionist cinematographic form, in which "le comble de l'artifice se marie avec la noblesse du vrai documentaire" ("the height of artifice blends with the nobility of true documentary") (see Godard 1989, 110). Godard also famously coined the adjective "Tashlinesque." Moreover, he included an extended homage to Tashlin and Lewis in the design of a cross section factory set in his film *Tout va bien* (1972). For more on Tashlin's grotesque style and resonances with Godard, see Ethan de Seife's *Tashlinesque: The Hollywood Comedies of Frank Tashlin* (2012).

8. In response to an impertinent interviewer's demand to know why there must be so much blood in *Pierrot le Fou*, Godard insists, "It's not blood, it's red." Indeed, the function of color in this film comes to exceed and even undermine its referential capacity (see Godard 1985, 108).

9. The album *La Bande des Pieds Nickelés,* illustrated by Louis Forton, uniting six episodes that appeared in the weekly magazine *L'Épatant* from June 1908 until January 1912, was originally published by Offenstadt in 1915. The copy of this album that appears in *Pierrot le fou* is from the Godard family's personal collection since 1948. The filmmaker's act to insert his own copy of the album echoes both the act of improvisation and of metacinematic reflection that Godard addresses in filmmaking (see de Baecque 2010, 287, 844n248).

10. "La Croisière Noire" was the name of colonial-era automobile expeditions across Africa (October 28, 1924–June 26, 1925). Together with "La Croisière Jaune" taking place across Asia (April 4, 1931–February 12, 1932), these expeditions were also called "traversées" (crossings), "raids" (a military term) or "croisières" (cruises). For more on French Trans-African expeditions in comics, see Chapter 4 in McKinney 2011.

11. Godard is referring to the OAS or *Organisation de l'armée secrète* (Secret Armed Organization), a French Far Right organization that used torture and assassination with the goal of preventing Algerian independence. Through the characters' narration, Godard explicitly refers to the war as "la guerre d'Algérie." As we have been discussing, Marianne's character is ambiguously constructed as having something to do with the OAS, while Ferdinand as adhering to circumstantial, reactionary politics regarding the inflictions of the war. Many of Godard's early works stage this vexed political engagement, despite the fact that Godard, along with the rest of *Cahiers du cinéma* group, avoided declaring a

direct statement on the role of the artist in the Algerian war. His film *Le Petit Soldat* is treating this subject most acutely, although it compares, or, as it has been critiqued, "it equates," Far Right and Far Left engagements (see de Baecque 2010, 162–68 and Godard 1985, 35–37).

12. Historian Benjamin Stora speaks of "Algeria: the war without a name" in *Emergencies and Disorder in the European Empires After 1945* (1994), specifically pages 208–16.

13. For a useful overview of the context of this reference, see Rabah Mahiout's *Le Pétrole algérien* (1974) and Philip C. Naylor's *France and Algeria: A History of Decolonization* (2000).

14. This text appears in the album *La Bande des Pieds Nickelés* (1915), p. 153. It is the album's fourth episode, originally published in *L'Épatant*, n.136–154 (November 10, 1910– March 16, 1911).

15. For more on the collaboration between Godard and Aragno on *Le Livre d'image*, listen to the interview with Aragno after the film's premiere at the Cannes Film Festival: vimeo.com/271516180.

16. For the atemporality of the digital image, see for example, Wolfgang Ernst's *Digital Memory and the Archive* (2013) and Jussi Parikka's *Archive Dynamics: Software Culture and Digital Heritage* (2012). For more on Godard and the implications of the digital image, see Godard and Ishaghpour (Éditions Farrago, 2000); Daniel Morgan, *Late Godard and the Possibilities of Cinema* (2012); and Timothy Murray, *Digital Baroque: New Media and Cinematic Folds* (2008).

17. Crary describes Godard's latest projects as "second-or-third-generation images, treated with effects of flickering, oversaturation, repetitive oscillations, flashings, extreme slow motion, and many more" (Crary 2012, 300).

18. Cone explains that Bécassine stopped publication before the golden age of comics, which began in the late 1950s, and before decolonization (for France and Belgium, the two countries that led the way in *bande dessinée)* (2011, 196–97).

19. Cone explains that although the albums of the 1920s and the 1930s picture France as containing ethnic minority characters, the representation of France does not exceed the national borders and the one of Bécassine is less adventurous and less daring, even tired, as the last album from 1939 demonstrates, incapable to respond to the upcoming geopolitical turmoil (2011, 197).

20. Antoine de Baecque explains that Godard himself often uses the term "rapprochement" to describe montage as an aesthetic form and possibility. The term is borrowed from a poem by Pierre Reverdy "L'Image," originally published in the French journal *Nord-Sud* in 1918: "L'image est une création pure de l'esprit. / Elle ne peut naître d'une comparaison mais du rapprochement de deux réalités plus ou moins éloignées. / Plus les rapports des deux réalités rapprochées seront lointaines et justes, plus l'image sera forte—plus elle aura de puissance émotive et de réalité poétique.

/ . . . Une image n'est pas forte parce qu'elle est brutale et fantastique—mais parce que l'association des idées est lointaine et juste" ("The image is a pure creation of the mind. / It cannot be born of a comparison, but only of the bringing together of two more or less distant realities. / The more the relations of the two realities brought together are distant and fitting, the stronger the image—the more emotive power and poetic reality it will have. / Two realities without any relation cannot be usefully brought together. Then there is no creation of an image. / . . . An image is not strong because it is *brutal* or *fantastic*—but because the association of ideas is distant and fitting"). See de Baecque 2010, 682–83. In a recent interview aired on *France Culture*, Godard talks about the notion of "rapprochement" in relation to the montage in *Le Livre d'image*. For more, the interview is available on www.franceculture.fr/cinema/jean-luc-godard-sentretient-avec-olivia-gesbert.

Works Cited

ARAGON, Louis. 1965. *Les Collages*. Paris: Hermann.

BAETENS, Jan, and Hugo FREY. 2015. *The Graphic Novel: An Introduction*. Cambridge: Cambridge University Press.

BENJAMIN, Walter. 1969. *Illuminations*, edited by Hannah Arendt. New York: Schocken.

CONE, Annabelle. 2011. "Strange Encounters During Wartime: *Bécassine chez les Turcs*," *European Comic Art* 4 (2): 181–97.

CONLEY, Tom, and T. Jefferson KLINE, eds. 2014. *A Companion to Jean-Luc Godard*. Chichester, UK: Wiley-Blackwell.

CRARY, Jonathan. 2012. "Jean-Luc Godard, *Histoire(s) du cinéma*." In *Sensible Politics: The Visual Culture of Non-Governmental Activism*, edited by Meg McLagan and Yates McKee, 299–303. New York: Zone Books.

CAMERY, Gautier-Languereau and Joseph Porphyre PINCHON. (1913) 1991. *Bécassine*. Paris: Gautier-Languereau.

DE BAECQUE, Antoine. 2010. *Godard: Biographie*. Paris: Grasset.

DELEUZE, Gilles. 1985. *Cinéma 2: L'Image-temps*. Paris: Les Éditions de Minuit.

DIDI-HUBERMAN, Georges. 2015. *Passés cités par LJG*. Paris: Les Éditions de Minuit.

FLETCHER, Alex. 2019. "Late Style and Contrapuntal Histories: The Violence of Representation in Jean-Luc Godard." *Radical Philosophy* 2.04 (Spring): 59–72.

FORTON, Louis. (1915) 1982. *Les Pieds Nickelés*. Paris: Éditions Henri Veyrier, 1982.

GODARD, Jean-Luc. 1985. *Godard par Godard: Les années Karina (1960 à 1967)*. Paris: Flammarion.

————. 1989. *Godard par Godard: Les années "cahiers" (1950 à 1959)*. Paris: Flammarion.

GODARD, Jean-Luc, and ISHAGHPOUR, Youssef. 2000. *Archéologie du cinéma et mémoire du siècle*. Tours, France: Farrago.

GROENSTEEN, Thierry. 1999. *Système de la bande dessinée*. Paris: PUF.

McKINNEY, Mark, ed. 2008. *History and Politics in French-Language Comics and Graphic Novels*. Jackson: University Press of Mississippi.

————. 2011. *The Colonial Heritage of French Comics*. Liverpool, UK: Liverpool University Press.

MILLER, Ann. 2004. "Les héritiers d'Hergé: The Figure of the *Aventurier* in a Postcolonial Context." *Shifting Frontiers of France and Francophonie*, edited by Yvette Rocheron and Christopher Rolfe, 307–23. Oxford: Peter Lang.

————. 2007. *Reading bande dessinée: Critical Approaches to French-Language Comic Strip*. Chicago: Intellect Books, University of Chicago Press.

ROSS, Kristin. 1996. *Fast Cars Clean Bodies: Decolonization and the Reordering of French Culture*. Cambridge, MA: MIT Press.

SONTAG, Susan. 1969. "Godard." In *Styles of Radical Will*. New York: Farrar, Straus, and Giroux.

STERRIT, David. 1999. *The Films of Jean-Luc Godard: Seeing the Invisible*. Cambridge: Cambridge University Press.

PART TWO
Comics, Photography, and the Photonovel

Figure 1: *Mickey au camp de Gurs*, panel 4.
©*Mémorial de la Shoah*, used with permission.

CHAPTER FOUR:
Remediating the Documentary: Photography and Drawn Images in *Mickey au camp de Gurs*

Charlotte F. Werbe

> "C'est un univers à part, totalement clos,
> étrange royaume d'une fatalité singulière."
>
> ("It was a world set apart, utterly segregated,
> a strange kingdom with its own peculiar fatality.")
> —David Rousset, *L'univers concentrationnaire.*

In this page from *Mickey au camp de Gurs* (*Mickey in the Gurs camp*, 1942) (Fig. 1), a comic booklet created by Horst Rosenthal while interned in Gurs in southern France, Mickey Mouse directs our attention to a bird's-eye view of the camp (Kotek and Pasamonik 2014, 3). In the black-and-white photograph, rows and rows of barracks stretch southward. On the horizon is a hazy outline of the Pyrénées. The teeming population alluded to by Mickey—nearly 22,000 passed through this space during World War II—is nowhere to be found. The provenance of this photograph and how Rosenthal came into possession of it is not clear. Perhaps it was taken before the camp was in operation, which would explain why the place looks deserted. Or perhaps, in what amounts to the same thing, the interned masses are simply not captured by the camera or the composition. Either way, the photograph, together with the cartoon alongside it, register one of the key features of the camp institution during World War II: namely, its duality as a site of incarceration, packed with captive bodies, and, on the other hand, as a zone of invisibility, where not only humans were made invisible or otherwise liquidated, but the very mechanism making them invisible was itself under erasure.

As well attested in the secondary literature, the internment, concentration, and extermination camps of World War II functioned as self-enclosed, autarkic sites that severed communication with the outside word. This separation allowed for the construction of a new social order, thereby creating what camp survivor David Rousset described as "un monde à la Céline avec des hantises kafkaïennes" ("a Céline-like world with Kafaesque angst") (1946, 69). The rules of society were not only deregulated, inverted, or otherwise disfigured, but the Nazi program of destruction also sought to eradicate any traces of the absolute erasure of targeted groups of people. In a speech delivered to members of the SS in 1943, Heinrich Himmler stated, "Among ourselves, this once, it shall be uttered quite frankly; but in public we will never speak of it . . . I am referring to the evacuation of the Jews, the annihilation of the Jewish people . . . In our history, this is an unwritten and never-to-be-written page of glory" (Facing History n.d.). Most killing orders were delivered orally so as to leave no written record. The rural locations of the camps—as in the case of Gurs, which was tucked away in the foothills of the Pyrénées mountains in southwestern France, only fifty miles from the Spanish border—were no mere coincidence, as they kept the system outside of view of everyday urban existence.[1]

Improbably surviving a regime of secrecy and oblivion, *Mickey au camp de Gurs* outlived its creator as a reflection on camp experience. Save for the date, 1942, and Rosenthal's signature on the last panel, little is known about the production and circulation of the text.[2] Some scholars have suggested that its first readers were children ("little Mickeys") interned at Gurs.[3] In fifteen pages of drawn panels and handwritten text, the narrative follows the famous cartoon mouse as he is arrested and interned at Gurs, where he encounters camp administrators, fellow prisoners, and the bureaucratic machinery of the camp. Although *Mickey au camp de Gurs* is not an autobiographical text, neither a memoir nor a diary, there are resonances between Rosenthal's and Mickey's journey through the camp. Rosenthal, a German-Jewish national, fled Germany in 1933 and was arrested and sent to Gurs in 1940. On September 11, 1942, he was deported in convoy 13, and all traces of him disappeared (*Mickey à Gurs* 93). Mickey, meanwhile, arrives at the camp as a foreigner—"Moi, pas papiers! Moi, international" ("Me, no papers! Me, international") (Fig. 2)—and, over the course of the comic, its cartoonish style makes visible the Kafkaesque bureaucratic and carceral machinery that ultimately disappeared Rosenthal.[4]

Figure 2: *Mickey au camp de Gurs*, panel 3.
©*Mémorial de la Shoah*, used with permission.

The past seventy years have been marked by a profound and concerted effort to accurately document the Holocaust and to recover the traces of individuals like Rosenthal. Nazi destruction of evidence, as well as enduring discourses of negationism, have sparked endless debates about the kinds of historiographical labor needed to establish what happened. In recent years, there has a been a trend toward the recovery of survivor testimony. However, in the immediate postwar period, the trend was toward a "perpetrator-focused, regime-centered . . . 'top-down' approach" (Hilberg 2008, 29).[5] As in Hilberg's landmark study of the Holocaust, *The Destruction of the European Jews* (1961), personal survivor accounts were often eschewed in favor of the official German documentation. This came at a time when individual testimonies were seen as unreliable in comparison to official paperwork, as well as to photographic modes of documentation, such as newsreel footage, which were perceived to be self-evident, unmediated, and objective. Where the "top-down" approach produced a unified narrative of the past, survivor testimony, it was thought, fragmented the historical record into individual recollection, inconsistent narratives, errors of memory, and so on.

Produced in the early 1940s, years before these questions began to be asked, challenged, and posed again in myriad ways by different generations of Holocaust scholars, Rosenthal's *Mickey au camp de Gurs* addresses the problem of documenting camp experience. Moreover, the design of the comic, especially its juxtaposition of colorful cartoons and a lone black-and-white photograph, stages a confrontation between different modes of documentation that anticipates subsequent debates about the ideal forms and media of historical evidence in Holocaust discourse. Putting Mickey Mouse, a quintessentially fictional figure, alongside the disembodied, self-evident facticity of the photograph brings the fictional or aesthetic and the photorealistic or documentary into a dynamic tension that evolves throughout the comic. In so doing, Rosenthal does not only transport us into "un univers à la Kafka où tout est étrange et arbitraire" ("a Kafka-like universe where everything is strange and arbitrary"), but renders strange the very media by which this "univers étrange" exists (Kotek and Pasamonik 2014, 103). In the following paragraphs, I examine how mixed-media in *Mickey au camp de Gurs* calls attention to the tensions that always belong to the work of documentation. I argue that the meeting of media—in particular the quintessentially documentary and quintessentially cartoonish properties of the images—invites readers to reimagine "documentation," thus mutually illuminating how truth and fact come into being.

*

Today, the copresence of photography and drawn images in comics is not unusual.[6] Rather, graphic novelists, especially travel journalists and memoirists, have taken significant advantage of this multi-modal medium, creating artworks that capture experience and memory in innovative ways. As a medium that promotes both the nonlinear and linear accumulation of information in order to achieve meaning—in a synchronic and diachronic process Groensteen dubs *braiding*—comics not only encode meaning—they lay bare the devices of that process of encoding and representation. For this reason, as Hillary Chute suggests, comics present themselves as a "rich location for the work documentation," as they always "call attention to the relationship of the part to the whole, to the self-conscious buildup of information" (2016, 17). When mixed-media are in play, for instance when photographs are inserted into a comic, as in *Mickey au camp de Gurs*, the part-whole dynamic activates a host of secondary dialectics between fictionality and realism, between private and public acts of remembrance, and between vernacular and state discourse.

Concerns regarding the transmission and representation of experience—the historical and the memorial—are at the heart of Holocaust discourse. As such, comics of recent decades about the Holocaust are always already engaged in a dialogue about the construction and circulation of Holocaust documentation. Some artists choose to explicitly address these concerns and do so by integrating photography into their work. Art Spiegelman, Miriam Katin, and Jérémie Dres, for instance, chose to insert photographs of family members in their graphic novels. Other artists shun photography, opting instead to draw images of iconic Holocaust photographs (e.g., Rutu Modan's *The Property*). It is interesting, nonetheless, that when artists do include photographs, they are typically family portraits. For instance, at the end of *We Are on Our Own* (2006), Miriam Katin's graphic retelling of her and her mother's survival in World War II, she chooses to include a single photograph of her and her mother. Similarly, Art Spiegelman includes three family pictures in *Maus*: him and his mother, Anja; his brother, Richieu; and his father, Vladek.[7] In this way, in graphic and comic representations of the Holocaust, photography figures the intimate and private relations destroyed during World War II.[8]

No such visual rhetoric of private memory or family intimacy appears in *Mickey au camp de Gurs*. Unlike contemporary comics, Rosenthal's use of photography is alienating and defamiliarizing; it depicts the absence of intimacy and personal connection. The high oblique and elevated vantage of the photograph, most likely taken from a nearby water tower, offers a distancing view on the Gurs internment camp. If taken from a water tower, it nevertheless approximates the gaze of the watchtower, which seeks to make things visible in order to better control them. Until the eighteenth century, this perspective was the principal mode for representing landscapes, where the "goal of showing as much as possible was outweighed by any concern for true perspective or straight sight lines" (Ford 2017). This preference for an Icarian or bird's-eye perspective was tied to its capacity to provide a visual inventory of wide spaces, a kind of panoptic and mastering vision of space. The effect, as Michel de Certeau suggests, is to stabilize the diversity and complexity of the world into a legible image, "transform(ing) the bewitching world by which one was 'possessed' into a text that lies before one's eyes" (1984, 92). Space, in other words, is made "readable," and therefore available to different kinds of organization, classification, and rationalization.

In this way, the aerial photograph in *Mickey* functions as a quintessentially documentary image. The properties of the photograph, as a "paragon of perfect visibility," in both vertical perspective and mechanical production, seem to present it as impersonal, objective, and unmediated (Saint-Amour 2011, 245). Indeed, aerial photography is most often associated with military reconnaissance and drone warfare, valued for its capacity to provide actionable information for instrumental purposes. But as Roland Barthes observed from atop the Eiffel Tower, where, looking down, "one can feel cut off from the world, yet owner of the world," the elevated perspective of the photograph in *Mickey au camp de Gurs* divorces the viewer from the scene in the same measure that it makes it visible and available to inspection. As I already mentioned, looking closely at the aerial image of the camp in *Mickey au camp de Gurs* reveals a conspicuous absence: There is not a single human being visible in the photograph. Considering the fact that the camps were premised on the exploitation and abuse of targeted groups of people, this incongruity is striking and puts into question the later valorization of photographic evidence in Holocaust discourse. If this black-and-white photo were to be used as proof, what could it immediately prove? If there were humans in Gurs, the photograph that provides an all-encompassing view of the camp—of its magnitude and internal order, of its surroundings—simultaneously keeps the prisoners out of focus.

In his research on aerial photomosaics, Paul Saint-Amour recounts an anecdote particularly relevant for the discussion at hand. In 1928, Major General Douglas MacArthur was shown an aerial photomosaic and upon being told that it is a map, he retorted, "You understand, young man, that's not a map . . . yet" (Saint-Amour 2011, 242). Saint-Amour glosses this perplexing statement by explaining that for MacArthur, the photomosaic aerial photograph is "too full of information to be legible or navigable; it too nakedly represents without representing" (243). Whatever the angle or composition of the aerial photograph, its perspective ultimately renders information unreadable. The space represented no longer "bear[s] any relation to visible, concrete objects" and as such, it abstracts reality by "disregarding . . . any discernible association of an object" (Baetens 2011, 102).

In *Mickey au camp de Gurs,* the paradoxical farseeing nearsightedness of bird's-eye photography enters into dynamic interrelation with the drawn images of the comic. The sketched and hand-colored cartoons not only point to the perceptive limitations of the view from the water or watchtower, although they certainly do this. More to the point, I argue that the comic images, like the black-and-white photo, are amalgams of mimesis and abstraction, immediacy and mediation, revealing as much as they conceal. That is to say, the visibility of what the photograph conceals is emphasized by the cartoon's own playful disguising and embellishing of reality. And in the meeting of these two media, both marked by exaggerated features of the fictional and the realistic, or the cartoonish and documentary, the comic raises the central question of postwar Holocaust discourse: How best to convey the camp experience?

In contrast to the mechanical production of photography, which presents itself as "an imprint or transfer of the real," drawings are artisanal, hand-made (Krauss 1981, 26). Although comics are, for the most part, made to be mass-produced, in the criticism there continues to an emphasis on the nonmechanical hand-madeness of these texts, as thematized in the works of Chris Ware, Alison Bechdel, Emil Ferris, and countless others. According to Emma Tinker, this emphasis on "the physicality of their texts reflects a desire to express something personal and individual, something of their identity through their comics" (2007, 1179). Comics' materiality, in other words, carries, as Pascal Lefèvre, Thierry Groensteen, Jared Gardner, and others have remarked, a human signature. Materially, comics' form bears the traces of authorial intention. For Jan Baetens and Hugo Frey, drawn lines "inevitably manifest themselves as agents and vehicles of storytelling . . . and behind or beyond each line emerges the source of any storytelling whatsoever: the nar-rator" (2014, 165). In this way, not only is a story told, but a familiarity and sympathetic connection between artist and reader is created, a phenomenon described by Philippe Marion as inviting the "reader-spectator to achieve a co-incidence of his gaze and the creative movement of the graphiateur" (Varnum and Gibbons 2001, 149).

Returning to the context of Holocaust discourse, the hybrid nature of comics as a mass- and mechanically- or digitally-reproduced form that is si-multaneously public and intimate, distributed and personal, makes comics a medium especially suited to the work of testimony, a communicative speech act that must negotiate between the private and public sphere. As Hillary Chute remarks, the very structure of the comics form is outward facing, as it is destined and created for a mass-consuming audience; at the same time, however, the form of comics balances this public vocation with dimensions of "intimacy, immediacy and crucial self-awareness" (2017). In this way, comics are uniquely suited to address the demands of bearing witness. In *Mickey au camp de Gurs*, the titular, pop-cultural Walt Disney character, perhaps one of the twentieth century's most emblematic figures of the industrial origin of most entertainment, becomes a vehicle for a personal, embodied tour of the camp in southern France. Public and private, the commercial and the intimate converge in the materiality of the text. Although it is a comic about Mickey, nothing about Rosenthal's text was informed by a commercial mo-tive. Numerous features emphasize its private, handmade quality, including the fact that there exists only one hardbound copy. Unlike in Disney anima-tions, mistakes are scattered throughout this text (Fig. 3). For instance, on pages 9 and 15, there are blotted out words, and it appears that page 11 was

Figure 3: *Mickey au camp de Gurs,* **final panel.**
©*Mémorial de la Shoah,* used with permission.

revised in order to add a missing sentence. As Spiegelman once stated about his own work, "If I make a mistake, I want you to have my mistake" (Witek 2007, 131). Indeed, he did not shy away from errors, choosing, for instance, to draw his panels in a one-to-one ratio, rather than drawing larger panels as many artists do. For Spiegelman, this emphasis on the one-to-one ratio would be consistent with the one-to-one relationship between him and his father represented in the text. The intimacy portrayed in the pages could be mirrored by the humanness of such mistakes. In *Mickey au camp de Gurs*, unedited imperfections similarly linger as reminders for the reader of the unique, individual, almost auratic quality of the comic.

But errors are, after all, only incidental, and there is a more systematic way in which the comic's form discloses an intimate world concealed from the all-seeing vantage of the photograph in *Mickey au camp de Gurs*. To use McCloud's classification scheme of dimensionality, the drawn images of *Mickey au camp de Gurs* are flat and one-dimensional. They do not figure the "real" features of the people in the camp, but instead an imaginary version of what they could have been. The choice to memorialize others through caricature offers a way of telling a story efficiently and comprehensively, without distraction. It is spare in detail but immediately recognizable. The high oblique aerial photograph, by contrast, gestures toward a three-dimensionality of space, with leading lines that stretch backward toward the Pyrénées and the border with Iberia. In a manner of speaking, the photograph is nothing *but* specific, clear, and real lines. But one of the disadvantages of the high oblique aerial photograph is what is dubbed "dead zones": the areas in shadow, behind large buildings and other structures that are hidden by virtue of the angle. The cartoon, on the other hand, in its one-dimensionality, hides nothing. Paradoxically, by flattening everything into a single plane, the comic achieves a merging of the internal and external, inner and superficial. Everything that exists in the world of this text is fully externalized, pure surface. In this way, the photograph, which appears to show the most, is covered in blind spots, whereas the cartoons, in their playful simplicity, focus on reducing information to its most salient, foreground information.

*

"A paradoxical and almost compulsive desire to narrate the single meaning behind the photograph defines our modern negotiation of the relationship between word and image," writes Megan Williams (2003, 5). Charles Hatfield remarks, "in fact comics . . . are always characterized by a plurality of messages" (2005, 36). Baetens brings both media together when he explains that "comics and photography are radically different in the sense that our basic vision of photography defines the medium in terms of 'single' images, whereas our basic vision of comics implies the notion of sequences of images" (2011, 103). There are, in effect, a number of significant differences—many of which have been discussed above—in how these photographs and comics are perceived—the former as an immutable, singular imprint of reality, the latter constantly reinvested with meaning through the accumulation of information. Given these seemingly different image regimes, how can one read the interaction of the photograph and the cartoon in *Mickey au camp de Gurs*?

If comics are already a system composed of "a complex combination of elements, parameters, and multiple procedures" (Groensteen 2007, 159), the presence of the photograph in the comic produces an excess of possible meanings. The aerial photograph, in relation to the drawn image, emerges as dominant (in interruption), subordinate (in quantity), and equivalent (in framing). This ambivalence *and* excess are pivotal to the reconstruction of documentation in *Mickey au camp de Gurs*. Georges Didi-Huberman remarks, in reference to the four photographs from Auschwitz, that "we often ask too much or too little of the image," and in this case, by putting together two distinct image regimes, Rosenthal invites readers to ask *both* too little and too much from each (2008, 32–33).

In *Mickey au camp de Gurs*, the photograph is subordinate in terms of number. It appears only a single time. This subordination can be interpreted in a few ways. On the one hand, it suggests that, while a plurality of drawn images is necessary to convey a message, a single photograph will suffice. On the other hand, its subordination may also suggest that it is simply not as useful as the drawn images. In other words, the drawn image is desirable and the photograph less so.

The photograph, in its singularity, also interrupts the reading, in this way dominating—even if momentarily—the reception of the story. Interruption is key to Alister Wedderburn's interpretation of *Mickey au camp de Gurs*. He argues that the text functions as an aesthetic disruption into the established order of the camp, a space premised on hyperrationality. Although few scholars have paid attention to the role of the photograph in Rosenthal's comic, Wedderburn comments on it briefly, suggesting that the media contributes to this interruptive mode by "[presenting] an encounter . . . between an actual place and an imagined, fabulous subject with no material referent at all" (2019, 182).

It is important to note, however, that the frames containing the photograph and the drawn images are identical in size, shape, and location. In the comics medium, this gestures toward a transparency or equivalency of meaning, as the size of the panel determines how time and space are conceptualized by the reader (McCloud 1993, 94–117). Both the photograph and the drawn panels are located on the right side, the line defining each panel is identical, and the size of the panels is the same. The format, therefore, is strictly ordered, reflecting a "conventional" page layout (Peeters 2006–2007). A page layout can be invisible in the sense that it remains constant throughout the narrative and is therefore almost imperceptible as a unit of meaning; this is achieved to great effect in Dave Gibbon and Alan Moore's *Watchmen* (1987) and in Jacques Tardi's *C'était la guerre des tranchées* (*It Was the War of the Trenches*) (2010). In the case of *Mickey au camp de Gurs*, the consistency of the page layout suggests that the photograph and the drawn images belong to the same order of reality, and that these two modes of representation are not as different as they may at first appear.

*

The way in which *Mickey au camp de Gurs* mediates between forms of visibility and invisibility, fiction and memory, anticipates what resistance member and camp survivor Jorge Semprún would later observe about representing camp experience. In Rosenthal's comic, Mickey's drawn figure cowers beside a photograph of the internment facility; in his memoir *L'écriture ou la vie* (*Literature or Life*) (1994), Semprún recalls a similarly disorienting encounter he had with mechanically-reproduced media.

Upon first seeing a newsreel showing footage of the Buchenwald concentration camp, Semprún was struck by the great disparities between the spectacle of the filmed or photographed and the embodied memory of what he lived. He describes the enormous breach between the seen (the *vu*) and the experienced (the *vécu*) when confronted with the newsreel's documentary images:

> Il en avait aussi [des images] de Buchenwald, que je reconnaissais. Ou plutôt : dont je savais de façon certaine qu'elles provenaient de Buchenwald, sans être certain de les reconnaître. Ou plutôt : sans avoir la certitude de les avoir vues moi-même. Je les avais vues, pourtant. Ou plutôt : je les avais vécues. C'était la différence entre le vu et le vécu qui était troublante. (1994, 259)

> (There were pictures from Buchenwald, too, which I recognized. Or rather: of which I knew for certain that they were from Buchenwald without being sure of recognizing them. Or rather: without knowing for certain that I had seen them myself. Yet I had seen them. Or rather: I had experienced them. The difference between what I saw and what I had experienced was confusing.) (Brink 2000, 148)

Strangely, then, while the documentary images aim to represent the reality of the camp *as it was*, they are, according to Semprún, inadequate. Any informed discussion of Holocaust testimony must take this fact into account. What, exactly, *is* a document representing events or experiences from the Holocaust? What can be counted as proof or attestation to the camps? What is that status of the document? Over the past seventy years, eyewitnesses and secondary witnesses alike have approached visual and graphic forms of evidence in myriad ways. Some have entirely eschewed newsreels, stock footage, or photography in favor of eyewitness interviews, as in the case of Claude Lanzmann's film *Shoah* (1985) or the archival recordings at the Fortunoff Video Archive for Holocaust Testimonies at Yale University. Others have opted to intersperse newsreels and other kinds of documentary footage with eyewitness testimony, for instance, in Marcel Ophül's film *Le Chagrin et la pitié* (*The Sorrow and the Pity*) (1969). Finally, others, such as the compilers of the Buchenwald footage Semprún saw, have opted for unadorned documentary footage.

The impetus to show newsreels, stock footage, and photographs is tied to the perception that such forms of documentation are unmediated, and

therefore serve as more adequate and direct means for reflecting the realities
of World War II. In a similar vein, memoirists tend to employ spare rather
than ornamental language, out of the concern that any emphasis on the aesthetic features of their texts would call attention to their mediatedness and,
therefore, their distance from reality.[9] In a context characterized by profound anxieties regarding the transmission of truth and fact, it is no wonder
that any semblance of artifice is abhorred. Nevertheless, beginning in the
1980s, these sorts of convictions were challenged as artists and eyewitnesses
devised new ways to preserve and transmit memory in innovative forms of
expression, leading a number of important scholars to reassess the relationship between truth and representation in Holocaust discourse. But even
after these developments, the conversation continues to be haunted by the
fear of the seeming unreliability of subjective or otherwise mediated modes
of bearing witness. *Mickey au camp de Gurs*, as a work that structures testimony as an interplay between observed, documentary fact and the playful
fictionality of a cartoon universe, offers a map for navigating the difficult
questions at the center of Holocaust studies. Years before Semprún's mature
work, and even before World War II was over, Rosenthal's comic anticipates
how the French-Spanish writer would later conceive of the inadequacy of
the *vu* without the *vécu*:

> Il aurait fallu travailler le film au corps, dans la matière filmique
> même, en arrêter parfois le défilement : fixer l'image pour en agrandir
> certains détails ; reprendre la projection au ralenti dans certain cas,
> en accélérer le rythme, à d'autres moments. Il aurait surtout fallu
> commenter les images, pour les déchiffrer, les inscrire non seulement
> dans un contexte historique, mais dans une continuité de sentiments
> et d'émotions . . . Il aurait fallu, en somme, traiter la réalité docu-
> mentaire comme une matière de fiction.

> (It would have been necessary to engage corporally with the film, with
> the filmic matter itself, to sometimes stop its scrolling: to stop upon an
> image in order to enlarge certain details; to resume the projection in
> slow motion in certain cases, to accelerate its rhythm, at other times.
> It would have been necessary, mostly, to comment on the images, in
> order to decipher them, to inscribe them not only in a historical con-
> text, but also in a continuity of feelings and emotions. . . It would
> have been necessary, in summary, to treat the documentary reality as a
> matter of fiction). (1994, 262)

In other words, while the footage provides the *vu*, it is the aesthetic devices that enable the *vécu* of the experience. Rather than denying reality, artifice—as Semprún sees it—is necessary to communicate the subjective, personal aspect of the experience: "Seul l'artifice d'un récit maitrisé parviendra à transmettre partiellement la vérité du témoignage" ("Only the artifice of a mastered story will succeed in partially transmitting the truth of the testimony") (1994, 16).

The counterpoint of photography and cartoon in *Mickey au camp de Gurs* can be read along similar lines. While comics are a "conspicuously artificial form" (Chute 2016, 17), Rosenthal calls attention to the way the interpretation of media is shaped through relation. The juxtaposition of two media of *Mickey au camp de Gurs* stages, more than an opposition or tension between photograph and comic, a basic interdependency between the two forms as modalities of documentation and creative memorialization. As I have argued in this chapter, and through a close reading of Rosenthal's singular text, it is only through establishing a relation between the photograph and the cartoons that the insufficiencies and possibilities, limits and conditions, rise to the surface, and, more than that, combine and recombine in unexpected ways, continually shifting the two poles of the problem, locating truth at one end, before displacing it the other side, and back again in a dynamic and circling interrelation. If all testimony aspires to represent, retell, or otherwise transmit the personal experience of the camps, the repurposing of Walt Disney's cartoon mouse confers a universality on memory—a universality that, under capitalism, commodities (and Mickey Mouse is certainly one) can uniquely sustain—while the drawings themselves intimate the personal, the subjective, the individual.

As I have explored, the photograph and drawn image, placed as they are in the text, suggest an ambivalence with regards to how they should be read. On the one hand, the lone photograph of *Mickey au camp de Gurs* sticks out as an anomaly, as if it possessed a kind of totemic significance. Seeing it alongside a children's cartoon, we might assume it to represent the single piece of factual evidence in the comic. On the other hand, the particular placement and design of the framed images, be it the photograph or the drawn image, suggest that no such hierarchy exists in this work—that, in other words, the two media belong to the same order of representation. And to the extent that they correspond to the same register, the meaning of the photograph and the drawn images can be said to lie precisely in the rapport or interplay that is created through their juxtaposition. That is to say, the photograph and the drawn image complete one another. Beyond the suggestion that "fictional" representations may be able to adequately capture the emotion, feeling, or social experience of the camps where documents fail, the placement of the photograph and the drawn image suggests not a hierarchy of meaning in documents—according to which one would be better or more adequate than the other—but rather, that establishing a relation between the documentary impulse and the cartoon's testimonial impulse, where the two inform, build upon, and contribute meaning to one another, is perhaps the best way to transmit and record the experiences from the camps. The breach between the *vu* and *vécu*, then, can be managed, not by denying or affirming either, but by bringing them into conversation, showing the places where they touch and the places where they disconnect.

In his writings on the four photographs from Auschwitz, Georges Didi-Huberman questions the treatment of images as either mere appearance or absolute evidence of some incontrovertible, almost Platonic truth. Relegating images to "the sphere of *simulacrum* [excludes] them from the historical field," but relegating images to "the sphere of the *document* [severs] them from their phenomenology, from their specificity, and from their very substance" (2008, 33). In its mixture of media, *Mickey au camp de Gurs*, by contrast, models a way of reimagining images as a way of both potentiating the document and verifying the fictional, thereby "putting the multiple in motion" (120).

Endnotes

1. But see Gordon J. Horwitz's *In the Shadow of Death: Living Outside the Gates of Mauthausen* for an account of local knowledge of these rural sites. Although the majority of internment, concentration, and extermination camps were established away from major cities, they were not necessarily hidden, in the sense that the general population was aware of their existence and at times interacted with the daily operations of the camp.

2. Rosenthal is the author of three small comic booklets: *Mickey au camp de Gurs*, *La journée d'un hébergé: camp de Gurs*, and *Petit guide à travers le camp de Gurs*. The first two were donated to the Mémorial de la Shoah in Paris by a survivor of Gurs, Rabbi Léo Ansbacher. The third is at the archives of the École Polytechnique Fédérale (ETH) in Zürich, Switzerland, donated by Elsbeth Kasser, a Swiss nurse who lived in the Gurs internment camp from 1940–1943, where she not only provided medical care for prisoners, but also contributed to the artistic activity in the camp.

3. See Philip Smith, "'Un livre pour enfants': *Mickey au camp de Gurs* as Picture Book" and Joël Kotek and Didier Pasamonik, *Mickey à Gurs: Les carnets de dessin de Horst Rosenthal*.

4. As Pnina Rosenberg argues, the verbal elements of *Mickey* also make visible the absurdist administrative apparatus of the camp. For instance, by identifying the date as "l'an II de la révolution nationale," Rosenthal places in direct contrast Pétain's regime and the French Revolution of 1789 (Rosenberg 2002, 276).

5. It is important to note that toward the end of World War II and in the few years immediately after the liberation of the camps, eyewitness testimonies were recorded, but typically for purely evidentiary purposes. Numerous centers were established with the explicit mission of documenting eyewitness experience of the Holocaust, such as the *Centre de Documentation Juive Contemporaine* (CDJC) in France or *The Central Jewish Historical Commission* (CZKH) in Poland, among many others. The number of testimonies recorded during this period is astonishing—approximately 18,000 testimonies and 8,000 questionnaires were collected. At a minimum, contributors numbered in the tens of thousands. By the early 1950s, the practice of interviewing witnesses virtually disappeared. For more, see Laura Jockusch, *Collect and Record!: Jewish Holocaust Documentation in Early Postwar Europe*; Boaz Cohen, "The Children's Voice: Postwar Collection of Testimonies from Child Survivors of the Holocaust"; and Beate Müller, "Translating Trauma: David Boder's 1946 Interviews with Holocaust Survivors."

6. Although there is a tendency to perceive the mixing of photography and comics as a new phenomenon, Nancy Pedri notes, quoting Thierry Smolderen, that since the birth of comics in the 1880s, photography "offered to cartoonists an almost unlimited source of new models that could be stylized, deformed, or redirected in empirical and intuitive manners to represent action and movement" (2015, 3).

7. For more, see Marianne Hirsch, "Family Pictures: Maus, Mourning, and Post-Memory."

8. As Ofra Amihay points out, other graphic novels make reference to widely circulated photographs and do so by relying "on the very iconicity of the photograph and its status as a collective *memento mori*" (2017, 174).

9. James E. Young suggests that the position in which the eyewitness testifying finds himself or herself is a double bind, whereby the desire to relate their experience requires recourse to literary strategies, and these literary strategies are what risk undermining the very truth that the testimony aims to impart. By these criteria, the truth can only emerge in accounts that are unmediated, which is, needless to say, an impossibility. Young writes: "The possibility that, once committed to paper, a witness's testimony could be perceived as a fabrication of reality and not the trace of it he had intended, would seem to mock a witness's very *raison d'être*. And to compound the dilemma, the more insistently a survivor-scribe attempts to establish the 'lost link' between his text and his experiences in the text, the more he inadvertently emphasizes his role as maker of the text, which ironically—and more perversely still— further undermines the sense of unmediated fact the writer had attempted to establish" (1988, 25).

Works Cited

AMIHAY, Ofra. 2017. "Take This Waltz, Take This Photo: Photography and Holocaust Memory in Israeli Graphic Novels." *Jewish Film & New Media* 5 (2): 161–98.

BAETENS, Jan. 2011. "Abstraction in Comics." *SubStance* 40 (1): 94–113.

BAETENS, Jan and Hugo Frey. 2014. *The Graphic Novel: An Introduction*. Cambridge: Cambridge University Press.

BARTHES, Roland. 1981. *Camera Lucida: Reflections on Photography*, translated by Richard Howard. New York: Hill & Wang.

BRINK, Cornelia. 2000. "Secular Icons. Looking at Photographs from Nazi Concentration Camps." *History and Memory*,12 (1): 135–50.

CHUTE, Hillary. 2016. *Disaster Drawn: Visual Witness, Comics, and Documentary Form*. Cambridge, MA: Harvard University Press.

———. 2017. "Why I Study Comics: An Interview with Hillary Chute." Interview by Robin Lindley. *History News Network*, November 6, 2017. historynewsnetwork.org/article/166047.

COHEN, Boaz. 2007. "The Children's Voice: Postwar Collection of Testimonies from Child Survivors of the Holocaust." *Holocaust and Genocide Studies* 21 (1): 73–95.

DE CERTEAU, Michel. 1984. *The Practice of Everyday Life*, translated by Steven Rendall. Berkeley: University of California Press.

DIDI-HUBERMAN, Georges. 2008. *Images in Spite of All*. Translated by Shane B. Lillis. Chicago: University of Chicago Press.

FORD, Lily. 2017. "Virtual Reality, 19th Century Style: The History of the Panorama and the Balloon View." *Open Learn*, April 13, 2017. publicdomainreview.org/2016/08/03/unlimiting-the-bounds-the-panorama-and-the-balloon-view/#fn1.

GROENSTEEN, Thierry. 2007. *The System of Comics*, translated by Bart Beaty and Nick Nguyen. Jackson: University Press of Mississippi.

HARBISON, Robert. 2000. *Reflections on Baroque*. London: Reaktion Books.

HATFIELD, Charles. 2005. *Alternative Comics: An Emerging Literature*. Jackson: University Press of Mississippi.

HILBERG, Raul. 2008. "The Development of Holocaust Research: A Personal Overview." *Holocaust Historiography in Context: Emergence, Challenges, Polemics and Achievements*, edited by David Bankier and Dan Michman, 25–36. Jerusalem: Yad Vashem.

HIMMLER, Heinrich. n.d. "Himmler Speech in Posen (Poland) in October 4, 1943." Facing History. www.facinghistory.org/holocaust-human-behavior/himmler-speech-posen-1943.

HIRSCH, Marianne. 1992–1993. "Family Pictures: Maus, Mourning, and Post-Memory." *Discourse* 15 (2): 3–29.

HORWITZ, Gordon J. 1990. *In the Shadow of Death: Living Outside the Gates of Mauthausen.* New York: The Free Press.

JOCKUSCH, Laura. 2012. *Collect and Record!: Jewish Holocaust Documentation in Early Postwar Europe.* New York: Oxford University Press.

KATIN, Miriam. 2006. *We Are on Our Own.* Montreal: Drawn & Quarterly.

KOTEK, Joël and Didier PASAMONIK. 2014. *Mickey à Gurs: Les carnets de dessin de Horst Rosenthal.* Paris: Calmann-Lévy.

KRAUSS, Rosalind. 1981. "The Photographic Conditions of Surrealism." *October* (19): 3–34.

MCCLOUD, Scott. 1993. *Understanding Comics: The Invisible Art.* Princeton, WI: Kitchen Sink Press.

MÜLLER, Beate. 2014. "Translating Trauma: David Boder's 1946 Interviews with Holocaust Survivors." *Translation and Literature* 23 (2): 257–71.

PEDRI, Nancy. 2015. "Thinking about Photography in Comics." *Image & Narrative* 16 (2): 1–13.

PEETERS, Benoît. 2006–2007. "Four Conceptions of the Page." Translated by Jesse Cohn. *ImageText* 3 (3). imagetext.english.ufl.edu/archives/v3_3/peeters/.

ROSENBERG, Pnina. 2002. "*Mickey Mouse in Gurs*—humour, irony, and criticism in works of art produced in the Gurs internment camp." *Rethinking History* 6 (3): 273–92.

ROSENTHAL, Horst. 2014. *Mickey au camp de Gurs.* Paris: Calmann-Lévy and Mémorial de la Shoah.

ROUSSET, David.1946. *L'univers concentrationnaire.* Paris: Éditions du Pavois.

SAINT-AMOUR, Paul. 2011. "Applied Modernism. Military and Civilian Uses of the Aerial Photomosaic." *Theory, Culture & Society* 28 (7-8): 241–69.

SEMPRÚN, Jorge. 1994. *L'Écriture ou la vie.* Paris: Gallimard.

SMITH, Philip. 2019. "'Un livre pour enfants': *Mickey au camp de Gurs* as Picture Book." *Children's Literature* 47 (2019): 104–19.

SONTAG, Susan, editor. 1975. *A Barthes Reader.* New York: Hill & Wang.

SPIEGELMAN, Art. 1996. *The Complete Maus.* New York: Pantheon.

TINKER, Emma. 2007. "Manuscript in Print: The Materiality of Alternative Comics." *Literature Compass* 4 (4): 1169–182.

VARNUM, Robin, and Christina T. GIBBONS, editors. 2001. *The Language of Comics: Word and Image*. Jackson: University Press of Mississippi.

WEDDERBURN, Alister. 2019. "Cartooning the Camp: Aesthetic Interruption and the Limits of Political Possibility." *Millenium: Journal of International Studies* 47 (2): 169–89.

WILLIAMS, Megan. 2003. *Through the Negative: The Photographic Image and the Written Word in Nineteenth-Century American Literature*. London: Routledge.

WITEK, Joseph. 2007. *Art Spiegelman: Conversations*. Jackson: University Press of Mississippi.

YOUNG, James. 1988. *Writing and Rewriting the Holocaust: Narrative and the Consequences of Interpretation*. Bloomington: Indiana University Press.

CHAPTER FIVE:
Photonovel Bodies:
Kitchen Sink Romance and Beyond

Jan Baetens and Fred Truyen

Photography is a key medium of the post-World War Two period, but as a social medium it cannot be separated from the changes in the broader cultural and economic field, more specifically the renewal of magazine publications using the *rotogravure intaglio* printing process, a subfield of media culture severely damaged by the war. Various publications that had been interrupted by the war resumed publication while new magazines and new formats were launched, and in most of them photography played a key role. In these pre-television years, the power as well as the presence of the daily, weekly, and monthly press was overwhelming, and so was the importance of photography—the years 1930 to 1950, those of triumphant photojournalism, have immediately been associated with the idea of photography's "self-reliance" (Lemagny and Rouillé 1986, 165). Already very present in prewar journalism and information, photography gradually superseded nonphotographic visual elements in the postwar period.

Yet photography and magazine culture—and we claim that both are two sides of the same coin—continue to be framed in quite narrow terms. Magazine culture is generally considered in terms of *politics* (even if not all magazines were directly oriented toward politics, or following a strict party line) or, more usually, *information* (even if infotainment was definitely already present). Photography, on the other hand, is commonly reduced to reportage and documentary; it may be a presentism-inflected rereading of the past to overestimate the role of autonomous art photography from that period in the culture at large, for instance. In order to have a broader view of the way in which photography actually functioned in society, it is time to propose a twofold reframing.

First of all, it is important to stress the wide circulation of numerous non-political weeklies and monthlies (Sullerot 1963). Entertainment magazines had a large market share in the newsstand, and their scope and range were rather different from the average information magazine: Escapism and sensationalism, for instance, were not always absent from their pages. Second, the type of photography that was highlighted in these magazines was very different from that of the other magazines. On the one hand, this kind of photography was often staged, if not overtly fictional. Granted, we do know that a lot of photo-documentary material was also staged and scripted. After all, Grierson had defined documentary as a "creative treatment of actuality" (1966, 147) and nearly all current discussions of photo-reportage tend to deconstruct the previously absolute distinction between staged and "real," that is unstaged photography (Blunck 2019). Yet the intended outcome of this creative manipulation was not fiction but truth, while entertainment magazines did not shy away from fiction. On the other hand, the photography one could discover in these week-lies and monthlies was less a duplication of the real than a replication of other, already existing images, for instance those of the movie world. The purpose of these blatantly fictional stories was not to question the traditional assumption of photography as an essentially realist medium, a copy of what had been, to paraphrase Roland Barthes's famous statement in *Camera Lucida* (1981), but to appropriate the medium in such a way that it could serve as an equivalent of Hollywood's dream factory. Even in the cases where there was a strong match with neorealist subject matters or production techniques (for these correspondences, see Pitassio 2019, 217–41), the emphasis was not on the mimetic dimension of the images but on the fictional character of their storytelling.

A good case in point is the photonovel (Faber, Minuit, and Takodjerad 2012; Baetens 2017), which is both a new genre (appearing overnight in 1947, first in Italy and somewhat later in France) and a very classic magazine format, as photonovels were only published in women's magazines featuring "drawn novels," that is an early form of romance comics whose style and content imitate the language of Hollywood and other movies. Quite a lot of them rapidly turned into full-blown photonovel magazines specializing in *serialized* photonovels, many running for several months, as neatly shown in an early short documentary by Michelangelo Antonioni, *L'amorosa menzogna* (*The Loving Lie*), which uses the shooting of the eponym photonovel to explore the production, distribution, circulation, and reception of the new magazine format (Figs. 1 and 2):

Figure 1: Michelangelo Antonioni,
L'amorosa menzogna **(1949)**
(screenshot of a publicity poster of the
eponym photonovel starring Anna Vita
and Sergio Raimondi, 2'31)

Figure 2: *Sogno* **no. 9 (1947),**
the actor Sergio Raimondi as
he appeared in "L'amorosa
menzogna"[1]

The Italian example, with the leading magazines *Sogno* (*Dream*) and *Bolero-Film*, was soon followed by France, with similar success. The French photonovel industry emerged in a different context, but it also presented a certain number of common features, and not only because of the strong industrial links between the French and the Italian production, mainly given the family and business ties between the publishers on both sides of the Alps (Antonutti). In the early years, much of the material published in France was even a translation or adaptation from the Italian, and it would take several years before a homegrown and rapidly independent French production would take off.

What the French and the Italian publications definitely shared was the reuse and update of the two most popular elements in the print media of the times: *comics* and *melodrama*, in this case with a certain sensationalist twist that can be explained by the competition with another type of magazine, namely the US "true confessions" format that was also introduced on the European market in the postwar years. The photonovel can be seen as the photographic merger and reshaping of all these elements, in ways that had never been conceived before. In both cases, the average price of a photonovel magazine was exceptionally low (between 0.5 and 1 euro, in today's money; see Baetens 2019, 4). This price point enabled the publishers to tap into a new audience, that of the female working class, never previously targeted by the typical middle-brow magazines of the prewar era, yet already quite familiar with a wide range of extremely cheap movie magazines, for instance those publishing "narrated films" (that is, illustrated novelizations in pulp magazine format; see Baetens 2018a, 16–25). In other words, the French photonovel had to compete with a type of magazine capable of offering a kind of glamour still missing in the first photonovels, which remained generally poor in aesthetic as well as narrative terms. In addition, these magazines mainly used images rather than texts, which helped cater to a semi-literate audience, and the hegemonic position of visuality continued to increase after the launch of these magazines. Over the years, one finds fewer and fewer serialized fictions or short stories, which were still quite present in the first years, and the same applies to other typical sections of a woman's magazine such as celebrity gossip, which tend to be more richly illustrated. However, in the case of France, where the literacy rate was much higher than in Italy, the presence of textual material was less felt as a handicap, even if here as well the dominant position of the image proved overwhelming.

A second common feature is the moral *panic*—we are using this term as an echo of similar debates around comic books in the United States a few years later—raised by the success of the photonovel. Already politically suspect before its very start, at least in France (Giet 1998), the photonovel business has been subject to three types of critique, all perfectly compatible with each other, as shown by the unusual alliance between right-wing and left-wing political groups and parties in their fight against the photonovel. First, the photonovel was considered an instrument of American soft power and thus accused of promoting the American way of life (on the tradition of French anti-Americanism, see Roger 2005). Second, for the Church, the "pursuit of happiness" highly endorsed by the photonovel was seen as a form of unacceptable individualism, while the dream of female emancipation—much more present in the photonovel than is commonly assumed—was considered an intolerable menace to the traditional gender roles. Third, the photonovel was also denounced as a hidden seducer—that is, a bridge to the introduction of consumer society and thus an obstacle to the realization of a society built and managed by the labor class. A special issue of *Regards* (*Views*), a cultural weekly that was a mouthpiece of the French Communist Party, epitomizes this rejection in crude ways (Figs. 3 and 4).

(*Left*) Figure 3: Front cover of *Regards* no. 352 (1952), special issue, "Les Secrets de la presse du coeur" ("The Secrets of the Romance Magazines"). Please notice the extremely gendered visual clichés of this new variation on the Adam and Eve motif, with for instance the highly stereotypical opposition between "blonde" (honest but naïve) and "dark" (cunning and calculating).

(*Right*) Figure 4: Back cover of *Regards* no. 352 (1952), with a pell-mell of the most important "bad" women's magazines of the era. (One easily recognizes: *Rêves, Intimité, Madrigal, Confidences, Eve, Festival, Nous Deux, Boléro,* and *A tout coeur*).

Needless to say, none of these critiques proved capable of stopping or even nuancing the success of the "capitalist" photonovel (on the subject of photonovel reading in strongly unionized communities, see Bravo 2003, 78 and after). Much more tolerant toward popular culture, thanks to its Gramscian heritage, the Italian Communist Party tried instead to customize the photonovel for its political propaganda, often with debatable results, given the equally reactionary gender politics of these publications (Bonifazio 2017).

It does not suffice, however, to stress the social, commercial, and cultural importance of the photonovel magazines, which suddenly became one of the print versions of cinema and even the very cheapest one, in all possible meanings of the word, according to its critics. At least as important is the fact that the photonovel also introduced and popularized a new type of photography.

At first sight, its main innovation may seem that of sequential photography in fiction, displayed in a layout strongly inspired by the language of comics, although the comics reference rapidly turns out to be deceiving upon a comparative close reading of both media. At the level of the individual image, there were also major changes, which have often been overlooked as a result of condescending critical attitudes toward the photonovel's material and intellectual poverty.

What are the major characteristics of the photographic image in the photonovel of the immediate postwar years? Leaving aside issues of sequential arrangement and larger questions of storytelling, it is possible to foreground a certain number of features that "serious" forms of photography and photo criticism and history tend to overlook, given the apparent banality of these elements (see Fig. 5 for an early but representative sample).

Figure 5: "Catene" in *Bolero* no. 1 (1947)

However, all of them are highly functional; their intrinsic *meaning* may be poor, but their actual *use* is dramatically rich:

1. Most pictures focus on characters, shown in a strange combination of action and pose, which means adopting a rather stiff pose while performing a certain action. Between action and pose, pose is however the pole that is clearly dominant. Nevertheless, the (relative) omission of action is less a disadvantage than an asset: it helps foreground the body of the character in a kind of pin-up or celebrity portrait style, a feature that is crucial for the emotional involvement of the reader, who is both impressed and attracted by the strongly gendered and sometimes highly sexualized bodies on display (Baetens 2013).

2. Most pictures are typically medium close-up shots, halfway between a mid-shot and a close-up, usually covering the subject's head and shoulders. Extreme close-ups are rare, for they interfere with the focus on the portrait, and wider shots are even rarer, since they raise issues of readability when presented in small size and poorly printed images.

3. The portraits in question draw attention to certain body parts (mainly the hair, the breasts, the lips, and the eyes) as well as clothing (even if in many cases this clothing is rather ordinary).

4. Just like in classic cinema, and in contrast to portrait photography, the subjects almost never look directly at the camera. This tends to detach the spectator from the scene (the reader is essentially a voyeur).

5. Moreover, the diagonal is used to render very gender-specific relations between the characters, such as power, trust, confidence, doubt, reservation, etc. Due to the chosen camera viewpoint and the use of indoor photography, photonovel pictures have little "depth": they juxtapose figures at the same level, projected on a virtually empty or at least never totally relevant background.

6. Finally, the characters are often shown in two shots and rely upon broad cultural stereotypes (the "good" blonde and the "bad" brunette, the "tall" man and the "small" woman"), with an equally stereotyped repertoire of facial expressions. Such a traditional visual politics has a powerful impact on the basic mechanisms of recognition and identification, which are vital to the medium's success: Photonovels are "scanned" rather than "read"—we should not forget

that the stories are most of the time dramatically formulaic, the only novelty in each story being not the narrative or the characters, but the bodies of the actors. Immediate recognition is therefore a must, as well as a springboard to identification.

However, the most distinctive feature of the photonovel's visual language, which one should examine not only at image level but also at sequence and page level, is the fact that photography in this case is a second-degree language, that is, a visual language superposed onto other, already existing, visual languages, one of them *con-textual* and the other *co-textual*.

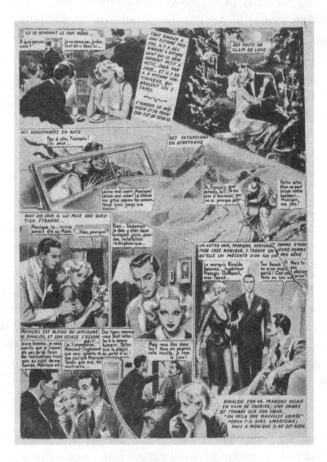

Figure 6: "Âmes ensorcelées" ("Souls under Spell") in *Nous Deux* no. 1 (1947), which was actually a translation/adaptation of *Anime Incatenate*, a drawn novel published in the first issue of the Italian sister magazine *Grand Hôtel* in 1946.

As already mentioned, the contextual underlying visual medium is that of the "drawn novel" (Baetens 2018b). Technically speaking, one could label "drawn novels" as pseudo-adaptations of nonexisting originals (Fig. 6). But it would certainly not be false to define them as an example of fake remediation. Less-well-intended critics would use the term plagiarism. The new women's magazines that emerged in the immediate postwar period were the first to introduce the drawn novel, which they replaced more or less rapidly by the even newer format of the photonovel, less expensive to produce and immediately welcomed by the drawn novel audience (Faber, Minuit, and Takodjerad 2012).

When comparing the drawn novel and the photonovel, at least those of the first years of the genre, it becomes clear that the publishing business aims at stressing the similarities between both formats, that is, the older and very successful one (the drawn novel) and the newer one, its competitor (the photonovel). A typical example of this "blending" strategy, which tries to make the differences as invisible as possible, is the introduction of the very first photonovel installment to be seen in *Nous Deux* (*The Two of Us*), the leading French women's magazine that had resisted for several years the shift from drawn novel to photonovel. (The magazine was commercially doing

(*Left*) Figure 7: "A l'aube de l'amour" ("The Dawn of Love"):
Appearance of the first photonovel in *Nous Deux* no. 165 (1950)
(*Right*) Figure 8: And the drawn novel installment on the opposite page

very well and could therefore afford to ignore the "vulgar" novelty of the photonovel.) This installment was segmented in different parts. The opening page of the photonovel on the left of a double spread (Fig. 7) was printed in front of a drawn novel page on the right (Fig. 8). It is easy to acknowledge the attempt to streamline both media: same types of characters, same setting, same storyline, same black-and-white balance, and even a more or less similar page layout. The photonovel format no longer consists of drawings imitating photographic movie images, as in the case of the drawn novel, but of photos initially imitating drawn images:

The last page of the photonovel installment was printed on the back cover of the magazine, in order to benefit from the possibility of being printed in color—only the front and back cover pages of the magazine could afford color—and thus be compared with the front cover illustration of the next issue. Since most readers used to keep their issues (just like comics, the photonovel is a medium with a strong transgenerational dimension) and even bind them in annual volumes, the back cover of issue no. 165 (Fig. 9) and the front cover of issue no. 166 (Fig. 10) eventually produced a double spread, and here as well the correspondences are crystal-clear, most blatantly of course at the

(*Left*) Figure 9: Last page of the first photonovel installment, back cover of issue no. 165 of *Nous Deux* (1950)
(*Right*) Figure 10: Front cover of *Nous Deux* no. 166 (1950)

level of the photonovel colorization (for the original pictures were in black and white). One is induced to believe that the photonovel is actually a . . . drawn novel.

In most cases, however, these similarities fall short, and one can only be struck by the relative poverty of the pictures in comparison with the lavish drawings. This should not come as a surprise, for it is much more difficult to photograph a world of luxury and glamour than to draw one, certainly in the case of the highly competitive magazine market where everybody was working on shoestring budgets. (*Nous Deux* is, comparatively speaking, a wealthy magazine, while the visual appearance of most other photonovel magazines is somewhat "lumpen.") This apparent deficiency is however more than compensated by a series of techniques that enhances the readers' involvement: The actors of the photonovel are not necessarily professionals, but "the girl and the boy next door" invited to become photonovel stars (and afterward, movie stars) by participating in casting events organized all over the country (on the laboratory function of the photonovel, which was used by the film industry as a test bench for good subjects as well as new stars, see Morreale 2011). Moreover, readers are also encouraged to communicate their ideas on plots and storytelling and thus to become cocreators, as clearly shown in the funny parody of the photonovel business in Fellini's 1952 *The White Sheik*, where the protagonist, a newly married woman secretly in love with the hero of her favorite photonovel, runs away from her husband in order to pay a short visit to the photonovel studio where she tries to get in touch with her "white sheik" (some second-rate Rudolph Valentino clone) by explaining to the secretary of the company how she would rewrite some captions.

That the bodies of the emerging photonovel genre are not as perfect or stereotyped as the Hollywood models of the drawn novel is therefore not a handicap: It enhances readers' participation, since both men and women, who are given many opportunities to participate, can identify more easily with the chosen models, whereas the celebrity and star system cult of the drawn novel sustains a very different, perhaps more alienated form of identification (which Adorno would call a form of *self-mutilation*).

Next to this *contextual* or intertextual reference, there is also a *co-textual* reference to, and remediation of, the visual elements present in other sections of the magazine issue. Some of them highlight celebrity culture: pictures of stars on the front and back covers, as well as illustrated gossip and movie news sections. But perhaps the most revealing ones are the advertisements. These images are either photographic or drawn, but this difference does not matter at all—as already hinted at above, pictures could be heavily retouched

(*Top left*) Figure 11: "Les Sept Gouttes d'or" ("The Seven Golden Drops") in *Nous Deux* no. 8 (1947)

(*Top right*) Figure 12: Back cover, *Nous Deux* no. 8 (1947)

(*Bottom left*) Figure 13: Advertisement for Axelle lipstick, *Nous Deux* no. 26 (1947)

(*Bottom right*) Figure 14: "Anges dans la tourmente" ("Angels in Torment"), fragment of a panel, *Nous Deux* no. 26 (1947) or colorized, so that the very distinction between drawing and photography does not have at all the significance that it will take afterward in art theory, at the heyday of the "index" debate in photography and art (see Krauss 1977).

Here is an early sample from *Nous Deux*, when the magazine was still running drawn novels in combination with photographic advertisements (Figs. 11, 12, 13, and 14, see previous page):

When looking at these advertisements, one is immediately struck by the proximity between what is shown outside the world of the drawn novel and the photonovel and what is shown inside it—there is a contrast between the external "real" world of consumer society, which is not primarily about stories but about objects, and the internal fictional world of the drawn novel as well as the photonovel, a "fake" world where it is only love that matters and where objects are almost absent, mainly for lack of a sizable production budget (the money available was used for makeup, not for props or settings). Yet there exists a strong match between the products on display and the specific features of the visual language implemented by the photonovel. This is logically the case as far as the type of products is concerned (Fig. 15): One may find advertisements for shampoo, lipstick, eyelash products, toothpaste, "natural" breast enhancement, but also, perhaps more surprisingly, rhinoplasty, birth control (sometimes under the guise of publicity for products helping to calculate fertility days, which is a nice euphemism for birth control), or, even more surprisingly, growth pills for adult men and women.[2] Such products are featured much more often than, for instance, furniture or clothing, which are clearly not associated with the general idea of the pursuit of happiness. Most of the latter products, at least those that are easy to visualize, can be discovered in the photonovel images.

Figure 15: Publicity page in *Nous Deux* no. 25 (1947)

Figure 16: "45 years old: don't give up, enjoy life"; advertisement for beauty products for women, *Modes de Paris* no. 73 (1948)

However, the connections between photonovels and advertisements are no less visible at the level of the storytelling that is involved: Body care and health products are indeed instruments of female seduction, which is not necessarily limited to bachelors or young adults, since quite frequently a certain emphasis is placed on the fact that "older" people can still enjoy life as well (Fig. 16), and this message perfectly matches the age of many photonovel actors, who are on average older than the characters of the typical love stories with which contemporary culture inundates its consumers.

But what to think of these interactions? The mere analysis of the visual material is not enough to grasp the broader social and cultural mechanisms at work. In order to understand why visual forms and the collective consciousness that supports them circulate between fictional and nonfictional representations, it is crucial to link the shift from drawn novel to photonovel on the one hand, with, on the other hand, the photographic and cultural dialogue between photonovel images and the photographic images and messages in the nonfictional sections of the magazines.

As seen above, the transition from drawn novel to photonovel was not immediately experienced as a radical change. Antonioni's documentary insists on the smooth, almost natural shift from drawn images to photographic images, while a magazine such as *Nous Deux* obviously tried to soften the move from one visual language to another. However, it cannot be denied that from the very beginning, the visual language of the photonovel was less sophisticated, less glamorous, less exoticizing, less adventurous than that of the drawn novel. A somewhat cynical point of view might be tempted to label this shift as a fall from heaven into real life. We should not forget that the photonovel appears during the heyday of gray and grim Italian neorealism. The move from Hollywood idealization to ordinary life, as witnessed in the photonovel, soon replaced the initial attempts to imitate the exuberant luxury of the drawn novel. It can be defined as a kind of "kitchen sink realism" *avant la lettre*, provided one puts a stronger emphasis on "kitchen sink"—as many photonovels were shot in extremely primitive studios, which once again can be seen in *L'amorosa menzogna*—than on "realism"—insofar as the romantic theme that continued to dominate the genre did not always escape from age-old melodramatic stereotypes.

It was of course the increased opportunity of empathy and identification, together with the perception of photography as a sign of modernity (as opposed to drawings, which were associated with the past), that explained the immediate and massive success of the photonovel and its rapid victory over the drawn novel. Yet the acceptance of the photonovel, a "poor" medium in comparison with the lavishly executed aesthetic fireworks of many drawn novels, had also to do with the way in which the magazines managed to establish a back-and-forth movement between its representations and the images that were published next to it in other pages of the publication, which generally alternated fictional and nonfictional sections. Photonovels did not appear as "complete stories," but as serialized installments, and each issue alternated advertisements and fictional fragments (photonovels, drawn novels, short stories, serialized classics, "true" confessions). In certain cases, both types were even gathered on double pages, so that the reader's eye was ceaselessly invited to go off-topic and to wander from fiction to nonfiction and vice versa. This was all the more logical and inevitable because the type of products that were advertised were limited to elements that could easily be illustrated in the photonovels, even when the bodies on fictional display were less perfect than the idealized figures of publicity. Any photonovel actor could use shampoo and have a haircut similar to the shampoo and the haircut presented in the advertisement section, for instance, while it was also relatively easy to find actors and actresses with the same physical features as the ones suggested in the advertisements (comparable nose, breasts, eye lashes, etc.) (Figs. 17 and 18). In this regard, it should be stressed that the gendering of the photonovel is a complex phenomenon, which involves men as much as women. In addition, the prices of these products were modest enough to be accessible to the less affluent readership targeted by the photonovel industry. By doing so, the photonovel magazines succeed in offering a dreamy counterbalance and upgrade to the danger of the "kitchen sink" aesthetics after the drawn novel period.

(*Left*) **Figure 17: Shampoo, haircut, eye lash, lipstick, etc., all in one image.**
Back cover of *Nous Deux* no. 13 (1947)
(*Right*) **Figure 18: "Aux portes du ciel" ("At Heaven's Gate"),**
***Festival* no. 5 (1949)**

The correspondence between fiction and nonfiction is further strengthened by two other aspects, both of which are typical of the photonovel magazines of that era. First, there is a blurring of boundaries between text (in this case, the fictional photonovel installments) and paratext (all the elements that surround and accompany the text in the magazine), the former losing much of its sequential character in order to become a mere set of portraits, the latter achieving a strong degree of sequentiality, so that it unfolds as a kind of narrative in itself (Baetens 2019). Second, one notices the dissemination of similar photographic material outside the two fields of fiction and advertisements. The special hairstyle of the (alleged) editor of a magazine like *Ève* (Figs. 19 and 20) is thus imitated by one of the (no longer alleged but real) readers of the weekly who participate in what we would call today a "discussion forum" under the flattering collective pen name of Évettes (little Eves) (Figs. 21 and 22). The absence of any formal separation between the magazine and its readership stimulates the bridging of the gap, within the pages of the same magazine, between the fictional world of the photonovel and the nonfictional world of the advertisements, which eventually see all their boundaries blurred: Readers, editors, actors, and models are all part of the same world, not just in an abstract or imaginary way, but in a very material and visual one.

(*Top left*) Figure 19: Front cover of *Ève* no. 144 (1949)

(*Top right*) Figure 20: "Ève vous guide et vous conseille" ("Eve guides and advises you"), Header of the letters to the editor section of *Ève* no. 144 (1949)

(*Bottom left*) Figure 21: "Papotages des Èvettes" ("Evettes' chat"), collective representation of the female readership of the magazine, *Ève* no. 144 (1949)

(*Bottom right*) Figure 22: Photo of a reader who sent letters to the editor, *Ève* no. 144 (1949)

Thus, the story comes full circle: Art imitates art, art imitates life, life imitates art, life imitates life. The line between fiction and reality becomes a very thin one, which of course does not mean that it does not exist, and no reader was fooling herself or himself. Everybody was dreaming of the Land of Oz, while realizing full well that the place to be was "home." The shift from drawn novel to photonovel, from Hollywood to kitchen sink, helps make the claim that popular audiences are anything but deceived by the dream world that cultural industries are offering them. Photonovels are no example of self-deception or manipulation; they are just one of the many ways in which material and imaginary forces of life interact.

Endnotes

1. Photonovels did not always have official "authors." It was the magazine rather than the director who "signed" these products of the new cultural industry. It should therefore not come as a surprise that it is the actor, not the photographer or the director, who is shown behind the camera, since the real and only stars of the photonovel were the actors.

2. At first sight, this could refer to an answer to the nutritional deficiencies of the postwar years, but in practice it was a crudely gendered problem, since most of these advertisements seem to suggest that it is shameful for a man to have a taller girlfriend.

Works Cited

ADORNO, Theodor. (1951) 1978. *Minima Moralia.* Translated by E. F. N. Jephcott. London: Verso.

ANTONIONI, Michelangelo. 1949. *L'amorosa menzogna.* Filums/Edizioni Fortuna. www.youtube.com/watch?v=1oMv4uIVNIs (last accessed May 15, 2020).

ANTONUTTI, Isabelle. 2013. *Cino Del Duca: De Tarzan à nous deux, itinéraire d'un patron de presse.* Rennes: Presses Universitaires de Rennes.

BAETENS, Jan. 2013. "The Photonovel: Stereotype as Surprise." *History of Photography* 37 (2): 137–52.

———. 2017. *Pour le roman-photo.* Brussels: Les Impressions Nouvelles.

———. 2018a. *Novelization. From Film to Novel.* Translated by Mary Feeney. Columbus: The Ohio State University Press.

———. 2018b. "The Postwar Drawn Novel." In *The Cambridge History of the Graphic Novel*, edited by Jan Baetens, Hugo Frey and Stephen E. Tabachnick, 75-91. Cambridge: Cambridge University Press.

———. 2019. *The Film Photonovel : A History of Forgotten Adaptations.* Austin: University of Texas Press.

BARTHES, Roland. 1981. *Camera Lucida: Reflections on Photography.* Translated by Richard Howard. New York: Hill & Wang.

BLUNCK, Lars. 2019. "Staged Photography." In *The Routledge Companion to Photography and Visual Culture,* edited by Moritz Neumüller, 228–38. London: Routledge.

BONIFAZIO, Paola. 2017. "Political Photoromances: The Italian Communist Party, the Catholic Press, and the Battle for Women's Heart." *Italian Studies* 72 (4): 393–413.

BRAVO, Ana. 2003. *Il Fotoromanzo.* Bologna: Il Mulino.

FABER, Dominique, Marion MINUIT, and Bruno TAKODJERAD. 2012. *Nous Deux présente: La Saga du roman-photo.* Paris: Jean-Claude Gawsewitch.

GIET, Sylvette. 1998. *Nous deux 1947–1997. Apprendre la langue du cœur*. Paris: Peeters & Vrin.

GRIERSON, John. 1966. "The First Principles of Documentary." In *Grierson on Documentary*, edited by Forsythe Hardy. London: Faber & Faber.

KRAUSS, Rosalind. 1977. "Notes on the Index: Seventies Art in America." October 3 (Spring): 68–81.

LEMAGNY, Claude, and André ROUILLÉ, eds. 1986. *Histoire de la photographie*. Paris: Bordas.

Morreale, Emiliano. 2011. *Così piangevano. Il cinema melò nell'Italia degli anni cinquanta*. Rome: Donzelli.

Pittasio, Francesco. 2019. *Neorealist Film Culture 1945–1954*. Amsterdam: Open Cinema & Amsterdam University Press.

Roger, Philippe. 2005. *The American Enemy. The History of French Anti-Americanism*. Translated by Sharon Bouwman. Chicago: University of Chicago Press.

SULLEROT, Evelyne. 1963. *La Presse féminine*. Paris: Armand Colin.

PART THREE
Comics, Reportage, and Memory

CHAPTER SIX:

BD Reportage or Exotic Travel Journal? *L'Afrique de papa* and the Intermedial Gaze

Michelle Bumatay

"Je garde malgré tout en permanence un carnet sur moi, pour l'exercice,
pour faire travailler l'œil et remplir ma bibliothèque imaginaire."

("Despite everything, I always keep a notebook on me, for exercise,
for working my eye and filling my imaginary library.")[1]
—Hippolyte

Introduction

Since the creation in 1991 of France-Info's *Prix de la bande dessinée d'actualité et de reportage* (*Prize for news-based and reportage comics*), BD reportage has become a well-established nonfiction genre in France, evidenced by the creation in 2008 of the quarterly French review *XXI*, which always features at least one BD reportage, and by the surge in other magazines dedicated to BD reportage (Bourdieu 2012; Dabitch 2009; Pollman 2015; Argod 2014; Flinn 2018).[2] Originally published in *XXI* in 2009, *L'Afrique de papa* (*Papa's Africa*) by French cartoonist Hippolyte (nom de plume of Franck Meynet) uses an intermedial blend of drawings, grayscale photography, and sketchbook reproductions to recount a two-week voyage he took to visit his retired father in the Senegalese seaside tourist retreat of Saly, located just south of Dakar. Reporting on Papa's Africa full of leisure and hedonism, Hippolyte also conveys his outsider's perspective steeped in observant reflection. The aesthetically bold result led to a second edition of the BD reportage as a one-shot album published in 2010 to launch Jean-Luc Schneider's newly created Reunion-based publishing house, Des Bulles dans l'Océan.[3] However, the one-shot differs from the *XXI* version in its use of extra materials that frame the text with a substantial series of photographs (the majority of which are absent from the original) and scanned images of Hippolyte's *carnet de voyage* (travel sketchbook) from his journey, comprised of written observations and sketches. Meant to enhance the BD reportage, this added material also complicates the original by revealing omissions and thus foregrounding the meticulously constructed nature of Hippolyte's intermedial choices for his first BD reportage.

L'Afrique de papa, Hippolyte's first foray into nonfiction, marks a crucial turning point in his career, and strong traces of lessons learned from both the two-week journey and the exploration of intermediality in *bandes dessinées* are found in his subsequent nonfiction work. In the foreword to the one-shot, Hippolyte explains that he had previously longed to produce *bandes dessinées* that were *carnets de voyage* before the popularity of the genre became, in his words "quelque peu surexploité" ("somewhat overused") (Hippolyte 2010). Similarly, in the introduction to the original *XXI* version, Hippolyte singles out as a model the seminal BD reportage, *Le Photographe* (2003–2006), by Emmanuel Guibert, Didier Lefèvre, and Frédéric Lemercier, as foundational to the development of his own approach, that, like *Le Photographe*, makes extensive use of photographs and drawings (2009,169). However, Hippolyte makes sure to underline that his work is not simply the result of imitation: "C'est le but de l'acte créatif: intégrer ce qui a été fait et tenter d'aller plus loin. La différence avec Guibert vient du fait que ce sont mes propres photos, ce qui induit un regard et un axe narratif différent du sien" ("It's the goal of the creative act: integrating what has been done and going further. The difference with Guibert comes from the fact that these are my own photos, which entails a gaze and a narrative axis different than his") (169). In effect, *L'Afrique de papa* can be read as his working through of the challenges inherent to this form of travelogue.

Hippolyte's intermedial approach dovetails with and is a function of the multivalent nature of the narrative that mixes different modes of communication, different genres—mainly BD reportage and travelogue—different visual mediums, as well as different versions of Africa.[4] While many point out that comics are, by nature, multimodal, employing verbal and visual modes of representation in addition to mobilizing layout as a field of signification, Hippolyte's nonfiction work is unequivocally and purposefully intermedial, being comprised of varied practices for engaging with the world, all of which are linked with ways of seeing and representing (Chute 2016; Kunka 2018; Køhlert 2019). In the foreword to the one-shot, Hippolyte explains that he always has his journal and camera on him so that he can "faire travailler l'œil" ("make his eye work")—this particular description of his artistic process is telling. Unquestioningly, he is referring to his ability to draw what he sees and to capture subtleties and shapes. Additionally, however, this description privileges the impact of sight on understanding. In fact, I argue that "faire travailler l'œil," a guiding principle for Hippolyte's artistic practice, becomes a central concern in *L'Afrique de papa*. In what follows, I examine Hippolyte's intermedial attempt to deliver a nuanced look of and beyond the exotic touristic view of Saly, an attempt that prompts Hippolyte to interrogate his own gaze and that has impacted his work since.

Reporting on Papa's Africa and Papa's Gaze

It is important to understand *L'Afrique de papa* in its original context—published in volume six of *XXI* as the featured BD reportage and flanked before and after with contextualizing information to guide readers' understanding of the text—since, presented as a piece of journalism, it is meant to shed light on a crucial contemporary issue overlooked in the twenty-four-hour news cycle (Beccaria and Saint-Exupéry 2009, 3). This BD reportage uses Hippolyte's journey to visit his retired father in Saly to inform readers of the neocolonial reality and drastically unequal power dynamics undergirding the hedonistic lifestyle and sexual tourism of the fishing village that was transformed in the 1980s through outside investment into a carefree, sun-soaked retreat for Europeans. Loosely structured around Hippolyte's journey to, arrival in, and exploration of Saly with and without his father, the story centers on the lifestyle of Hippolyte's father and other European tourists and residents like him, a lifestyle that takes as a given (because of gross economic imbalances) the privileged right to the land and all its resources, including the people, for individual pleasure.[5] Indeed, the title—*L'Afrique de papa*—all at once suggests a personal connection to the continent of Africa through familial ties, conveys ownership through possession, and links the current state of affairs to a paternalist and colonialist past whose effects persist even well after Senegal's independence from France in 1960, albeit in new configurations.[6]

As with other BD reportages published in *XXI*, *L'Afrique de papa* is directly followed by a two-page spread of information that allows readers to delve deeper into the story and the current event issues with which it engages. For *L'Afrique de papa*, the content of the left-hand page attests to the veracity of Hippolyte's portrait of Saly; professional aerial and landscape photographs provided by L'Agence France-Presse of the Western-style housing projects and beaches are accompanied by a list of facts about the fishing village's transformation into one of the largest European tourist destinations in West Africa and the fallout of such rapid and largescale development, namely prostitution, pedophilia, and the spread of sexually-transmitted infections. The right-hand page features a range of other texts (essays, novels, a film, a photography book, and a *bande dessinée*) that provide more insight into the themes touched upon, including critiques of the power imbalance between the Global North and the Global South, sexual tourism, Senegalese wrestling, and immigration. The information provided in these two pages leaves no doubt that Hippolyte's father's lifestyle is caught up in the socioeconomic and political complexities of neocolonialism and that, though Saly might stand as an impressive example of the predatory and exploitative potential of Western tourism, it is by no means the only example.

As a featured BD reportage in *XXI*, *L'Afrique de papa* had a set limit of thirty *planches* (pages) and a story about current events to transmit, two nonnegligible external constraints that undoubtedly influenced Hippolyte's decisions.[7] The crux of *L'Afrique de papa* lies in Hippolyte's continual juxtaposition of his father's African paradise with the ongoing struggle to escape the economic hardships and lack of social mobility that the local population faces in direct response to the hedonistically-driven appetite for indulgence made possible, supported, and even encouraged by such an industry. While the first is predicated on the unrestrained and unapologetic pursuit of pleasure, the second is dependent upon an economy of black bodies and their performance, whether in the form of the local fishing tradition, sport—namely wrestling and soccer—or prostitution. Narratively and verbally, this duality is crafted through two key characters: Hippolyte's own father and Dodo, a Senegalese artist and musician whom Hippolyte meets on the beach at dusk while watching local Senegalese men during their daily wrestling practice. From the first moment to the last moment that Hippolyte's father appears, he repeatedly sums up his life with the phrase "Elle est pas belle la vie!" ("Isn't life grand!") (Fig. 1). Each time, he is also depicted with an arm or two raised, gesturing to all that is around him and taking up as much physical space as he likes. Conversely, Dodo offers an alternative summation: "Ici, pour t'en sortir, tu as le sport ou les Européens. Être un champion ou un étalon. C'est toujours ton corps que tu donnes" ("Here, to get by, you have sports or Europeans. Being a champion or a stallion. It's always your body that you give"). Though Dodo's bleak account of the limited options for getting by made available to Senegalese through the use of their bodies occurs only twice (and is slightly altered the second time), its importance is indicated by the fact that these occurrences lie directly in the middle of the story (when Hippolyte meets Dodo) and at the end of the story.

Figure 1: Hippolyte's arrival in Saly and the reader's introduction to Papa's Africa. Reprinted with kind permission from

DES BULLES B DANS L'OCÉAN

These two versions of Saly manifest in the text intermedially and at multiple levels as a pronounced duality, which is instantly captured on the cover of the one-shot: on the top half, a high-contrast grayscale photograph of a Senegalese wrestler practicing a left jab with his fist extended horizontally across the frame; on the bottom half, a drawn panel of an energetic club scene dominated by a warm yellow with orange, red, brown, and pink in which older European men dance with scantily-clad African women. Many of the men have their arms raised as they dance with music notes and CFA francs floating around their heads and their red faces emphasizing their intoxication. The warm watercolors, jubilant atmosphere, curved bodies, and visual density of the bottom panel clash jarringly with the stark photograph. At the same time, the same gesture—a raised fist—connotes different meanings. In the top half, the wrestler's jabbing left fist is but a part of his composed movement, completed by his clenched right fist poised to deliver a second blow and his determined and focused expression. This fist represents a practiced and precise attack and a demonstration of force. In the bottom half, the fists of the dancing men fling out at various angles as extensions of their unselfconscious and unrestrained delight. In contrast to the wrestler's calculated move, these raised fists are but one way in which the Europeans in Saly unapologetically take up space, and use it and everything in it for their own pleasure. Visually mimicking the wrestler's strong punch, the raised fists of the men at the club establish a complex subtext on the question of power in Papa's Africa: Though the wrestler is undoubtedly physically strong, the carefree economic authority of the dancing men signaled by the floating stream of CFA francs encircling them cannot be denied.

In his review of *L'Afrique de papa*, Christophe Cassiau-Haurie latches on to the obvious binary between drawings and photographs as the guiding force for the two visions of Africa; yet, this facile assessment, which mischaracterizes in-text sketches, fails to address the complex play of focalization markers in the drawings (that let readers see Papa's Africa *and also* Hippolyte seeing such a vision) and the range of strategies employed for framing the photographs (that hint at Hippolyte's examination of his own gaze).[8] In her analysis of photography in documentary *bandes dessinées*, Margaret Flinn explains that "frequent redundancies between the representation of a place or object in drawn panels and the photographs do not negate the bédéiste's hand as valid documentary mediation, but the shift in style calls attention to the differing mediations: camera and hand" (2018, 141–42). For Flinn, photographs in documentary comics, like documentary films' "juxtaposition of different visual registers," leads to "an aesthetic of intermediality that exceeds aesthetic positioning," and that thus "challenges the primacy of narrative as the most useful category for understanding what photography is doing in the comics text" (142). In *L'Afrique de papa*, photographs have much more than a narrative function, and Hippolyte's decision to encapsulate each photograph in a thick, evidently hand-drawn frame highlights rather than obscures their subjective framing.

As suggested by the cover, in addition to juxtaposing photographs and drawn panels, Hippolyte develops his multivalent and intermedial representation of the two worlds that cohabitate Saly through design, layout, framing, and color. In all of his work, he mobilizes layout as an aesthetic, figurative, and narrative element composed of a collection of two-page spreads, intimately understanding that "different modes offer different potentials for making meaning" (Kress 2010, 79). The thirty *planches* are broken up into discreet sections: an introduction to the beach where wrestlers train as Hippolyte's plane arrives; his journey from the airport to his father's villa; his time on the beach first with his father and then alone; an afternoon and evening in which Hippolyte's father introduces him to his friends, his lifestyle, and one of his favorite clubs, L'Étage; Hippolyte's exploration of the fishing village and his description of other European tourists who dare to explore beyond the touristic circuit; and the denouement that crosscuts between photographs of a televised professional wrestling match and drawn panels depicting what transpires at L'Étage at the same time. Hippolyte purposefully plays with the relationship between the left- and right-hand pages, switching to dynamic interactions between the two or purposefully repeating the same layout. Furthermore, there are only two moments in the text when Hippolyte opts for a more fluid layout, thus distinguishing their content as crucial. Not surprisingly, one such moment is Hippolyte's encounter with Dodo, while the other depicts Hippolyte's arrival via plane in "Papa's Africa."

For this arrival, Hippolyte crafts a dreamlike scene around the plane ferrying him from France to Senegal, but paints a rather ugly picture inside it that prefigures "Papa's Africa" and generates a cyclical story. The light-orange tinted clouds billowing around the plane contrast sharply with the blue and grays of the plane's cabin, all of which is a metaphor for the discrepancy between the European paradisiac perception of what Senegal represents and the lived reality of the locals. European passengers on the plane start to notice a particular trio: two white men sitting on either side of a silent young black man with his knit cap pulled low over his face. Realizing that this young man is in the process of being deported, European passengers start to congregate near the row, making jokes with the two policemen at the expense of the

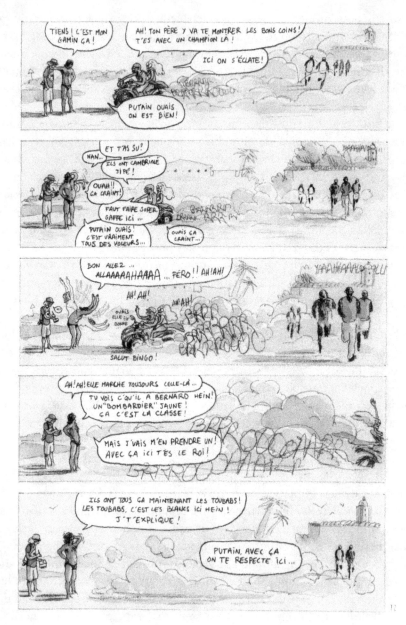

Figure 2: Papa's expansive notion of the beach.
Reprinted with kind permission from

young man. In narrative textboxes, Hippolyte condemns such behavior, but visually portrays himself in silent solidarity with the young man. This short scene achieves two important functions. First, it demonstrates that "Papa's Africa" is not confined to any physical geography, but rather an ideology. Second, since the young man visibly resembles the character at the very end of the text, it suggests a closed-circuit existence for those who make "Papa's Africa" possible.

Repetitive page layouts become a form of "iconic solidarity" typically used for depicting Papa's Africa and thus serve as a marker of narrative focalization (Groensteen 2007, 17). To emphasize his father's notion of the beach, for example, Hippolyte uses horizontal panels that span the width of the page and repeats them for three pages; this connotes an openness only interrupted, much to Hippolyte's father's dismay, by the locals (young men jogging as part of their daily wrestling training and vendors hoping to sell souvenirs to tourists) (Fig. 2). Horizontal panels such as these, reserved for Hippolyte's interactions with "Papa's Africa," contrast with the smaller panels containing images—both drawings and photographs alike—of the local residents who, with the exception of Dodo, are confined to smaller spaces within the makeup of the text, a deliberate choice that foregrounds the privilege of Europeans in Saly.

Complementing the layout, color helps convey geographic locations and time of day, sets the tone, and serves as another marker of focalization. Scenes depicting the local population going about their daily routines feature colors that imply natural lighting—mauves and tans for sunrise and sunset, yellows for daytime, and blues and grays for nighttime—whereas pink is thematized to convey the skewed vision of Papa's Africa. When we first see Hippolyte's father, he is relaxing on his veranda framed by a pink-flowering bougainvillea and exclaims, "Alors, elle est pas belle la vie!" ("So, isn't life wonderful!") as a greeting to his son (Fig. 1). The sarcastic tone of the two affixed text boxes of Hippolyte's narration—". . .le rêve" ("the dream") and "Bienvenue dans l'Afrique de papa" ("Welcome to Papa's Africa")—leave little room for mistaking Hippolyte's impression of Africa with that of his father's. The pink of the flowers becomes a marker of what Kai Mikkonen calls "mind style" and what Silke Horstkotte and Nancy Pedri term as "aspectuality" (Mikkonen 2015, 114; Horstkotte and Pedri 2011, 332). Pink as the marker of Papa's Africa figuratively alludes to *la vie en rose* vision of life in Saly for Europeans. Scenes showing Hippolyte's father and his friends (little more than carbon copies) are awash in the warm yellow of the sunny beach and blanketed in a rosy pastel palette maintained through Hippolyte's father's pink floral shirt

Figure 3: The zoom effect to critique the exotic gaze and consumption of Papa's Africa. Reprinted with kind permission from

DES BULLES **B** DANS L'OCÉAN

and the constant presence of sunbaked, barefoot, and almost-nude Europeans wearing bathing suits as their everyday attire and often sporting rosy cheeks due to intoxication. Moreover, the projection of this mind style on Saly and what it ostensibly has to offer Europeans is enhanced by the pink exterior of L'Étage, Hippolyte's father's preferred club, and the pink, skin-tight clothing of the Senegalese prostitutes there. Hippolyte critiques this lifestyle by exposing the exoticizing gaze at work in this mind style though a zoom effect on a European man at L'Étage eating a pizza while lustfully ogling the prostitutes (Fig. 3). In eight panels on a single page, Hippolyte draws the same man, first as part of the scenery, then zooming in on his face as he consumes pizza and women, and finally moving in even closer to just his smiling, pizza-smeared mouth. These "memorable panels" that are "incongruent . . . with their syntagmatic surroundings" suggest the grotesqueness inherent in such unabashed consumption (Horstkotte 2015, 41).

To be sure, Hippolyte, critical of Papa's Africa, works to expose its hypocritical and exploitative nature by embracing Dodo's summation as the narrative frame for his father's lifestyle (the story starts and ends with wrestling) and by establishing a correlation between Senegalese wrestling and prostitution as the economy underlying such a lifestyle. Hippolyte's approach is most explicit in the denouement, which crosscuts between photographs of a televised professional wrestling match and drawn frames of the scene at L'Étage at the same time. As an introduction to the match, Hippolyte juxtaposes equally-sized frames representing the two sides of Saly: The first is a drawing of his father home alone as he stumbles upon the match on television, while the second is a densely-packed photograph of the hundreds of Senegalese fans in the stands eager to witness the match. Hippolyte's father pokes fun at wrestling and dismisses the muscled athletes (as he does those in training on the beach in Saly) as "feignants," or lazy idlers. Hippolyte makes sure that the irony of such a statement is not lost; in contrast to the fit Senegalese wrestlers, prostitutes, and fishermen who work and train seemingly without rest, European bodies are often drawn as flabby, flaccid, and either leisurely loafing about or unreservedly partaking in physical pleasure. From the facial expressions in the scenes at L'Étage, it is clear that the Senegalese consider Hippolyte's father and those like him as the real "feignants." Interestingly, just a few panels later, a photograph of a young Senegalese boy turning to look back directly at the camera provides an unsettling moment that both challenges the aestheticizing gaze of Hippolyte's camera and dramatizes the kind of looking perpetuated by Hippolyte's father, which Hippolyte thematizes on the adjacent page, where there is an almost one-to-one parallel between the

Figure 4: Crosscutting between wrestlers and prostitutes as the denouement
begins. Reprinted with kind permission from

DES BULLES **B** DANS L'OCÉAN

objectification of black female and male bodies (Fig. 4). To complement the drawn images of the scantily-clad women heading to the club, the photographs of the male wrestlers are cropped to highlight their physical attributes. In both cases, Hippolyte crops out the women's and men's heads, thus further exoticizing and eroticizing their bodies. Energy builds in both settings as Hippolyte's father, who stopped watching the match to dance at L'Étage, basks in his paradisiac version of Africa while the wrestlers prepare to battle.

Over the course of the final four pages, the depicted wrestling match becomes a dramatic metaphor for the internal struggle that some Senegalese face when deciding between either side of Dodo's equation. Hippolyte employs a staggered layout that repeatedly alternates between the photographs of the match that remain horizontally wider than drawn frames of yellow-washed close-ups of a black male body and an older European woman at L'Étage. Up to now in the text, prostitution was presented solely in the context of black women and white men. Here, however, Hippolyte reverses the situation, pointing out that it is not just European men seeking the attention of African companions, but also alerting readers to European women's participation in sexual tourism (Blanchard et al. 2018, 468–69). Juxtaposing wrestling with the close-ups of the man and woman points to the struggle for physical dominance and the submission of one body to another. Ultimately, the woman wins, as evidenced by the last strip giving way to a single centered drawn panel as the woman and man disappear into the night, a panel surrounded by the silent whiteness of the page due to the lack of a competing photograph. Though Hippolyte chooses not to represent himself in either location, his take on the situation occurs in text boxes superimposed over the staggered frames that riff on Dodo's equation: "Ici, pout t'en sortir. . . tu as le sport . . . ou les Européens . . . Être un champion . . . ou un étalon . . . C'est toujours ton corps qui t'aide. . . ou qui te perd" ("Here, to get by, you have sports or Europeans. Being a champion or a stallion. It's always your body that helps you or that wastes you"). Though this closing statement communicates a strong critique of Papa's Africa, there is a noticeable silence around the in-text representation of Hippolyte.

Hippolyte and His Gaze in Papa's Africa

Describing Hippolyte's portrayal of his father's version of Africa, the editors of *XXI* and *Des Bulles dans l'Océan*, as well as reviewers of *L'Afrique de papa* (taking their cue from the editors), remark upon Hippolyte's silence and his recourse to drawing in his sketchbook rather than responding to his father (Cassiau-Haurie 2010; Bourdieu 2012). This is due in large part to

Hippolyte's own representation of himself within the narrative as a character with little to no dialogue and almost never without his camera and sketchbook. On the one hand, this silence boosts reader identification with Hippolyte; on the other, it hints at a broader reflection on subjectivity and the gaze. As with other practitioners of BD reportage, Hippolyte chooses to include visual depictions of himself in the story-world to highlight his subjectivity and to authenticate the story being told (Sacco 2012, xiii; Bourdieu 2012, 5; Pollman 2015, 500). When we first see Hippolyte, he is on the plane for Senegal, absorbed with filling in his sketchbook-cum-*carnet-de-voyage*, a deliberate choice meant to solidify a direct link between what the character is doing and the end result that the reader is in the process of reading. The other few scenes that include drawings of Hippolyte fall into two categories. The first consists of scenes in which his father introduces him to his lifestyle. In these scenes, Hippolyte visibly contrasts with other Europeans; he always has on much more clothing than those around him and even a hat to shield his eyes and he tries to take up as little space as possible, quietly huddling in his seat, lingering on the edges away from others (including his father), calm in his demeanor, and often sketching or writing rather than contributing to conversations. The second category consists of the two-page spread in the center of the text depicting Hippolyte's encounter with Dodo. Over these two more loosely organized pages, Hippolyte provides four drawings of himself as he watches wrestlers practice at dusk on the beach, each time also supplying a drawing of Dodo.

The importance of this moment for Hippolyte cannot be overstated, and he goes to great lengths to encode important lessons learned while finding the intermedial means to walk readers through such a life-altering encounter. At first glance, one instantly notices the much less rigid layout and the copresence of at least three different modes of visual communication (grayscale photographs, detailed drawings with color, and sketches) and two different modes of verbal communication (Hippolyte's narration and speech balloons). Working through the various elements, one realizes the profound narrative experimentation taking place as Hippolyte grapples with having his own gaze under scrutiny. The yellow background of the two pages continues from the previous section, in which static frames depict Hippolyte's father's version of the beach, thus establishing that Hippolyte is still on the beach, but his father is not. The pages start with grayscale photographs in two columns with Hippolyte's narration between them that describes the images captured by his camera: "Quand la journée tire à sa fin, les lutteurs se retrouvent et commencent leur échauffement final. Ils laissent derrière eux les maisons 'africaines' des toubabs et leurs différents joujous high-tech. Ils vivent leur vie" ("When the day draws to a close, the wrestlers regroup and start their final warm-up. They leave behind them the Toubabs' 'African' houses and their high-tech toys. They live their life") (2010, 13) (Fig. 5). The photographs, all the same size, generate a narrative flow: The first strip contains a medium shot of a man jogging to join others already gathered and a long shot of the men gathered; the two photographs in the second strip are taken from much closer to the men and show various pairs in mid-practice; the third strip features a photograph from equally close of other men watching attentively while waiting their turn, but rather than follow up with a second photograph, Hippolyte provides a drawing of himself holding his camera while writing in his book with someone behind him who says, via speech balloons, "Ils n'aiment pas trop être pris en photo tu sais . . . comme des curiosités" ("They don't very much like being photographed you know . . . like curiosities") (13). This comment, in the moment, sparked a shift in Hippolyte, which he reproduces in the text by interrupting the continuation of photographs; the purposefully uneven layout of the photographs signifies the immediacy and impact of the comments. The framing of this first drawn floating panel obscures the identity of the person making the comment and provides dramatic irony in that the character Hippolyte is unaware that he is also being observed. The next floating panel, on the left-hand side of the next strip, continues to depict the storyworld, this time from another angle showing the character Hippolyte and the man, who turns out to be Dodo, with the wrestlers in the background. In this panel, the character Hippolyte's camera is slung by his side, and he has switched to sketching in his journal as Dodo goes on to explain, in speech balloons, "Ici, c'est une parenthèse dans Saly . . . c'est un moment à eux, pas un show" ("This here is an aside in Saly . . . it's their moment, not a show") (13). To demonstrate that he understood what Dodo meant, Hippolyte not only draws himself as sketching rather than taking pictures, but he also chooses to include reproductions of his sketches to finish out the page.

The visual shift from more detailed storyworld panels to floating pencil sketches, some with shadowing or watercolor, attempts to vouch for Hippolyte's realization that while he works to capture what he sees, his act of gazing is itself a kind of spectacle for others (Dodo as well as the readers) to watch. Up to now, his in-text incarnation had been an almost silent observer whose desire to capture and to convey Papa's Africa privileged his outsider status as ostensibly less intrusive and less exploitative than that of

**Figure 5: Left-hand page of Hippolyte's intermedial account of meeting Dodo.
Reprinted with kind permission from**

DES BULLES **B** DANS L'OCÉAN

other Europeans in Saly. Yet Dodo's simple remarks shatter this assumption, making Hippolyte aware of his own gaze. The shift from photographs to sketches on the page represent different modes of looking. For while there is indeed a "temporal aspect of image 'capture' characterized by the quickness of both the sketch and the camera's shutter," as Margaret Flinn suggests, there is also a different physicality associated with each activity (2018, 143). The interruption and unevenness in layout of the photographs at the beginning of the page and the sketches following Dodo's comments work as a kind of indexicality of Hippolyte's actions in the moment. Readers supposedly have the proof that Hippolyte's desires are different from those of his father. Yet his presence during the wrestlers' daily practice represents an intrusion, and the narrated text accompanying the two-page spread reveals Hippolyte's quest for access in the moment. Rather than respond verbally to Dodo's comments in the text, Hippolyte shifts to sketches and narrative text that describes the importance of wrestling in Senegal. It is as though, having been deprived of his camera out of the desire to avoid being seen as treating the wrestlers as curiosities, Hippolyte cannot help but fill the void with other forms of representation (verbal descriptions and sketches).

On the accompanying page dedicated to Dodo, the tension of Hippolyte's desire to differentiate himself from Papa's Africa while also wanting to learn and capture all that he can plays out through composition and repetition. As with the previous page, Hippolyte eschews a grid pattern, presenting instead a more fluid layout featuring drawings, sketches, and photographs. There is no doubt that this page is about Dodo, since he and his guitar are represented no less than eight different times; the page is roughly divided into four bands starting with a detailed portrait of Dodo and ending with two photographs of him.[9] Hippolyte also includes himself in two of the drawings of Dodo; these two floating panels represent their conversation in the storyworld. In both instances, Hippolyte is seated below Dodo on the seawall as he learns from him while sketching him implied by the repetition of Dodo's portrait in the second strip. The framing in these storyworld panels suggests Hippolyte's status as pupil and cast Dodo as a wise sage, all of which works together to posit Dodo's knowledge about himself and his take on life in Saly as authentic. The floating narrative text that captions the first portrait of Dodo explains that he is not a wrestler but an artist from the interior of Senegal who has come to Saly to profit from booming tourism. For him, dusk on the beach when he plays music is, after a whole day of "faux-semblants" ("pretenses") or subterfuges, "une parenthèse enchantée" ("an enchanted aside") (2010, 14). Over the course of the second strip, Hippolyte provides three different portraits of

Dodo that run into one another as he plays guitar and describes his family, to whom he sends money and whom he rarely gets to visit. The following strip starts with a storyworld panel that depicts Dodo asking, "La prostitution?" followed by a speech balloon with an ellipsis and no pointer to determine whether it is Dodo's hesitation or Hippolyte's. Nevertheless, the fact that Dodo asks the question implies that Hippolyte has already prompted him to speak on this topic. Hippolyte does not completely withhold the fact that he is responsible for introducing the topic to the conversation, but he abstains from representing himself as the topic's origin. To accompany Dodo's take on prostitution as a means to get by, Hippolyte inserts two more sketches of wrestlers from his journal. Juxtaposing sketches of men wrestling with Dodo's comments can be read as a metaphor for the struggle that prostitution might represent for those looking to get by (which, as previously mentioned, is what happens during the denouement). These sketches have the added function of foreshadowing Dodo's next statement, the one that Hippolyte pits against his father's motto—that, to get by, Senegalese either have sports or Europeans, and that in either case, it is always one's body that one gives.

This summation's cold calculatedness and Dodo's own unaccounted position within such an equation seem to be brushed off or even undermined in the last strip that begins with a narrow column of floating text attributed to Dodo and two photographs of him that, in juxtaposition with the many colorful and expressive portraits above, feel crammed into the bottom of the page. In the text, Dodo laughingly reveals that since he is neither handsome nor strong, he paints and writes songs. He then goes on to tell Hippolyte, "Mais moi si tu veux tu peux me prendre en photo!" ("But me if you want you can take my photo!") (2010, 14). As with the sketches of the wrestlers, the abundance of sketches of Dodo before the two small photographs suggests a hungry camera. That is to say, the immediacy of the two photographs after Dodo's permission stand in opposition to the entire rest of the page, where Hippolyte tried multiple times, ostensibly unsuccessfully, to capture Dodo's image. The return to photography right away, without any hesitation, and the diagonal bookending photographs on these two pages imply Hippolyte's dissatisfaction with only sketching and hint at his reliance on the mediated gaze supplied by the camera as a means of objectively interacting with Senegal. Put another way, the aestheticizing gaze of Hippolyte's camera is meant to be distinct from the hedonistic appetite of the European tourist gaze conveyed through the focalization of Papa's Africa, but perhaps it is not. For example, in the back-and-forth between wrestling and prostitution during the denouement, Hippolyte's consumption of wrestling is much like his father's;

while Hippolyte's father's experience of the match is mediated through the television, Hippolyte, who was physically in attendance (and ostensibly the only non-Senegalese person present based on the photographs presented in the text), his experience of the match is also mediated, though through his camera, not a television. Furthermore, the decision to crop the photographs of the male wrestlers so as to generate an explicit comparison with prostitution, rather than differentiating his gaze, reinforces its exoticizing power. In this way, his photographs mimic passages about black male bodies in some French colonial novels, in which "while not overly homoerotic, might point to a homoerotic voyeurism which allows a predominantly European male authorship and readership access to a covert and indirect erotic engagement with black male bodies" (Everett 2018, 8).

Another key moment when these tensions play out is during Hippolyte's visit to the fishing village during Tabaski, the Senegalese term for the Muslim holiday Eid al-Adha. This two-page spread features nine photographs in the top half of the left-hand page flanked by drawings of the village mosque and school and seven photographs in the bottom half of the right-hand page under drawings with a sketch-like quality of those gathered at the foot of a giant baobab where the sacrificial steer is being butchered. The minimal scale of the photos gives priority to the drawings, which suggests that Hippolyte internalized Dodo's lesson. Through text boxes superimposed on the drawing of the sacrifice, Hippolyte is sure (and quick) to inform readers that since his presence intrigued those gathered, he was invited to get closer and that the villagers demanded that he take their photo near the sacrificed animal. In spite of this avowal, there exists a palpable tension in Hippolyte's presence and his photographer's gaze, to which he seems to allude, or at least to the impossibility of being certain when he explains that "les villageois semblent heureux que je m'intéresse à eux" ("the villagers seemed happy that I was interested in them") (2010, 20). Though a far cry from the sexual tourists in Saly, Hippolyte is nevertheless a consumer of Africa and of Africans. As with the photographs of Dodo, the text box informing readers that the villagers asked to be photographed instantly triggers a rapid succession of photographs from a range of various angles and proximities to the animal that are equally crammed into the lower third of the page. These traces of Hippolyte's physical movement in the moment do not suggest the quiet Hippolyte character who restricts his presence. Here, Roland Barthes's observation of and concern for photographers' bodies and actions seems apt: "For me, the Photographer's organ is not his eye (which terrifies me) but his finger: what is linked to the trigger of the lens, to the metallic shifting of the plates (when the camera still has such things)" (1981, 15). It is both Hippolyte's eyes and fingers that work to capture the scene.

The specialness of this experience is underscored through manipulation of the photographs in the addition of red for both the blood of the sacrificed animal and the shirts of some of the young participants. These "memorable" photographs, treated differently than the rest of the photographs, suggest a certain reverence for the subject of the camera's lens, yet still confine the people in small-scale frames pushed to the edge of the page. One potential signification of these choices might be found in the use of pink in the drawings on these pages, here a metaphor for the reach of Papa's Africa. Though this event takes place in the traditional village whose existence predates the development of the tourist enclave, it is not out of reach of the tourists. It is, however, at the periphery, a marginal "backstage" space where tourists in search of "authenticity" are "an obvious intrusion" (Urry 2011, 10). As with Hippolyte's presence during Dodo's "parenthèse enchantée," his presence on the morning of Tabaski in the fishing village and the implied hesitation in his narration of the scene attest to his awareness of the tensions of such encounters. As an interesting counterpoint to his own experience and an attempt to downplay his encounter as spectacle, on the next page, following the "memorable" photographs, Hippolyte offers a rare one-page vignette that comments on tourism from which he, his father, wrestlers, and prostitutes are absent. Additionally, unlike the rest of the text, this left-hand page does not visually correspond to its right-hand companion, establishing a unique occurrence. In the text box at the beginning of the page, Hippolyte explains sarcastically that certain tourists "osent 'l'aventure'" ("risk 'the adventure'") by visiting the fishing village (2010, 21). The vignette depicts a European couple whose bohemian beachwear imply that they are perhaps a different type of tourist than those represented by Hippolyte's father. Over the course of the page, the couple superficially take in what the village might have to offer. They browse in a shop where the owner, a silent but welcoming host, offers them tea only to be met with clichéd remarks from the woman about the supposed differences between Western feminism and polygamy. The couple also discuss in front of the shop owner how the cheap price of the clothes means nothing to them, but would be a great sum to the shop owner; without making the purchase, they leave offering an insincere promise that they will pass by later (an echo of Hippolyte's father's strategy on the beach with vendors). While this scene might also represent clichéd stereotypes about Western tourists, one can read Hippolyte's desire to distance himself and his own practices from such superficial behavior.

Reframing the Report

This desire is much more prevalent in the one-shot version of *L'Afrique de papa* published by Des Bulles dans l'Océan, whose self-stated mission includes introducing readers to the various kinds of Africas that exist today.[10] While the extent to which writers and cartoonists have control over the paratextual spaces of their work is not always obvious, given the content of the inside covers and front and back matter, one could convincingly argue that Hippolyte worked closely with the Des Bulles dans l'Océan's editor on the entire project. Ultimately, the one-shot adds a total of twenty-four extra pages to the original text. The photo collages of the inside front and back covers generate a nuanced tableau of local geography, traditions, culture, and people. The Senegalese landscape, flora, and fauna are complemented by local people happily posing for the camera. Hippolyte even includes a small photograph of himself. These photographs not only paint a much different picture than that of Hippolyte's father but also work to frame the constructed perception of his father's African paradise. Additionally, Hippolyte provides scanned images of his *carnet de voyage* preceding the text and full-page reproductions of his photographs directly following the text. Though the genre of *carnets de voyage* is steeped in an exotic view of the other and the elsewhere, Hippolyte's scanned pages display a self-reflexive and self-conscious approach to cultural difference. The scanned pages are ripe with dense text and detailed sketches which, together, speak to the time and effort Hippolyte employed to understand and examine the complexity and richness of his experiences. They also tell a slightly different story than the one presented in the BD reportage. First, the handwritten title page of the *carnet*, "Carnet de mai: Sénégal, Gambia, Casamance, 2008" belies the sole focus on Saly. Second, though the densely-packed handwriting is difficult to read, there is one page on which Hippolyte reproduces a conversation between his father, someone named Adam, and his mother. This small detail, the presence of Hippolyte's mother during the journey, is easy to miss and begs the question of what else Hippolyte omitted from the BD reportage. Similarly, directly following the somber end of *L'Afrique de papa*, in which the young Senegalese stallion succumbs to the older European woman and leaves the club with her, ten full-page photographs offer a counternarrative that celebrates local culture. All but the last two photographs show the local population on the beach using it and enjoying it for their own purposes. However, I would argue that the doubly twinned nature of the last two photographs once again recall the dual nature of life in Saly. Hippolyte establishes a correlation between the two through composition, for in both instances the two people in the photograph are turned away from the camera. While the left-hand photograph of two local boys walking together suggests a positive easiness, the proximity of the right-hand photograph of two older European women walking along the beach hints at a potentially bleak future for the two boys. To end the text with the photograph of the two women—a photograph that also appears in *L'Afrique de papa*—echoes the ending of the BD reportage, thus leaving readers to ponder the price of such a leisurely stroll.

Drawing from a preexisting interest in *carnets de voyage*, inspired by Emmanuel Guibert's use of photography in *Le Photographe*, and encouraged by Patrick de Saint-Exupéry (co-founder and editor of *XXI*), Hippolyte mobilized his first BD reportage, *L'Afrique de papa*, to explore the many possibilities of an intermedial approach to storytelling. This process has had a profound impact on the rest of his work, and Hippolyte gestures to the importance of *L'Afrique de papa* in the foreword to the one-shot version stating that working with Patrick de Saint-Exupéry at *XXI* was "très important dans l'approche que je me fais maintenant du récit de voyage" ("very important in the approach that I now have for travel writing") (Hippolyte 2010). This intermedial approach invites readers to work through both his journeys and the self-reflective process of recounting his experiences, at the center of which is a theorization of the gaze. For example, the zoom effect for the scene in which the man eating a slice of pizza at L'Étage draws readers' attention to the violence of his neocolonially-tinged masculine gaze; in a sense, readers witness Hippolyte's gaze of the man's gaze. This technique has become a hallmark of Hippolyte's nonfiction work for two primary reasons. First, the zoom effect, whether through photography (as is the case in *Les enfants de Kinshasa*) or drawing (as is the case in *La fantaisie des Dieux: Rwanda 1994*), works to authenticate what one has witnessed. Second, and more importantly, this technique, I argue, is a telling byproduct of Hippolyte's coming to terms with and working through his own gaze. The two-page spread in the center of *L'Afrique de papa* that abounds with images of Dodo conveys the palpable desire to capture Dodo through sketches, drawings, and photography. As explained, this pivotal scene shapes how Hippolyte *sees* Senegal and also how he *understands* it. For Hippolyte, "faire travailler l'œil" at work in *L'Afrique de papa* is an intermedially embodied practice directly linked to one's cognitive process. While this does not result in total knowledge, it can, and should, help us interrogate our own gaze.

Endnotes

1. All translations are my own unless otherwise stated.

2. Patrick de Saint-Exupéry, cofounder of *XXI* with Laurent Beccaria, singles out Joe

Sacco, Emmanuel Guibert, and Jean-Philippe Stassen as key figures in the emergence of BD reportage, citing 2000 as an important year for the genre due to the publication of *Le Photographe* and *Déogratias* (Beccaria and Saint-Exupéry 2012, 5).

3. The press release for *L'Afrique de papa* on Des Bulles dans l'Océan's website features the cover image and many high-quality reproductions of key *planches* (https://dbdo-editions.com/wp-content/uploads/2019/07/L-afrique-de-papa-DBDO.pdf). Quality reproductions from the *XXI* version can be found in Christophe Cassiau-Haurie's review of *L'Afrique de papa* for Africultures (http://africultures.com/lafrique-de-papa-9576/).

4. Many comics studies scholars point to the difficulty of categorization of such texts. For example, Benjamin Woo problematizes Joe Sacco's self-applied term "comics journalism," while Nina Mickwitz and Margaret Flinn advocate for the term "documentary comics" rather than comics journalism (Woo 2010; Mickwitz 2016; Flinn 2018).

5. In the short introduction to *L'Afrique de papa* in *XXI*, readers are informed that Hippolyte's father, a former travel agent and car salesman who was twice married and twice divorced, sold his house in Haute-Savoie and, for the same price, purchased a small villa (part of which he rents out) that stretches along the Atlantic beach eighty kilometers south of Dakar (Hippolyte 2009, 168).

6. See Pascal Blanchard, et al., editor, *Sexe, Race & Colonies* (Paris: La Découverte, 2018), in particular, the preface by Achille Mbembe and Jacques Martial and the third and fourth sections on "Décolonisations" and "Métissages."

7. In *Grands reporters: 20 histoires vraies*, the massive 2012 anthology of twenty of *XXI*'s BD reportages (654 pages in total), all but two tell their true tale in thirty *planches*. The two exceptions are Jean-Philippe Stassen's *Les visiteurs de Gibraltar* at twenty-nine *planches* (published in the very first issue of *XXI*) and a collaborative effort by Emmanuel Guibert, Alain Keler, and Frédéric Lemercier, *Des nouvelles d'Alain*, at thirty-nine pages divided into four chapters, originally published in installments from the fall of 2009 to the spring of 2010 (issues 8, 9, 10, and 11) and often alongside another thirty-page BD reportage.

8. "Les scènes avec les Européens passent essentiellement par des dessins et croquis. La photographie retrace les tranches de vie et les rencontres faites par Hippolyte durant son séjour au Sénégal. Le travail des pêcheurs sur la plage, l'entraînement des lutteurs, les scènes de marché, telle est l'Afrique d'Hippolyte. Celle qu'il était aussi venu chercher et qu'il est condamné à observer à travers l'objectif d'un appareil" ("The scenes with the Europeans go through drawings and sketches. Photography recounts slices of life and encounters that Hippolyte made during his trip to Senegal. The work of the fishermen on the beach, wrestlers' training, market scenes, such is Hippolyte's Africa. One that he had come in search of and that he is condemned to observe through the lens of a camera") (Hippolyte 2010).

9. One of the photographs of Dodo also graces the back cover of the one-shot album published by Des Bulles dans l'Océan.

10. According to the press release for *L'Afrique de papa* on Des Bulles dans l'Océan's website, founding editor Jean-Luc Schneider wanted to promote stories from the Indian Ocean and Africa to demonstrate the range of Africas in existence today, and he wanted to create beautiful books in a digital era. He chose *L'Afrique de papa* as the first title since it pleased him for what it reveals about Africa, and, overall, for the ways in which the story is told and realized.

Works Cited

ARGOD, Pascale. 2014. "Du reportage graphique et du carnet de reportage: images géopolitiques, regards de reporters et témoignages du réel." *Belgeo: Revue belge de géographie*, no. 2. https://doi.org/10.4000/belgeo.12843.

BARTHES, Roland. 1981. *Camera Lucida: Reflections on Photography*. Translated by Richard Howard. New York: Hill & Wang.

BECCARIA, Laurent and Patrick DE SAINT-EXUPÉRY. 2009. "Foreword." *XXI*, no. 6 (Spring): 3.

BECCARIA, Laurent and Patrick DE SAINT-EXUPÉRY, ed. 2012. *Grands reporters: 20 histoires vraies*. Les Arènes.

BLANCHARD, Pascal, Nicolas BANCEL, Gilles BOËTSCH, Christelle TARAUD, and Dominic THOMAS, eds. 2018. *Sexe, Race & Colonies*. Paris: La Découverte.

BOURDIEU, Séverine. 2012. "Le reportage en bande dessinée dans la presse actuelle: un autre regard sur le monde." *COnTEXTES: Revue de sociologie de la littérature* 11.

CASSIAU-HAURIE, Christophe. 2010. "*L'Afrique de papa* de Hippolyte." *Africultures*, July 5, 2010, africultures.com/lafrique-de-papa-9576/. Accessed September 1, 2019.

CHUTE, Hillary L. 2016. *Disaster Drawn: Visual Witness, Comics, and Documentary Form*. Cambridge, MA: Harvard University Press.

DABITCH, Christophe. 2009. "Reportage et bande dessinée." *Hermès, La Revue* 54 (2): 91–98.

EVERETT, Julin. 2018. *Le queer imperial: Male Homoerotic Desire in Francophone Colonial and Postcolonial Literature*. Boston: Brill-Rodopi.

FLINN, Margaret. 2018. "Photography as Narrative, Aesthetic, and Document in Documentary Bande Dessinée: Emmanuel and François Lepage's *La lune est blanche* (2014)." *Inks: The Journal of the Comics Studies Society* 2 (2): 137–59.

GROENSTEEN, Thierry. 2007. *The System of Comics*. Translated by Bart Beaty and Nick Nguyen. Jackson: University Press of Mississippi.

GUIBERT, Emmanuel, Didier LEFÈVRE, and Frédéric LEMERCIER. 2010. *Le Photographe: édition intégrale*. Charleroi, Belgium: Aire Libre/Dupuis.

HIPPOLYTE. 2009. "L'Afrique de papa." *XXI* 6: 168–201.

———. 2010. *L'Afrique de papa*. Réunion: Des Bulles Dans l'Océan.

———. 2012. "Les enfants de Kinshasa." *XXI* 17: 168–201.

HIPPOLYTE and Patrick DE SAINT-EXUPÉRY. 2014. *La Fantaisie des dieux: Rwanda 1994*. Paris: Les Arènes.

HORSTKOTTE, Silke. 2015. "Zooming In and Out: Panels, Frames, Sequences, and the Building of Graphic Storyworlds." In *From Comic Strips to Graphic Novels: Contributions to the Theory and History of Graphic Narrative*, edited by Daniel Stein and Jan-Noël Thon, 27–48. Berlin: Walter de Gruyter GmbH.

HORSKTKOTTE, Silke and Nancy PEDRI. 2011. "Focalization on Graphic Narrative." *Narrative*, 19 (3): 330–57.

KØHLERT, Frederik Byrn. 2019. *Serial Selves: Identity and Representation in Autobiographical Comics*. New Brunswick, NJ: Rutgers University Press.

KRESS, Gunther R. 2010. *Multimodality: A Social Semiotic Approach to Contemporary Communication*. London: Routledge.

KUNKA, Andrew J. 2018. *Autobiographical Comics*. New York: Bloomsbury Academic.

MBEMBE, Achille and Jacques MARTIAL. 2018. "Préface." In *Sexe, Race & Colonies*, edited by Pascal Blanchard, Nicolas Bancel, Gilles Boëtsch, Christelle Taraud, and Dominic Thomas, 7–11. Paris: La Découverte.

MICKWITZ, Nina. 2016. *Documentary Comics: Graphic Truth-Telling in a Skeptical Age*. New York: Palgrave Macmillan.

MIKKONEN, Kai. 2015. "Subjectivity and Style in Graphic Narratives." In *From Comic Strips to Graphic Novels: Contributions to the Theory and History of Graphic Narrative*, edited by Daniel Stein and Jan-Noël Thon, 101–23. Berlin: Walter de Gruyter GmbH.

POLLMANN, Joost. 2015. "Comics and Journalism: Witnessing the World with Pen and Paper." *IJOCA* 17 (1): 500–504.

SACCO, Joe. 2012. *Journalism*. New York: Metropolitan Books, 2012.

SCHNEIDER, Jean Luc. 2010. *"L'Afrique de papa."* Press release. Des Bulles Dans L'Ocean website. dbdo-editions.com/wp-content/uploads/2019/07/L-afrique-de-papa-DBDO.pdf. Accessed 15 September 2019.

Urry, John and Jonas Larsen. 2011. *The Tourist Gaze* 3.0. London: SAGE Publications.

Woo, Benjamin. 2010. "Reconsidering Comics Journalism: Information and Experience in Joe Sacco's Palestine." In *The Rise and Reason of Comics and Graphic Literature: Critical Essays on the Form*, edited by Joyce Goggin and Dan Hassler-Forest. Jefferson, NC: McFarland & Co: 166–77.

CHAPTER SEVEN:
(Re)Negotiating Memory: *Panama Al-Brown ou l'Énigme de la Force*, or the Black Boxer vs. the Graphic Novel

Maxence Leconte

On a freezing Manhattan morning in November 1950, a police patrol stopped by 42nd Street near Times Square; in spite of the biting cold, a black homeless man was lying in the middle of the sidewalk. When the policemen nudged his body, the vagabond did not move, nor did he speak, and the patrol was compelled to take him away. After a few hours at the local station, the homeless man was still fully unconscious in his cell; in a state of confusion and panic, an ambulance was called. Six months later, on April 11, 1951, in a grim Staten Island hospital, the destitute man passed away, knocked out by tuberculosis. His name was Alfonso Teofilo Brown, former bantamweight champion and first Latino to ever claim a boxing world title. The medical superintendent, Dr. Klein, informed the press that the champion died penniless, "sans un ami ou un parent connu et, si personne ne le réclame, son cadavre sera enterré comme on enterre les indigents" ("without any known friend or parent and, if no one claims it, his body will be buried like those of indigent people") (Boisse 1982, 24). The very next day, a group of three unknown men arrived at the hospital to collect Al-Brown's body. They loaded the coffin in a white van and drove straight to Harlem. All night long, the men visited one bar after another, and with the casket open, begged patrons to buy them and the late champion one last drink. The next day, they did the same. Finally, the coffin was returned to the Staten Island hospital, the body buried near Long Island City, eventually exhumed, and shipped to Panama City.

The story of boxing dilettante Alfonso "Panama" Al-Brown, perhaps one of the most ubiquitous and electrifying figures of both the Parisian sport and nightlife scenes during the *Années Folles*, remains contested and—at times—hidden from the general public. Spanish painter and essayist Eduardo Arroyo completed the first biography of the boxer in 1981, three decades after the

black champion's death. More recently, essayist and historian José Corpas elu-
cidated some of the shadowy details of Al-Brown's life in his book *Black Ink: A
Story of Boxing, Betrayal, Homophobia, and the First Latino Champion* (2016).
While both biographies did justice to the late boxing champion, a missing link
remained all too visible. What happened to the French cultural contributions to
Al-Brown's memory? How could there be no trace of the man who dwelled in
Paris for years and considered the city one of the greatest loves of his life? Had
the memories of Brown simply faded, or had we consciously avoided them?

A partial response ultimately appeared with Alex Inker's[1] *Panama Al-Brown
ou l'Énigme de la Force* (*Panama Al-Brown or the Enigma of Force*) (2017), a
graphic novel joining the long tradition of comics dedicated to the sweet science of prizefighting. Since the early publications of the 1930s and the cult
figure of *Joe Palooka*,[2] the connections between boxing, the graphic novel, and
social issues have extended far beyond borders of time and space, as recent examples demonstrate.[3] With the aim of renegotiating the memory of the boxer
of color, Alex Inker takes his readers further with a *bande dessinée* that echoes
the methods of the *reportage*. By doing so, *Panama Al-Brown ou l'Énigme de la
Force* demonstrates the graphic novel's position as a literary medium embedded
in a fabric of intermediality, stressing "the interconnectedness of modern media" as "constituents of a wider social and cultural environment" (Jensen 2016,
1). As a result, Inker's work complicates our understanding of postcolonial
history and therefore reshapes our approach to its discourse. In the following
pages, I examine the particular significance of the French graphic novel as both
an aesthetic and political medium (Clark and Cromer 2007; McKinney 2008,
2013) capable of reconstructing and empowering the memory of marginalized
identities such as that of Panama Al-Brown. Using Inker's *bande dessinée* as my
main focus, I demonstrate how both the body of the text—or hypertext (Purves
1998), integrating images and words in symbiosis—and the body of its main
character Alfonso Brown are combined to offer new possibilities for the depiction and the understanding of blackness, immigration, racism, and resistance in
France during the interwar period. A character simultaneously admired and reviled, Al-Brown's multifaceted personality displays the fundamental paradoxes
and the genuine complexity inherent to the life of the boxer of color during the
Années Folles, a puzzle most eloquently explored through the prism of a literary
medium such as the graphic novel.

To begin, a brief introduction of Al-Brown's sinuous journey to and
within Paris will be superimposed on the French historical and social climate
of the 1920s and 1930s. The Third Republic's ambivalent stance toward color
and race certainly affected the memory of the Panamanian boxer in France

and deserves to be underlined. Given the importance attributed to the medium of the graphic novel in this work, I then proceed to a swift analysis of the early cultural significance of the *bande dessinée* during the same time period in France. Finally, I turn to Inker's work and analyze it as a particularly noteworthy example of the graphic novel's aptitude to renegotiate memory thanks to the concept of *reportage*, thus not only partaking in the reworking of the French postcolonial and postmodern literary landscape (Miller 2007; McKinney 2013) but also functioning as a perfect instance of intermediality. By drawing on the theories of Said (1993) and Groensteen (2007), I demonstrate that Inker's *modus operandi* is to playfully yet authoritatively destabilize the reader's vision of history and memory through characteristic components of the *bande dessinée* such as rhythm and framing.

A study in contrasts, confronting the literary canon on the one hand and hegemonic social constructions on the other, this chapter underlines the value of nonlinear, fluid readings of both texts and identities made possible by the graphic novel, a literary medium that celebrates them and their "hybridity as a way of looking at the Self and the Other and their variegated appearances" (Iggers, cited in Clark and Cromer 2007, 575). I logically conclude by suggesting that such hybridity, by challenging the normative spaces of high literature and white-centered, heteronormative self, functions as an apt platform to encourage a renewed understanding of both memory and history and their subsequent teaching (Clark and Cromer 2007).

Paris and the Dark Side of Blackness
During the Interwar Period

What did the French people even know about boxing, and what was the status of the sport in France during the 1920s? In a few words, they adored it. Or more precisely, they loved boxers and considered them to be as important as any popular actor or singer. For instance, the social and cultural impact created by a boxer such as Georges Carpentier[4] can hardly be measured: hundreds of fights in Paris and around France, tens of thousands of spectators, and more money that organizers could count. Yet, for all the distractions boxing brought to the urban life of the French capital and other cities, the impact created by one's skin color was fundamental to the perception of the audience: Invariably, white prizefighters were hailed as heroes whereas men of color were seen as hereditary foe. While historian Tyler Stovall assertively claimed in his masterful *Paris Noir* (1996) that the many African Americans who immigrated during the interwar period found a peaceful and colorblind society when arriving in the French capital, we must be wary of such strong allegations. Undeniably, the likes of dancers and entertainers such as Josephine Baker and Ada Bricktop, along with the many jazz musicians who dwelled in France for many years, enraptured Parisian society: The *Tumulte Noir* (*Black Tumult*), as Jody Blake coined it (1992), was a welcomed break for a shaken French society who lost an entire generation during World War I.

Nonetheless, the black body remained a source of anxiety, especially when juxtaposed to white masculinity. As studied by Sylvain Ville, the first wave of black boxers who took over Paris in the 1910s was met with a mixture of great respect and untenable fear. Men such as the mighty Jack Johnson, nicknamed the "Galveston Giant," turned Parisians on their heads for multiple reasons. First, their success in the ring earned them a new social status and quite a bit of money. But more importantly, and all too suddenly, a black man could, by the mere use of his fists, transform an entire history of racial domination used to justify the imperialist drive of a country like France. One can easily forget, in the liberating context of the *Années Folles*, that this time period was also the apex of the French Colonial Empire. In addition to the temporary Universal Exhibitions of 1900 and 1937, the *Jardin d'Acclimatation* served as a permanent structure in northeast Paris, which put on display families of diverse races from around the world for over seventy years, subsequently "turning the myth of the savage into a reality" (Bancel 2004, 5) to emphasize the so-called superiority of Western civilization. As Tyler Stovall suggested, perhaps African Americans were never considered to be as primitive as other people of color hailing from the French colonies; yet, the racial and cultural biases remained remarkably strong against the black men donning gloves. As Marjet Derks astutely claimed, "boxing contributed to the knowledge that white Europeans formed about blacks in pre-war modernity, next to con-structions that were based on the jazz and music scene" (2016, 198); notably, this construction only created greater prejudices toward men of color. Theresa Runstedtler phrased it to perfection in her essay on Jack Johnson: if "French sportsmen enjoyed gazing at African American pugilists on stage and in the ring, they ultimately viewed black men not only as different from white men, but also as fundamentally removed from Western civilization" (2012, 441). This notion was certainly visible in art and literature, part of which was the unique genre of the *bande dessinée*.

During the interwar time period, this particular literary medium had "already been collected in high-quality albums"[5] according to Christopher Murray, and with themes and styles relevant to its era, the graphic novel played a central part in shaping the literary mind of young adults in twentieth-century France. One certainly recalls the beloved work of Hergé, whose famous reporter Tintin and his faithful dog Milou came to life in the late 1920s. While Belgian, Hergé's drawings immediately found a home in *l'Hexagone* since Tintin spoke French, incidentally still considered the world's most important language during the time period. A glimpse at one of the artist's early works suffices to re-contextualize the connection between popular culture and racial beliefs during the interwar period. Published in 1931, *Tintin au Congo* presented its readers with a clear representation of the colonial and civilizing mission entrusted to the white man. In Hergé's work, black characters were unsophisticated, spoke an imperfect French, and were depicted as childlike—in other words, as entirely primitive. The album contained enough racism that the original version has since been modified. Compelled to apologize in the wake of decolonization, Hergé claimed his work simply mirrored the racial zeitgeist of imperialist times:

> "Les nègres sont de grands enfants . . . Heureusement pour eux nous sommes là, etc." Je les ai dessinés, ces Africains, d'après ces critères-là, dans le plus pur esprit paternaliste qui était celui de l'époque, en Belgique.

> ("Black people are big children . . . Fortunately for them, we are here [to help them], etc." I drew them, these Africans, according to those criteria, in the purest paternalistic spirit that was characteristic of that era, in Belgium.) (Sadoul cited in Girard 2012, 81)

It is in this context that Panama Al-Brown set sail from New York to Paris in October 1926, after spending four years in the United States. As opposed to his first journey between Panama and Harlem, Brown had a suitcase and a passport this time around and was expected to step in the ring as soon as possible. As World War I came to an end, a number of American boxing organizers migrated to Paris, including the turbulent yet clear-sighted Jeff Dickson. While the United States raved about heavyweight fighters, France certainly enjoyed the tenacity of smaller boxers. In his *Encyclopédie de la Boxe* (*Encyclopedia of Boxing*), Claude Droussent quotes Dickson: "Ici, il n'y a pas de sport, pas de spectacle. On peut tout faire" ("Here, there is no sport, no spectacle. One can do anything") (Droussent 1990, 85). The American organizer understood that fighters like Al-Brown were France's new El Dorado. And surely, it took the Latino fighter less than three months and as many victories to become a known figure of the Parisian world, in and out of the ring, for over a decade.

Nevertheless, and despite his status of great champion in the Paris of the *Années Folles,* no remarkable novels, plays, or cultural productions focusing on Al-Brown were penned during the time period. A close analysis of the boxer's multidimensional self helps illuminate some of the reasons that led to these mishaps and their subsequent forgetting, especially visible in the French cultural and literary discourses. This threefold analysis, examining Al-Brown as boxer, entertainer, and lover, is fundamental in our study, as it emphasizes the subsequent reworking of history and memory achieved by Alex Inker in his graphic novel as both a cultural and a political gesture.

Panama Al-Brown: Boxer, Entertainer, Lover

Certainly, Panama Al-Brown was an authentic champion and proved it in the ring over two decades. His size and his reach were so unconventional for a bantamweight that he surprised the vast majority of his opponents who often underestimated the power contained is his slender body. As a result, "ce poids coq à la morphologie étrange, tout en jambe et en bras, le corps épais comme un fil de fer" ("this bantamweight fighter with a strange morphology, all legs and arms, with a body as thin as a wire") (Droussent 1990, 85), managed to record some of the most outrageous wins the sport ever witnessed at the time. On January 29, 1929, the up-and-coming Gustave Huméry, depicted as a young "tueur" ("killer") (89), squared off against Brown, who lethargically stepped in the ring, taking a drag from his coach's cigarette. Yet, at the sound of the bell, the Panamanian took two steps forward and knocked Huméry unconscious at an impossible speed with his favorite right hook. The fight lasted a mere eighteen seconds, count included, and left the French public baffled, screaming for a refund. A few months later in 1930, the swift and brash Eugène Huat, nicknamed "le chat tigre" ("the tiger cat"), decided to insult Al-Brown in the press, calling him a nobody, a monkey who fell from a coconut tree. This example demonstrates that despite his boxing abilities, Al-Brown first and foremost mirrored the fear and loathing of white French fighters, and this, throughout his entire life. Moreover, while the French press acknowledged his victories, it rarely showed regard for Al-Brown as a man worthy of respect. In his *Champions dans la Coulisse* (*Champions Behind the Scenes*) published in 1944, the prominent journalist Gaston Benac described Al-Brown as "un nègre étrange" ("a strange black man") (127), incapable of fighting scientifically, with little to no endurance, and virtually no regard for the sport. More importantly, the racial overtone of Benac's words and his stereotyping of Brown were hard to miss: "les cheveux ébouriffés, dépeignés depuis l'heure du corps à corps, accrocheur en diable, M. Alfonso n'était alors pas beau à voir" ("with tousled hair, uncombed since the start of the hand-to-hand fight, tenacious like a devil, M. Alfonso was not a pretty sight") (127). Nevertheless, in the span of twelve years, Al-Brown stepped in the ring forty times in France. He consistently drew large crowds, as many as 20,000 spectators one night in April 1927 at the Vélodrome d'Hiver. He left *l'Hexagone* claiming thirty-three wins over three draws and a mere four defeats. His record may not be stellar, but his accomplishments in the ring undeniably possessed a bit of magic. Not simply because he conquered France, almost proceeding to a reversed form of colonization by showing how tenacious and resilient black boxers could be, but also because Al-Brown was more than a fighter: He was a man full of life, easily influenced and, most of the time, a slave to his ominous passions.

Indeed, the electric fighter in the ring was purely the reflection of the man outside of it. Al-Brown was one of Paris's most prized entertainers during the interwar period. And there was nobody Al-Brown enjoyed entertaining more than himself. He knew Montmartre like the back of his hand, and frequented Paris's finest nightclubs as well as its sleaziest bars. Brown was certainly no fan of the prohibition reigning supreme in the United States. One day, he famously claimed that "une journée sans champagne n'est pas une journée" ("a day without champagne is not a day") (Droussent 1990, 87), and while most boxers celebrated with champagne once victorious, Al-Brown grew accustomed to drinking it before stepping in the ring. Over time, owning multiple luxurious cars and betting on horses became part of his lifestyle, too. And when the opium came, the life of the boxer began to spiral out of control. Al-Brown remained an efficient boxer, but his multiple managers, including the scandalous Robert "Bobby" Diamant, knew how to exploit his weaknesses. To fulfill his passions, Al-Brown needed money and had to keep fighting; fighting despite a broken right hand that never fully healed; fighting despite the unquantifiable amount of pain medication present in his system at all times. Rather than a boxing manager, Arroyo described Bobby Diamant as a chemist, "tant il adorait les drogues, les potions et les remontants" ("so much he loved drugs, potions, and stimulants") (Boisse 1982, 9). The manager's methods, Arroyo continued, were akin to modern slavery. Al-Brown did have a share of responsibility in his exploitation, for he signed the contract tying him to Diamant that gave his manager 75 percent of any cash prize earned during his fights. More than anything, Al-Brown was a slave to his own passions, in a world with little to no guidance for men of color, in a sport run by white businessmen who knew how to make money off colored bodies. Against all odds, it was one of Al-Brown's most contested passions that enabled his return to boxing and transformed him into a legend of the ring.

In 1935, after a terrible disillusionment and the loss of his world title in Spain, the Panamanian dropped out of the ring. A keen entertainer and a great dancer, Al-Brown had decided that he would instead play music in cabarets all night, then sleep and smoke opium all day. A year later in 1936, Jean Cocteau stepped into a Parisian club, the Caprice Viennois, and saw him perform. The two men fell in love. Indeed, if Al-Brown's skin color and extravagant lifestyle had much to do with the constant adversity he faced throughout his life, his homosexuality did not make things less complicated. Undeniably, the Paris of the *Années Folles* was a vibrant city, where the queer community felt at home and thrived (Tamagne 2014). Evidently, the transgressive nature of Al-Brown's sexuality had much to do with his professional occupation. It was unthinkable that a black boxer knocking out France's white hopes and virility all at once could be a charming man's man. Cocteau, who called the boxer his "poème à l'encre noire, un éloge de la force spirituelle qui l'emporta sur la force tout court" ("poem in black ink, a tribute to the spiritual strength that prevailed over regular strength") (Peeters 2002, 12), took it upon himself to become Al-Brown's manager. In an effort to clean up their lives and keep off the champagne and the drugs, both men moved to the countryside thanks to a pension provided by none other than Coco Chanel. After months of training, and to the surprise of many, the boxing magic reappeared. At the advanced age of thirty-six, Al-Brown reclaimed the bantamweight World Title in Paris, by defeating Baltasar Sangchili at the Palais des Sports in 1938. Cocteau and Al-Brown remained friends, but their story ended abruptly. Jean Marais, Cocteau's newest lover at the time, steadily pushed Al-Brown away. The ex-lovers nonetheless traded letters in the newspapers *Ce Soir* and *L'Auto*, where the writer begged the fighter to retire at the helm of his success:

> Tu m'avais promis de reconquérir ton titre et je t'avais promis de t'aider jusqu'au bout dans cette étonnante entreprise. La chose est faite. . . . Profite de ton triomphe. N'imite pas les vedettes qui se prolongent et qui s'accrochent . . . jamais personne n'accepte de sortir à la bonne minute. Sois un sage, n'imite personne, sors de scène. C'est mon dernier conseil.

> (You had promised me that you would regain your title and I had promised you that I would help you until the end of this amazing enterprise. Now it is done. . . . Make the most of your triumph. Do not imitate the stars that linger and hang on . . . no one ever agrees to leave at the right time. Be a wise man, do not imitate anybody, walk off the stage. It's my last advice.) (1938b, 2)

In 1939, after a final fight in Paris, Al-Brown set sail for New York, never to return to France. The Panamanian champion quickly vanished from the French cultural landscape: His complex and controversial identity as a black man who was at once a boxing champion, an entertainer consumed by his passions, and an open homosexual made his memory all the more frightening to a rebuilding France post-World War II, at a time when the country strived to salvage its national pride and keep its colonial empire alive. In other words, the black boxer was a problematic actor of the French cultural landscape of the interwar period, and for this reason, his memory was soon erased. Recollections of Al-Brown only re-emerged in France recently, thanks to Inker's *Panama Al-Brown ou l'Énigme de la Force*, published in 2017. How and to what extent does this graphic novel contribute to the revamped memory of the black champion will be my main examination, and its answer my primary focus, for the remainder of this study.

L'Énigme de la Force (2017): From the Canvas of the Ring to the Canvas of the Graphic Novel

Interviewed by the newspaper *L'Auto* on the day of Al-Brown's return bout for the World Title against Sangchili, Jean Cocteau, in his capacity as manager and writer, offered the following words to the reader:

> Je me suis attaché au sort d'Al-Brown, d'abord parce que Brown me représente le sommet de la boxe, une sorte de poète, de mime, de danseur et de magicien qui transporte entre les cordes la réussite parfaite et mystérieuse d'une des énigmes humaines : l'énigme de la force.

> (I became attached to the fate of Al-Brown, first because Brown represents for me the pinnacle of boxing, a kind of poet, of mime, of dancer and magician who carries within the ropes the perfect and mysterious achievement of one of the human enigmas: the enigma of force.) (1938a, 1)

The concept of enigma brought up by Cocteau likely guided Alex Inker throughout the conception of his *bande dessinée*. The illustrator's decision to shape his graphic novel as an ongoing journalistic investigation or *reportage* taking place in 1955, the year Cocteau received his appointment at the *Académie Française*, is not simply telling, but also strategic. In his introductory discourse to *l'Académie*, Cocteau, an influential French writer, painter, and filmmaker acclaimed during his lifetime, briefly mentioned

Figure 1: Jean Cocteau's speech in *Panama Al-Brown ou l'Énigme de la Force*.
©Éditions Sarbacane.

the name of his black lover who passed away four years earlier in complete
anonymity (Fig. 1). Placed between literal parentheses in the text, the name
of Al-Brown was most likely overlooked by the distinguished in attendance.
However, Cocteau's remark does not go unnoticed by Jacques, Inker's fictional, ingenious, and good-natured reporter who then elects to connect the
dots of Al-Brown's life so as to revamp the memory of the boxer. The illustrator
makes use of several ingenious and distinctive techniques to convey the re-
habilitated portrait of Al-Brown's memory through the medium of the *bande
dessinée*. His first discernible gesture is to engage his readership in his
graphic novel by entrusting the mission of uncovering Al-Brown's secrets
and forgotten existence to a journalist such as Jacques. Indeed, and while
his character initially strikes the reader as a reporter lacking seriousness,
with his indolence and apparent casual interest toward his profession, we gradually discover a man whose beliefs evolve and who subsequently strives to
erase any prejudice caused to the memory of the boxer (Fig. 2). The reporter
becomes so obsessed by the ghost of Al-Brown's presence that he refuses to
let any impediment stop him from unveiling the truth about the fighter.
By discovering the value of pushing against the discourse, or status quo, in
order to re-inscribe his subject in the cultural memory of the interwar period,
Jacques's valiant attitude and effort serve as a teaching moment for readers and
scholars alike. As a result, a new vision of the medium arises, which focuses
on its intermedial nature in regard to the notion of *reportage*.

As explained by Ann Miller in her comprehensive study *Reading Bande
Dessinée: Critical Approaches to French-language Comic Strip*, "reportage, in a
fictional version, is an indelible part of the history of *bande dessinée*, having
provided the pretext for Tintin to open up the world . . . As a non-fictional
genre, it became prominent in the 1990s," and "has since been pursued by
French-language artists" (2007, 57). In opposition to the colonialist and

self- righteous style of Hergé, contemporary instances of *reportage* are now used in French graphic novels to prompt "a revisionist treatment of history which has sought to uncover some areas that had been repressed" (57). Alex Inker makes an apt demonstration of Miller's theories in his graphic novel. To solve Al-Brown's enigma, the reporter Jacques engages in a lengthy investigation: His journey to Panama, Harlem, and of course all over Paris, takes the form of a time-consuming and demanding battle, a metaphor echoing the numerous bouts, real and symbolic, Al-Brown engaged in throughout his lifetime. Situated in the context of the graphic novel, the conceptualization of *reportage* as an ongoing battle, a fight for truth and memory, is facilitated thanks to the particular element of rhythm.

According to Thierry Groensteen in *Comics and Narration*, "the 'text' of comic art obeys a rhythm that is imposed upon it by the succession of frames. This is a basic beat that, as in music, can be developed, nuanced, layered over by more elaborate rhythmic effects emanating from other 'instruments'" (2013, 241); as such, the process of reading and interpreting any graphic novel can be understood as a "rhythmic operation of crossing from one frame to the next" (241). Following Groensteen's definition, I contend that the unique rhythm of Inker's *bande dessinée* stems from its connection to the notion of

Figure 2: Reportage in *Panama Al-Brown ou l'Énigme de la Force* (25).
©Éditions Sarbacane.

battle I previously described. By alternating the size of his frames and avoiding any structural repetition in his pages, Inker's rhythmic process echoes what Groensteen coined as "periodic alternation" (263), which both destabilizes and signals the vastly different forms of experiences undergone by the characters in the graphic novel and, consequently, by the reader. Indeed, the latter begins to apprehend the difficulty one encounters through journalistic research by following Jacques's arduous battles to collect the fragments of Al-Brown's life. The journalist's efforts to rehabilitate the memory of the boxer of color are mediated by the unpredictable rhythm of a graphic novel whose frames accelerate or slow down his progress. In contrast with the high intensity experienced by Jacques during Jean Cocteau's discourse, made visible by the multiplication of small frames that underline the rapidity of the events unfolding before his eyes, the successive visits of the journalist to Panama or New York are marked by larger, more detailed and slower frames, emphasizing the sizable task of his investigation. By creating these nuances in rhythm, Inker's *bande dessinée* not only renders visible and appealing the content of the issues that Jacques strives to elucidate; it is also the form of the graphic novel, and the use of multiframes that creates a "power of attraction that entices the reader forward" (247), thus helping the reader experience the laborious nature of Jacques's mission.

Figure 3: Remembrances of Al-Brown (89). ©Éditions Sarbacane.

Building on the complexity of Inker's frames, I suggest that the illustrator's work is also attentive to the ways in which memories of Al-Brown are presented to the reader. As opposed to the strictly squared frames found in traditional graphic novels, Inker inserts wavy frames to distinguish between the past and the present in his work (Fig. 3), thus highlighting the sometimes-fuzzy nature of our recollections: In the *bande dessinée*, past images and remembrances of Al-Brown are intertwined with their present state, showcasing the role of the literary medium as one able to reconcile and restructure our memories. Put in contact, the lines of each frame are juxtaposed to create what Mark McKinney describes as an "a-frontier" (2013, 33), a delicate boundary that acknowledges the separation of time and space yet brings these categories much closer than is possible in a traditional novel. Beyond the rhythm imagined by the illustrator, the graphic novel encourages its readers to let their eyes wander beyond the simple textual elements, in order to seize the particularities of each frame, thus allowing each of us to construct connections and reconstruct meanings based on our own sensibility.

Consequently, delving into a *bande dessinée* is at times akin to a voyage where reading and viewing collide into each other. The notion of voyage, in relation to both Al-Brown's story and the medium of the graphic novel, carries a central connotation in this study. In his book *Culture and Imperialism* (1993), Edward Said discusses the expression of the *voyage in*—which characterizes the return journey made by migrants toward formerly colonized countries and spaces, a homecoming usually tinted with the hope to repair the past, or at least, better understand where one comes from. This notion, since reprised by Mark McKinney (2013), finds natural echoes in my study and provides a renewed understanding of *Panama Al-Brown ou l'Énigme de la Force*. In the graphic novel, Panama Al-Brown's voyage to Paris and his meandering must be interpreted as a unique type of *voyage in*, where the boxer returns to the mind of the reader—this space previously colonized by assumptions or prejudices—to transform it, and change the reader's perception of how a black man ought to behave and what a black boxer ought to look like. This *voyage in* created by the graphic novel also complicates the relation previously established between color and immigration in France, for the champion was no ordinary migrant; Panamanian by birth, Harlem resident by necessity, Parisian by heart, the character of Al-Brown was by essence unbounded, thus proving that "genealogies produced in comics . . . contest or otherwise rework the racist closing off of French national belonging and, perhaps more rarely, the masculinist gendering of nationalism and national 'patrimony' including the colonial heritage of French comics" (McKinney 2013, 16–17).

Certainly, and while noting that Groensteen in *The System of Comics* calls the graphic novel an "art of space and an art of time" and emphasizes that "these dimensions are indissociable" (2007, 36), I posit that the graphic novel also functions as an art of contest, made especially visible in *Panama Al-Brown ou l'Énigme de la Force*. Indeed, if both boxing and *reportage* are reflections of the literary medium as unique arts of space and time, all three are also integrated to the essential concept of âgon[6] theorized by Roger Caillois in his canonical *Les jeux et les hommes* (*Man, Play and Games*) (1961). In Inker's work, the notion of âgon is placed at the intersection of the graphic novel, the journalistic investigation, and the sport of boxing, and underlines the deliberately competitive nature found at the heart of these enterprises. Caillois defines the agonistic drive as "the desire to win," made possible by "discipline and perseverance," leaving the participant "to his own devices, to evoke the best possible game of which he is capable, and it obliges him to play the game within the fixed limits, and according to the rules applied equally to all" (15). In order to win the contest of reaching a renewed truth regarding the boxer of color, the illustrator must proceed methodically as he depicts Al-Brown and his companions, mixing artistry and political engagement.

Without a doubt, the illustrative qualities of the *bande dessinée* carry as much significance as the textual content in communicating the revamped story of the black champion for Alex Inker, and as such, the visual discourse representing the boxer and other actors in *Panama Al-Brown* deserves to be highlighted. To begin, I contend that the character of Jacques could not possess a more stereotypical demeanor than the one imagined by the illustrator. His round body and affable face, his naïve gaze, along with distinctive markers such as his old hat and a thin mustache, are truly reminiscent of the caustic appearance of *monsieur tout-le-monde* (*Mister Everyman*) in the 1950s. Such outward form not only makes Jacques all the more relatable to a general audience, but it also underlines the fact that the transformation of the unremarkable journalist into an engaged advocate for the unjustly forgotten in the course of the story is attainable by anyone. The illustrator furthermore plays with the exaggerations formerly used to describe Al-Brown back in the 1930s in order to create a compelling image of the black champion. The many conversations initiated by Jacques with strangers, offering the reader fragments of the boxer's past life, trigger an array of memories and tales immersing the reader into a unique and multidimensional portrait of the Panamanian. Under the illustrator's pencil, Al-Brown's slender physique first appears to be the object of parody. Inker's lines often make the boxer's heavy gloves look disproportionate in comparison to his slight frame, or his suits too wide for his lean body. However, if the facial features emphasize the boxer's flat nose, large smile, and pronounced forehead, we understand these traits as a particular gesture made by the illustrator to mock the physical description once purported by writers such as Gaston Benac; indeed, this time around, Al-Brown never fails to walk around with a gracious air in his impeccable and bespoke clothing, constantly catching eyes from the crowd in and out of the ring, while typically being placed in the center of the frames. In this sense, and going back to the non-ironic and scornful depiction of black figures like king M'Hatuvu[7] in *Tintin au Congo*, similar visual techniques of exaggeration and flamboyance are used this time around by Alex Inker in his contemporary graphic novel as a way to enforce an ameliorative vision of the black man. By doing so, the *bande dessinée* proceeds to a conscious reversal: By humorously yet authoritatively playing with the reader's expectations, in what could be described as a pastiche, cultural codes are subverted in the graphic novel and the figure of Al-Brown duly empowered. This idea is taken further by the illustrator thanks to his use of a minimal black and white color palette. Surely, if the use of these two colors mirrors once again the style of the original comics of the 1930s, it also underlines the constant dichotomy of the racialized world in which Al-Brown lived, which, put in today's postcolonial context, underlines the constant divide created by the color line. These visual elements are essential but only frame the main thread of Alex Inker's work.

Even more ingenious is the storyline, which reuses through the categories of the *bande dessinée* and journalism two of the main tools traditionally used during the interwar period to undermine people of color, only this time, to revalorize the memory of Al-Brown, and complete this notion of pastiche, aptly defined by Ann Miller: "Jameson has argued that in the postmodern period, parody, which has a political and moral intent, has given way to pastiche, just as a sense of history has given way to the nostalgic recreation of the past through retro styling and the imitation of surface appearances" (Miller 2007, 142). By playing with rhythmic, structural, and "retro" codes in his work, Alex Inker presents both a political and cultural critique of the original use of the graphic novel, perfectly contesting what Mark McKinney defines as "the pervasive but insufficiently acknowledged presence of colonialism within a canon of French comics" (2013, 30). In this sense, *Panama Al-Brown ou l'Énigme de la Force* can be construed as an act of resistance echoing those performed by Al-Brown, as a homosexual and man of color, both in and out of the ring during the 1930s. Concurrently, "l'Énigme de la Force" raised by Jean Cocteau found an apparent solution uncovered by the medium of the graphic novel. An intermedial assemblage of texts and images, the literary

Figure 4: A conversation between the journalist and the boxer's ghost (151).
©Éditions Sarbacane.

medium of the *bande dessinée* teaches us that one cannot look at memories from a fixed perspective, and that rather, a multiplicity of vantage points creates a more compelling understanding and appreciation of the multifaceted lives of marginalized characters such as Al-Brown. In connection to the many possibilities created by the graphic novel to rehabilitate or transform memories, one last uncanny yet formidable intervention imagined by Alex Inker in his work deserves to be examined.

At the end of his journey, Jacques, unable to complete his investigation of Al-Brown, is fired by his newspaper company. On a starry night in Paris, a bottle of champagne in his hand, the journalist takes a seat on a bench overlooking the river when the ghost of Al-Brown appears. The conversation between the two men is brief. Jacques apologizes to the boxer for failing to complete his mission and remind the world of the fantastic fighter, entertainer, and lover Al-Brown used to be. In return, the Panamanian laughs heartily, and claims that he forgot a number of people himself, because such is life. While everyone eventually ends up forgotten, Al-Brown continues, one should simply strive to live liberated from people's expectations in order to experience no regrets (Fig. 4).

By imagining this conclusion to his graphic novel, the author-illustrator reaches far beyond the philosophical advice pronounced by the black boxer. In *Panama Al-Brown ou l'Énigme de la Force,* the boxer has the last word, and thus concludes his own story, an ending that, as explained by Ben Carrington in his book *Race, Sport and Politics: The Sporting Black Diaspora,* hardly ever occurs throughout history:

> The meaning of the black athlete has been contested from within and without . . . During certain historical periods the black athlete has been despised and lionized, blamed for the woes of the black community and held up as its savior, seen as signaling a post-racial future and confirming the indisputable facts of racial alterity in the present. (2010, 13)

Remarkably, Carrington continues "only rarely has the black athlete spoken, or been allowed to speak. It is normally spoken for" (2010, 13). In *Panama Al-Brown,* this discourse of silence is rejected and gives way to a novel and revised vision of history, in the form of a graphic novel that brings the voice of the black man back to the center stage, with an emphatic punch.

Conclusion: Reclaiming History, Informing Teaching Practices

Giving his voice back to the black boxer functions as a powerful way to rehabilitate the memory of Al-Brown and offers a necessary corrective to the biographical works of both Eduardo Arroyo and Jose Corpas. In his work, Alex Inker demonstrates that the medium of the graphic novel has the potential to push back against oversimplification and deserves to be treated as a significant contribution to various academic fields. By demanding a transdisciplinary approach from scholars (Bandy 2016), the study of *Panama Al-Brown ou l'Énigme de la Force* is placed at the intersection of both history and literature. As Clark and Cromer remind us in their essay "Getting Graphic with the Past: Graphic Novels and the Teaching of History,"

> In a graphic novel, the print is incomplete without the visual text, and the visual text is incomplete without the print. One form does not simply accompany and expand the meaning conveyed in the other; rather, the two are co-dependent, with each equally necessary to meaning-making. (2007, 579)

Much like the story of Panama Al-Brown, the strength of the graphic novel is found in its multidimensional character. By stressing the importance of inclusion—both in its form and its content—the graphic novel caters to a larger, often younger and more diverse audience, thus multiplying the effect generated by both history and literature as it renders stories once overlooked finally accessible to all. If "graphic novels are rich and multi-layered" and "are one means to help students appreciate the complexity of history" (Clark and Cromer 2007, 583), they also deserve to be perceived as genuine creations enabling both the reworking and the critique of history not only thanks to their content, but also to their form, making them an art of resistance. Subsequently, I conclude this study by stressing the critical importance of a work such as *Panama Al-Brown ou l'Énigme de la Force*, which invites us to rethink our approach not just to research but also to teaching, for the medium of the graphic novel epitomizes the value of looking at the world from different perspectives, something we should always encourage ourselves and our students to pursue.

Endnotes

1. Alex W. Inker, MA (Film Studies), graduated from *l'École Supérieure des Arts de Saint Luc* in 2006 (Tournai, Belgium). His publications, which include *Apache* (2016), *Panama Al-Brown ou l'Énigme de la Force* (2017), and *Servir le Peuple* (2018), all demonstrate a particular attention to the reworking of French historical and cultural discourses. Credited for the graphic novel, Jacques Goldstein's contribution consists of a separate biographical conclusion placed at the end of the work.

2. Imagined by Ham Fischer, *Joe Palooka* recounts the story of a naive yet good-natured boxer, whom we may perceive as emblematic of American middle-class values: hard work, politeness, social obedience. Published in installments between 1930 and 1984 in several newspapers, the comic was publically acclaimed and even served as inspiration for a dozen films.

3. Recent examples include: *Le Chemin de l'Amérique* by Baru, Ledran and Thévenet (1990), *L'Enragé* by Baru (2006), *Le Boxeur* by Kleist (2013), *Young: Tunis, 1911—Auschwitz 1945* by Vaccaro and Ducoudray (2013), and *Succombe qui doit* by Rica and Ozanam (2014).

4. Active from the 1910s to the 1930s, Georges Carpentier was widely considered to be the first French athlete to reach the status of global superstar. Thanks to his boxing prowess, which included a light heavyweight world title in 1920, Carpentier rose to preeminence to embody a certain vision of Frenchness in the public eye; consequently, his image was used in commercials, films, and other commercial ventures. For more on the subject, refer to Sylvain Ville, 2016, "Georges Carpentier, Naissance d'une Célébrité Sportive," *Genèses* 103: 49–71.

5. Christopher Murray, "Graphic Novel," Encyclopedia Britannica online. www.britannica.com/art/graphic-novel.

6. Sociologist Roger Caillois defined âgon as one of the central components driving mankind toward play, alongside *alea* (luck), *mimicry* (role playing), and *illinx* (vertigo).

7. "M'Hatuvu" or "m'as-tu-vu," a play on words imagined by Hergé, functions as a derogatory expression meaning "have you seen me?" otherwise used to describe an attention-seeker.

Works Cited

ARROYO, Eduardo. 1981. *Panama Al-Brown: 1902–1951*. Paris: JC Lattès.

BANCEL, Nicolas. 2004. *Zoos Humains: Au Temps des Exhibitions Humaines*. Paris: La Découverte.

BANDY, Susan. 2016. "The Intersections of Sport History and Sport Literature: Toward a Transdisciplinary Perspective." *The International Journal of the History of Sport* 33 (14): 1577–591.

BENAC, Gaston. 1944. *Champions dans la Coulisse*. Toulouse: Editions de l'Actualité sportive.

BOISSE, Delphine. 1982. *Panama Al-Brown*. Paris: Adaptations.

BLAKE, Jody. 1992. *Le Tumulte Noir: Modernist Art and Popular Entertainment in Jazz-Age Paris, 1900–1930*. University Park: Penn State University Press.

CAILLOIS, Roger. 1961. *Man, Play and Games*. Urbana: University of Illinois Press.

CARRINGTON, Ben. 2010. *Sport, Politics, Race: The Sporting Black Diaspora*. New York: SAGE.

CLARK, Penney and Michael CROMER. 2007. "Getting Graphic with the Past: Graphic Novels and the Teaching of History." *Theory and Research in Social Education* 35 (4): 574–91.

COCTEAU, Jean. 1938a. "L'Ombre d'Al-Brown." *L'Auto*, March 4, 1938, 1.

———. 1938b. "Lettre Ouverte à Al-Brown." *Ce Soir*, April 5, 1938, 2.

CORPAS, Jose. 2016. *Black Ink: A Story of Boxing, Betrayal, Homophobia, and the First Latino Champion*. Iowa City, IA: Win by KO.

DERKS, Marjet. 2016. "The 'Negro Boxer' as Contested Cultural Icon: 'Negrophilia' and Sport in Pre-War Europe." In *Building Bridges: Scholars, History and Historical Demography*, edited by P. Puschmann and T. Riswick, 196–215. Nijmegen, Netherlands: Valkhof Pers.

DROUSSENT, Claude. 1990. *Encyclopédie de la Boxe*. Paris: Ramsay.

GIRARD, Eudes. 2012. "Une Relecture de Tintin au Congo." *Études* 417 (7): 75–86.

GROENSTEEN, Thierry. 2007. *The System of Comics*. Jackson: University Press of Mississippi.

————. 2013. *Comics and Narration*. Jackson: University Press of Mississippi.

HERGÉ. 1931. *Tintin au Congo*. Brussels: Éditions de Petit Vingtième.

IGGERS, Georg. 1997. *Historiography in the Twentieth Century: From Scientific Objectivity to the Postmodern Challenge*. Hanover, NH: Wesleyan University Press.

INKER, Alex W. 2017. *Panama Al-Brown ou l'Énigme de la Force*. Paris: Éditions Sarbacane.

JENSEN, Klaus Bruhn. 2016. "Intermediality." In *The International Encyclopedia of Communication Theory and Philosophy*, edited by Klaus Bruhn Jensen and Robert T. Craig, 1–12. Chichester: Wiley Blackwell.

McKINNEY, Mark, ed. 2008. *History and Politics in French-Language Comics and Graphic Novels*. Jackson: University Press of Mississippi.

————. 2013. *Redrawing French Empire in Comics*. Columbus: The Ohio State University Press.

MILLER, Ann. 2007. *Reading Bande Dessinée: Critical Approaches to French-language Comic Strip*. Bristol: Intellect.

PEETERS, Georges. 2002. *Monstres Sacrés du Ring*. Paris: La Table Ronde.

PURVES, Alan. 1998. "Flies in the Web of Hypertext." In *Handbook of Literacy and Technology: Transformations in a Post-Typographic World*, edited by David Reinking et al., 235–51. Mawah, NJ: Lawrence Erlbaum.

RUNSTEDTLER, Theresa. 2012. *Jack Johnson, Rebel Sojourner: Boxing in the Shadow of the Global Color Line*. Berkeley: University of California Press.

SAID, Edward. 1993. *Culture and Imperialism*. New York: Penguin Random House.

STOVALL, Tyler. 1996. *Paris Noir: African Americans in the City of Light*. Boston, MA: Houghton Mifflin Harcourt.

TAMAGNE, Florence. 2014. "Paris, Resting on its Laurels?" In *Queer Cities, Queer Cultures: Europe since 1945*, edited by Matt Cook. London: Bloomsbury.

VILLE, Sylvain. 2016. "Portrait des Boxeurs de Métier en France, 1904–1913." *Le Mouvement Social* 254: 13–29.

CHAPTER EIGHT:
Mediated Martyrdom in Marjane Satrapi's *Persepolis*

Renée Altergott

In the opening episode of Marjane Satrapi's fourth volume of *Persepolis,* Marji has just returned home to Tehran. It is June 1989. Although the Iran-Iraq War has ended, the city has been transformed in her absence into a veritable mediascape of martyrdom propaganda and memorialization. Struggling to find her bearings now that so many streets have been renamed after martyrs, she sighs: "J'avais l'impression de marcher dans un cimetière" ("I felt as though I were walking through a cemetery") (2007b, 4.1 "Le Retour" ["The Return"]). Speculating that her upcoming art school entrance exam would likely include a question on "martyrdom," she spends two months training by sketching a photograph of Michelangelo's marble sculpture, *La Pietà* (1499). The day of the exam, having guessed correctly, she alters her drawing to adhere to the Islamic codes of martyrdom iconography: "Ce jour-là, je l'ai reproduite en mettant un tchador noir sur la tête de Marie, un vêtement militaire pour Jésus, ensuite, j'ai rajouté deux tulipes, symboles des martyrs, de chaque côté pour qu'il n'y ait pas de confusion. J'étais très contente de mon dessin" ("On that day, I reproduced it by putting a black chador on Mary's head, an army uniform on Jesus, and then I added two tulips, symbols of the martyrs, on either side so there would be no confusion. I was very pleased with my drawing") (4.4 "Le Concours" ["The Contest"]). In other words, Marji believes that inscribing her own Islamic icon within a Western foundation constitutes an act of subversion. This achieves an effect similar to what Typhaine Leservot has termed the "hybridization" of Satrapi's choice of title, "Persepolis," which is "the western name for this pre-Islamic city central to Iranian identity" (2011, 128). For Thierry Groensteen, hybridity is the fundamental condition of the *bande dessinée,* whose icons are "at once a production of the imagination and a recycling of icons from every provenance" (2007, 42).

Figure 1: 4.1 "Le Retour" ©Marjane Satrapi & L'Association, 2007.
Reprinted with kind permission of the publisher.

However, readers of this *bande dessinée* should experience a moment of déjà vu, as Marji's exam drawing evokes the propaganda mural she just saw upon her return to Tehran three episodes prior. Within a single frame, Marji stares up, incredulous, as two buildings loom menacingly over her: a twenty-meter-tall mural extolling the virtues of martyrdom on the left, and a bombed-out building on the right, its gaping windows and snow-covered windowsills evocative of the rows upon rows of empty graves at the Behesht-e Zahra cemetery (Fig. 1). In fact, if we compare these two frames side by side, we see that Marji's drawing is essentially a *mirror image* of the propaganda mural, down to the shirt pocket detail: A woman in a black chador cradles a fallen, bearded soldier, surrounded by tulips (Fig. 2).

POUR RENTRER À LA FACULTÉ D'ART, EN PLUS DES TESTS, IL Y AVAIT UNE ÉPREUVE DE DESSIN. J'ÉTAIS CERTAINE QU'UN DES SUJETS SERAIT "LES MARTYRS", ET POUR CAUSE! JE M'ÉTAIS DONC ENTRAÎNÉE, EN RECOPIANT UNE VINGTAINE DE FOIS UNE PHOTO DE "LA PIETÀ" DE MICHEL-ANGE. CE JOUR-LÀ, JE L'AI REPRODUITE EN METTANT UN TCHADOR NOIR SUR LA TÊTE DE MARIE, UN VÊTEMENT MILITAIRE POUR JÉSUS, ENSUITE, J'AI RAJOUTÉ DEUX TULIPES, SYMBOLES DES MARTYRS* DE CHAQUE CÔTÉ POUR QU'IL N'Y AIT PAS DE CONFUSION.

J'ÉTAIS TRÈS CONTENTE DE MON DESSIN.

* ON RACONTE QUE LES TULIPES ROUGES POUSSENT DU SANG DES MARTYRS.

**Figure 2: 4.4 "Le Concours" ©Marjane Satrapi & L'Association, 2007.
Reprinted with kind permission of the publisher.**

Despite westernizing the "reading" direction of the mural by moving the gravitational pull of the martyr's head from right to left, Marji's drawing is so similar that it verges on plagiarism. The minor changes in color of the background and the uniform are not enough to refute this charge. The similarity between the two images has not gone unnoticed, but it has only summarily been addressed. For example, in Hillary Chute's elaboration of the *bande dessinée* as an "idiom of witness" and Satrapi's ethical gesture of "retracing" in the animated film, she relegates this key scene of graphic "retracing" to a footnote, and claims that Satrapi simply "calls attention to her facility in adopting the codes of this visual culture" (2010, 248 n47). To my mind, the reader's familiarity with this image calls into question Marji's claim to artistic subversion and therefore demands a more rigorous critique. Not only are there further repetitions of the Pietà pose within the same album, but protesters appropriated one of these additional frames as a piece of martyr iconography for Neda Agha-Soltan during the 2009 Iranian election protests. This chapter seeks to shed light on the significance and legacy of Marji's drawing by bringing key works of written and visual Iranian Islamic propaganda into dialogue with theories of media, witnessing, and the formal aesthetics of the *bande dessinée*.

Defining the Pietà Constellation

To fully account for the implications of Marji's drawing, we must first situate it within a broader constellation of interconnected images within the album. In addition to the mural and Marji's drawing, the Pietà pose already appeared in the ultimate panel of Tome 2, when Taji faints into Ebi's arms at the airport (2007b, 2.10 "La Dot" ["The Dowry"]) (Fig. 3). In Tome 1, there are two instances where God is shown cradling Marji: 1.7 "Les Héros"

**Figure 3: 2.10 "La Dot" ©Marjane Satrapi & L'Association, 2007.
Reprinted with kind permission of the publisher.**

LA JUSTICE, JE NE SAVAIS PAS CE QUE C'ÉTAIT.
MAINTENANT QUE LA RÉVOLUTION ÉTAIT BEL ET BIEN
FINIE, J'ABANDONNAIS LE MATÉRIALISME DIALECTIQUE
DE MES B D. LES BRAS DE MON AMI ÉTAIENT LE SEUL
ENDROIT OÙ JE ME SENTAIS EN SÉCURITÉ.

**Figure 4: 1.7 "Les Héros" ©Marjane Satrapi & L'Association, 2007.
Reprinted with kind permission of the publisher.**

("The Heroes") (Fig. 4), where she is smiling, eyes closed, with her head on the right-hand side of the frame, and 1.1 "Le Foulard" ("The Scarf") where Marji's face expresses concern, and her head is on the left-hand side (Fig. 5).

Satrapi's oriented network of Pietà citations thus culminates in both the scene of drawing and the revelation of the "prographic" origin of her (allegedly) subversive artistic practice, or the preexisting image that serves as its basis (Groensteen 2007, 41). If Patricia Storace did previously identify Taji and Ebi's posture as "unmistakably based on the Pietà" (2005, 42), the significance of the constellation as a composite unit and formal technique in *Persepolis* has yet to be fleshed out.

For example, Groensteen's concept of *tressage* ("braiding") (2007, 146) is a productive measure for the relations between discontinuous images and raises the additional questions of rhythm and sequence. On the one hand, if the third iteration does appear in the privileged site of the last panel of Tome

Figure 5: 1.1 "Le Foulard" ©Marjane Satrapi & L'Association, 2007.
Reprinted with kind permission of the publisher.

2, and thus, the very last panel of certain editions, Satrapi does not go as far as to "rhyme" episodes by placing the motif in the same location on the page. On the other hand, in emphasizing the sequentiality of images in an oriented network (2007b, 174), *tressage* enables us to argue that the accumulative order of interconnected images actually *says something*. As it turns out, bringing these three additional, previous occurrences to bear on Marji's exam drawing only further destabilizes her claim to subversion. Whereas Marji (the character) appears to reproduce the mural she has just seen in the diegesis (in 1989), one could argue that Satrapi (the author) has already infused representations at the narrative level with this Western iconographic motif in three previous sites. The sequence of this constellation therefore increases the ambiguity of the fourth instance, by introducing the possibility that the propaganda mural itself has *already been subverted by the author*.

Of course, the very notion that *any* of Satrapi's graphic citations of the Pietà pose, but especially the propaganda mural, are "subversive" hinges on this pose *not* being used in Islamic propaganda. In researching Islamic propaganda symbolism, conventions, and teachings, we may begin to recover the distinction between imaginary and prographic underlying the mural seen by Marji in "Le Retour," that has since been obscured at the hand of Satrapi's homogenizing artistic execution.[1] In the absence of a singular prographic origin of Satrapi's propaganda mural, I will show that its basic elements—the physical disposition of the figures and the slogan, "The martyr is the heart of history"—both appear separately in Iranian Islamic visual culture.[2] First, I focus on two artists, Kazem Chalipa and Hamid Qadiriyan, whose paintings depict the martyr/mourner figure in contrasting styles and were transformed into multi-story murals in Tehran. Second, I trace the origins of the slogan back to the influential teachings of key figures of the revolution and the war to uncover a deeper, symbolic connection between martyrdom and mediation.

Every Battle is Karbala

Kazem Chalipa was born in Tehran in 1957 to Hasan Isma'ilzadeh, a well-known Iranian coffeehouse painter (De Sanctis Mangelli 2014, 253). In the early 1980s, he produced a wide array of paintings that explored the Iran-Iraq War in both its brutal reality and powerful symbolism. One of his first paintings from 1980, entitled *17 Shahrivar* (a date that falls during the sixth month of the Iranian calendar), depicts the aftermath of the Black Friday Massacre of September 8, 1978 (84). Done in the style of Socialist Realism, this scene could have easily been painted from a photograph and shows a veiled woman cradling a male protester, bleeding from his neck and seemingly deceased.[3] The massacre of dozens of demonstrators in Zhaleh Square, Tehran, was a pivotal incident that contributed to the Iranian Revolution. Peter Chelkowski and Hamid Dabashi offer translations of the red and black revolutionary slogans in the background, such as the left shutter: "Praise to Khomeini, death to the Shah" (2000, 109).

This scene is sharply contrasted by a painting from the following year bearing the Arabic title *Ithaar*, which has been translated as either "Altruism, giving in abundance" (Chelkowski and Dabashi 2000, 162), "Sacrifice" (Khany et al. 2017, 58), or "Certitude of Belief" (Middle Eastern Posters, Box 3, Poster 67, U. of Chicago). As opposed to *17 Shahrivar*, this painting brings the two symbolic worlds of Karbala and the Iran-Iraq War together beneath the frame of a *mihrab* inscribed with the *Surat as-Saff*, the 61st chapter (*Sura*) of the Qur'an. The white background, featuring rows of the headless martyrs

Figure 6: Kazem Chalipa, *Ithaar*, 1981.
Poster reproduction.
Special Collections Research Center,
University of Chicago Library. Image
reproduced with kind permission of
the University of Chicago.

of Karbala in paradise, parallels the red foreground, where embryonic soldiers are developing within rows of tulips on the left and soldiers are marching to battle and being put to death on the right, to converge at a central vanishing point. In the center, the ghostly figure of a headless Imam Husayn mounted on a white horse, holding a sword and the Qur'an, stands directly behind an older woman dressed in a black chador, holding a fallen soldier. The fabric of his uniform drapes below his lifeless body to complete the cycle of martyrdom as it transforms into a giant, red tulip (Fig. 6).

It must be noted, however, that the figure of the sustained mourner is not restricted to women. *Shahid* (Martyr), an Iranian magazine published by the Martyr's Foundation (*Bunyad-i Shahid*), includes many artistic works of propaganda that show men and boys on the battlefield assuming the same pose.[4] One such painting by Hamid Qadiriyan entitled *Shahid* appeared on the back cover of Issue 253 (*Khordad* 1375, ca. May 1996), and depicts a veiled, glowing Imam Husayn, the paradigmatic Shiite "Prince of Martyrs," holding a deceased, anonymous martyr of the Iran-Iraq War.

Of interest to this study, all three paintings underwent intermedial transformations, ranging from the singular, multistory mural to mass reproduction via printing in posters, stamps, or magazines. Whereas Chalipa's *17 Shahrivar* eventually appeared on the cover of Issue 256 of *Shahid* magazine (*Shahrivar* 1375, ca. August 1996), Chelkowski and Dabashi note that *Ithaar* was reproduced on postage stamps and at least one mural in Tehran. Their book, *Staging a Revolution*, includes a photograph of one such mural that was located close to the former American Embassy, to the right of

Figure 7: Christia, Fotini (Photographer). July 2006. *The Duty of the Teacher Is to Guide, to Train and to Lead* (photograph), part of *Tehran Propaganda Mural Collection.* Cambridge, MA: H.C. Fung Library, Harvard University. Detail. Retrieved from http://id.lib.harvard.edu/images/olvgroup11882/urn-3:FHCL:1268159/catalog. Image reproduced with kind permission of Fotini Christia.

a mural of Khomeini's portrait with a deep blue background (2000, 162). Fotini Christia provides a more precise location of this mural: "Saadi Street (Darvazeh Dolat), Pamenar, Tehran" (2008, 5).[5] Although the accompanying photograph shows that the mural had already greatly faded by 2006, we can still make out the same horse, the headless saints, and the "mihrab" frame; unfortunately, the satellite dish atop a new construction obscures the bottom half, including the woman (Fig. 7).

Along the same vein, Christiane Gruber gives a detailed account of the intermedial transposition of Qadiriyan's painting into a mural along the Modarres Highway in northern Tehran, which entailed minor censorship of its violence (Fig. 8). It was sponsored by the Cultural Center of the "Prince of Martyrs" and executed on March 14, 2003, in honor of 'Ashura (2008, 28–29).

Figure 8: Mural of Imam Husayn and an anonymous war martyr on Modarres Highway at the Resalat Street exit, Tehran. Photograph by Christiane Gruber. Image reproduced with kind permission of Christiane Gruber.

On the one hand, the Pietà pose acts as an anchor, implying a direct link between the sacrifices expected of young men and the foundational martyrdom of Imam Husayn at the battle of Karbala. On the other hand, the two more symbolic paintings deviate from general mural culture in Iran, which combines idealized photographic portraiture with colors and symbols of the Islamic Republic.[6]

Zayneb's Message

It may be tempting to conclude that the Christian Pietà pose is present in Islamic visual culture and legible as such to the Western viewer. The scholarly critical apparatuses accompanying Chalipa's works imply as much;

Chelkowski and Dabashi write of *17 Shahrivar*: "A *pietà*-like figure of a woman holding the head and shoulders of a dying male demonstrator takes up the center and foreground of the painting" (2000, 109). Likewise, in her write-up of the University of Chicago's Iranian poster archive, Elizabeth Rauh describes the female posture of *Ithaar* as "reminiscent of Christian Pietà scenes."[7] On the surface, there is a strong parallel between Shiite Islam and Christianity, at least with regards to a founding martyr. However, further investigation into the propaganda slogans that appear in *Persepolis*, and their theoretical underpinnings, reveals further significance behind the "Islamic Pietà" figure in question.

Let us begin with the partially obscured slogan of the mural Marji sees in "Le Retour." Of the three translations of martyrdom slogans she offers the reader—"Le martyr est le cœur de l'histoire" ("The martyr is the heart of history"); "J'espérais être un martyr moi-même" ("I hoped to be a martyr myself"); and "Le martyr est vivant à jamais" ("A martyr lives forever")—the visible script of the mural matches the first. The fuller view afforded by the animated film version of *Persepolis* (2007) allows us to complete our transcription of the Persian slogan: "shahīd qalb-e tārīkh ast" ("The martyr is the heart of history"). This phrase alone carries an overwhelming resonance for Iranians, as it can be traced back to the influential lectures of Dr. 'Ali Shari'ati (1933–1977), an intellectual revolutionary often hailed as the chief ideologue of the Islamic Revolution. Shari'ati completed his doctorate in Paris, collaborated with leaders of the Algerian FLN, and translated works by Frantz Fanon into Persian. Many of Shari'ati's phrases served as ready-made revolutionary slogans, and as such, were shouted and painted on protest banners during the Islamic Revolution, and later inscribed onto the graves of those who were killed during demonstrations (Fischer and Abedi 1990, 212). The phrase in question originally appeared in a 1970 lecture, and has been translated by Mehdi Abedi and Gary Legenhausen as follows:

A shahīd is the heart of history. The heart gives blood and life to the otherwise dead blood-vessels of the body. Like the heart, a shahīd sends his own blood into the half-dead body of the dying society, whose children have lost faith in themselves, which is slowly approaching death, which has accepted submission, which has forgotten its responsibility, which is alienated from humanity, and in which there is no life, movement, and creativity. (1986, 248)[8]

Chelkowski and Dabashi even provide photographic evidence of the continued use of Shari'ati's slogan in mural propaganda during the

Iran-Iraq War.[9] It is sometimes misattributed to Ayatollah Khomeini, who echoed this phrase in his own teachings after Shari'ati's death, asserting that the martyr is "the heart of history and the blood of each martyr is like a bell which awakens the thousands" (*Iran Times*, November 16, 1982, 12, qtd. in Dorraj 1997, 512 n60). In any case, in their writings, Shari'ati, Khomeini, and Ayatollah Mutahhari (1920–1979) all elaborated a vivid, and sometimes shocking, imagery that insisted upon the regenerative powers of the martyr's blood, which, as we have seen, is not usually portrayed literally, but rather symbolized through red tulips. Thus, it is not surprising that the other slogan that appears in *Persepolis* (2007, 2.6 "La Cigarette") comes from Mutahhari: "Shahādat means the transfusion of blood into a society, especially into a society suffering from anemia. It is the shahīd who infuses fresh blood into the veins of the society" (1986, 136). Instead of following the aesthetic conventions of mural composition, Satrapi offers the reader a literal translation of this slogan in the following frame to capture the way she interpreted such propaganda as a naive young girl.

Even more pertinent to our study is the way these ideologues use two separate figures to argue that martyrdom and witnessing are in fact intertwined, inextricable imperatives of the Islamic Republic. Although this interdependence is already contained in the etymology of the word "shahīd" with "martyr," having been derived from "witness,"[10] Manochehr Dorraj has argued that the concept of martyrdom withstood a "complete metamorphosis" after World War II (1997, 511). First, Ayatollah Taleqani defined "witnessing truth" as the condition for martyrdom: "Anyone who has understood this truth and divine goal and has stood for it, sacrificing his life, is called 'shahid' in the terminology of the Qur'an and jurisprudence. The 'shahid' is the one who has experienced the 'shuhud' (vision) of truth" (1986, 67). By ascribing a clear intention to the act of martyrdom that had not necessarily been explicit, Taleqani further politicized the concept, and ultimately mobilized a volunteer army for the Iran-Iraq War. However, for Dr. Shari'ati, martyrdom alone did not suffice. In his same previously-discussed 1970 lecture, "After Shahādat," he argued that the paradigmatic sacrifice of Imam Husayn would have been forgotten if it weren't for his sister Zaynab, whose duty it was to bear witness to his martyrdom by spreading the message. Shari'ati condenses this dual relationship between martyrdom and bearing witness into the opposition of "the blood" and "the message" (249). The older-looking women in Chalipa's *Ithaar* and Satrapi's propaganda mural may therefore be evoking Zaynab, who was fifty-four when her brother died (October 10, 680 CE). In the most cited passage of Shari'ati's lecture, which often appears in visual martyrdom propaganda, he declares: "All battlefields are Karbala, all months are Muharram, all days are Ashura . . . One has to choose either the blood or the message, to be either Husayn or Zaynab, either to die like him or survive like her" (251). In sum, martyrdom is nothing without the subsequent transmission of its message. Witnessing is understood, then, to be an act that both precedes and follows martyrdom, the condition and the result; it is not enough to simply witness; one must bear witness.

Ultimately, the main artworks cited above—in their original, mass-produced, and mural forms—precede the publication date of Satrapi's fourth and final volume (August 3, 2003), and could have, at least in theory, inspired the mural in *Persepolis*. While there is no direct evidence that she was familiar with these specific images, they nevertheless point to a broader saturation of the martyr/mourner pose in the visual culture of both the Islamic Revolution and the Iran-Iraq War. Moreover, Islamic teachings, writings, and slogans leading up to the war suggest that what Western viewers identify as a "Pietà-like figure" actually evokes the coupling of Husayn and Zayneb, who embody the Islamic imperatives to self-sacrifice and to bear witness to sacrifice. Acknowledgment of the Islamic roots of this pose further reinforces the link between Satrapi's formal repetition of this *specific* figure within *Persepolis* and her own "injunctions to 'never forget'" (Chute 2010, 143).

This brings us back to Marji's scene of drawing as retracing. On the one hand, since the Pietà-like pose is not foreign to Islamic martyrdom iconography, it should not be enough on its own to truly constitute formal subversion, neither during the act of drawing represented diegetically in 4.4, nor on Satrapi's behalf in the interwoven iterations of this pose throughout the album. Neither East nor West can lay claim to such a universal experience and ubiquitous pose. Put another way, within the closed space of Satrapi's album, the subversive aspect of Marji's drawing is illegible as such. On the other hand, as soon as the reader brings external references to bear on this question, it becomes readily apparent that Marji's drawing is much closer to a literal reproduction of Michelangelo's statue than the previous iterations, through the precise angle of Jesus's head tilted backward, Mary's right-hand fingers bracing him beneath his armpit, and the angle of his right arm as it dangles by his side (Figs. 9 and 10).

(*Left*) Figure 9: Michelangelo, *La Pietà*, 1499. St. Peter's Basilica, the Vatican. Photo by Stanislav Traykov, March 6, 2008.
Reprinted under Fair Use.

(*Below*) Figure 10: 4.4 "Le Concours" ©Marjane Satrapi & L'Association, 2007. Reprinted with kind permission of the publisher.

Although Ebi and Taji's pose comes close, Ebi's face is in shadow, his hand is under her head, and her head is not tilted back. To my mind, in having Marji name the prographic source of her submission, Satrapi upends the obscuring homogenization of her own style, thus restoring the legibility of the intermedial subversion of her drawing. Furthermore, the fact that her reproduction of this statue in particular would have entailed sketching a mostly nude, male body *also* registers as subversive, as this is precisely the type of artistic training that will subsequently be denied to Marji and her female classmates later in Tome 4.

But what of the rest of the constellation? The revelations concerning the final iteration need not discount the ethical work underlying Satrapi's formal *tressage*. Let us recall that Chute's theorization of the ethics of "retracing" ultimately rests on the fact that Satrapi inscribed her own movement and gestures into the animated film version of *Persepolis*, thereby restricting said work to the author alone, during a moment of intermedial transposition (2010, 172–73). Bearing this in mind, I would like to propose that the formal technique of *tressage* already serves to implicate the reader as a witness, using repetition to teach her to "never forget" Satrapi's own graphic testimony by raising her memory of previous occurrences throughout the act of reading. In the following section, I will show how an alternative instance of intermedial transposition marks the apotheosis of Satrapi's constellation of Pietà poses, by taking that last step from passive reception to active transmission.

Politicizing *Persepolis*

The imperative to bear witness, as conveyed by Dr. Shari'ati, seems to find resonance in John Durham Peters's seminal essay on media studies, entitled "Witnessing." By reframing witnessing in terms of "mediation," he pinpoints the necessary operation from reception to transmission, whereby the passive viewer must become an active speaker:

> A witness is the paradigm case of a medium: the means by which experience is supplied to others who lack the original. To witness thus has two faces: the passive one of seeing and the active one of saying. . . . What one has seen authorizes what one says: an active witness first must have been a passive one. (2001, 709)

The cell phone video capture of the murder of Neda Agha-Soltan during the 2009 election protests in Iran has raised new questions about the incursion of media into the process of witnessing and bearing witness that, according to Peters, is *already* mediation. In this final section, I will first assess what has been placed at stake by this recent intermedial turn of witnessing. Second, in the modern digital age, it has become nearly impossible to account for the myriad forms and endless variations of martyr iconography for Neda that were produced around the world in the months that followed her murder. However, the fact that one of the icons in question was the first frame from Satrapi's constellation of Pietà poses opens a new line of inquiry into intermediality, propaganda, and the *bande dessinée* beyond the pages of *Persepolis*. Drawing from the writings of Shari'ati and Peters, I will therefore compare three main media formats of Neda's iconography—video, portraits, and the *bande dessinée* frame—to determine the extent to which intermediality enhances, or hinders, the imperative to bear witness.

Witnessing at Stake

On June 12, 2009, Iranian President Mahmoud Ahmadinejad declared an early reelection victory of 63 percent over his main opponent and leader of the reformist "green movement," Mir-Hossein Mousavi. In the following weeks, millions of Iranians took to the streets to protest what they considered to be controversial results. Neda Agha-Soltan, a twenty-six-year-old who aspired to become a tour guide abroad in Turkey, joined the protests starting June 15. What had largely begun as peaceful—or even silent—demonstrations quickly grew violent once Ayatollah Khamenei officially endorsed Ahmadinejad and warned that protests would be met with consequences.[11] Neda's mother recalls that three *basiji* (volunteer militia) women had even approached Neda to discourage her from participating, explaining that the *basiji* men viewed female beauty as a threat and were likely to target her, or even shoot her (Thomas 2010). On June 20, on her way home from protests in Amir-Abad, Neda was shot directly in the chest by a sniper, "seemingly unprovoked" (Mortensen 2011, 6). Despite the efforts of her music teacher, Hamid Panahi, and another bystander, author and translator Dr. Arash Hejazi, she died within minutes. To this day, no one has been charged with her murder, but it is widely reported that a *basij* soldier essentially carried out Khamenei's warning.

Two protesters captured Neda's final moments on cell phone video, the longer of which was uploaded onto Facebook and YouTube later that evening by an Iranian asylum seeker in Holland, to attract global attention to the injustice (Tait and Weaver 2009). The second video consists of a fifteen-second close-up of Neda once she is already unconscious and bleeding heavily. Despite their poor image quality, even the earliest models of the camera cell phone offered a new individualized mode of capturing irrefutable proof, sufficient to counter the authoritative media of the State. Then again, it places both passive acts of witnessing at stake: the original moment of witnessing and the subsequent reception of testimony. For the spectator-witnesses who observed Neda's final moments through their cell phone screens, the original "moment of witnessing" collapsed onto the mediated object it produced, or in the words of Paul Frosh and Amit Pinchevski, mediation has blurred the line between testimony production and consumption (2014, 595). The subsequent intermedial shift in transmission from social media platforms to international news networks subjected the footage to a seemingly infinite repetition loop evocative of the mediatized collapse of the World Trade Center towers. The argument that the media's treatment of 9/11 footage evacuated the horrific events of their history and meaning (Gleich 2014, 161) could just as easily have been about Neda. Therefore, if *Time* magazine would declare Neda's death "probably the most widely witnessed death in human history" that year (Mahr 2009, n.p.), the global reach of the rebroadcasted cell phone video testimony came at the expense of ethical engagement, as its facile reproducibility disallowed meaningful, ethical retracing of trauma.

The Birth of an Icon

Shortly after June 20, a still frame from the shorter, close-up cell phone video—at which point the life has left Neda's eyes and blood is streaming from her nose and mouth—was reproduced as an icon of her martyrdom. As an image, the increased iconicity of Neda's bloody portrait flouts the aesthetic conventions of traditional Iranian martyr iconography by literally conveying the "blood" instead of the "message." However, its circulation on the internet and transformation into protest posters points to an engaged viewership committed to not only bearing witness to the *facts* of her murder but transmitting this video testimony to others around the globe.

Of course, not all protest posters displayed the same icon. Other posters used the same still frame, but stylized her dead gaze by filtering it through Shepard Fairey's signature aesthetic (best known from the "Obama Hope" campaign poster of 2008). More common still were two beautiful portraits of Neda: a conservative one of her wearing a black chador and a family photo showing her in a pink button-up shirt, smiling and unveiled. Apart from public demonstrations in the streets, many paid tribute via the trending hashtag #IamNeda, or even assumed Neda's identity in their online avatars by swapping out their Facebook profile names or photos with hers. Paris-based

Iranian artist Reza Deghati synthesized this slacktivist expression of solidarity with public protest through his "Neda Masks" projects, realized on July 25, 2009, in Paris and June 12, 2010, in Washington, DC. Participants were invited to visit his website to find instructions on how to download, print, and transform Neda's smiling, unveiled portrait into a mask (Fig. 11).[12] The artist's condition for the photo shoot was that no other words be visible, besides the poem "Ma hame yek Nedaeem, Ma hame yek sedaeem" in both Persian and English, "We are all one Neda, We are all one calling." The fact that "Neda" means "voice" or "calling" in Farsi brings further symbolism to her silencing by the Iranian State.

Similar to the way video-capture confused the act of witnessing with the consumption of a mediated object, some have called out the objectifying nature of Neda's martyr iconography. For example, Carsten Stage has analyzed a few of these visual items through the lens of Scott Lash and Celia Lury's concept of "thingification" (2007), arguing that Neda "increasingly became an 'image-object' after her death" (2011, 421). Nima Naghibi expresses ambivalence toward the Fairey filter, for its evocation of Andy Warhol's critique of consumer culture necessarily predestines Neda's icons to be "forgotten and discarded upon quick consumption" (2016, 30). To my mind, through

Figure 11: Reza Deghati, "Neda Masks," Paris, July 25, 2009.
Idea and photograph: REZA/Webistan.
Image reproduced with kind permission of Reza Deghati.

this gesture of donning the Neda mask and taking to the streets, demonstrators enact a sort of bodily retracing not unlike Satrapi's bodily inscription of trauma in her animated film, the main difference being that they look forward in empathy and solidarity, imagining a shared future trauma by coming to terms with their own vulnerability.

The Accidental Martyrdom of Neda Soltani

While the reproduction, dissemination, and wearing of portraits, be they bloody or conservative, all constitute acts of engaged "bearing witness" beyond the passive "witnessing" of the video loops, the viral nature of such transmission unfortunately also came with severe consequences for one woman in particular: Neda Soltani (b. 1977). Under pressure to quickly identify the victim in the cell phone videos, journalists took to Facebook and, confusing their last names, ended up entering a fourth portrait into the mix of icons in circulation in the news and on the streets. Soltani had uploaded her profile photo to Facebook on June 7, 2009, which depicted her in a dark, flowered headscarf. In her self-published memoir, *My Stolen Face*, Soltani recalls with bitter irony the naive incredulity with which she learned, through a flood of emails and Facebook invitations from strangers around the world, that she had supposedly been martyred. Her attempts to contact the networks and correct this error backfired, and her passport photo continues to be confused with Agha-Soltan's *to this day*. In her own words: "Not only did they have no interest in correcting their error, but they also had to maintain it, because the world had by now identified my face as the symbol of resistance and opposition. My face was engraved in the collective consciousness of the world" (Soltani 2012, Chapter 8, n.p.). As opposed to the episode in *Persepolis* where Ebi laughingly recounts the harmless transformation of a dead cancer victim into a martyr of the people (2007, 1.4 "Persepolis"), the endless circulation of Soltani's portrait placed her life at stake, and, for all intents and purposes, produced a second martyr. Once Ahmadinejad requested an investigation into Agha-Soltan's murder, accusing various Western forces of plotting against Iran's government by killing Neda, Soltani was threatened, detained, and questioned. After a narrow escape to Greece, she arrived as a refugee in Germany, where she still lives in exile. The plight of Neda Soltani illustrates how "bearing witness" in the modern digital age, in the form of viral dissemination, may look like active engagement, but still evacuates images of meaning much like the video loops of Neda Agha-Soltan's final moments.

Recasting Marji as Neda

This brings us to one last item of Neda's martyr iconography, in the form of a recycled *bande dessinée* frame. First, from June 20–27, 2009, Payman and Sina (pseudonyms) created a ten-page adaptation of *Persepolis* using Photoshop and Adobe Illustrator. Both artists were of Iranian origin but had been born after the 1979 Revolution and had thus spent most of their lives outside Iran. As of June 2009, both were living in Shanghai, and Sina specialized in viral marketing. Satrapi and her editor gave them full permission to use images from *Persepolis* (Delorme 2016, 210), and they ultimately used forty-four vignettes, reordering them to tell the story of the 2009 election protests, with new speech bubbles and captions in English for a global audience. The resulting ten-page work, *Persepolis 2.0*, was posted on www.spreadpersepolis.com on Saturday, June 27, 2009, and culminates with the frame of God cradling Marji in the Pietà pose from 1.1 "Le Foulard" ("The Scarf"). A caption was added to recast Marji as Neda, which reads: "Don't cry Neda. Your death will not be in vain . . . " (Fig. 12).

**Figure 12: Payman and Sina, *Persepolis 2.0*, 27 June 2009, 10.
Reprinted by Fair Use.**

As opposed to the photo-realism and specificity of the propaganda murals, which were intended to highlight individual sacrifice, it is precisely Satrapi's homogenized aesthetic that enables this representational shift from Marji to Neda. In a fitting extension of Satrapi's constellation, what once conformed to martyrdom propaganda has since been turned into liberal propaganda contesting the Islamic regime. If I previously proposed that the interplay between repetition and memory in Satrapi's use of *tressage* simulated the act of witnessing, this remains in the passive realm, as it stops short of bearing witness. The viral dissemination of various portraits of Neda may have gone a step beyond the spectatorship of either the repeated Pietà or the video loop, but, as the case of Neda Soltani has proven, the stakes are exponentially higher. The appropriation of Satrapi's frame as a protest icon accomplishes the shift from passive witness to active bearing witness without placing anyone at stake. What is more, this has the potential to impact future readings of Satrapi's Pietà tressage, as new readers of the *bande dessinée* may now in fact recognize the first image of the constellation from Neda's global martyr iconography.

Earlier, I argued that the subversive aspect of Marji's drawing was not fully legible without consulting Iranian propaganda, Islamic teachings on martyrdom, and Michelangelo's statue. As for Neda Agha-Soltan, it is also true that viewers only learn of her "Westernized looks" through two of the main photographic sources of her iconography—the cell phone videos and the pink portrait. Much like the women Marji encounters upon her return to Tehran, Neda's choice of clothing (a baseball hat, blue jeans, and Adidas-style sneakers), her thin figure, sculpted eyebrows, and "signature Iranian nose job" (Sabety 2010, 123, qtd Naghibi 2016, 25–26) have been interpreted as small acts of defiance to the imposed conservative Islamist dress code. Nima Naghibi gives a rather cynical reading of Neda's rapid transformation into a martyr icon, arguing that global outrage over Neda's murder was largely dependent upon her legibility as a Westernized woman (2016, 26). To my mind, learning of Neda's Westernized looks validates the use of Satrapi's Pietà constellation to commemorate her, as she embodied the subversive hybridization to which Marji aspired with her drawing. At the same time, the pose, subject matter, and homogenized style of this frame do not explicitly evoke Michelangelo's *Pietà* as Marji's drawing does, leaving room for the Islamic imperative to bear witness embodied by Zayneb.

Endnotes

1. Groensteen cites the Hergéan line as an example of a unifying or "homogenizing" aesthetic style, which conceals the "double origin" of the BD icon, or its joint imaginary and documented inspiration (2007, 42). For the relationship between Satrapi's aesthetic style and trauma, see Chute 2010, 145–46; for the context and significance of Satrapi's choice of black and white, see Baetens 2011, 111–18.

2. Although it does not have any direct bearing on our analysis, it is worth noting that Satrapi's animated film version of *Persepolis* (2007, in collaboration with Vincent Parronaud) does depart from the graphic novel in that it cites the iconic mural outside the former US Embassy (or "Den of Spies") in Tehran, showing a skull-faced Statue of Liberty.

3. This was recently displayed alongside three of his other paintings in an exhibit entitled *Unedited History: Iran 1960–2014* at the Musée d'Art Moderne de la Ville de Paris, from May 16 to August 24, 2014, and then at the MAXXI (Museo nazionale delle arti del XXI secolo) in Rome, December 11, 2014 to March 29, 2015 (De Sanctis Mangelli 2014, 82–85).

4. For example, the cover of Issue 66 (15 *Mordad* 1363, or August 6, 1984) depicts two men in this position, and the children's insert of Issue 78 (15 *Bahman* 1363, or February 4, 1985) features a drawing of a young boy cradling a fallen adult soldier.

5. Christia originally displayed her personal research photographs in an exhibit entitled *Walls of Martyrdom: Tehran's Propaganda Murals*, which was held at Harvard's Center for Government and International Studies from May–July 2007.

6. For an overview of the artistic guidelines for propaganda murals put out by the Artistic and Cultural Bureau of the Qom Seminary's Office of Propaganda in the mid-1980s, see Chelkowski and Dabashi 2000, 291. For more on the role of photography in public and private martyr memorialization beyond the mural, see Varzi, *Warring Souls* (2006), along with her documentary film, *Plastic Flowers Never Die* (2008); and Fromanger, "Variations in the Martyrs' Representations" (2012).

7. https://www.lib.uchicago.edu/collex/exhibits/graphics-revolution-and-war-iranian-poster-arts/new-battle-karbala/.

8. Lecture originally delivered "the day after 'Shahadat,' in 1970 in the Grand Mosque of Narmak in Tehran, the night after Ashura" (Shari'ati 1986, 252 n1).

9. In one panel of a series of murals along Imam Khomeini Avenue in Andimeshk, the phrase appears in calligraphy alongside the logo of the Martyrs' Foundation (Chelkowski and Dabashi 2000, 108, Fig. 7.1).

10. There is some speculation that the semantic evolution from "witness" to "martyr" in both Farsi and Arabic is in fact calqued from the derivation of "martyr" from Ancient Greek μάρτυς ("mártus" or "witness"). It is interesting to note that Fischer and Abedi indicate that there is some ambiguity to the term "shahīd" in Shari'ati's phrase: "shahīd qalb-e tārīkh ast (martyrdom/witnessing is the heart of history)"

(1990, 212). Fischer and Abedi have therefore altered their citation of Abedi and Legenhausen (1986, 248; cited n97), who originally left the term "shahīd" untranslated. While the Farsi terms for "martyr" and "witness" are related, there is in fact a distinction between the two terms, indicated by different vowel lengths: "shāhid" means "witness," and "shahīd" means "martyr."

11. Looking back on the tragic events, Dr. Arash Hejazi, one of the men caught on film trying to save Neda's life, said: "He virtually signed Neda's death sentence on that day" (Antony Thomas 2010).

12. http://wearealloneneda.wordpress.com/

Works Cited

BAETENS, Jan. 2011. "From Black and White to Color and Back: What Does It Mean (Not) to Use Color?" *College Literature* 38 (3): 111–27.

CHELKOWSKI, Peter, and Hamid Dabashi. 2000. *Staging a Revolution: The Art of Persuasion in the Islamic Republic of Iran.* London: Booth-Clibborn.

CHRISTIA, Fotini. 2007. "Walls of Martyrdom: Tehran's Propaganda Murals." Center for Government and International Studies South Concourse Gallery, Harvard University, May–July 2007. library.harvard.edu/collections/tehran-propaganda-murals.

CHRISTIA, Fotini, and H.E. CHEHABI. 2008. "The Art of State Persuasion: Iran's Post-Revolutionary Murals." *Persica* 22: 1–13.

CHUTE, Hillary L. 2010. *Graphic Women: Life Narrative and Contemporary Comics.* New York: Columbia University Press.

DE SANCTIS MANGELLI, Flavia, ed. 2014. *Iran: Unedited History, 1960–2014.* Rome: Cura Books.

DELORME, Isabelle. 2016. "*Persepolis 2.0*, adaptation éphémère d'une œuvre durable?" In *Persepolis: Marjane Satrapi et Vincent Paronnaud, Dessin de vie*, edited by Barbara Laborde, 209–29. Lormont, France: Le bord de l'eau.

DORRAJ, Manochehr. 1997. "Symbolic and Utilitarian Political Value of a Tradition: Martyrdom in the Iranian Political Culture." *The Review of Politics* 59, no. 3 (Summer): 489–521.

FISCHER, Michael M. J., and Mehdi ABEDI. 1990. *Debating Muslims: Cultural Dialogues in Postmodernity and Tradition.* Madison: University of Wisconsin Press.

FROMANGER, Marine. 2012. "Variations in the Martyrs' Representations in South Tehran's Private and Public Spaces." *Visual Anthropology* 25, no. 1–2, (September): 47–67.

FROSH, Paul, and Amit PINCHEVSKI. 2014. "Media witnessing and the ripeness of time." *Cultural Studies* 28 (4): 594–610.

GLEICH, Lewis S. 2014. "Ethics in the Wake of the Image: The Post-9/11 Fiction of DeLillo, Auster, and Foer." *Journal of Modern Literature* 37, no. 3 (Spring): 161–76.

GROENSTEEN, Thierry. 2007. *The System of Comics.* Translated by Bart Beaty and Nick Nguyen. Jackson: University Press of Mississippi.

GRUBER, Christiane. 2008. "The Message is on the Wall: Mural Arts in Post-Revolutionary Iran." *Persica* 22: 15–46.

KHANY, Minoo, Christophe BALAY, and Mostafa GOUDARZI. 2017. "The Analysis of War Reflections in Kazem Chalipa's Paintings According to Panofsky." *Bagh-e Nazar* 14, no. 47 (April): 55–70.

LASH, Scott, and Celia LURY. 2007. *Global Culture Industry: The Mediation of Things.* Cambridge: Polity.

Leservot, Typhaine. 2011. "Occidentalism: Rewriting the West in Marjane Satrapi's Persépolis." French Forum 36, no. 1 (Winter): 115–30.

MAHR, Krista. 2009. "Nedha Agha-Soltan." *Time*, December 8, 2009.

Middle Eastern Posters. Collection, Special Collections Research Center, University of Chicago Library.

MORTENSEN, Mette. 2011. "When citizen photojournalism sets the news agenda: Neda Agha Soltan as a Web 2.0 icon of post-election unrest in Iran." *Global Media and Communication* 7 (1): 4–16.

MUTAHHARI, Ayatullah Murtada. 1986. "Shahīd." In *Jihād and Shahādat: Struggle and Martyrdom in Islam,* edited by Mehdi Abedi and Gary Legenhausen, 125–52. Houston, TX: Institute for Research and Islamic Studies.

NAGHIBI, Nima. 2016. *Women Write Iran: Nostalgia and Human Rights from the Diaspora.* Minneapolis: University of Minnesota Press.

PAYMAN and SINA. 2009. *Persepolis 2.0.* June 27, 2009, www.spreadpersepolis.com.

PETERS, John Durham. 2001. "Witnessing." *Media, Culture & Society* 23 (6): 707–23.

SABETY, Setareh. 2010. "Graphic Content: The Semiotics of a Youtube Uprising." In *Media, Power, and Politics in the Digital Age: The 2009 Presidential Election Uprising in Iran,* edited by Yahya R. Kamalipour, 119–24. Lanham, MD: Rowman and Littlefield.

SATRAPI, Marjane. 2007a. *The Complete Persepolis.* Translated by Blake Ferris and Mattias Ripa. New York: Pantheon.

———. 2007b. *Persepolis.* Paris: L'Association.

SATRAPI, Marjane, and Vincent PARONNAUD, directors. 2007. *Persepolis.* DVD Video. Paris: Diaphana.

SHARI'ATI, Dr. 'Ali. "After Shahādat." 1986. *Jihād and Shahādat: Struggle and Martyrdom in Islam,* edited by Mehdi Abedi and Gary Legenhausen, 244–52. Houston, TX: Institute for Research and Islamic Studies.

SOLTANI, Zahra Neda. 2012. *My Stolen Face: The Story of a Dramatic Mistake.* Munich: Ariadne-Buch.

STAGE, Carsten. 2011. "Thingifying Neda: The Construction of Commemorative and Affective Thingifications of Neda Agda Soltan." *Culture Unbound* 3: 419–38.

STORACE, Patricia. 2005. "A Double Life in Black and White." *New York Review of Books*, April 7, 2005, 40–43.

TAIT, R., and M. WEAVER. 2009. "The accidental martyr." *The Guardian,* June 23, 2009.

TALEQANI, Ayatullah Sayyid Mahmud. 1986. "Jihad and Shahadat." In *Jihād and Shahādat: Struggle and Martyrdom in Islam,* edited by Mehdi Abedi and Gary Legenhausen, 47–80. Houston, TX: Institute for Research and Islamic Studies.

THOMAS, Antony, director and producer. 2010. *For Neda.* Film. HBO Home Etnertainment.

VARZI, Roxanne, 2006. *Warring Souls: Youth, Media, and Martyrdom in Post-Revolution Iran.* Durham: Duke University Press.

———, director. 2008. *Plastic Flowers Never Die.* DVD Video. Watertown, MA: Documentary Educational Resources.

CHAPTER NINE:
Children in Graphic Novels: Intermedial Encounters and Mnemonic Layers

Maaheen Ahmed

This chapter proposes a new concept for considering intermediality in comics: media memories. Inspired by cultural historian Aby Warburg's use of the montage for his incomplete *Mnemosyne Atlas* and philosopher John Sutton's concept of porous memories, I use the concept of media memories to better understand how media remember other media and how certain images and tropes persist over time and across media (M. Ahmed 2019, 3). Media memories are tropes, styles, and images that travel from medium to medium, adapting to fit each new habitat. They are loaded images and techniques that persist in varying forms across media. In this chapter, I consider the media memories channeled through children and childhood "geographies." "Geographies of childhood include social imaginaries inhabited by both children and others," writes developmental psychologist Erica Burman (2019, 1). Childhood geographies, like Peter Hollindale's concept of childness, are useful in that they account for adult roles in creating, remembering, and reforming ideas of children and childhood: Child and adult perspectives coalesce, with the former often dominating the latter in most cultural productions, the vast majority of which is produced by adults.[1] The graphic novels discussed here are no exception.

In this chapter, I turn to contemporary graphic novels in French and in English, focusing in particular on glimpses of childhood and the presence of children in Lynda Barry's *What It Is,* Dominique Goblet's *Faire semblant c'est mentir* (*Pretending is Lying*), the fourth volume of Manu Larcenet's *Combat ordinaire* (*Ordinary Victories*), Steven T. Seagle and Teddy Kristiansen's *It's a Bird . . .* , and, very briefly (in order to deepen the connection between North American childhood memories and superhero comics), Jeff Lemire's *Essex County.* Published between the 1990s and 2010s, these works are situated in the move toward comics for an adult audience that do not shy away from experimentation. Belonging to a privileged state of (relative) legitimation, these comics are pseudo-autobiographical. They are imbued with the specific childhood geographies of children's image-making practices and children reading comics (the latter with a focus on the North American context). These geographies, which are intermedial in their essence, are fleshed out and activated by media memories.

In focusing on media memories, I am interested in both the interaction between media and memories evoked during those interactions; I would go so far as to suggest both are closely interlinked, especially in the case of the figure and idea of the child. Memories, in turn, are inevitably tied to affect: They both channel and evoke affects. Child figures and other elements related to childhood (elements of children's culture, manifestations of childishness) are especially laden with affects, triggering (for adult readers) nostalgia but often also wistful joy. Before turning to the close readings, I will draw connections between Warburg's and Sutton's concepts of memory to highlight their relevance for considering comics history and the workings of comics.

Porous Memories, the *Mnemosyne Atlas,* and Comics Form

In *Wide Awake in Slumberland,* Katherine Roeder masterfully shows how Winsor McCay was influenced by at least three forms of modern popular culture: dime museums that combined circus entertainment with fair attractions, films, and advertisements. All of these forms are remediated by the comic strip and filtered through the different kinds of memories captured by comics: We encounter dream worlds but also action-packed sequences, slapstick comedy, and other manifestations of modern entertainment. These elements coexist with, or are sometimes surpassed by, more existential concerns in the comics examined here, especially of troubled familial and collective memories (*Faire semblant c'est mentir, Combat ordinaire*) and death (*It's a Bird . . . , Essex County*). In other words, these graphic novels interweave clashing media memoires, such as those of the modern entertainment industry and historiography, as well as literary autobiography.

Such a vast scope of media memories is comparable to Aby Warburg's project to map memories across cultural production. The evolutionary biologist Richard Semon's concept of the "Engramm" had a strong influence on Aby Warburg's cultural memory work: Engrams are the imprints resulting from powerful shocks. They capture Warburg's interest in the transposition of intense emotional experiences, initially "stored as 'mnemonic energy,'" engraved in collective consciousness and later channeled into art (Assmann 2011, 198, 358). According to art historian Matthew Rampley, Warburg sought "to explore the specifically *visual* forms of the engram," which he called dynamograms (1999, 104). The *Mnemosyne Atlas* turned into a broad cultural and historical project of tracing visual memories and their transformations across diverse forms of cultural production, from popular, everyday images to those ranked among the higher arts.

The concept of an organic transfer of memories across people, generations, and objects remains influential and resurfaces in philosopher John Sutton's concept of "porous memories." Even though porous memories, which imply that memories leave physical traces on people and travel through objects, have not been validated by neurobiological research, they are related to concepts used in literary and cultural studies for capturing, for instance, the transfer and mutation of tropes. For Sutton, porous memories capture experience that is essentially bodily and sensory, based on allusions rather than logical connections.

Comics can reveal—and revel in—connections in a way that is comparable to Sutton's "porous memories": the exograms or "objects which embody memories and which combine in many different ways with the brain's distributed, context-ridden 'engrams'" (Sutton 2004, 130). If comics are likened to Sutton's imaginary South Sea sponges from the 1630s that replayed messages recorded earlier when squeezed, we can hear the reverberations of more than a century-long practice of capturing fantasies interacting with familiar realities that is closely linked to the techniques of popular entertainment, especially illustrated magazines and moving pictures, which developed at the same time as the modern comic strip.

Georges Didi-Huberman sees the montage practice of the incomplete *Mnemosyne Atlas* (1927–1929) as an expression of the chaos and ruptures of its time as well as its maker: Warburg began the atlas three years after his breakdown (a result of the First World War) and two years before his death. There is, then, a strong emotional element in Warburg's concept of cultural memory. Moreover, there is an underlying assumption of cyclicality and recurrence in cultural memory, which assures the continuation of collective memory while also being indicative of traumatic memory (Roth 2011, 133). The universal trauma of growing up, which implies giving up childhood and complying with adult constraints is a central tension anchored in the practice of reading, making, and, ultimately, judging comics (cf. Pizzino 2016 and 2017, and Gordon 2019 for insights on how critique and graphic novels themselves have internalized the notion of comics' "growing up." I turn to these concerns further below).

The montage or collage work of comics, which is to a certain extent a given in every comic, evokes the ruptures and fragments associated with the modern age (and traumatic memories). Hillary Chute reads the collage work of Lynda Barry's *One Hundred Demons* as "a literal re-collection, [visualizing] a process of recollection and re-narrativization that well figures the assimilation of traumatizing experience" (2011, 292; my modification in brackets). But, as Alan Gibbs has shown, fragmentation and collage are not necessarily an expression of traumatizing experience but are more about modernity itself. What Barry calls "bumpiness," or the materiality of the collage is not only an expression of "trouble"—a recurrent theme in Barry's work that made it difficult to sell in the late 1970s (Chute 2011, 282)—but more a means of expression, since most of Barry's books on comics making, such as *Syllabus* and *What It Is*, retain the technique but not the trauma. This in turn can be tied to the "ordinariness" observed by Chute: In combining "the amusing with the appalling, insisting on both as the lived reality of girlhood," Barry, "the author-subject makes political, collective claims by testifying to the very ordinariness of her trauma" (289).

The relatability of such ordinariness, which contains the seeds of empathic connections with readers, precedes (and paves the way for) its political implications. The impact and affects of ordinariness are activated by another kind of publication that plays a key—albeit often overlooked—role in comics history: fanzines, which regularly use collages and maintain a degree of directness or unconventionality of tone and roughness of production that reappear in some comics autobiographies and convey a sheen of authenticity. Brian Cremins brings out another aspect of fanzines, which was mentioned by none other than Frederic Wertham. Wertham "tells the story of 'a little goblin' that swaps 'all the solemn church bells' in Rotterdam 'with tinkling sleigh bells'": The goblin is the mischievous outsider, the one who effects small but joyful changes in consciousness. If fanzines, often filled with stories of favorite childhood characters and comic books, are these "tinkling sleigh bells," then their creators are the "little goblins" who produce the vital, exuberant tinkling (Cremins 2016, 133). Here, Wertham suggests that the revolutionary potential of these amateur magazines lies in their sense of childlike mischief and entertainment. This also exemplifies one of those slippery, hard to grasp instances when child and childhood remain stuck (in the sense of Sara Ahmed's concept of stickiness, see S. Ahmed 2004, 89–92) to comics and even determine their intermedial connections to memories of childhood readings and childlike modes of visualization, for instance.

The ways in which comics instrumentalize the memories concretized through other media and those memories themselves reveal media awareness, while affirming the necessary role played by the imagination in construing information, be it personal or collective, stemming from the here and now or from an only vicariously experienced past. If "cinematic memory was a world of affronted senses and collapsed time" (Matsuda 1996, 174), comics memory is a collage of visual experiences reflecting the confluence of the personal and the collective, the perceived and the imaginary.

Thierry Smolderen's concept of "polygraphy," through its emphasis on the allusions ingrained in the often-conflicting drawing techniques feeding into comics (2014, 9), can be read as a materialization of Sutton's porous memories, which in turn have strong connections with Warburg's interest in the power and transfer of images. In a related vein, Gert Meesters has shown how the multiple styles in Dominique Goblet's *Faire semblant c'est mentir* and Olivier Schrauwen's *Mon fiston* (*My Son*) evoke diverse references to the world of comics as well as the fine arts. Meesters turns to two linguistic concepts, Ferdinand de Saussure's theorization of associative connections between words and the more contemporary notion of "conceptual blending spaces" suggested by Gilles Fauconnier and Mark Turner, which are activated through references. Given the dependence on a reader for the activation of such references and the associative manner through which references are triggered and the amorphous forms they ultimately acquire, it is perhaps more useful to talk about *memories* in order to capture the blurry, fuzzy manner in which references and inclinations travel and mutate.

Media Memories Around Children and Comics

In the editorial for the "Comics and Childhood" special issue of *ImageText*, Charles Hatfield paraphrases essayist Adam Gopnik's observation that "caricature . . . is a modern form associated as much with the learned and politically factious as it is with the ingenuous doodling of children" (2006–2007, n.p.). While Gopnik was writing about Spiegelman's *Maus*, Hatfield goes on to point out the close connections between children and comics, whereby "many of the best—the most stimulating, most troubling, most psychologically questing, ideologically fraught, and artistically vital—comics for adults have as their subject matter *childhood* and its possibilities: its potential for tenderness, awe, terror, and social critique" (2006–2007, n.p.).

Chris Foss, Jonathan W. Gray, and Zack Whalen note that the exaggerations in *Little Nemo* reflect a child's view of the world (2016, 3). As mentioned by Rosemarie Garland-Thomson in the foreword to the same volume, exaggeration is also a recurrent characteristic of comics (2016, xii). Comics, therefore, can be said to embody a playful imagination, which is childish in its liberties. This is comparable to the easy, taken-for-granted transitions between reality and fantasy, a recurrent feature of children's literature (Nodelman 2008). Writing about the cartoonish style and its affective hold on readers in Alison Bechdel's work, Vera Camden draws connections with medieval art and its disregard for academic perspective and forms. According to Camden, "it is perhaps more accurate to observe that comics are childlike in that even when their content is adult and profoundly disturbing, their images remain transfixing, even regressive in their magnetism, and drawn to the depiction of the child's perspective and childhood memory" (2019, 95). I agree with Camden about the underlying impact of childhood memory in graphic novels with autobiographical and nostalgic inclinations (see Baetens and Frey 2014) but not comics at large. While Camden does not unpack the childish element of such drawing—perhaps because it risks only stating the obvious?—her discussion of the affective hold of seemingly unschooled drawing is pertinent and at least partially indebted to the Romantic associations stuck to childhood. In a similar vein, Daniel Worden considers both children and melancholy to be an inevitable part of comics. He, too, makes this claim with reference to graphic novels rather than mainstream comics.

Writing about Chris Ware's edited issue of *McSweeney's Quarterly Concern* (no. 13), Worden suggests a certain melancholy is endemic to comics as is the presence of children. He adds that "the hallmark of this 'language' [of comics] is a direct access to emotion" (2015, 896). As in Camden's article, the role of children and childishness in facilitating and even forming such emotionality calls for further unpacking. Many of the emotions in the graphic novels discussed here are generated from media memories of childhood: from children, child versions of protagonists, childish protagonists to objects of childhood, and, of course, childish drawing styles. Correspondingly, comics artists' autobiographical accounts and remembrances often go back to their love, as children, for stories and drawing and usually comics: In *L'Ascension du Haut Mal* (*Epileptic*) David B.'s younger self, Pierre-François, is highly imaginative and loves stories and drawing. The children we encounter in the graphic novels discussed here are no different in their eagerness to draw and even to make and read comics. Such children combine the media memories of the arts and comics, as well as ideals of imaginative and creative childhoods. Perhaps most crucial in the light of graphic novels and comics legitimation is the bridge drawn between the early twentieth-century avant-garde movements' acceptance of children's art and childlike drawing styles and the graphic novel's sometimes shy references to such drawings.

Unsurprisingly, the first question in Lynda Barry's *What It Is* is about the image, and it opens with her childhood memories (2009, 5–12). Barry returns to her childhood experiences and memories repeatedly throughout the comic (25–28, 37–40, 51–54, 63–66, 89–92). While these earlier references are usually about her use of imagination to counter stark, everyday realities, we later see Barry drawing and making collages often in the face of adult adversity (75–80). After a hiatus of a few years, Barry starts drawing again, this time concentrating on copying (100–105)—copying comics (105) but also old children's books (111)—discovering underground comics, and eventually enrolling in a painting course; we follow Lynda growing up through her encounters with and processing of different kinds of image-making (114–122). Finally, in the narrative within a narrative "Two Questions" (123–135), we see how Barry's childhood and adolescent anxieties haunt her adult self: It is here that the younger and older personas of Barry become inextricable. As foreshadowed by Barry's art, however, the two were always interconnected, since Barry does not shy away from "childish" images. On the contrary, she activates them to make her points about comics creation and visual storytelling in general: Sometimes adult standards, and ways of judging and looking, have to be shunned in order to create.

The two questions—"Is this good? Does this suck?" (Barry 2009, 123)—are intended to weed out "bad drawings" from the "good" ones, Lynda's child self explains (128). This imposition of adult standards contributes to the potential stigma of comics drawing, comics reading, and comics themselves (especially, and even today, those comics that strive to entertain through tried and tested formulas and shun literary and artistic aspirations). Barry asks another question that is similar to the title of Dominique Goblet's book discussed below: "What is the difference between lying and pretending?" (72). While Barry affirms that "there is no lie in pretending," the question captures the anxieties of potential artists as well as media like comics that are not recognized as art. Of the books we see Barry reading, the inclusion of Marion Milner's *On Not Being Able to Paint* is particularly significant because of its pioneering role in art therapy and its insistence on encouraging adults to channel their feelings through free drawing (133). Such "free" drawing and art therapy are at the heart of Barry's work. She frequently evokes children's ability to draw without restraint. This scruple-free image-making is seen as a form of play: "At the center of everything we call 'the arts' and children call 'play' is something which seems very alive . . . the way memory is alive" (14). This "something" is the image for Barry.

The importance of retaining some childish qualities into adulthood is reinforced by the recurrent presence of playing, appearing in the beginning but also at the very end of *What It Is* (Barry 2009, 208). This playing is closely tied to role playing and exercising the imagination. Correspondingly, much of the latter half of *What It Is* takes the form of an "activity book" (137–213). The activity book combines DIY aesthetics with a familiar childhood practice and educational tool with which adults are rarely confronted.

If Barry's child self appears only intermittently, her collages almost always contain some references to the world of childhood. This fits Barry's regular evocation of children's art-making to understand how images and, eventually, comics images can work. Collages themselves can be seen as counter-artistic and even childish practices. To bolster the latter impression, Barry incorporates images that evoke childhood such as cartoon figures and animal drawings. The simple text complements the "childish" element. That the pages are drawn on yellow notebook pages (like many of Barry's works) further strengthens the connection to childhood and children's practices.

In *What It Is,* the young Lynda starts as an imaginative child and eventually turns into a comics maker. This trajectory is similar to the one found in David B's *Eplipetic* and Jean-Christophe Menu's *Krollebitches*. In Menu's memoir, subtitled *Souvenirs même pas en bande dessinée (Memories not even in comics)*, we encounter a similar kind of child as in Barry's *What It Is*: a child comics reader, nascent comics fan, who also starts drawing and eventually making his own comics—a passion which, in rejection of acceptable grown-up behavior, the artist sticks to in his adult life. Mark McKinney discusses a similar episode in Farid Boudjellal's *Petit Polio*, where the child protagonist is shown reading and eventually entering a comic in an effort to better understand his identity in the real world (2013, 197–98).

Yasco Horsman's concluding claim about "maintaining a relation to an embarrassing infantile comic enjoyment may be the source of the comics' 'exuberant' creative energy, a force that only lives on in its refusal to grow up" is only part of the complex attachment to comics (2013, 333). As suggested by the graphic novels discussed here, this attachment is embodied by the child but also refracted by it through the media memories it interweaves.

The role of the child in graphic novels is imbued with personal and collective media memories of, and around, childhood. Decades before the countercultural movement, the avant-garde had embraced childish forms of drawing and even bricolage, dragging it from the realms of outsider art to the mainstream of fine arts (Kunzle 2019, 85). In illustration, this incorporation of childish drawing styles goes even further, to Cham and even Hogarth and later Töpffer (Kunzle 2019, 85; Smolderen 2014, 8, 25). Media memories channeled through childlike drawing styles and other indicators of children's worlds and childishness, such as toys, play, or childish modes of narration encapsulate, on one hand, affects such as nostalgia and, on the other hand, a curious legitimizing impulse that conjures the media memories of both modern art and the DIY, untutored culture of fanzines, or édition sauvage (wild publishing) that resists institutionalized and established publishing (for the application of Jacques Dubois's concept of *littérature sauvage* to fanzines, see Crucifix and Moura 2016). The confluence of (goblinesque) "wildness" and childish drawing—which is not too far from the "primitivity" that was once the goal of the modernist avant-garde—structures crucial moments in Goblet's *Faire semblant c'est mentir*.

Faire semblant c'est mentir: Childishness and the Drawn Line

Begun in 1995, Dominique Goblet's pseudo-autobiographical graphic novel famously took twelve years to complete. In his preface, Menu sees time as the "raw material" of this book. Given the centrality of time, the presence of child figures is particularly loaded since child characters are in many ways figurations of temporality: They are inevitably caught up in the process of "growing up," physically but also socially. Unsurprisingly, Dominique's daughter, Nikita, is the character the reader encounters the most when the first chapter opens. The last panel on this page even offers a partially cut off, full frontal view of the smiling girl, drawn as if by a child.

Jan Baetens describes the first of the many destabilizing elements in Goblet's art as stemming from the blending of adult and childish styles "to the extent of becoming indistinguishable and generating a friction between past and present within the images" ("au point de devenir indissociables et de provoquer une friction entre passé et présent au cœur même des images") (2014, 173). Goblet also incorporates a collage aesthetic since her style is often a collage of different techniques.

Pretending Is Lying is preceded by a prologue that recounts what we realize later are Dominique's—pet-named Nikske or "little nothing"—memories. Drawn with smudged red pen, which makes the drawing seem old, almost neglected, the prologue recalls how Dominique fell and tore her leggings on her way to school. It captures a tender moment between the mother and the daughter that has a bittersweet edge since Dominique's mother addresses the source of the child's chagrin—her torn leggings—by magically making them disappear, when in reality she reverses the leggings so that the holes are at the back and not in the front. Nikske however believes her mother can work magic. This very personal (fictional or nonfictional) moment foreshadows the issue of pretending as equivalent to lying, an indispensable component of the media memories of image-making, as suggested above. The episode also evokes another emotion channeled through child figures in the comics discussed here, which constitutes the media memories of childhood: emotional attachment, more specifically, parent-child love. Each square panel is cut out and pasted, evoking the collage and, ironically, the practice of making disparate elements connect. This in itself figures memory work.

Children and childhood memories are, in many ways, central to the story, since Dominique's memories of her own unhappy childhood and tensions with her father, Jean-Pierre, are a recurrent theme. We encounter Nikske again in the third chapter as Dominique recalls how disconnected Jean-Pierre was from his wife and daughter: While Dominique and her mother fall out and make up, the father only drinks and raves about the 1973 Grand Prix in Zandvoort where Roger Williamson had a fatal accident. At the beginning of the mother-daughter quarrel, Dominique's mother tries to occupy her fidgety daughter by encouraging her to draw and then to paint. However, Dominique is briefly locked up in the attic as punishment for having left watercolor stains on the table and on the freshly ironed laundry. This is an avant-gardist rebellion comparable to the rebelliousness of graffiti. It is also a comicsy stain on acceptable, comfortably categorized academic drawing. The recollection ends with the mother and daughter playing a "popular" game titled "Ne t'en fais pas!" ("Don't worry!")—this game serves as the transition into the narrative's present, where Jean-Pierre's partner, Cécile, has unpredictable and hysterical reactions that lead to an abrupt, dramatic break in the dinner with the grown-up Dominique and her daughter. In what can be read as a typical twist for the comic, the joyful, collective (familial and communal) act of boardgame playing acquires a painful tinge.

Adults and children are, significantly, not very different in *Pretending Is Lying*. Jean-Pierre is a megalomaniac who stretches the truth and loves to tell stories with himself as the hero. His partner Cécile clings to her past grandeur, or illusion thereof, and has an unpredictable, volatile temperament. Cécile's hysteria is already present in the early pages of the graphic novel. Her reaction to Nikita's drawing of her friend leads to two of the most fascinating pages in the graphic novel and also includes its title: "Pretending is lying!" Cécile shouts out when Nikita says that her friend does not have long hair, unlike the picture she drew of her. "What is it then?" Cécile insists, her stick figure towering over a tiny, flabbergasted Nikita. "Pretending is LYING, it's LYING. PRETENDING is lying!" (Fig. 1). Cécile accuses Nikita of lying several times even though, for the child, the drawing was only pretend or play. The contrast of opinions and Cécile's demagogic reaction suggest that

Figure 1: Goblet, *Faire semblant c'est mentir*: Cécile explodes and accuses Nikita of lying. ©Dominique Goblet & L'Association, 2007. Reprinted by kind permission of the author and publisher.

this is not only a dramatic moment in the comic. The drawing style conjures up media memories of childhood drawing and its recuperation by the fine arts. All this is framed in a system of comics that is stretched to its limits: During Cécile's tirade, words no longer remain confined to word balloons but spill all over the panel; figures lose all sense of proportion, and the space is deliberately confused as Nikita becomes interchangeable with her imaginary friend's drawing.

The childish drawing expresses the chaos of the situation and gives form to the childish, unpredictable adults. Baetens considers such blurring of lines between adult and child and similar absolute categories as characteristic of Goblet's work (2014, 176). Such deliberate garbling of categories re-evokes the issues of both temporality and the relationships between time and space and writing and drawing (176). Cécile's equating of unrealistic art with "false" art or non-art evokes the legitimation issues of comics as a popular medium for the masses and not for those who set and apply the standards of art.

Combat ordinaire: Planter des clous: Poetry and the Stuff of Childhood

The next graphic novel I turn to also has a bone or two to pick with the notion of art, which is again connected, loosely but significantly, to the child, childhood, and childish drawing. Manu Larcenet's four-volume *Combat ordinaire* juxtaposes personal issues, the "extreme nervousness" of the protagonist, Marco, a photographer (whose name and appearance bear a close resemblance to Manu), and collective memory (particularly that of the Algerian War), with a focus on the daily business of living, telling, and remembering. This ordinariness is reinforced by the comic's obsession with everyday moments and objects. In *Combat ordinaire*, which is characterized by its playful cartoony style and often cheerful pastel colors, the moments of self-insight are expressed through black and white panels maintaining an allusive relationship between words and images, which in turn echo psychoanalytical methods of associative thinking (2008, 18).

While the third volume, *Ce qui est précieux* (*That Which Is Precious*) traces the stages of Marco's grief after his father's death, the fourth volume, *Planter des clous* (literally: *Nailing*) takes on a different tone with the birth of Marco's daughter, Maude. This volume taps into the media memories surrounding the concept of childhood and, inevitably, the relationship between children and comics; the most prominent of these elements are the exaggerated emotions, which are already evident in the young child's tantrums (Larcenet 2008, 10), the playfulness, spontaneity, and brashness associated with children's drawings, as well as their simplicity and directness. In this final album, the sequences of reflection, which usually unfold across panels of still lifes drawn in a realistic style, show Maude's stuffed animals (9, 24). The first sequence is about the love and fascination Marco feels for his daughter. Each panel shows a different stuffed animal from a different perspective, as Marco admiringly adds how his child has taught him about reconsidering and questioning everything from different angles. The child, as well as the child's point of view, is partially equated with the smiling stuffed animals, which provide unconditional comfort and companionship to their young owners, just like Marco's daughter does for him. In the second sequence, however, the stuffed animals accompany a reflection on how Maude makes him see the world in a different way and helps him accept that there is nothing logical about the world (9). Such insights build on connections between the child, toy, play, and the consequent disruption of adult logic.

During the kindergartners' Picasso exhibition (Larcenet 2008, 16), Marco is the only one who seems interested in the children's drawings (including but not limited to Maude's), while the other parents chat and eat. This exhibition not only pokes fun at the recuperation of infantile styles by high art but also prefigures a certain leveling of artistic practices. This leveling becomes more evident when Marco reflects, over images of Maude's stuffed animals, about "what is precious": poetry (24) (Fig. 2). He expands his concept of poetry to

Figure 2: Marco's reflections on the redemptive power of poetry.
Le Combat ordinaire 4: Planter des clous **(30).**
©DARGAUD 2008, by Larcenet (www.dargaud.com).
Reprinted by kind permission of the publisher.

include popular singers, cartoonists, comedians, painters, and photographers to conclude that "poetry redeems everything." Just like the Picasso exhibition, the juxtaposition of these thoughts to different kinds of stuffed animals is not merely an act of irreverence against the hierarchies of art; it is an affirmation, much like Barry's encouragement, to celebrate creativity without judgment, to see and appreciate in a childlike way.

Having tracked down a few media memories at the intersection of children's image-making practices and comics, I will now focus on the media memories attached to children's comics reading, especially in the North American context.

It's a Bird . . . and Essex County: Growing up with Superhero Comics

It's a Bird . . . interweaves personal engagement through the autofictional protagonist with the superhero figure. Tellingly enough, the comic begins with a childhood memory, one of the protagonist and his brother's rare moments of comics reading. The two brothers initially quarrel over holding the comic, which emphasizes the precious materiality of the book for the young readers, the desire for ownership and control over comics reading (Kristiansen and Seagle 2004, 5). The materiality and magic of the comic book are further accentuated by the book's brightness, which contrasts with the bland colors of the hospital scene (5–6). And while neither of the two brothers read many comics during their childhood, Steve read vociferously and "*consumed* stories" (8), enacting the connection between the figure of the child and imagination already seen above. As historian Carolyn Steedman has shown, the child became a figuration of interiority from the end of the eighteenth century onward and into the twentieth century when the concept was theorized by Freud under "another name as 'the unconscious,' or 'the unconscious mind'" (1995, 4). "The idea of the child," Steedman continues, "provided the largest number of people living in the recent past of Western societies with the means of thinking about and creating a self: something grasped and understood: a shape, moving in the body . . . something *inside*: an interiority" (20).

In contrast to the previous two comics, the relationship between children and adolescents and comics in It's a Bird . . . is more prominent and closely tied to the figure of the superhero. For Cremins, "the tropes and obsessions of even the most sophisticated, experimental comic narratives still draw on a lineage which, if mapped, will bring the curious reader back to the characters present at the inception of the form, heroes like Superman and

Batman, those apocalyptic pulp fantasies of the Great Depression" (2013, 303). Even though they appear only briefly, the children in *It's a Bird* . . . are always associated with comics, and, of course, Superman, who in many ways embodies the media memory of American comics. The actual story quickly establishes a link with childhood and the child comics reader who is "baby-sat by half a *Superman* comic" (Kristiansen and Seagle 2004, 19). Even though he is unable to read, Steve remains fascinated by the red S and the story he constructs through the pictures.

It's a Bird . . . (superficially) breaks down the comics form, as well as the thought processes of a writer brainstorming for a new comic book idea while grappling with the possibility of his succumbing, like his grandmother, to Huntington's disease, which becomes Steve's kryptonite in this interweaving of personal and fictional stories that are under development. Steve's girlfriend Lisa's reference to the Spin Doctors' song, "Jimmy Olsen's Blues" (Kristiansen and Seagle 2004, 35) suggests a generational shift from identifying with Superman to identifying with Jimmy Olsen, the far more ordinary, unimpressive photographer for the *Daily Planet*. The song paints Olsen as a geeky, loser type who is most likely to spend his evenings alone, reading Shakespeare in his low-rent downtown apartment. The boy fan of Superman has turned into a resentful, lonely youth who does not shy away from literary classics (that were once themselves popular entertainment). This is exactly what has happened to Steve, who finds himself unable to believe in Superman in the beginning but who eventually realizes the character's universal significance.

The deconstruction of Superman and his relationship to this world and its readers in *It's a Bird* . . . simulates the processes of creation by emphasizing the interaction between subjectivities (in this case, that of the writer) and popular culture memories. This interaction is materialized by the presence of the hand. The hand is both a creative part of the body and one that establishes emotional bonds. A sign of human connection that extends beyond the comic book to touch the reader, the hand is significant, especially in the world of comic books, where exaggeration and expressionism are the norm and the focus on the unabashedly intimate and the personal was limited before the appearance of graphic novels and the confessional comics popularized by underground publications from the 1960s onward. Particularly noteworthy for the affective import of media memories surrounding children and comics is the emphasis on the hands holding the comic: from the children's hands as they bicker over the only comic book their father could find in the hospital store (Kristiansen and Seagle 2004, 3), to the moment when they decide to hold the comic together (6), to Steve's own hands (35).

It's a Bird . . . ends on a note of affirming the role of the imagination over logic and rationality, much like *What It Is* and *Combat ordinaire*: As two children (who are identical to the child versions of Steve and his brother) try to decide whether it's a bird or a plane they see in the sky, Steve suggests they can see Superman if they really want to (Kristiansen and Seagle 2004, 124). This plays on the link between (childlike) imagination and creativity. But the child is not only linked to playful creativity; it also evokes the specter of growing up and of grown-ups. It harbors, as Steedman's notion of interiority suggests, the origins of the adult it will turn into.

When Steve obsesses about Huntington's disease and the Superman project his editor forces on him, the first "s" in Huntington's becomes the "s" symbolizing Superman (Kristiansen and Seagle 2004, 104)—these visual connections trace a train of thought linking mortality with the superhero, the presumed childhood distance from mortality, and the adult realization thereof. Childhood and death similarly collide in *Essex County*, which opens with Lester's mother's death. Personal battles and fictional, even impossible Superman stories, become one, thereby emphasizing the personal value of those stories for individual readers and other comics artists. *Tales from the Farm*, the first book in Jeff Lemire's *Essex County*, captures the role of superhero comic books as both a channel of escapism for young, troubled children and the kind of reading that "normal" adults disparage. Besides Lester, the story's young protagonist (who is a comics artist and reader), the only other avid or once-avid reader of comics is Jimmy Lebeuf, Lester's unacknowledged father, as confirmed later in *Essex County*, a promising ice hockey player whose career ended after a head injury.

Through including rough comics drawings on notebook sheets, the stories in *Essex County* merge with Lester's comics (Lemire 2009, 58–64, 435–436). Unsurprisingly, while the first one contains a traditional, straightforward superhero versus supervillain battle, the second comic, made by a slightly older Lester, begins with a battle but ends in a personal trauma: the sudden loss of the hero's father, after which the hero takes his father's Captain Canada costume and tailors it to his size. Once again, personal and collective memories are intertwined with personal elements affecting the fictional (we read the second comic just before Lester finds out that Jimmy Lebeuf is his father), and the fictional affecting the personal (most prominently through Lester's taking recourse to making comics and occasionally living in a comics-inspired alternative world) to help the young protagonist come to terms with reality.

Children and Comics:
Legitimation Hauntings and Entanglements

Comics scholar Christopher Pizzino makes a case for comics as a "traumatized medium" (2016, 17). This trauma is expressed by "autoclastic" or self-breaking images, and is, thus, to be distinguished from other traumas through the very fact that it is expressed (71). While speaking of a trauma in this context seems farfetched, as Pizzino himself suggests, it is more fruitful to consider the role of troubled memories of comics, stemming from the marginal, low cultural standing of the medium, which is a recurrent reference in comics and is one of the factors contributing to the effectiveness of the self-conscious visual vocabulary in *Maus* (Pizzino 2017). These associations are both blatant and subtle, underlying the technique of drawing, drawing style, but also the more abstract components of the story. Following Pizzino's autoclastic train of thought, it is possible to consider comics as a haunted medium, channeling media memories through their distinctive, hybrid idiom that tap into the issues of "cultural power and prestige" (2017). Nowhere is this more evident than in the presence of children in graphic novels. The child in graphic novels, the preferred site of comics legitimation, is multifaceted in spite of its relatively unvarying manifestations in the works discussed here, where the figure is essentially a conglomerate of interiority and pastness. It evokes the childish side of comics, interrogates and even repurposes the sometimes suppressed, embarrassing facets of comics (Worden 2015).

In the guise of a conclusion, I would like to turn to Peter Blake's 1954 painting *Children Reading Comics* to sum up the media memories stuck to child figures (Fig. 3). Based on a family photograph (Grunenberg and Sillars 2007, 19), the painting shows the artist's younger self and his sister sitting on a bench reading (or displaying), not books, but *Eagle*, the British comics periodical launched in 1950. The iconic image of the (middle-class) reading child is repositioned by these working-class children: moved out of the confines of the domestic space and, given the big, ephemeral, richly illustrated and advertisement-laden comics magazine, into the fragmented, quick entertainment that characterizes modern mass culture. The intimacy of home is traded for the public space of the park. This is the first of many "ticks" or aspects of the drawing that challenge assumptions. Another tick is the monumentality of the children: The brother and sister dominate the painting and are even too big to be fully contained by it. Such disregard of proportions evokes the so-called primitive and naive strains of modernist art. The young Blake looks uncomfortable and somewhat dissatisfied, probably because he has been given the black-and-white pages that have more advertisements than comics, while his sister holds on to the brightly colored front page. His sister wears an eye patch that, despite being a medical device, evokes childish role playing or pretending. It could also explain why she got to hold the cover page. Given that the *Eagle* catered to boys rather than girls (as confirmed by the Mecano ad), the painting challenges the gendering of comics readership. The two children consequently queer the situation. I use queer here in the sense of "un sujet qui bouge" (a subject that moves), that resists being pinned down and raises questions (Baetens 2014, 177). These children, like the children in the graphic novels discussed here, combine memories, a personal one that activates a broad range of collective memories and that is channeled through media memories. They have an autobiographical hold as well as a sociohistorical one, invoking, simultaneously, the individual child that the artist once was and the shared image of the child. The child in comics goes off on many tangents.

Figure 3: Peter Blake, *Children Reading Comics*, 1954. From the collection of Tullie House Museum, Carlisle, UK. ©SABAM Belgium 2019. Reprinted with permission.

In addition to the intimate, holdable size of the painting (36.7 cm x 41.7 cm), perhaps the most noteworthy element is the way the children hold on to the periodical and the space accorded to the comics: The two hands holding the papers put the comics on display for the viewer. The pages merge with the children's bodies and dominate them. This image embodies the close connections between children and comics that I have tried to tease out and interweave in this chapter. Finally, the painting is intermedial on multiple counts: Based on a photograph, the painting incorporates the mass medium of comics. Another version of *Children Reading Comics* painted two years later replaces the public space with a dingy lounge with a television in the background. The strokes here are thicker, savage in their distortion of reality. The image on the television screen is blurred and even the children's faces are almost unrecognizable. The comics pages, taking up almost two-thirds of the painting, are the most dominant and lucid element. Once again, the children are not reading but displaying their comics in a manner that makes the comics substitutes for their bodies.

In drawing out connections with Warburg's and Sutton's memory projects, I try to show how comics remember and layer their stories, through (a version of) their own history but also through mining a rich source of images and techniques from a wide range of media. Media memories help point toward the media historical layers guiding these intermedial exchanges. They also help trace the affective bearings of such interactions. The children's drawings in the comics discussed above are instances of intermediality that simultaneously provoke a dialogue of memories and legitimation stories. Perhaps that is what the figure of the child shows best in comics: the impossibility of separating the child, its intermedial essence as a mediator between art worlds and comics worlds, its mnemonic load that combines the personal and the collective. As Steedman suggests, it channels the formation of modern self-consciousness, doing so in a particularly affective way: "The figure of the child, released from the many texts that gave birth to it, helped shape feelings, and structure feeling into thought" (1995, 19). As already suggested by the comics examined above, childish presences capture the struggle of canonical hierarchy, but also of expression, and hence, of establishing emotional, affective, and consequently powerful connections.

The multiple strands connecting children and comics stretch across media and cultural productions. While it might be impossible to disentangle all of these strands, especially in the scope of one book chapter, media memories help trace the trajectories and uncover the workings of individual strands.

This chapter is an outcome of the COMICS project funded by the European Research Council (ERC) under the European Union's Horizon 2020 research and innovation program (grant agreement no. 758502).

Endnotes

1. Exceptions do exist: The title page of *Planter les clous* (literally: *Nailing*) includes a drawing by Larcenet's daughter of her family and herself. This is one of the rare instances in which a real child's presence is asserted. Dominique Goblet's *Chronographie* (2010), drawn with her daughter Nikita Fossoul, is perhaps the strongest example of an artist's collaboration with their child: The book collects portraits Goblet and Fossoul drew of each other over a period of ten years (see Erwin Dejasse's Chapter Ten in this collection).

Works Cited

AHMED, Maaheen. 2019. "Instrumentalising Media Memories: The Second World War According to *Achtung Zelig!*" *European Comic Art* 12 (1): 1–20.

AHMED, Sara. 2004. *The Cultural Politics of Emotion*. Edinburgh: Edinburgh University Press.

ASSMANN, Aleida. 2011. *Cultural Memory and Western Civilization: Functions, Media, Archives*. Cambridge: Cambridge University Press.

B., David. 2011. *L'Ascension du Haut Mal*. Paris: L'Association.

BAETENS, Jan. 2008. "Of Graphic Novels and Minor Cultures: The Fréon Collective." *Yale French Studies* 114: 95–115.

———. 2014. "Dominique Goblet: écrire au féminin ?" *Interférences littéraires/ Litteraire interferenties* 14 (October): 163–77.

BAETENS, Jan, and Hugo FREY. 2014. *The Graphic Novel: An Introduction*. Cambridge: Cambridge University Press.

BARRY, Lynda. 2009. *What It Is*. London: Jonathan Cape.

BURMAN, Erica. 2019. "Found Childhood as a Practice of Child as Method." *Children's Geographies*, January 14, 2019. DOI: 10.1080/14733285.2019.1566518.

CAMDEN, Vera. 2019. "'Cartoonish Lumps': The Surface Appel of Alison Bechdel's *Are You My Mother?*" *Journal of Graphic Novels and Comics* 9 (1): 93–111.

CHUTE, Hillary. 2011. "Materializing Memory: Lynda Barry's *One Hundred Demons*." *Graphic Subjects: Critical Essays on Autobiography and Graphic Novels*, edited by Michael Chaney, 282–309. Madison: University of Wisconsin Press.

CREMINS, Brian. 2013. "Bodies, Transfigurations and Bloodlust in Edie Fake's Graphic Novel, *Gaylord Phoenix*." *Journal of Medical Humanities* 34 (2): 301–13.

———. 2016. *Captain Marvel and the Art of Nostalgia*. Jackson: University Press of Mississippi.

CRUCIFIX, Benoît, and Pedro MOURA. 2016. "Bertroyas dans la jungle. Bande dessinée et édition sauvage." *Mémoires du Livre* 8, no. 1.

DIDI-HUBERMAN, Georges. 2003. "Dialektik des Monstrums: Aby Warburg and the Symptom Paradigm." *Art History* 24 no. 5 (December): 621–45.

FOSS, Chris, Jonathan GRAY, and Zack WHALEN, eds. 2016. *Disability in Comic Books and Graphic Narratives*. Basingstoke, Hampshire: Palgrave.

GARLAND-THOMPSON, Rosemarie. 2016. "Foreword." In *Disability in Comic Books and Graphic Narratives*, edited by Foss, Chris, Jonathan Gray, and Zack Whalen, x–xiiv. Basingstoke, Hampshire: Palgrave.

GIBBS, Alain. 2014. *Contemporary American Trauma Narratives*. Edinburgh: Edinburgh University Press.

GOBLET, Dominique. 2014. *Faire semblant c'est mentir*. Paris: L'Association.

GORDON, Ian. 2019. "Bildungsromane and Graphic Narratives." In *A History of the Bildungsroman*, edited. by Sarah Graham, 267–82. Cambridge: Cambridge University Press.

GRUNENBERG, Christoph, and Laurence SILLARS. 2007. *Peter Blake: A Retrospective*. London: Tate.

HATFIELD, Charles. 2006–2007. "Comics and Childhood." *ImageText* 3, no. 3. imagetext.english.ufl.edu/archives/v3_3/introduction.shtml.

HOLLINDALE, Peter. 1997. *Signs of Childness in Children's Books*. Stroud, UK: Thimble Press.

HORSMAN, Yasco. 2013. "Infancy of Art: Comics, Childhood and Picture Books." *Journal of Graphic Novels and Comics* 5 (3): 323–35.

KRISTIANSEN, Teddy, and Steven T. SEAGLE. 2004. *It's a Bird . . . .* New York: Vertigo.

KUNZLE, David. 2019. *Cham: The Best Comic Strips and Graphic Novelettes*. Jackson: University Press of Mississippi.

LARCENET, Manu. 2008. *Combat ordinaire 4: Planter des clous*. Paris: Dargaud.

LEMIRE, Jeff. 2009. *Essex County*. Atlanta: Topshelf.

MATSUDA, Matt K. 1996. *The Memory of the Modern*. New York: Oxford University Press.

McKINNEY, Mark. 2013. *Redrawing French Empire in Comics*. Columbus: The Ohio State University Press.

MEESTERS, Gert. 2010. "Les significations du style graphique." *Textyles* 36–37: 215–33.

NODELMAN, Perry. 2008. *The Hidden Adult: Defining Children's Literature.* Baltimore, MD: John Hopkins University Press.

PIZZINO, Christopher. 2016. *Arresting Development: Comics at the Boundaries of Literature.* Austin: University of Texas Press.

———. 2017. "Comics as Trauma: A Postmortem and a New Inquiry." *ImageText* 9 (1). imagetext.english.ufl.edu/archives/v9_1/pizzino/.

RAMPLEY, Matthew. 1999. "Archives of Memory: Walter Benjamin's *Arcades Project* and Aby Warburg's *Mnemosyne Atlas.*" In *The Optic of Walter Benjamin*, edited by Alex Coles, 94–117. London: Black Dog Publishing.

ROEDER, Katherine. 2014. *Wide Awake in Slumberland: Fantasy, Mass Culture and Modernism in the Art of Winsor McCay.* Jackson: University Press of Mississippi.

ROTH, Michael. 2011. *Memory, Trauma and History: Essays on Living with the Past.* New York: Columbia University Press.

SMOLDEREN, Thierry. 2014. *The Origins of Comics: From William Hogarth to Winsor McCay.* Translated by Bart Beaty and Nick Nguyen. Jackson: University Press of Mississippi.

STEEDMAN, Carolyn. 1995. *Strange Dislocations: Childhood and the Idea of Human Interiority, 1780–1930.* Cambridge, MA: Harvard University Press.

SUTTON, John. 2004. "Porous memories and the cognitive life of things." In *Prefiguring Cyberculture: An Intellectual History*, edited by Darren Tofts, Annemarie Johnson, and Alessio Cavallero, 130–41. Cambridge, MA: MIT Press.

WORDEN, Daniel. 2015. "The Shameful Art: *McSweeney's Quarterly Concern*, Comics and the Politics of Affect." *Modern Fiction Studies* 52 (4): 891–17.

PART FOUR
Comics, Cultural Capital, and the Artistic Tradition

CHAPTER TEN:
Art Brut and Alternative Comics: Reciprocal Sympathies

Erwin Dejasse

> *"The child is innocence and forgetting, a new beginning,*
> *a game, a self-rolling wheel, a first movement, a sacred Yes."*
> —Friedrich Nietzsche

"J'ai toujours aimé l'art brut, ça part des tripes,
tout comme mon travail."
("I've always loved Art Brut, it comes from the gut,
just like my own work.")
    —Dominique Goblet (Snoekx 2019)

"Au moment où j'ai rencontré les gens de l'art brut . . . ça m'a filé la pêche et
ça m'a changé un petit peu les pendules dans ma tête."
("When I met the Art Brut people . . . it gave me energy and it reset the
clock in my head a little bit.")
    —Pakito Bolino (Tran 1999)

"Je ne plaisante pas . . . lorsque je dis être soufflé par
le dessin d'enfant, l'Art dit Brut, singulier, ou tout tracé élémentaire jeté
avec force, conviction et spontanéité."
("I'm not kidding . . . when I say I'm blown away by children's drawings, the
so-called Art Brut, Art Singulier, or any elementary tracing executed with
force, conviction, and spontaneity.")
    —Olivier Josso Hamel (Crucifix 2015, 26)

These three testimonies coming from major figures of alternative
comics, active from the origins of the movement, are indicative of
their obvious interest—expressed within their creations—in works that are
commonly brought together under the terms of *Art Brut* and "Outsider Art."

At the time of writing, this is a phenomenon that remains diffuse but which is nonetheless revealing of the aspirations that drive the actors of alternative publishing. Among these, more than anyone else, Jean-Christophe Menu, cofounder of the publishing house L'Association, has been working to formulate a discourse that would distinguish the identity and issues of alternative comics. Although Menu is not the sole and undisputed spokesperson for this movement, his contribution remains unparalleled in the French-speaking field, as an *in vivo* testimony of his triple practice as author, editor, and critic. Furthermore, he has written a few pages devoted to *Art Brut* and Outsider Art, which I will consider in light of his own creations, as well as the other comics works that he helped to put out as a publisher—all of which form a whole that he describes as a *meta-work* (2008, 93). Therefore, in this chapter, I will primary consider the achievements published by L'Association that were designed during the period spanning from 1990 to 2011, when Menu was presiding over its editorial structure. I will aim to highlight a certain number of artistic sympathies or correlations between such alternative comics publications and *Art Brut* or Outsider Art by focusing more particularly on the following works: *Gnognottes* from Jean-Christophe Menu himself (1999) and three volumes by the authors quoted in my epigraph, respectively *Spermanga* by Pakito Bolino (2009), *Chronographie* by Dominique Goblet, produced jointly with her daughter Nikita Fossoul (2010), and *Au travail* (volume 1) by Olivier Josso Hamel (2012).[1]

However, before discussing the connections that can be drawn between these two creative fields, it is necessary to clarify certain terms. Forged by the painter, writer, and collector Jean Dubuffet, the notion of *Art Brut* is extremely difficult to pinpoint because it seems so fluctuating. Céline Delavaux's study of Dubuffet's texts on the matter proposed a most convincing hypothesis: *Art Brut* is not strictly speaking an artistic category but the expression of the artistic ideal of Dubuffet. While its most often quoted definition describes *Art Brut* as "des ouvrages exécutés par des personnes indemnes de culture artistique" ("works produced by persons unscathed by artistic culture") (Dubuffet 1967a, 201–2), the author constantly rethought his subject matter as his thinking and his perception evolved. The success of this notion has led to its reappropriation by new actors in the field who have often considered it in a broader sense, while competing designations such as *Folk Art*, *Art Singulier* or *Self-Taught Art* have also emerged. The most frequently used equivalent term is "Outsider Art." Coined by British art historian Roger Cardinal, Outsider Art originally was only an English equivalent to *Art Brut*. Nevertheless, this term is used today to describe a group of artworks that includes roughly all the creations that have no place or voice in the usual artistic institutions (museums, galleries, specialized magazines, etc.). However, the matter became even more complex from the moment these artistic institutions became more open and began to give more and more credence to these types of works. Attempting to strictly delimit any specific set of works can only lead to an impasse. Therefore, for lack of a better term, I will use in the remainder of this essay the expression *Art Brut and Outsider Art movement* to designate an artistic field whose contours will necessarily remain imprecise.

As I have already shown in a previous essay ("Bande dessinée, art brut et dissidence," 2010), a number of Art Brut and Outsider Art works reactivated the narrative function of visual art, which the twentieth century had largely neglected. During this period indeed, many creators widely broke with the primacy of representation that had governed graphic and pictorial creation since the Renaissance in favor of formal research—which led in particular to abstraction—and conceptual approaches. Conversely, *Art Brut* and Outsider Art did not have the same disdain for telling stories, often breaking the *taboo of narrative* that pervaded what was commonly referred to as *contemporary* or *modernist art*, as defined by Clement Greenberg (1961). On the other hand, many of these works also coalesce within the same platform a heterogeneous set of signs. They often bring together texts and images—as in most comics—but also, sometimes, elements as diverse as collages, pictograms, musical notes, and imaginary alphabets, ranging from visible to readable. Admittedly, in the twentieth and twenty-first centuries, there are numerous poems or novels that make use of graphic elements and paintings embellished with texts, but to a much lesser extent than in the Art Brut and Outsider Art movement. In spite of more or less frequent "overflows" and overlaps, the traditional literary and pictorial categories continue to govern artistic practices. Voluntarily or not, Outsider artists free themselves from these dominant practices and reuse devices at work in the field of comics.

"Numerous and Troubling" Points in Common with Comics

In 2006, in the second issue of *L'Éprouvette*, the short-lived critical magazine that he co-founded one year earlier, Jean-Christophe Menu wrote a praiseful article about Charlotte Salomon (1917–1943), a Jewish painter who died in Auschwitz and whom he discovered through an exhibition held at the Museum of Jewish Art and History in Paris. During the last months of her life, Salomon completed a series of 871 drawings in a single volume entitled *Leben? Oder Theater? (Life? Or Theatre?)*. If Menu is enthusiastic about its artistic qualities, he also comments on the similarities between Salomon's work

and comics: "Les points communs avec la Bande Dessinée, telle que nous
la défendons, sont nombreux et troublants" ("The points in common with
comics, as we conceive of them, are numerous and troubling") (2006,
129). Upon reading *Leben? Oder Theater?*, one may indeed conclude that
it brings together the quintessence of Menu's aspirations. He describes it
as a "work of incomparable richness," which would be the most complete
incarnation of the comics medium—although the author obviously never
thought of it as such.

Menu emphasizes from the outset that Charlotte Salomon's creation
is an autobiography, linking it with a trend that has been at the core of
alternative comics and that largely contributed to forging the identity
of L'Association. Besides the highly acclaimed *L'Ascension du Haut-Mal*
(*Epileptic*) by David B. or *Persépolis* by Marjane Satrapi, Menu has published several dozens of autobiographical works, including *Au travail* by
Olivier Josso Hamel, in which the author tries to reconstruct his memory
while questioning his childish emotions, especially through the prism of
the "classics" of the French-speaking comics that he discovered at a very
young age. *Chronographie* by Dominique Goblet and Nikita Fossoul is also
connected to this current. The book shows a succession of double portraits—
the mother draws her daughter and vice versa—made over a period of ten
years. Although it does not describe any facts, it conveys the evolution of an
emotional and affective web. Jean-Christophe Menu has also created numerous comics in which he is the central character. The short stories gathered in
Gnognottes offer an extremely wide range of such comics. In these, he describes
his childhood memories, recounts his most delirious dreams, portrays himself
as an unlikely messiah in a story imbued with surrealism, and constructs an
equally improbable avatar in the person of Plumaga Plupürrh (a creature with
a skull covered with strange tentacles and dressed as the cartoonist, always
wearing the same striped sweater). Finally, the book shows many episodes
featuring the Mune—"La Lune de Menu" ("The Moon of Menu") (1999,
36)—a planet shaped like a feminine posterior contrasting with the black sky
of a desert landscape, who engages in endless conflictual dialogues with the
author. In his later iterations, this universe will continue to grow and expand
organically, building an *individual mythology*.

Beyond autobiography in the strict sense of the word, the catalog of
L'Association presents a wide range of different ways of looking at self-representation. These cover a range of related territories such as autofiction or
fantasized autobiography. Such approaches are ubiquitous in the Art Brut and
Outsider Art movement, where the artists' own personal experiences are often

the main topic of their works, even if they freely reinterpret them. Although Charlotte Salomon gives her characters substitute identities in *Leben? Oder Theater?*, Menu claims that this work is a "total" autobiography (2006, 133). The approach of Dominique Théate—with whom Dominique Goblet also wrote comics[2]—appears quite different. His captioned drawings form a monumental diary in which he evokes his daily life (describing his father-in-law who is a truck driver, the theater plays or the hippotherapy sessions offered at the center for people with mental disabilities that he is attending) (Fig. 1). With an ironic distance, he also imagines that he is a golden boy displaying all the outward signs of economic success, dressed in an elegant suit and driving a luxurious BMW car. Théate has built up a universe of recurring characters, places, and situations that he recombines infinitely to constitute, as Menu, an *individual mythology*.

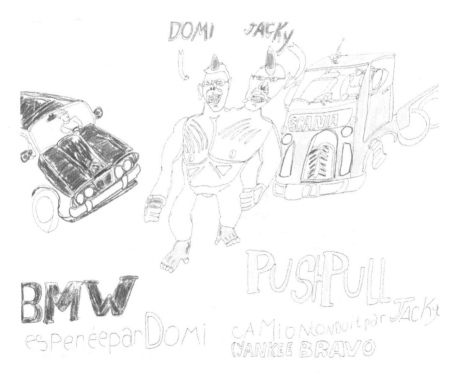

Figure 1: Dominique Théate, untitled, 2017,
pencil on paper, 50 cm x 65 cm, coll. La "S" Grand Atelier.

In *Plates-bandes*, Jean-Christophe Menu writes that the creation of L'Association was the brainchild of a group of authors who had found that the editorial landscape of the late 1980s was incompatible with their "désir d'utiliser la Bande Dessinée comme moyen d'expression au sens absolu du terme (disons de *nécessité* intérieure plus que d'*aptitudes* extérieures)" ("desire to use comics as a means of expression in the absolute sense of the term (let's say of inner *necessity* more than exterior *aptitudes*)") (2005, 25). In view of the works that make up the catalog of L'Association, we can hypothesize that a comic strip born of *inner necessity* would be a work resulting from an imperative need for expression, even if it were only reaching a limited audience; a creation that involves a personal investment that can go as far as unveiled intimacy, the expression of the author's anxieties, or even trauma. On the tenth page of *Au Travail*, Olivier Josso Hamel writes:

> Orphelin de père depuis peu, j'identifie mal la perte que je vis. Agité par des émotions indéfinies, je piste mon trouble au travers des miroirs qui s'offrent à moi. Dans cette entreprise de reconnaissance, la muette puissance d'évocation n'est pas le moindre mérite des cases qui m'aspirent . . .
>
> (Having recently lost my father, I misidentify the loss I'm experiencing. Agitated by undefined emotions, I track my trouble through the mirrors that offer themselves to me. In this endeavor of recognition, the mute power of evocation is not the least merit of the panels that suck me in . . .) (2012, 10)

The previous pages—in which the author describes the emotions that overwhelmed him when he discovered *Tintin, Spirou, Lucky Luke,* or *Astérix*—suddenly take on a special resonance when they are overcome by the loss of the father and the need to grieve for him. Reactivating memory in such a way can hardly be conceived without a personal investment by the author. As he describes it himself, this creation responds to a wider motivation than the sole desire to deal with a particular comics subject:

> *Au Travail* est bien le fruit d'une réelle nécessité, et à plus d'un titre. À mes yeux, ce projet représente un tournant salutaire dans mon parcours: la quête active d'un gain d'énergie et de liberté, au sens humain comme artistique. Depuis le début, ma pratique de l'autobiographie a toujours répondu au besoin impérieux d'exprimer la vie intérieure.

(*Au Travail* is indeed the fruit of a real necessity, and in more ways than one. In my opinion, this project represents a salutary turning point in my career: the active search for a gain of energy and freedom, in the human and artistic sense of the word. Since the beginning, my practice of autobiography has always responded to the compelling need to express inner life.) (2012)

To my knowledge, the idea of *inner necessity* has never been expressed in these particular terms by Dubuffet. Nevertheless, it runs through all his writings. Indeed, he speaks of "manifestations directes et immédiates du feu intérieur de la vie" ("direct and immediate manifestations from the inner fire of life") and of artistic creations regarded as "libération des vraies voix profondes intérieures" ("liberation of true inner deep voices") (1967a, 214, 222). The Art Brut creations—some of which were not even designed to be seen by a public, except by the artist himself—were often made to escape a confinement, to remedy a state of extreme suffering or to exorcise a drama. Dominique Théate started drawing after a very serious motorcycle accident that caused a cerebral palsy. He therefore invented a double who could live the existence that life's circumstances did not allow him to access. *Leben? Oder Theater?*, which Menu says is "une des œuvres autobiographiques les plus charnellement ancrées dans la vie qui soient" ("one of the most carnally entrenched autobiographical works") (2006, 139), is also a matter of a fundamental, imperious *inner necessity*. Charlotte Salomon knew she was threatened with deportation. She was also facing a dozen suicides in her family—including her mother's and her grandmother's—that seemed to prompt her to kill herself as well. Menu quotes from the catalog of the exhibition at the Museum of Jewish Art and History in Paris: "[elle] se vit donc placée devant ce choix: mettre fin à ses jours ou bien entreprendre quelque chose de vraiment fou et singulier" ("[she] was thus faced with a choice: to end her life or to undertake something really crazy and peculiar") (130).

The Explosive Richness of an Expanding Cultural Constellation

In the same essay, Menu explains that Charlotte Salomon "se retrouve face à elle-même, à inventer un langage, son propre langage, qui va lui permettre de tout mettre dans cet ouvrage, qui ne ressemble à rien" ("is face to face with herself, inventing a language, her own language, which will allow her to put everything in this work, which looks like nothing else") (2006, 130). Menu's discourse is part of a double and apparently contradictory argument that

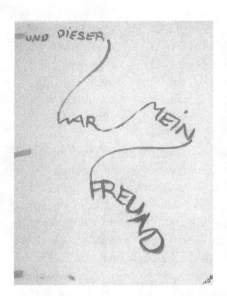 

Figure 2 (a & b): Charlotte Salomon, *Leben? Oder Theater?* p. 19, 1940–1942,
gouache on paper (including texts painted on tracing paper), 32.5 × 25 cm.
Collection Jewish Historical Museum, Amsterdam
© Charlotte Salomon Foundation

asserts the unclassifiable character of Salomon's work while at the same time
claiming that it belongs to the realm of comics. Yet, its links to the medium
are not necessarily obvious when viewed through normative definitions. The
textual elements, directly integrated into the images, are often transcriptions
of dialogue; however, they are never inscribed within speech balloons. Every
page is a bleeding-edge composition that can be grasped as an autonomous
image. The way in which Charlotte Salomon combines verbal signs and images is idiosyncratic. Among other configurations, she draws music notes to
indicate the tunes in which the words spoken by the characters are hummed,
and she paints texts on tracing paper that "overlay" on the next page (Fig. 2).

In spite of its resolutely singular character, there seems to be a consensus
that *Leben? Oder Theater?* belongs to the field of comics. After Menu, Paul
Gravett included it in his guide *1001 Comics You Must Read Before You Die*
in 2011. Four years later, the French art publisher Le Tripode published a
luxurious edition as close as possible to the original format, with a descriptive
blurb stating unequivocally that the work is a graphic novel. This late assimilation into the comics corpus keeps up with the times; the work of Charlotte
Salomon would probably not have generated the same interest twenty years

earlier, at least in the context of its reception in France. The 1990s marked the end of a long period when the practice of comics tended to be confused with the the use of *prototypical devices*. By this, I mean a set of visual-narrative devices that characterize the overwhelming majority of productions to the point of being perceived as the norm for the medium. These conventional configurations establish what the average reader understands as the "standard" comics format: They display straight-lined frames juxtaposed to form strips that are laid on top of each other; they contain mostly drawings with texts placed inside balloons; the panels are fragments of space-time that have to be read in a fixed sequence; they are apprehended one after the other in order to follow the evolution of a character or a group of characters. The preeminence of these *prototypical devices* may give the impression of a formally stable medium and, therefore, encourage the development of essentialist definitions, capable of subsuming all of its incarnations.

In *Gnognottes*, one can read a page originally published in *Les Cahiers de la bande dessinée*. It was originally intended to support the report of the symposium *Bande Dessinée, récit et modernité* held at Cerisy-la-Salle in 1987, a venue in which Jean Ricardou often advocated for anti-narration throughout the 1970s and 1980s (1999, 14). Menu depicts a controller of the "specificity brigade" requiring that a character in tears provide, among other proofs of identity, a "*certifikat* de spécificité" ("*certifikat* of specificity"), a "permis de béder" ("license to practice comics"), and an "autorisation de phylactériser" ("authorization to write speech balloons"). This page seems to mock the debate on the specificity (or specificities) of the medium that kindled numerous critical and analytical discourses during the period when the Cerisy symposium took place.[3]

Indeed, L'Association—and more broadly all the alternative publishing structures—has been driven since its inception by a quest for new *affordances* of comics. Driven by a dynamic of renewal of its practices, it has been rethinking its subjects, as well as its aesthetics and narrative structures; this implies de facto an attempt to move beyond the prototypical devices to which I previously referred (an approach that had already been initiated by comic strips from the counter-culture since the mid-1960s). It is fueled by an emancipatory dynamic aiming to take the medium out of its essentialization by no longer considering comics as a language defined by its specificities, but by adopting instead an approach that Éric Maigret and Matteo Stefanelli describe as "constructivist," which "refuse la limitation de la bande dessinée et propose une ouverture du champ des possibles . . . croyant en la diversification et en la richesse explosive d'une constellation culturelle en expansion" ("refuses the limitation of comics and offers to open up the field of possibilities . . . believing in diversification and in the explosive richness of an expanding cultural constellation") (2012, 9).

In this regard, *Chronographie* by Nikita Fossoul and Dominique Goblet is a work that largely escapes narrow definitions. This succession of double portraits is actually even further away from the prototypical devices of comics than *Leben? Oder Theater?* Despite its singularity, it nevertheless presents some written dialogues associated with drawings in order to produce a narrative, in the strongest sense of the term. The radicalism of *Chronographie* is indicative of the degree of openness that L'Association allows in terms of narrative construction. If the visual-narrative devices that characterize *Au travail* may seem less *eccentric*, the work is nonetheless far removed from the dominant uses. Olivier Josso Hamel's graphic avatar takes multiple forms, passing without transition from adulthood to childhood, turning into an octopus or a spider screwed onto an anthropomorphic body. He renounces an objectifying representation of the diegetic universe, preferring to visually translate the wandering of his thoughts into a heterogeneous whole of images, including his own children's drawings and redrawn excerpts of the comics that permeated his early years. The author attempts to "pick up the pieces" of his childhood and opts for a narrative construction that complies with the always fragmentary nature of human memory.

The issue of fragments in comics is a matter that Jean-Christophe Menu actually addresses in his Visual Arts doctoral thesis entitled *La Bande dessinée et son Double* (*Comics and their Double*), published by L'Association in 2011. Both in his own work as a comic artist and in his *meta-work* as an editor, one of his distinguishing achievements was to produce and publish creations largely freed from plot-based schemes. He also championed the state of incompleteness:

> Mon postulat à propos des projets inachevés a parfois du mal à être compris: ces faux départs, ces tentatives avortées, font pour moi part de mon "œuvre" au même titre que les récits dûment poussés à leur terme. Ils contiennent autant de richesse et de potentialités que les travaux finis, sinon plus du fait de leur mystère.

> (My assumption about unfinished projects is sometimes hard to understand: these false starts, these aborted attempts, are for me part of my "work," to the same extent as the stories that are duly pushed to their conclusion. They contain as much richness and potentiality as the finished work, if not more because of their mystery.) (2011, 327)

Gnognottes perfectly illustrates this statement. In the notes that conclude the volume, Menu writes: "There are among my works 15 or 20 book projects that have not been made for x reasons, and 'never mind the bollocks,' I think in the end that these GNOGNOTTES look much more like me (16)" (1999, 126). Although publishing unfinished works is quite a common practice in the literary field, comics publishers, for their part, never considered it useful before the rise of alternative outlets—with the notable exception of *Tintin et l'Alph-Art* whose publication was justified only because of Hergé's unique status. By contrast, a state of incompleteness characterizes numerous graphic narratives from the Art Brut and Outsider Art movement, in which "incomplete" works are likely to be even more numerous than "finished" ones. This can be explained by the fact that many of these works were created anonymously without the assistance of a "mediator" who would ensure their preservation and dissemination, which often results instead in the dispersion of the work and its partial loss. Fragments can also be inherent elements of the creator's poetics. Such is the case of Dominique Théate, already mentioned above, or of the Dutch artist Wouter Coumou,[4] whose drawings are quickly

Figure 3: Wouter Coumou, untitled, around 2000,
felt pen on paper, 21 cm x 29.6 cm. Coll. Trink Hall Museum, Liège.

sketched with a ballpoint pen; most of them show speech balloons and are often divided into panels (Fig. 3). His work is akin to a logbook that describes the daily life of his family yet without abiding by an exact transcription of the facts; for instance, his parents are still depicted as a couple, whereas in real life they have been separated for a long time. Both quite prolific, Théate and Coumou have made several hundred works that are not meant to be read and looked at in a specific order; their approach consists of making each drawing a new version of a fictional universe in perpetual expansion.

These artists deviate from the principle that a worthy narrative has a beginning and an end. Furthermore, their stories often are nearly unintelligible. The author is frequently the only person capable of explaining what is being told—assuming that he or she has the desire or the actual ability to express it orally. Such is the case of Japanese artist Katsutoshi Kuroda.[5] Inspired by mangas like *Dragon Ball, Fist of the North Star,* or *Battle Royal,* he writes ultraviolent comics that are often set in the Edo Period (1603–1868), in which the same character rarely survives beyond a few panels (Fig. 4). Drawn with felt-tipped pens, they form volumes of several hundred pages. For the uninformed reader, they appear as a never-ending succession of colored explosions that border on abstraction.

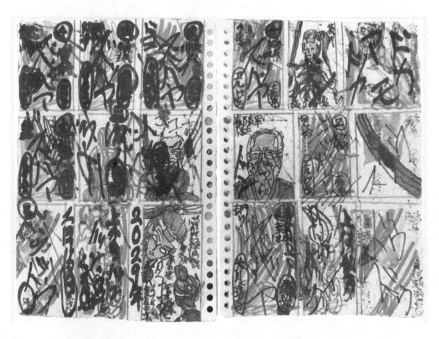

Figure 4: Katsutoshi Kuroda, untitled, 2019, felt pen on paper, 30 cm x 40 cm. Coll. *Nishiawaji Kibou-no-ye,* Osaka.

Figure 5: Pakito Bolino, *Spermanga*. ©L'Association, 2009.

The way in which Kuroda's creations are likely to be experienced has obvious similarities with a whole area of works related to comics less by the production of a narrative generated by a succession of panels than by the proliferating nature of the drawings. The reader is also a viewer who delights in the visual power of the images, their articulations, the graphic currents that run through them, without necessarily worrying about reading a story that may very well be embryonic, if not almost nonexistent. This is the approach that was adopted by publications related to the "graphzine movement" that emerged at the end of the 1970s, which is notably being continued today by Marseille publisher Le Dernier Cri, founded by Caroline Sury and Pakito Bolino in 1993, and only directed by Bolino since 2009. To my knowledge, it is the first alternative comics outlet to have published works made by Art Brut and Outsider Art creators. The absence of artistic norms in such publications allowed them to welcome all kinds of graphic virtualities, including creations that did not conform to any visual-narrative constraints and that were made by creators who were self-taught, marginalized, mentally ill, or mentally disabled. Le Dernier Cri also published at irregular intervals a voluminous anthology whose title clearly refers to the artistic movement theorized by Jean Dubuffet: *Hôpital Brut*.

Pakito Bolino's *Spermanga* is full of monstrous creatures that copulate, make mincemeat of each other, perform strange surgeries, or invent weapons of mass destruction. There is no exposition, no climax or outcome; no more heroes, helpers, or opponents. The narrative structure seems totally improvised, as if the author were driven by the sole desire to show as much semen and blood as possible (Fig. 5). Pakito Bolino's visual style is congruent with his subject matters and with his anarchic narrative structures. His untamed line betrays a feverish motion, and the *horror vacui* compositions never sacrifice the power of expression in favor of legibility. The motto of Le Dernier Cri synthesizes the essence of its intentions and aesthetic biases: "Vomir des yeux" ("To vomit from the eyes").

Likewise, the drawings of many creators associated with the Art Brut and Outsider Art movement, such as Wouter Coumou or Katsutoshi Kuroda, are unfinished and do not try to be seductive; they do not coincide with accepted definitions of what is considered "well drawn." At the very end of the 1990s, in an interview with Lionel Tran, Bolino states that Art Brut "gave [him] energy" and reset "the clocks in [his] head" (Tran 1999). He discovered creators with whom he finally felt in symbiosis, contrary to what he saw in the galleries and museums dedicated to contemporary art. According to him, his creations were not acceptable there: "Pendant des années je me suis senti comme un pauvre con qui fait des gribouillages et qui dessine comme un mongolien. Ça je l'ai ressenti" ("For many years, I felt like a poor scribbling schmuck who drew like he had Down's syndrome. That's how I felt") (1999).

By the same token, Jean-Christophe Menu's drawings are crude and seem hastily made. Breaking with the polished design of the *Ligne Claire*, they do, however, reconnect with one of the fundamental insights of comics initiated by Rodolphe Töpffer. In *Le Mickey maudit*, a two-page self-reflective story dedicated to Étienne Robial, the founder of Futuropolis publishing house, the latter makes a confession: "De toutes façons, tu vois bien la vitesse avec laquelle c'est dessiné alors!" ("Anyway, you see how quickly it was drawn!") (1999, 35) (Fig. 6). *Gnognottes*, a compilation of fragments published in various anthologies and magazines, is an eloquent demonstration of the unstable character of Menu's *graphiation*.[6] Clean compositions coexist with panels overloaded with hatching, and the drawings can range from mimetic representation to expressionist distortion, all of which breaks with dominant uses in the West, where comics are generally stylistically homogeneous (Fig. 7).

**Figure 6: Jean-Christophe Menu, *Le Mickey maudit* (1987),
reprinted in *Gnognottes*. ©L'Association, 1999.**

**Figure 7: Jean-Christophe Menu, *Le Mickey maudit* (1987)
Reprinted in *Gnognottes*. ©L'Association, 1999.**

In this respect, Olivier Josso Hamel's graphic evolution from his previous comics to *Au travail* is extremely eloquent. Benoît Crucifix notes that, in his former works, "[il] avait développé une signature graphique particulière, entre autres reconnaissable par un usage du noir et blanc en lavis et un système laborieux de hachures et d'ondulations, mais dont le poids risquait de le 'scléroser' et de l'"enfermer"" ("[he] had developed a particular graphic signature, notably recognizable by the use of black and white wash and a laborious system of hatching and undulation, but whose influence could risk 'stunting his work' and 'imprisoning him'") (2017). The author switched from a drawing style based on a system of graphic codes—where the manner in which he draws eyes, hair, or the folds of pants is immediately recognizable—to a graphiation just as unstable as that in Menu's work. In *Au travail*, he comments on this evolution:

> Enfin je lâche prise pour plonger dans le vide. Vive le trait libre, le premier jet sans filet, la plume qui crache et le pinceau qui tache . . . Un bain de jouvence dans l'encre noire et la blanche pâte du correcteur, qui ici se transforme en couleur.

> (Finally, I let go and dive into the vacuum. Long live the free line, the first draft without a safety net, the nib that spits and the paintbrush that stains . . . A fountain of youth into black ink and the white paste of White-Out, which here turns into color.) (2012, n.p.) (Fig. 8)

Figure 8: Olivier Josso Hamel, *Au Travail 1*. ©L'Association, 2012.

The idea of drawing "without a safety net" is consubstantial with the project of *Chronographie*, which is based on a fundamental "rule" that the mother and the daughter set for themselves prior to its effective implementation: Every fortnight, they would draw each other's portrait. This principle is neither a self-imposed structure nor a script that one must follow; it is about letting the work develop organically. The possibility of failure did not discourage the two authors from starting their project. Dominique Goblet concedes that some of the drawings in *Chronographie* are flawed but insisted upon keeping all of them to avoid presenting a truncated work (2010, 7). The "botched" portraits remain an integral part of the creative process. The very long period of time during which *Chronographie* was composed further accentuates the unstable nature of the *graphiation*. The stylistic heterogeneity appears even more obvious in the case of Nikita Fossoul, whose naive first drawings reveal her very young age—she was seven at the time—while the last ones that conclude the book are made by a young woman with an already assertive artistic personality (Figs. 9 & 10).

Figures 9 & 10: Nikita Fossoul & Dominique Goblet, *Chronographie*.
©L'Association, 2010.

Giving Up the Artistic Aspect

L'auteur s'efforce de s'extraire complètement de soi et de faire chanter ou parler les personnages avec leurs propres voix. Pour y parvenir, il aura fallu en grande partie renoncer à l'aspect artistique, ce qu'on pardonnera je l'espère, compte tenu du travail accompli pour pénétrer au plus profond de l'âme.

(The author strives to completely extract herself from herself and to make the characters sing or speak with their own voices. To achieve this, it was necessary in a large part to give up the artistic aspect, which I hope people will forgive, taking into account the work accomplished to penetrate the depths of the soul.) (Salomon 2015, n.p.)

In this excerpt from the introductory text of *Leben? Oder Theater?*, the fictional double of Charlotte Salomon says she had to "give up the artistic aspect" of her work. The author had previously studied at the prestigious Berlin Academy of Arts at a time when acquiring a technical mastery was still a major objective in learning how to paint. Charlotte Salomon, far from being "unscathed by artistic culture," decided, in essence, to unlearn—a willful technical impoverishment akin to the practice of *deskilling* in modern visual arts (Roberts 2010)—while the majority of creators from the Art Brut and Outsider Art movement simply never learned. In light of current notions, we should therefore understand the term "artistic aspect" as referring to a certain "know-how," the mark of professional artists. In 1946, facing some public disapproval of his own works, Jean Dubuffet writes:

Il est vrai que la manière du dessin est, dans ces peintures exposées, tout à fait exempte d'aucun savoir-faire convenu comme on est habitué à le trouver aux tableaux faits par des peintres professionnels, et telle qu'il n'est nullement besoin d'aucunes études spéciales, ni d'aucuns dons congénitaux pour en exécuter de semblables. A cela je répondrai que je tiens pour oiseux ces sortes de savoir-faire et de dons, leur seule action me paraissent être d'éteindre les spontanéités, couper les courants, frapper l'ouvrage d'inefficacité.

(It's true that the manner of drawing in these exhibited paintings is completely free of any agreed upon know-how as we are used to finding in the paintings made by professional painters, and that it is such that it is not necessary to undertake any particular studies or have any congenital gifts to make similar ones. To this, I would answer that I see these kinds of know-how and gifts as pointless, because it seems to me that they only extinguish spontaneity, cut off the streams, make the work inefficient.) (1967b, 63).

Au Travail, Chronographie, Spermanga, and the comics fragments gathered in *Gnognottes* also embody the rejection of the "know-how" and of "professionalism" through their heterodox—if not openly shaky—narrative constructions and their "unfinished" drawings that sometimes give off an impression of profound flippancy. Olivier Josso Hamel talks about "les méfaits du 'bien fait'" ("the harms of the 'well done'"). Although the concepts of "know-how" and "professionalism" have undoubtedly lost much of their relevance in the field of visual arts today, they often remain evaluation criteria in the field of comics, judging by the appreciation found in most of the book reviews published by the general press.

The refusal of know-how and professionalism is also an essential feature of the punk movement, like Dada before it. François Keen describes it as a reaction to "la starisation à outrance [et] à l'inflation de 'savoir-faire' des groupes 'progressifs'" ("the over-starization [and] the inflation of 'know-how' of 'progressive rock' bands"). Evoking the most iconic punk band the Sex Pistols, he adds that "[les punks] ont défini de nouvelles règles du jeu, ou plus exactement ont inventé les règles d'un nouveau jeu, et toutes les façons de jouer sont encore possibles. Une seule idée fédère tous les nouveaux venus: 'Do-It-Yourself' qui devient le fin mot de l'esthétique punk" ("[the punks] have defined the new rules of the game, or more exactly have invented the rules of a new game, and all ways of playing are still possible. Only one idea unites all the newcomers: 'Do-It-Yourself,' which becomes the final word on punk aesthetics") (1999, 503). This statement sheds a light on an opposition between "know-how" and DIY. Alternative comics—notably those of L'Association—grew out of a rejection of the normalizing publishing standards that prevented new affordances of comics. Their identity was built on a similar game of opposition. Rather than celebrating the mastery of proven formulas, they aimed to once again reshape the medium as an uncharted territory, open to every peculiarity. Moreover, Pakito Bolino, Jean-Christophe Menu, and Olivier Josso Hamel openly acknowledge the heritage of the punk movement. Bolino also makes noise music, while Menu designed the logo of the French band Les Satellites as well as several of their album covers. Many comics from L'Association have a punk aesthetic. They show expressive and no-frill graphics, the visual equivalents of musical pieces based on a maximum of three chords, a saturation of the page space similar to the saturation of the soundscape.

One of Menu's pages, originally published in the fanzine *Sortez la chienne* (*Take the Bitch Out*) and reprinted in *Gnognottes*, takes the form of a manifesto. It shows a creature with amphibian features praising improvisation, the freedom of letting go, and the practice of a "first draft without safety net." The author makes pronouncements such as "Le Pourquoi Faire est l'ennemi du Faire"; "Avec trop de pourquoi faire, il n'y a plus de faire!!"; "Si tu commences à penser au lecteur tu es foutu" ("The 'Why Do' is the Enemy of 'Doing'"; "With too many 'why do,' there is no more 'doing'!!"; and "If you start thinking about the reader, you're screwed") (1999, 70). While the making of comics is often seen as very laborious work, close to the job of a miniaturist, Menu expresses a need for urgency that prohibits wondering about the conditions under which the work will be done or how it will be received. He also highlights the value of urgency—which in this case implies the literal survival of the artist—in Charlotte Salomon's work: "Ce que cette urgence a généré de particulier, c'est la remise en question radicale, à des fins impérieuses, du savoir-faire dont l'artiste disposait parfaitement, au profit de quelque chose de nouveau et d'inimaginable" ("For imperative reasons, this urgency has generated a fundamental questioning of the know-how the artist perfectly mastered for the benefit of something new and unimaginable") (2006, 140).

The *Do-It-Yourself* philosophy that drives the punk movement also brings it closer to childhood, a period of intense engagement in craftsmaking and creativity: Children invent songs and stories, build their own games; with rudimentary means, they throw themselves into short-lived projects. In *La Bande dessinée et son Double*, Menu is a tireless promoter of "[la] *part d'enfance* qui (est inhérente à la bande dessinée) et qui contribue à la garder, dans son essence, quelque peu *irrécupérable*" ("[the] *part of childhood* that (is inherent to comics) and that helps to keep them, in their essence, somewhat unrecoverable") (Menu 2011, 17). The issue of childhood is also central in *Chronographie*, where half of the portraits were actually done by a child. Her lack of "professionalism" and her technical "blunders" did not prevent their publication alongside the drawings of her mother, who is much more experienced and who enjoys a greater reputation. Finally, childhood is at the center of the endeavor of memory reconstruction in *Au Travail*, a work that advocates primal energy and ingenuity:

> Comme tout enfant, je dessine . . . Car enfant, on dessine tous ou presque, me semble-t-il. Du moins jusqu'à un certain âge . . . Après

quoi seuls quelques-uns continuent, alors que la majorité lâche l'affaire. Quel est donc ce mystère ? . . . Si l'on appelle "don" la séparation arbitraire des prétendus bons et des soi-disant mauvais, alors je ne crois pas au "don." En revanche, je crois au plaisir, à l'éveil, au goût, à leur circulation fertile comme à la perpétuelle construction. C'est pourquoi j'ai toujours un peu de mal lorsque j'entends quelqu'un regretter de n'avoir pas continué à dessiner.

(Like any child, I draw . . . Because as children, we all draw, or almost all of us, I think. At least until a certain age . . . After which only a few continue, while the majority gives it up. So, what's the mystery? . . . If one calls a "gift" the arbitrary separation between the so-called good and the so-called bad, then I don't believe in "gift." On the other hand, I do believe in pleasure, in awakening, in taste, in their fruitful circulation as well as in perpetual construction. That's why I always have a little trouble when I hear someone regretting not having continued to draw.) (Josso Hamel 2012, n.p.)

Olivier Josso Hamel makes this often-heard, disappointed observation: in most cases, children stop drawing when they become teenagers or even adults. Only a few "good" ones will go on to pursue a career as professional cartoonists. However, if the Art Brut creators continue to draw (or paint, sculpt, or make music, or even all of these at once), they do not fit into the category of professionals. They remain, like the children they were, DIY handymen whose possible technical weaknesses will not stop them from drawing. Josso Hamel also notes: "Qu'on l'appelle art brut, naïf, primitif, punk, œuvre de fou ou dessin d'enfant, c'est à mon sens de la même sève essentielle dont il s'agit" ("Whether one calls it art brut, naive, primitive, punk, the work of a madman, or a child's drawing, it is in my opinion the same essential force") (Josso Hamel 2012, n.p.).

Passing the Hand Through the Looking Glass

As early as in his very first column in *Les Cahiers de la bande dessinée*, devoted to *In Vitro* by Marc Caro, Jean-Christophe Menu writes: "Il s'agit bien avec cet album de passer la main à travers le miroir, et de voir que derrière le cadre bien galvaudé de la bande dessinée, il peut encore tout se passer" ("This book is all about passing your hand through the looking glass, and seeing that behind the well-worn frame of comics, anything can still happen") (Menu 1987, 62). The metaphor of the looking glass already announces the issue of the *Double*, which will be the subject of his doctoral thesis published in 2011. Borrowing this concept from Antonin Artaud, he defines the *Double* as "le symbole de ce qui peut encore être réel et vrai dans l'Art, figé par les académismes ou galvaudé par le divertissement" ("the symbol of what can still be real and true in Art, [which is often] frozen by academicism or devalued by entertainment") (2011, 41).

Menu's thesis adopts a contentious posture, defending "la Bande Dessinée comme moyen d'expression au sens absolu du terme" ("comics as a means of expression in the absolute sense of the term") against standard productions that would only be the "degraded reflection" of the medium (Menu 2005, 25). However, the notion of *Double* also refers to works commonly associated with other forms of expression. Jean-Christophe Menu has written an entire chapter about the "*hors-champ* corpus" of comics, which he describes in these terms:

> le microcosme BD tient à distance tout un corpus d'œuvres relevant cette fois indéniablement de son domaine mais qu'elle n'intègre pas dans son Histoire, et donc qu'elle ne reconnaît pas comme partie intégrante de son champ. . . . Parmi ces exemples, on peut distinguer ceux qui ont pratiqué une certaine forme de bande dessinée sans vraiment le savoir (Charlotte Salomon) et ceux qui en ont fait en toute connaissance de cause (Buzzati, Di Rosa) sans être intégrés par le secteur de la BD.

> (the comics microcosm[8] keeps at a distance a body of works that definitively belongs to comics but that it does not integrate into its History, and therefore does not recognize as part of its field. . . . Among these examples, one can distinguish those who have practiced a certain form of comics without really knowing it (Charlotte Salomon) and those who have done so with complete awareness (Buzzati, Di Rosa) without being integrated by the "comics sector.") (2011, 432)

The author thus takes into consideration a whole series of works that he considers as fully pertaining to the realm of comics, although they are commonly associated with other fields of expression. He returns to the subject of Charlotte Salomon's *Leben? Oder Theater?* but also mentions several achievements associated with the Art Brut and Outsider Art movement, such as Henry Darger's work, *Soft City* by Norwegian cartoonist Hariton Pushwagner, and the first collaborations between authors published by Frémok (including Dominique Goblet) and creators from La "S" - Grand Atelier, an art studio for people with mental disabilities.

The notions of *Double, hors-champ,* and even *alternative comics* can only be defined by considering them in opposition with "something else." As in Dubuffet, whose positions extend those of Antonin Artaud (2011, 41), Menu's writings are guided by a rhetoric of otherness. "True art" for Dubuffet, "Comics in the absolute sense of the term" for Menu, are opposed to usurping forces that threaten what they consider to be the ideal of the medium.

Translated from the French by Erwin Dejasse,
Fabrice Leroy, and Shelly Miller Leroy

Endnotes

1. The making of the first volume of *Au Travail* began in 2007 and was entirely conceived in close dialogue with Jean-Christophe Menu. The book was published in 2012, the year following his departure from L'Association (Crucifix 2015).

2. Goblet, Dominique, and Dominique Théate. 2019. *L'Amour dominical*. Brussels: Frémok. For the work of Dominique Théate, see the 2017 exhibition catalog *Dominique Théate: In the Mood for Love*. Paris: Galerie Christian Berst.

3. Dejasse, Erwin. 2021. "Les Cahiers de la bande dessinée «période bruxelloise»: la critique à l'âge ingrat." In Chris Reyns-Chikuma, *50 ans d'histoire des éditions Glénat : Des marges bédéphiliques au centre économique en passant par une quête du capital symbolique*. Liège, Belgium: Presses Universitaires de Liège: 65–100.

4. For the work of Wouter Coumou, see Gronert, Frits. 2002. *Folly Drawings: over in- en outsiders in de kunst*. Rotterdam, Netherlands: Gallery Atelier Herenplaats.

5. A brief presentation of Katsutoshi Kuroda's work can be found on the organization's website, Diversity in the Arts: https://www.diversity-in-the-arts.jp/en/stories/16541.

6. Philippe Marion proposes to "name 'graphiation'" "cette instance énonciatrice particulière qui 'traite' ce matériau graphique constitutif de la BD et lui insuffle, de manière réflexive, l'empreinte de sa subjectivité singulière, la marque de son style propre" ("this particular enunciating instance that 'treats' the graphic material constituting comics that, reflexively, infuses them with the imprint of its singular subjectivity, the mark of its own style") (Marion 1993, 35).

7. Personal testimony of Dominique Goblet to the author, Angoulême, 2010.

8. In his writings, Menu distinguishes between "bande dessinée" and "BD." The second term is commonly used as a simple abbreviation of the first one. Nevertheless, Menu uses "BD" to designate the standard products from the comics industry.

Works Cited

BOLINO, Pakito. 2009. *Spermanga*. Paris: L' Association.

CRUCIFIX, Benoît. 2015. *Entre deux traits*. Interview with Olivier Josso-Hamel, unpublished.

———. 2017. "Mémoire de la bande dessinée dans *Au travail* d'Olivier Josso Hamel. Cases remémorées, redessinées." *Comicalités* 2017, n.p. journals. openedition.org/comicalites/2415.

DEJASSE, Erwin. 2010. "Bande dessinée, art brut et dissidence." *neuvième art 2.0*. neuviemeart.citebd.org/spip.php?article39.

DELAVAUX, Céline. 2018. *L'Art brut, un fantasme de peintre*. Paris: Flammarion.

DUBUFFET, Jean. 1967a. *Prospectus et tous écrits suivants*, vol. 1. Paris: Gallimard.

———. 1967b. *Prospectus et tous écrits suivants*, vol. 2. Paris: Gallimard.

FOSSOUL, Nikita, and Dominique GOBLET. 2010. *Chronographie*. Paris: L'Association.

GREENBERG, Clement. 1961. *Art and Culture: Critical Essays*. Boston: Beacon Press.

JOSSO HAMEL, Olivier. 2012. *Au travail 1*. Paris: L'Association, "Éperluette."

KEEN, François. 1999. "Punk." In *Le Siècle rebelle. Dictionnaire de la contestation au XXᵉ siècle*, edited by Emanuel de Waresquiel, 501–504. Paris: Larousse.

MAIGRET, Éric, and Matteo STEFANELLI. 2012. *La Bande dessinée: une médiaculture*. Paris: Armand Colin / INA.

MARION, Philippe. 1993. *Traces en cases. Travail graphique, figuration narrative et participation du lecteur*. Louvain-la-Neuve: Academia.

MENU, Jean-Christophe. 1986. "Caro: *In Vitro*." *Les Cahiers de la bande dessinée* 76: 60–63.

———. 1999. *Gnognottes*. Paris: L'Association.

———. 2005. *Plates-bandes*. Paris: L'Association.

———. 2006. "Le grand livre de Charlotte Salomon." *L'Éprouvette* 2: 129–40.

———. 2008. "Passage des écoliers." *Neuvième Art* 14: 93–95.

———. 2011. *La Bande dessinée et son Double. Langage et marges de la bande dessinée: perspectives pratiques, théorique et éditoriales*. Paris: L'Association.

ROBERTS, John. 2010. "Art After Deskilling." *Historical Materialism* 18: 77–96.

SALOMON, Charlotte. 2015. *Vie? Ou théâtre?* Paris: Le Tripode.

SNOEKX, Kurt. 2019. "L'Amour dominical: le fulgurant coup de foudre de Dominique Goblet pour Dominique Théate." *Bruzz*. https://www.bruzz.be/fr/culture/expo/lamour-dominical-le-fulgurant-coup-de-foudre-de-dominique-goblet-et-dominique-theate-2019.

TRAN, Lionel. 1999. "Les 7 Familles de la bande dessinée: Le Dernier Cri." *Jade* 17. Republished online: www.pastis.org/jade/novembre/dernier_cri.htm.

CHAPTER ELEVEN:
Belgo-Swiss "Pop Art"? Appropriation and the Making of Euro-Modernity in Hergé's *L'Affaire Tournesol*

Hugo Frey

The Tintin series has been subject to vast, global patterns of reme-diation. On the one hand, this was always a marketing strategy to promote the works themselves and to maximize their value by using images from the strips for multiple and numerous public and commercial purposes, such as in film adaptation or through use in derivative products ranging from chocolate bars to children's toys. On the other hand, as the Tintin charac-ters became globally recognized, they have been subject to countercultural and unofficial appropriation. This has been in "homemade" new commercial products and replicas, such as, for example, the new t-shirt designs targeting backpackers in Asia ("Tintin in Vietnam" is a t-shirt that is quite iconic, but not based on one of Hergé's albums) or the statues found in African street markets that represent new artisanal sculptures of Tintin. The boy-hero has also of course figured in unofficial new comics albums sometimes with por-nographic content, while others are more serious, like in the work of Charles Burns (2010) or Seth (1996). The contemporary fine art scene again "takes from Hergé" with his style and subjects being reworked, for example, by the important—albeit controversial—creatives Anton Kannemeyer and Conrad Botes. One might add that to some extent the hard commercial control of the Tintin franchise by its owners has spurred on these more polemical "wild" ap-propriations; and, in contrast, it has certainly magnified their power to shock. Of course, relatively gentle independent pastiches of Hergé's work developed in his own lifetime by artists such as Joost Swarte (1980). Never forget too that Art Spiegelman and Françoise Mouly featured a reimagined Tintin figure on the cover of their compilation edition of *Raw* magazine (1987).

This chapter develops a new close reading of appropriation, cross-refer-encing, image swapping, and repurposing from inside the Tintin series itself. Its focus is one of the least studied works, the 1956 album *L'Affaire Tournesol* (*The*

Calculus Affair). The plot of the adventure features each of the main "family" of Tintin protagonists, including Tintin himself, Captain Haddock, Dupont and Dupond, Milou, and the eponymous Professor Tournesol. The adventure follows the kidnapping of the Professor, whose military-scientific work has attracted the attention of two competing sets of international spies from the fictional Balkan nations Borduria and Syldavia. We follow Tintin's search for the Professor from the "family" stately home in Belgium, Moulinsart, to Geneva, and on to the Nyon home of a fellow scientist, Professor Topolino. The work concludes with the heroes rescuing Tournesol from the grip of the Bordurian state.[2] The denouement is that the secret microfilmed formula had been hidden all along inside the handle of Tournesol's umbrella. The "chase" to capture him had been therefore a "*fausse piste*" (false lead). Finally, just when the heroes collect the umbrella from a lost property office in Geneva, Tournesol is surprised to find that the microfilm is again missing. This Cold War wild goose chase concludes back at Moulinsart, where the secret item has been located all along.

This spy plot is commonly linked to Hergé's knowledge of a bizarre Cold War news item that had interested him. According to Benoît Peeters (2002, 355), it was reported in the Belgian press that a short piece of road situated between Portsmouth and Guildford, on the Hampshire-Sussex-Surrey borders, in southeast England, had witnessed a number of bizarre traffic accidents. The press linked this odd set of coincidences to a mysterious scientific military establishment located nearby.[3] Be that as it may, the storyline is also quite close to the contemporary novel from Egon Hostovsky, *The Midnight Patient* (1954), which was first printed in English translation from the Czech in 1954 and was translated into French in 1955 during the run of *L'Affaire Tournesol* in *Journal de Tintin*. It also narrates the story of a peaceful scientist trapped between competing spy groups and also makes use of a significant plot twist toward its conclusion. In 1957, the same work was adapted to cinema in France by Henri Georges Clouzot as *Les Espions*. Publicity for the film was provided in poster art by the cartoonist Siné, which further linked the work in the mind of the public to the world of comics. Clouzot's vision of some of the many spies that besiege a hospital mansion house also evoke the humor of the Tintin books. Nonetheless, the influence of Hergé's work on cinema is much sharper in the later cult classic *Les Tontons flingueurs* (1963, directed by Georges Lautner, with the important script by Michel Audiard), in which there is a short passage that pays tribute to *L'Affaire*.[4]

Yet, this chapter is not about the influences on Hergé's spy adventure strip, nor for that matter how he was an inspiration for others (alongside the cult film by Audiard and Lautner, a whole music composition by contemporary artist Klaus Schulze is dedicated to *L'Affaire*). Rather, in this chapter, my aim is to dig deeper into the pop art aesthetic stylizations that are to be found in the work and to essay that this a significant theme for rethinking *L'Affaire*. In the rest of this analysis, I will continue to explore *L'Affaire* for its use and reuse of mass media graphic design, insignia, iconography, advertising, and publicity material. It is my contention that this album represents Hergé's "little," always minimized, "microfilmed down," version of pop art. Far from being a dull formulaic work of spy genre material, this album warrants a rereading that takes into view and sheds new light on its use of advertising iconography, logos, militaria, repetition of classic Tintin images, and others. In fact, when one starts exploring this material, one quickly finds that the album is suffused with this kind of imagery. So, already in the mid-1950s, Hergé became his own, quiet, under-the-radar, pop artist.

It is no coincidence that the plot of *L'Affaire* begins with an image of a shattered mirror, for through much of the rest of the album the reader is presented with endless shards and fragments of reworked, appropriated, and reimagined old and new symbols and icons. Throughout the work, in Hergé's depiction of Belgium and Switzerland, the reader is saturated with redrawn or reimagined real-life advertising iconography. Tintin and Haddock descend from their flight from Belgium to Geneva using a branded Swiss Air ladder. They have flown on a Sabena (Belgium's national airline) flight, with the craft drawn in perfect blue and white livery. The Hôtel Cornavin, in Geneva, is similarly authentic and its modernist front doors are also meticulously redrawn. Cars from manufacturers such as Citroën and Mercedes fill the pages, each with their famous logos recreated in great detail. The press media of the period is similarly referenced, with local and international magazine titles pictured in the work: *Marie Claire, Paris Match, Life,* and the *Journal de Génève.* It is also worth adding here that there is a coded borrowing and reference to the world of comics publishing too. In the use of the name Topolino for a character, one thinks quickly of *Topolino*, the Italian comic that introduced Disney to Italy (first published in 1932).

Alongside these redrawings of authentic advertising art and graphic design, what Peeters calls "hyper-realism" (1990, 100), Hergé included a significant number of invented advertisings of his own. Fresh dairy milk is delivered to Moulinsart in a van branded as a "Lactas" delivery company. Sanzot the butcher is also equipped with a company vehicle and it too is given its own iconic branding. This very commercially designed van sports a Sanzot graphic designed name, a red and white side coloring, and an iconic pig logo. Lactas uses a circular poster shape including a bottle and cow to advertise itself. A packet of cigarettes left behind by a spy is beautifully designed with a tobacco leaf motif. When the Moulinsart mansion house is shown to be besieged by film crews, there is also a "Friture" (a French fries takeaway van) outside, and a poster is pinned on the wall of the stately home: "Souvenirs de Moulinsart" ("Souvenirs from Moulinsart"). In Switzerland we see yet another advert, this time: "Pour voir clair. Lunettes Leclerc" ("To see clearly. Eyeglasses Leclerc").

Earlier Tintin books feature many objects and specific real-world items. This was particularly the case for the inclusion of exotic, non-European, museum artifacts and treasures that Hergé found in Brussels's museums and placed inside the adventures (typically in 1937's *L'Oreille Cassée* (*The Broken Ear*), which is partly set in an ethnographic museum). However, what is distinct in this new work from the mid-1950s is that this earlier kind of material, associated with colonial-era anthropology, has been here removed and replaced with the ephemera of European postwar modernity. This is a pattern shared in fine art if one compares the inter-war Surrealists' focus on the exotic and the non-European with postwar pop art's predominant focus on the subject of domestic mass consumer society.

The plenitude of commercial advertising material in the imagined Western Europe in the first part of *L'Affaire* is neatly followed by an equivalent excess of iconography in the depiction of the Soviet bloc-style country of Borduria. Whereas Western Europe has many different icons (all performing the same sales function, one should note, and sharing some design features quite directly, as in Sanzot and Lactas design works featuring circles and bold product emphasis—pig; milk bottle), in Borduria, it is the image of the leader that is reflected everywhere in the form of reproductions of images of his mustache. These are to be found in the language of the state that uses a mustache-like circumflex accent over the vowel "o" (thus: "ô"). It is included on statues dedicated to the leader; military medals and uniforms; and the front fenders of state cars. But it is also featured in decorative arts: The lamp base in Tintin's hotel shares the same mustache curves set into its fetching blue and black ceramic. The same is true, of course, of hotel fixtures and fittings (the corridor light fittings have a sweeping insignia, too), and the wooden table on which the lamp sits has carefully designed emblems of the leader. The theater where the opera star Bianca Castafiore performs is decorated with a sculpted bust of the dictator. The Bordurian dictator himself resembles a cartoon redrawing of Stalin. The focus on facial hair of the dictator is of course also very funny in its own way.[5]

Later American pop art is often criticized for its neutral or at best ironic relationship to the material that it represented. This is not the case with Hergé's take on the modern worlds of signs in his imaginary Western and

Eastern Europe. Two strong inferences can be deducted in his use of this kind of material besides mirroring the economic and political climate in the news and popular culture of the time. First, through showing each side of the Cold War enemies being equally saturated with images, one can infer that Hergé is adopting a critical overview of each position. For him, neither side is much better than the other; on the one side, the advertising and other logos function to sell consumer objects, whereas on the other side, they glorify an official state leadership. Each world is just as overloaded with superficial iconography as the other. It is in fact a line of interpretation not dissimilar to that which evolved in France under De Gaulle (1958–1970), in which the French-European foreign policy position aimed to navigate an independent role sitting between capitalism and Soviet communism (at least rhetorically). It is also an interpretation Hergé magnified further in the final finished work, *Tintin et les Picaros* (1976), where two different competing Central American political leaders are shown to be both equally unable to address poverty in their slums. It is another sign of Hergé adopting the "plague on all your houses" ideology that Pascal Ory (1985) describes as a component of the tradition of right-wing anarchism. This is the political and cultural milieu in France and francophone Europe that emerged after the Second World War that countered Christian democracy and socialism and communism. Instead of supporting the Center-Right or the Left, its proponents (often working in literature or cultural fields) argued for a conservatism that deliberately mocked and provoked the ideological mainstream and the rise of modern social democracy. The right-wing anarchists employed comedy to critique contemporary society and governance, but were often much less clear as to what should replace it (see also Hewitt 1996).

Second, the treatment of the growth of West European capitalism in the work displays a particularly strong satirical streak. The capitalist world that the advertising signs represent is mostly viewed as a society that is upsetting and frustrating. Readers will recall that at the beginning of the work, Haddock is plagued by the forces of capitalism when a number of wrong number phone calls looking for Sanzot Butchery are directed to him at Moulinsart. Next, Séraphin Lampion of Assurances Mondass is an additional rude intervention that further plagues Haddock. Lampion is portrayed as representative of the new upwardly mobile working class, now working in white-collar professions such as insurance sales. Similarly, when Dupond and Dupont leak news of a new mystery, the media and commercial world again descend on Haddock. The quiet repose of his mansion is soon besieged by commercial activity. Later in the story, in Switzerland, perpetuating the same consistent theme,

Haddock is the victim of an accident when the optician's advertising sign crashes down on his head. In the comic mode, the album therefore certainly resembles the cinema of Jacques Tati, which provided more explicit humorous critique of the import of American capitalism to Western Europe. His films—*Jour de Fête* (*The Big Day*) (1945), *Mon Oncle* (*My Uncle*) (1958), and later *Playtime* (1967)—are masterpieces of satire on the rise of the new commercialism in postwar France. Of course, Haddock preceded the invention of Tati's *Monsieur Hulot* by several years, but one can be sure that the influences run in each direction.

Let me add that when Hergé was writing *L'Affaire,* the Tintin business was itself advancing greatly and was a part of the rise of modern capitalism in postwar Europe. It is also the case that in the 1920s and 1930s, Hergé's work had also directly embraced commercial art and graphic design. As well as making the Tintin books, he had worked in publishing, providing editors with dust jacket images for a range of political and religious tracts. Similarly, he had taken on design work for sweet manufacturers and also for the Belgian food company Habi, as well as for the national railway company.[6] When the Tintin series directly included images of postwar capitalism, the authenticity and credibility of the designs were advanced by this professional experience in the field. Moreover, the borderlines of commercial design, comics, and fine art are permeable. Benjamin Rabier, for example, invented not only a precursor to Tintin (Tintin-Lupin) but also the logos for the French cheese brand "La Vache qui rit" and "Baleine" salt, while Salvador Dali imagined the logo for a children's sweet company selling lollipops. In fact, there are some design similarities between Rabier's iconic cheese wrapper and the materials Hergé invented for Lactas and Sanzot milk and beef providers.[7]

Speaking of dust jacket design, one should note that this art is also featured directly in *L'Affaire.* The work is well known for its inclusion of a real-life book and its dust jacket illustration: Leslie E. Simon, *German Research in World War Two* (1947). This is one of the only, if not the only, "real-world" book cover illustrations that is redrawn inside the pages of any of the books in the Tintin series. In *L'Affaire,* it is repurposed into a single-panel image, as if being held in the hands of Tintin. The cover is recreated with a high level of verisimilitude and continues to feature the image of a V-2 rocket missile and a small aircraft. The red-and-white checkered pattern on the rocket is maintained from the original illustration. Unlike in pop art, however, the cover is not magnified but reduced to a single small panel. Yet, just as in Roy Lichtenstein's famous works of some years later, in his recreation Hergé also adapts and makes tiny edits to the original version of the dust jacket. His technique here was to almost copy the original cover but to also remove the still politically sensitive swastika emblem that is visible in the image on the original cover of the short print run, English academic tome. Furthermore, the V-2 rocket appropriated into *L'Affaire* resembles the space rocket that the heroes had just used in the previous adventures—*Objectif Lune*; *On a marché sur la Lune* (*Destination Moon*; *Explorers on the Moon*)—and it shares the same colored design as that machine. One can add that by openly linking the image of the V-2 Nazi missile (responsible for significant deaths and casualties in London at the end of the war and manufactured by prisoners held in slave camp conditions) to his idea of a space rocket in the moon adventures, the father of Tintin inadvertently pointed out some real-world connections. After all, it was precisely the German-Nazi scientist Werner von Braun that the US intelligence services had redeployed into working at NASA in the early Cold War space race.[8] The rise of Werner von Braun to NASA pioneer was in complete contrast to the Belgian collaborator and extreme right-winger, Raymond de Becker, for whose political tracts Hergé had designed cover images back in the 1930s. De Becker never recovered such a professional role as the German rocket engineer and instead, after the war, published on the margins in esoteric reviews, writing a history of gay sex, which was radical in its day, and titles such as a study of male film stars. Hergé maintained a correspondence and friendship with him (Peeters 2002, 334). Pierre Assouline suggests that it was de Becker who inspired the Belgian graphic novelist to take an interest in Jungian psychoanalysis (1998, 660).

Next, let me underline that here we have an original kind of pop art. Hergé in *L'Affaire* shares pop art's general aesthetic by redrawing advertising and mass media iconography. In the repetitious inclusion of the material, it coincides with the idea of serial representation better known in the later works from Andy Warhol (multiples of Campbell's Soup tins, Brillo boxes, or Dollar signs). What it necessarily does differently is to reduce the scale and size of the publicity images to include them inside the panels or, to be more precise, in illustration details in drawings inside panels (a maximum reduction mode rather than the magnification in the Warhol or Lichtenstein tactic of blow-up). Nevertheless, it is the case that the cover of the album is close to the later blow-up stylization. It takes a single-panel image from late in the adventure (Hergé 1956, 58) and then maximizes it to fit the full cover size. This image is framed by shards of broken mirror, alluding to the story's initial episode. The original panel is subject to small alterations and organization to give more narrative power in the enlarged format. Thus, from the original panel, a small piece of car metal is removed entirely, while for the cover a military tank is added to the background. One should note that this same design approach had been used previously, particularly when redesigning prewar dust jackets for the postwar market. In 1946, a "cleaned" and "sharper" cover was used for the new colored edition of *Le Lotus bleu* (*The Blue Lotus*), for instance.[9] The publication history of *L'Affaire* is of further importance in this regard. In its serialized prepublication in *Le Journal de Tintin,* it was printed in a larger size "Italian" format for some of the run—appearing in the double middle pages of the magazine. In the magazine version, the panel images were larger (featuring only three tiers of panels on a double page), whereas the standard issue of the album reduced their size to fit the A4 page layout. This original "Italian" printing did mean that there was more space on the page to include more content, to fit inside the panels the many drawings of the marketing icons and propaganda emblems.

But why really were there so many symbols and images, signs, and repetitions in one Tintin story? The saturation of signs and emblems in the work has an important narrative and poetic function that is worth recalling. The inclusion of so many capitalist and communist adverts, signs, logos, and insignia fulfills a powerful narrative function, as well as a social-political, aesthetic one. All of this material adds to the creation of the work's double conclusion that the secret microfilm formula was in the Professor's umbrella all along (and then the next discovery that it was always at home at Moulinsart in the first place). The bombardment of icons and adverts in the work distracts the viewer from seeing the umbrella. Our eyes are turned to follow Tintin and Haddock and likewise we are invited to focus on the depictions of Switzerland and Borduria and not to pay much attention to Tournesol's umbrella. The umbrella features in the plot in a number of panels and is "there to see" but our vision is distracted with all of this additional backdrop and descriptive material. At one point in the story, Milou seems to "know" the secret of the umbrella, as he first finds it at Topolino's house and then repeatedly carries it through many panels of the story, but the reader is too distracted by the spectacle of so many signs to really take in this critical information.[10]

Furthermore, the appropriation of signs in the work also expands to a high level of internal copying and borrowing of images preexisting inside the extended Tintin story-world itself. The work bombards the reader with images that are seemingly familiar from many of the other Tintin books. The similarities are in fact striking and recurrent at the level of individual panels and sequences of action. Thus, there are images of "thunder bolts" that are repetitious of similar panels from *Les Sept Boules de Cristal* (*The Seven Crystal Balls*) (a work that narratively shares the same plot development of the abduction, search, and rescue of Tournesol). The identification of tobacco as a "clue," in *L'Affaire*'s packet of cigarettes, looks back and repeats a trope from *Les Cigares du Pharaon* (*Cigars of the Pharaoh*). Another panel in which Haddock knocks over Lampion calling out "En avant à Genève" ("Off to Geneva") echoes numerous similar scenes from the series when the Captain finally decides to accept an adventure. More directly, the sequence when Haddock waits patiently for Tintin and Professor Topolino to open a bottle of wine returns the reader to the comparable passage in *Au Pays de l'Or Noir* (*Land of Black Gold*), where the same joke is played out. Similarly, the denouement in which the search returns to Moulinsart to be resolved is a direct copy of the conclusion to *Le Trésor de Rackham le Rouge* (*Red Rackham's Treasure*). As noted above, the V-2 rocket image depicted herein repeats the space rocket design from *On a marché sur la lune*. Repetition is important to build up reader loyalty, and this aspect of repeated panel images or very similar images and sequences is central to how and why the Tintin series is so powerful. While of course the works have many aspects that stand out as moments of individual aesthetic or narrative innovation and skill, by the postwar period they were also creating a deeply familiar visual and narrative world of webs of recurrent material that gave readers not only new stories but also a sense of nostalgia for the earlier works. As indicated above, this was through direct panel-to-panel duplication of imagery (e.g., the thunderbolt); or reworked comedy sequences that shared setting and humor; or less direct but very clear repetitions. One may go as far as to suggest that the new foregrounded images of contemporary advertising (in Western Europe) and political insignia (in Eastern Europe) in their bold and brash originality conceal these many internal repetitions from the previous Tintin books precisely because they are new and have not featured in previous works.

Similarly, *L'Affaire* established panel-images and sequences of panel-narrative that pointed the way forward to later works from the series. The opening pages of the work where Haddock and Tintin are walking in the countryside together are very suggestive of the similar introduction to *Les Bijoux de la Castafiore* (*The Castafiore Emerald*). Lampion's invasion of the Moulinsart house that occurs at the very end of *L'Affaire* is almost exactly replicated with the "Arab invasion" scene in *Coke en Stock* (*The Red Sea Sharks*). The plot denouement in *L'Affaire* similarly prepares the way for the modernism of *Castafiore* (as well as looks back to the conclusion of *Le Trésor de Rackham Le Rouge*), which again ends happily after an extended "wild goose chase." Redundancy on the levels of narrative and panel imagery provides readers with the familiar world they can return to and reexperience. For quite some time, most critics have stressed the uniqueness of the storytelling of the

Tintin albums. The point here is not to deny that important critical work, or the power of individual albums, but to add that there is a great deal of familiarity inside the complete storyworld that was created. Repetition is a key aesthetic strand in comics and the Tintin books, while seemingly very different from, say, Batman or Superman, share this disposition far more than is often given credit. Furthermore, this world of repetitions helps readers of all ages to engage with and start reading the works. The familiarity of the works provides reassurance that one can read individual works in almost any order, as the visual language is common, even if the stories are different. The repetition of materials also provides an intradiegetic timelessness that justified the repeated agelessness of the characters, even while world historical events and indeed fashion for design (cars, clothes, objects) were evolving across the decades. Indeed, it is a unique feature of the Tintin storyworld that history does move forward, while characterization (drawing and psychological) and iconic imagery, discussed here, remain constant. Such meta-disposition across the storyworld can (a) reassure us that much remains familiar and safe, but also (b) perturb us to wonder why nothing evolves or reflects the clear passage of time that is being marked in the always contemporary and updating *mise-en-scène* of the backdrops and plot-contexts.

L'Affaire is a very "meta" work that clearly remixes many previous aspects from the series and prepares the reader for several others in subsequent albums. It is a key work on these grounds alone, but also a good example of how a serial narrative comic creates cohesion between a very long running period of sub-stories (the albums) and the storyworld of the albums as a totality. In 1959, the idea of a full "Tintin universe" was itself raised in contemporary criticism by Pol Vandromme (1959). However, Vandromme emphasized the importance of the recurrent characters rather than implicit repetitions of panel imagery or passages of similar plot development.

Finally, there is also a further level of image appropriation and recuperation that in the 1950s most readers would not have recognized in this work. Hergé included redrawn images of real people from his own circle in this book that few outsiders would notice. In itself, this was not new, as there were already references to collaborators in other contemporary postwar works. (Famously, Hergé's sometime colleague, E. P. Jacobs, is referenced on the postwar cover of *Les Cigares du Pharaon*, 1955 edition.) In *L'Affaire*, Hergé included his own self-portrait in two passages. First, there is a journalist figure who closely resembles a depiction of Hergé in the media circus outside Moulinsart panel referenced above. Much later in the story, at Castafiore's performance at the opera in Borduria, a clear shape of Hergé's body is featured (1956, 52). There, Hergé appears to be sitting in front of Tintin, and then in the final panel of the same page we are shown Tintin, Milou, and Haddock from the perspective of the same Hergé-like figure. It is a most original panel, as across the whole series very rarely are the heroes placed behind another figure, or viewed from the perspective of an intra-diegetic figure. Therefore, there is a genuine playfulness to *L'Affaire* that opens up more and more as one interprets it as a game of signs and icons. The Hergé panels are a good example of the imagery being created for readers familiar with the artist's body shape, a small group on its original publication. It is also possible that this inclusion mirrored Alfred Hitchcock's familiar film technique of placing himself briefly in his own work as a backdrop figure.[11] If so, Hergé was offering a beautiful homage to the director as well. In fact, it was not so unusual in contemporary comics to find this kind of secret self-portraiture. For example, the much younger and less famous Hugo Pratt added an image of himself to one of his illustrations for the British war comics of the same period, *War Picture Library*.[12] Let me speculate further on Hergé in the context of *L'Affaire*. The same sequence in the opera house may have another explanation. On the same page, and between these panels, a group scene includes another redrawing of a figure from Hergé's milieu. Here we can discern that Hergé has included a representation of the young colorist Fanny Vlamynck, whom he had first employed in his studio in November 1955 and with whom he would fall in love and later marry (see Peeters 2002, 368). The sequence therefore has surely some romantic connotations: Hergé showing himself and his female colleague close to each other, with Tintin, at the social occasion of the opera. In the same panel an older woman looks directly into Fanny's eyes, suggesting annoyance or jealousy. One may speculate that in this image Hergé was projecting his own sense of guilt for falling in love with Fanny by including a representation of his then wife, who is glaring at her. This section was first printed in *Le Journal de Tintin* in late 1955, so the dates make this thesis quite possible. Benoît Peeters notes that Hergé was quickly fond of Fanny and that this was very evident by the Toussaint holiday in 1956 (2002, 368). This secret sequence from *L'Affaire* underlines the point that the couple were probably quite close to each other a little earlier than that date, or that Hergé had desired this to be the case. Tintin himself is given some words to indicate something is occurring in these panels in the opera house. Positioned in front of the probable representation of Fanny and next to the panel that shows Hergé's back, the boy-journalist remarks: "Mais oui, capitaine, c'est encore dans la foule qu'on a le plus de chances de passer inaperçus" ("It's true, Captain, when you're in a crowd there's always less chance of being noticed") (52). This material not only shows Hergé's playfulness and audacity but also his mastery of his art, where the control and rhetorical use of words and images works on multiple levels. Indeed, in this passage, Tintin is talking to Haddock about hiding from the Bordurian police in the crowd; yet if the image is of Fanny and Hergé's then wife, the words are also a bold and daring commentary on that situation as well, one that is only open to those who could read the images of the women at a time when neither was very well known publicly, if at all.

Extracting images in panels of seemingly not much consequence to explore their similarity with real-life figures is a fascinating project. However, it would probably be exploiting the grounds of critical plausibility to raise one further final example from *L'Affaire*. Instead, readers are invited to examine a much earlier passage in this work and judge for themselves. In the scene where Tintin and Haddock are being driven in a taxi from Geneva to Nyon (Hergé 1956, 20), pause to dwell on the drawing of the taxi driver. In this book that features a dictatorship that uses the insignia of a mustache and a historical research book on Nazi military technology, one of the images of the taxi driver does look very close to a representation of . . . Adolf Hitler! Hergé may have found it an amusing internal code of graphic design to remove the swastika from the book dust jacket he appropriates a few pages later, but to have nonetheless smuggled in the image of the Führer himself, now embodied as a neutral Swiss taxi driver (perhaps a linguistic pun also on the similar sound of the German word for leader, "Führer," and the verb "fahrer," to drive). It is plausible to suggest that Hergé certainly knew that neutral postwar Switzerland was a common safe location for former wartime collaborators and the like. One has to also admit that image-text-context are complex matters here and that "turning" images away from intra-diegetic storyworld cohesion is a speculative luxury on the part of the critic. All that we do know is that the taxi driver "looks a little like" the Nazi dictator and that Hergé and artists in his studio knew how words and images worked together to either signal information or to play around with them to make hints and odd suggestions.

To conclude, as in the early British pop art scene of Richard Hamilton, Eduardo Paolozzi, and others, Hergé's work mirrors the growing consumer society of the postwar years that were seeing remarkable economic growth and new social opportunities. In the two main Western European locations, Belgium and Switzerland, many of the military, political, and economic restrictions that had followed the liberation of Europe from Nazism were now slowly lifting. A developing capitalist culture of increased domestic consumption and leisure and entertainment culture was gradually accessible, if only in small ways, to a growing number of members of society. Geneva itself was an important hub for international political institutions and had, in the summer of 1954, held the major peace talks on the future decolonization of French Indochina (just months before *L'Affaire* was first serialized in *Le Journal de Tintin*). Thus, this Tintin book captures the social and political realities of a given time and a specific place (although Hergé's depiction of Geneva shows no sign of the delegates from North Vietnam or China ending French power in East Asia). Nonetheless, using the genre of the spy thriller, the work is a historically important document of its time.

What this chapter has also unpacked is the high recurrence of types of images inside the images (advertising; political insignia; repeated self-referential imagery from inside the total Tintin storyworld); moreover, it has speculated on the role of remediated depictions of figures from Hergé's inner circle. In so doing, I have underlined how significant this material and tactic is for the composition of the album. The work is not only a continuation of the Tintin adventures but also an extended play on the importance of logos, iconography, and semiotics for society at large, both democratic and totalitarian. It is a response to the saturation of signs and messages that artists like Warhol and Lichtenstein replied to a little later on. The repetition of classic Tintin images adds subtly to the mythology of the series and shows a knowing understanding of what "typical" (if not stereotypical) Tintin material looked like—a knowingness that was also a good way to further conceal the personal autobiographical depiction that the work included but concealed to most contemporary readers.

Finally, let me note by way of an epilogue that appropriately enough it is a panel from the same work that provides one of the best contemporary street art appropriations in the form of a mural on the streets of Brussels today (Fig. 1). On the rue de l'Etuve, a panel from *L'Affaire* is magnified and presented on the side of the building. Cleverly, this street art blown-up excerpt from *L'Affaire* works as *trompe-l'œil* to suggest a real-life hotel fire escape. Thus, when looking at the building it is as if the characters are really making their way down an exterior stair into the street. The further reason this is a successful street art installation is precisely because the original source material remains current and modern and hence fits the contemporary street scene. Work from this album of remediated advertising signs functions now as a tourist-poster for the Tintin series and its heritage role in twenty-first-century Belgium.

With many thanks to Jan Baetens
and Fabrice Leroy for their suggestions on this piece.

Figure 1: The Brussels mural reproducing an iconic scene from *L'Affaire Tournesol*. Photo courtesy of Benoît Majerus.

Endnotes

1. Serialized in *Journal de Tintin* December 1954 to February 1956.

2. The name of the country Borduria clearly evokes the French word "ordure," meaning excrement or filth, or a place of filth. It is a good example of the comedy subtext to the Tintin series, especially where language is modified to suggest double meaning.

3. Noting here that also Peeters suggests the important role of Jacques Martin in the making of *L'Affaire*.

4. For more on the backdrop to Audiard see Frey 2014, 175–177.

5. For a different approach to Borduria, facial hair, and Dupond and Dupont, see Jan Baetens 1987, 75–80.

6. A helpful visual survey of this material is offered in Steeman 1991.

7. See also Lachartre 1986 and the current research led by Myriam Boucharenc.

8. For what it is worth, in popular culture, this is the background subject matter of the new Amazon Prime television series *Hunters* (2020).

9. The first edition cover of *Le Lotus bleu* was smaller and more intricate. The original artwork was probably itself inspired by film poster materials for *Shanghai Express* (1932). An auction of this original work occurred in fall 2020 and was reported in the European press to likely make millions.

10. A further warning perhaps is given when Haddock is knocked down by the optician's sign. A metaphor on vision and concealment if ever there was one.

11. This occurred throughout his career.

12. See Pratt, "Up the Marines!", *War Picture Library* (1960), no 58. reprinted in Hugo Pratt (2009, 252). Photographs of Pratt's friend, Gisela Dester, have a passing resemblance to his iconic character Corto Maltese. Adapted a little, certainly.

Works Cited

Assouline, Pierre. 1998. *Hergé*. Paris: Gallimard, Folio.

Baetens, Jan. 1987. *Hergé écrivain*. Brussels: Éditions Labor.

———. 2006. "Hergé, auteur à contraintes? Une relecture de *L'Affaire Tournesol*." *French Forum* 31 (1): 99–112.

Burns, Charles. 2010. *X'ed Out*. London: Jonathan Cape.

Frey, Hugo. 2014. *Nationalism and the Cinema in France*. New York: Berghahn.

Hergé. 1956. *L'Affaire Tournesol*. Brussels: Casterman.

Hewitt, Nicholas. 1996. *Literature and the Right in Postwar France*. Oxford: Berg Books.

Hostovsky, Egon. 1954. *The Midnight Patient*. New York: Appleton Century Crofts.

————. 1955. *Le Vertige de Minuit*. Paris: Robert Laffont.

LACHARTRE, Alain. 1986. *Objectif Pub*. Paris: Robert Laffont.

ORY, Pascal. 1985. *L'Anarchisme de droite*. Paris: Grasset.

PEETERS, Benoît. 1990. *Le Monde d'Hergé*. Brussels: Casterman.

————. 2002. *Hergé, fils de Tintin*. Paris: Flammarion.

PRATT, Hugo. 2009. *WWII. Histoires de Guerre*. Brussels: Casterman.

SIMON, Leslie E. 1947. *German Research in World War Two*. New York: J Wiley.

STEEMAN, Stephane. 1991. *Tout Hergé*. Brussels: Casterman.

SPIEGELMAN, Art, and Françoise MOULY. 1987. *Read Yourself RAW*. New York: Pantheon Books.

SWARTE, Joost. 1980. *30/40*. Paris: Futuropolis.

VANDROMME, Pol. 1959. *Le Monde de Tintin*. Paris: Gallimard.

CHAPTER TWELVE

Salammbô in the Third Degree: From Novel to BD to Video Game
Ana Oancea

G ustave Flaubert began his novel *Salammbô* (1862) out of a desire to escape the present, which he had examined so closely in *Madame Bovary* (1857)—"j'éprouve le besoin de sortir du monde moderne, où ma plume s'est trop trempée" ("I feel the need to exit the modern world, where I too often dipped my pen") (1927a, 164). The leap is both geographic and temporal, with the novel taking ancient Carthage, rather than the author's contemporary France, as its setting. It recounts a love story against the background of the Mercenary Revolt (240–238 BC) following the First Punic War. Mâtho, the Libyan leader of mercenaries shortchanged by Carthage, dreams of Salammbô, daughter of the city's leader and priestess of its most important deity, even as he engages in a complex plot to unite various disgruntled armies and confront her father's forces. It is thus set on a grander, more epic scale than his previous novel, but Flaubert also leaves room for invention by taking on a lesser-known event and location, and eschewing Rome, Greece, or Egypt.

Contemporary reviews were primarily negative, suggesting that the book was lifeless and boring, even unreadable, due to its accumulation of detail in the reconstruction of the ancient world (Flaubert 2013, 1226). Flaubert suggests that in writing it he merely employed the "procédés du roman moderne" ("devices of the modern novel") (1219), elaborating fiction in the margins of reality, as in *Madame Bovary*. But his copious research, which the novel showcased with great precision, remained problematic to his readers. The combination of Flaubert's realist working method and his topic was deemed strange by literary critic Sainte-Beuve, while his use of historical information was regarded as unscientific by archaeologist Guillaume Frœhner. On this account, *Salammbô* became the subject of a minor literary quarrel over the mix of science and literature, which contributed to its high volume of sales. The novel's exoticism made it very popular, and it also surprised its public through the vivid depictions of violence and scenes of sensuality it contained.

As Adrianne Tooke shows, Flaubert's detailed rendering of grandiose and grotesque Carthage can also be linked to his notion that the purpose of writing was "faire voir" ("to show"). The author also credited his travels to Africa and the Middle East with teaching him the proper approach to a subject, that of "être œil" ("to be an eye"). Because he conceived of his work in such visual terms, Flaubert opposed illustration, writing, "Jamais, moi vivant, on ne m'illustrera, parce que la plus belle description littéraire est dévorée par le plus piètre dessin. Du moment qu'un type est fixé par le crayon, il perd ce caractère de généralité, cette concordance avec mille objets connus qui font dire au lecteur 'J'ai vu cela' ou 'Cela doit être'" ("As long as I live, I will never allow my books to be illustrated, because the most beautiful literary description is swallowed up by the most wretched little drawing. As soon as something is represented pictorially it loses its general nature, that resemblance with one thousand familiar objects that makes the reader say, 'Oh yes, I've seen that' or 'It must be like that'") (1927b, 221). To the author, then, illustration impoverished the text by fixing the form or meaning of what was portrayed, and by taking over the work of the reader's imagination, which was open to a different range of associations.

This chapter considers two adaptations of Flaubert's novel that rely nevertheless on illustration, Philippe Druillet's *bande dessinée, Salammbô* (1985), and Cryo Interactive's eponymous video game (2003), as its expansions into other media. It argues that in addition to the subject matter shared, each successive iteration relies on medium-specific elements from its predecessor (text from the novel, flowing illustrations from the BD), to which it assigns different functions in the new context. Druillet's adaptation takes a visual approach to exposition, often relying on full-page illustrations or two-page spreads to draw the reader into a futuristic Carthage reimagined in hallucinogenic colors and intricate designs. His BD treats the excerpts from Flaubert it cites as images: Displayed alone on a page, they are encased in ornate frames and lettered distinctively from captions or speech balloons. Like illustrations in a novel, the quotes from Flaubert are complementary to the visual storytelling.

Cryo's take on Druillet's *Salammbô* is focused on visual fidelity to the BD, which a brief reading of the developer's most successful previous project indicates is a key element in their method of adaptation. The game's use of panels, borders, and page layout shows the similarities between *Salammbô* and other games that reference comic book elements, such as *XIII* and Atlus's *Persona 5* (2016). A look at the extent to which they are integrated into game themes or fulfill functions specific to the medium will suggest that *Salammbô* achieves the greatest degree of intermediality. Through a discussion of the gameplay inherent to the genre into which the BD was adapted, I will conclude that the game recreates the experience of reading the album.

Salammbô as BD

Druillet began working on his adaptation of *Salammbô* in 1978, in the wake of his album *La Nuit* (*The Night*) (1976), an apocalyptic narrative to which he refers as a requiem for his first wife. Despite the change in subject, Marie Barbier suggests a possible continuity between the two projects. Flaubert's characters drowning under the weight of his verbal construction of Carthage can be perceived as the novel's dystopian side, similarly to *La Nuit*'s last survivors disappearing in the ruins of their civilization. The project was initially suggested to Druillet by Philippe Koechlin, the editor of *Rock & Folk* magazine, which had published his previous album. Though he was not previously familiar with the novel, the artist recounts being immediately fascinated once he started reading it. He cites the novel's ability to incite his visual imagination as the reason for his captivation and acknowledges that he undertook the project despite some trepidation at the idea of combining the BD medium with the work of a classic author (Barbier 2017, 17).

Stretching to three volumes and representing seven years' work, *Salammbô* was a great critical success, contributing to Druillet's being awarded three years later the prestigious Grand Prix de la ville d'Angoulême (1988). In interviews, he refers to this period as one spent steeped in Flaubert's world, but the BD represents a synthesis of two creative sources. Indeed, the artist casts his own recurring character, Lone Sloane, an intergalactic traveler, as Flaubert's protagonist Mâtho. This substitution determines the genre of the BD as science fiction, and also influences its aesthetic. The four Lone Sloane albums preceding *Salammbô* (1966–1978) were characterized by psychedelic colors, monstrous characters and environments, the use of geometric patterns in backgrounds, and irregular page layouts, with a predilection for splash pages and unconventional panel structures. The encounter of the two universes, Druillet's and Flaubert's, is also staged diegetically, with the recognizable Carthaginian plot being bookended by chapters in which Lone Sloane engages in his characteristic adventures. The character assumes his solitude by killing the crew on his ship so that he can pursue Salammbô, whom he has seen in a vision, thereby becoming Mâtho. Once he is killed at the end of Flaubert's plot, Lone Sloane is reabsorbed back into his original world by his friend Yearl the neo-Martian, who also destroys the city, thus closing both narratives.

The relation of the two versions of *Salammbô* and of the two media is further encapsulated in six distinctive pages featuring only text and facing illustrations to which they bear a close relationship. They offer insight both into Druillet's adaptation of Flaubert and Cryo's adaptation of Druillet, to the extent that this layout is reused in the video game, which, as I argue, strives to reproduce the look of its specific BD source—one of whose markers are the six pages with decorated borders, to which the game assigns the role of transitions. A point of continuity between the game and the BD, these pages also reveal a great difference in the approaches to adaptation of the two.

Five of the six passages featured are drawn from Flaubert, like the majority of the BD text.[1] However, they stand out in that they feature typographical indications that they are cited from Flaubert.[2] Rather than creating tension, the use of ellipses in these passages suggests omission, which alludes to the existence of a source from which they are cited. They thus bear the markings of what Antoine Compagnon called "le travail de la citation" ("the work of citation"): Druillet's operations on the Flaubertian text. According to the critic, quotes in a text should be read as the interaction of *"un énoncé répété et une énonciation répétante"* (*"a repeated utterance and a repeating enunciation"*), *which places them* "dans cette ambivalence, la collusion, la confusion en elle de l'actif et du passif" ("in this ambivalence, the collusion, the confusion herein of the active and the passive") (Compagnon 1979, 56). They are informed by their context, being commented on by the surrounding text, even as they serve to clarify it, aiding it in making its point more resoundingly.

These passages are decorated with accompanying illustrations. Depending on the pagination, they either face an illustrated page or are followed by one that relates to the plot points mentioned in the citation. The text may add some background information or allude to the relevance of the developments, but the emphasis is on repetition, with text and image echoing each other. One could read a concern for fidelity in the act of citing from Flaubert as much as possible, and in matching text and illustration, but instead, these passages make it clear that Druillet is not concerned with the letter of text.

As points of direct intersection between Flaubert and Druillet, novel and BD, these passages attest to a contest of text and image. The condensation of the Flaubertian text and the visual disposition of the passages with decorative borders make them comparable to illustrations in a novel, with a reversal of the positions and of the roles of the two media. As Newell explains, illustrations are commonly thought to make difficult novels easier and to provide a "gateway" for readers into the work. Believing that the collaboration between text and images can lead to the reader's higher level of comprehension assumes that images are transparent and subordinate to the text, while text is open to a multitude of meanings. But as Fischer suggests, illustrations can "add metaphorical comment, extend the story, alert the reader to significant patterns, and supply visual types of the characters" (1995, 61). Newell further shows that the production of illustrations for novels is "always inflected by numerous intertexts, among them the artist's other works, or . . . the meanings and significations a reproduced work has accumulated from previous contexts and reproductions" (2017, 79). Concluding on the relationship of illustrations and the texts in which they appear, she writes that they fulfill the same need as adaptations on the part of the public, noting that "audiences consistently want more: more explanation . . . more clarification, more expansion, more story—they want more of the same but different, but not too different" (94).

In reversing the places of text and image, *Salammbô* casts the text as the gateway into the illustration, seemingly enacting Barthes's schema, whereby "polysemous," images evocative of "a 'floating chain' of signifieds," are juxtaposed with a "linguistic message," which helps the reader "to choose the correct level of perception," and clarify the meaning of the image by letting them focus "[their] gaze but also [their] understanding" (1977, 39). But given the minimalist approach to citation in the BD and the editing of the decorated passages, this text is reduced to the most practical of comments and the most limited extension to the story. It is, moreover, displaced from its network of allusions and intertexts and cannot supply the much-desired "more story." Encased in its borders, the Flaubertian text merely signifies its provenance and medium, providing a skeleton upon which the illustration can grow.

The angular, repeated pattern of the borders casts the Flaubertian text as inert, stressing its difference from the visual narrative into which it is inserted. But the encasement of the text in these ornamental pages can also be seen as showcasing it. It appears a special find, rendering the passages akin to the results of a Flaubertian archaeological dig.[3] Read at the time of its publication as an "archaeological novel," *Salammbô* is the fruit of five years of intensive research by its author into ancient Carthage. The visibility of this labor makes the novel akin to an encyclopedia of Antiquity (Neefs 1974), condemned by prominent literary critic Sainte-Beuve as well as archaeologist Guillaume Frœhner over its claim to scientific erudition and its ability to represent the past. To summarize such criticisms, the first commentator considered that *Salammbô* was not a realist novel because the archaeological details were not used in a realist manner, in that they did not help to elucidate the psychology of the characters. The latter found it "unscientific" because Flaubert's use of novelistic conventions impeded proper scientific communication. Explicating Frœhner's critique from the epistemological point of view of archaeology, Corinne Saminadayar-Perrin shows that Flaubert failed to achieve the standard goals of the discipline—he did not render the past intelligible, but merely described it through its artifacts. She further observes that *Salammbô*'s "dense matérialité des objets qui occupent le devant de la scène revêt une fonction essentiellement ornementale" ("dense materiality of the objects in the foreground takes on an essentially ornamental function") (2011, par. 24). Neefs relates this tendency to Flaubert's project of reconstructing an inaccessible model: The accumulation of research evident in the text was needed to occlude the gap at its center (1974, 64).

These two notions, of the decorative artifact and the absent model, inversed, define Druillet's adaptation and his operations on Flaubertian text. To Druillet and his readers, the model is all too present—as he notes, "Pendant sept ans, je travaille sur *Salammbô*. Non sans appréhension, car adapter Flaubert n'est pas chose aisée. C'est un monument de la littérature et Flaubert lui-même avait souhaité bon courage à ceux qui voudraient l'illustrer" ("For seven years, I work on *Salammbô*. Not without apprehension, because adapting Flaubert is not an easy thing. It is a monument of literature and Flaubert himself had wished good luck to those who would want to illustrate it") (2010, 197–98). The novel's decorative artifacts, details that the nineteenth-century author had carefully researched in order to accurately represent Carthage, are visually substituted with elements of Druillet's own science fiction universe. For example, antagonist Hamilcar Barca's elephants, the various races in the mercenary army, and their weapons become futuristic alien creatures and technologies, which are nevertheless not addressed as such. Through their inversion of text and image, the pages with decorated borders present the Flaubertian model and denote its role in the new work: a seed enveloped by a much larger, differently shaped, colored, and textured fruit. The narrative follows the aesthetic, with the opening pages of the BD, in which Druillet sets up the substitution of the protagonist (his Lone Sloane as Flaubert's Mathô) integrating Flaubert's *Salammbô* into a larger body of (illustrated) work as a further voyage of Lone Sloane, echoed in the closing pages by the hero's reabsorption into his own universe.[4]

The Video Game: *Salammbô*'s Production

Reviewing the catalog of *Salammbô*'s publisher, the now-defunct Cryo Interactive, we note a thematic predilection for historically based games:

Versailles 1685 (1996), *Egypte 1157 av. J.C.* (1997), *Chine* (1998), as well as a methodological preference for adaptations from other media.[5] Drawing on literary sources appears a creatively productive area for the company, as indicated by titles such as *Ubik* (1998), *The New Adventures of the Time Machine* (2000), *Dracula* (2001), *Jekyll & Hyde* (2002), and *The Mystery of the Nautilus* (2002). The games entertain diverse relationships with their sources, ranging from the simple appropriation of the novels' titles or characters into new narratives (*The Mystery of the Nautilus* keeps only Verne's submarine and its captain), to what can be termed "loose adaptations," in which the player reproduces key actions or scenarios from the literary texts in new locations or for new purposes (*Ubik*, *Jekyll & Hyde*). Games inspired by other media include *Aliens* (1995) and *Hellboy* (2000), which are based on comic books, and *Les Visiteurs* (1998) and *From Dusk till Dawn* (2001), based on films.

The diversity of these examples suggests that Cryo's interest in adaptation derives from the commercial appeal of an already-vetted story, which also stands to attract an already constituted public. Starting in the 1980s, video games have been perceived as a valuable tie-in market for films (Fassone 2018, 108), with blockbusters being at the forefront of franchises to adapt. Independent companies and European companies, however, found it more difficult to secure the rights for these films, with Ubisoft's acquisition of *King Kong* in 2005 representing the first French project of such magnitude (Blanchet 2015, 186). Even though Cryo's adaptations are not of the same scale, they do follow trends in film-to-game adaptation by promising a close relationship with their source, allowing users "yet another opportunity to buy into the film franchise" (Moore 2010, 186). The closeness of the relationship between game and film is primarily signaled through visual means, but Cryo's biggest commercial success, *Dune* (1992), also adapts plot and character development through its gameplay. A look at how this is achieved will help us identify the key elements in the developer's method of adaptation, which will frame the discussion of *Salammbô*.

The two projects are very similar in terms of their sources, which are high-profile science fiction texts. Both are layered adaptations, with *Dune* based on David Lynch's film (1984) of Frank Herbert's novel (1965) by the same name.[6] The games thus take on a classic text, but as an adapted version into a new, more popular medium, with the latter installment being visually predominant. *Dune* used the likeness of the actors playing the main parts and used some film sequences. For *Salammbô*, this is manifest in the game's association with Druillet: The artist's involvement in development is featured in its advertising campaign and on the front of the game box, while the back features his picture. His sigil is the first image presented to the user when launching the game, indicating that the artist was viewed as being of greater relevance to the game's intended audience than Flaubert, and he is also credited with graphic design and artistic direction.

While the David Lynch adaptation was found unsatisfactory by viewers and critics alike,[7] the game's positive user reception can be attributed to the close match between the film narrative and the genre into which it was adapted. The game offered more to its players than the typical film-to-game adaptation, which provided a pale imitation of its source through visual resemblance, unsupported by a strong narrative or gameplay (Fassone 2018, 111). Cryo's *Dune* took advantage of Lynch's paring down of the first novel of Frank Herbert's space opera to a handful of key characters, locations, and conflicts centered on the exploitation of a valuable commodity (spice). It also followed its secondary focus on the messianic nature of the main character, Paul Atreides, and his mastery of psychic powers, which would assist him in triumphing over his rivals. Like the film, it excised the novel's philosophical meditations and political intrigue, reducing its worldbuilding to a few essential elements.

The close relationship between game and film was achieved through gameplay. *Dune*'s core element is real-time strategy gameplay in which the user, cast as Paul Atreides, gathers resources, both human (an army) and material (tools, weapons, spice) and manages them in a series of conflicts with various antagonists keen on attaining the same objectives. The adventure side of the game entails conversations with other characters that allow the player to obtain necessary information to advance the plot. This is conveyed to the user as the building of relationships with the inhabitants of the alien planet, and its effect is to open access to superior types of resources. The development of the main character's psychic powers, which happens as the plot advances, offers increased communication range and access to better transportation, which render the resource management easier. A close fit between story and mechanics is thus evident. The practical effect of the game's adventure side is to make available different iterations of the strategy gameplay, while, narratively, it integrates the game mechanisms into the specific parameters of the *Dune* diegesis.

Visually, the game recommends itself as an adaptation of its film source by styling the main characters on the actors playing them and by including footage from the film. Offered as an enhancement of the playing experience in the Sega Mega CD release of the game, this addition renders the encounter of the two adaptations very visible. The inclusion is meant to underline the continuity between Lynch's and Cryo's versions of *Dune*, but the juxtaposition in fact reminds the user that the two are distinct. That one is "playing the film" is much more convincingly suggested by the gameplay, which reproduces the main character's story arc through its combination of strategy and adventure mechanisms. The apposition of the two media, while desired for commercial reasons, remains jarring by not being integrated into the conceit of the game or being given a game-specific function.

The adaptation of *Dune* thus indicates that, in analyzing *Salammbô*'s engagement with its BD source from the point of view of its production, the following elements are key: the game as the adaptation of an adaptation, the producers' desire to stress the intermedial nature of the adaptation, and the visual signaling of the correlation of the game and its source. *Salammbô*'s box appears to address the last point by informing that the game is developed "d'après le roman de Gustave Flaubert et la bande dessinée culte de Philippe Druillet" ("based on Gustave Flaubert's novel and Philippe Druillet's cult comic"). This suggests a synthesis of Flaubert and Druillet, perhaps even an equality in prestige. In this regard, the game is promoting an institutional recognition of the BD, which first appeared in *Métal hurlant* (1980, no. 48–54), a French science fiction magazine with a profound influence on the genre,[8] to great critical reception. As the author remarks, "Pour la première fois, un auteur de bande dessinée illustre un classique de la littérature. Les deux mondes ne s'affrontent pas, ils se complètent. Avec *Salammbô*, j'ai fait entrer la bande dessinée dans les musées" ("For the first time, a comics author illustrates a literary classic. The two worlds do not clash but complete each other. With *Salammbô*, I helped comics enter museums") (Druillet 2010, 197–98). Because of this newly acquired symbolic capital, and in similar fashion to the case of *Dune*, Cryo's approach to the adaptation of an adaptation is more focused on the second layer than on the source material, making Druillet's BD the model to replicate in video game format.

But unlike Lynch's *Dune* as an adaptation of Herbert's novel, the BD does not distill, reduce, or tidy up the source narrative for easier consumption. Instead, it expands the diegesis through Druillet's own science fiction universe, and transitions to visual exposition. Druillet's world disperses through Flaubert's *Salammbô* when he casts his recurring hero, Lone Sloane, as the novel's protagonist Mathô.[9] The two characters may share this profession, but they have few other similarities, as Sloane is an interplanetary traveler, who engages in epic conflicts, being once used by the gods in their battle for supremacy (*Lone Sloane: Délirius 2*).

As Paula Rea Radisch has observed, Druillet "stretches and expands his frames" (1993, 104), one of his trademarks being the two-page spread, which accommodates non-linear reading patterns that emphasize energy and

movement. The reader is drawn both to observe vignettes of action in freely
defined sequence and to contemplate the whole. In contrast, pages that serve
"only as visual display" also occur, as a paradoxical visual intrusion within a
visual story (110). Writing about such panels, Karin Kukkonen notes that
they have a tendency to embed the characters they represent in their surroundings (2018, 60). She observes a certain automation of their actions
and subordination to their environment even in illustrations in which their
movement is emphasized (64). Integrating characters into elaborate borders
that obscure backgrounds effaces to a certain extent their role as characters,
turning them into decorative objects. Their new abstract existence splits them
from their narrative function, impacting narrative flow. A similar disruption
occurs due to the great variety of spans of diegetic time and space shown in
Druillet's large compositions. Thus, though Sonia Lagerwall has shown that
the "transmediation faithfully follows the story" (2014, 46), despite necessary
ellipses and synthesis, it is very differently articulated in the BD.

This is one of the elements of *Salammbô* that is adapted, rather than
merely transferred, in Cryo's game, which reuses Druillet's characters and locations.[10] Though the game reduces the plot to a simpler quest and divides it
into different episodes, the transitions are effectuated in panels that employ
borders drawn from the BD and adopt the look of distinctive pages in the
album. In the following section, I argue that in the case of Cryo's *Salammbô*,
the encounter of the two media is not discordant, as it was in *Dune*, with the
function given to BD elements being particular to the video game. This integration renders the game an intermedial extension of *Salammbô*, conferring
the "doubled pleasure of the palimpsest: more than one text is experienced—
and knowingly so" (Hutcheon 2006, 116).

Reading *Salammbô* as a Comic Book and Video Game

Salammbô is a point-and-click adventure game in which the player is
cast as Spendius, an escaped slave enlisted by the titular character to contact
Mathô and eventually help the lovers meet. The choice of a secondary character as hero is explained by Luis Pimenta Gonçalves as ensuing from the de-
velopers' desire to reduce the complexity of the plot,[11] which in its modified
form could not be assigned to Mathô in a faithful adaptation (2014, par. 17).
He goes on to note also that the player does not "become" the character—the
point of view remains in the third person, as does the voice-over narration
in referring to Spendius (par. 18). This distancing between player and game
narrative maintains the separation of reader/novel or BD and constitutes one
way that *Salammbô* indicates its nature as an adaptation.

Despite these changes in plot and character, what is much more closely adapted from the BD are the game visuals. The overall look of the game is darker, but the design of key locations (for example, the aqueduct and the temples of Tanith and Moloch) as well as characters (Mathô, Spendius, Salammbô) bears a strong resemblance to their graphic novel versions. The complexity of structures has been maintained, and they continue to be inhabited by strange animals and alien races. The three-dimensional rendering of characters and their adaptation to the expectations of a gameplaying public have made them more static in their appearance and more exaggerated in features, but they are easily recognizable to readers of Druillet's work.

The game also borrows distinctive layout elements of the BD, to which it attributes medium-specific functions. To transition between locations, the game adopts the arrangement specific to six pages in the BD that feature only text encased in an elaborate border, on a slightly patterned background, and face illustrations.[12] The transition sequences treat the square gameplaying screen as a comic book page divided into a variable number of panels, with a larger column on the right used to display subtitles corresponding to the voice-over narration (Fig. 1). It recounts the consequences of the player's

Figure 1: Transition screen in *Salammbô*

actions, with two-dimensional images in Druillet's style enclosed in panels of irregular shapes. These renderings of the game's three-dimensional elements are meant to more closely match the visuals in the BD, making the transitions one of the points in which the adaptation and its source can be seen simultaneously.

The design inherited from Druillet is associated with a break in gameplay. It is a visual element that the user does not control, but which summarizes the episode's events and their significance or consequences. In so doing, it fulfills a further game-specific function, that of bridging the gap between the greater narrative developed by the game and the user's actions. In a point-and-click adventure game, the user advances by solving puzzles, the answers to which depend on conversations or the location and correct arrangement of different objects. Progress occurs in small steps, and not in real time, so these transitions help the user master the magnitude of the character's achievements and their chronology. Through these screens, gameplay appears logically organized, independently of player trial and error.

The Flaubert and Druillet narratives of *Salammbô*, and their respective media, are entwined along the nodes provided by the decorated passages. The novel's distinctive features, and those of its writing, are encapsulated in these pages, becoming embedded in the BD version. In the game, the layout of these pages is used in a function specific to the genre, that of conveying the impact of the player's actions and projecting the action into new locations or launching new episodes. In these instances, the player is reminded that the game is an adaptation, and that a change in medium has occurred, but much more seamlessly than in *Dune*. Motivated by the logic of visual adaptation, the integration of the two media in *Salammbô* is very close.

The game draws on the visual characteristics of its source and integrates the distinctive elements of its medium into gameplay. In a point-and-click adventure game, the player progresses in a linear story by solving various puzzles, including conversations in which a series of correct replies must be given, different objects gathered, organized, or transferred to other characters. In *Salammbô*, visual cues dominate, with the character's main activity being the careful observation of spaces with complex architecture and décor. Plot points are broken down into smaller steps, which reduce the action to the puzzle mechanisms. For example, the initial task of giving Salammbô's statue to Mathô entails six further actions—a conversation with him (1), in which Spendius is instructed where to go to remove his chains (2); a game played with the character that owns blacksmithing tools (3); a conversation with the artisan to obtain glue (4); putting the statue back together (5); and another conversation with Mathô (6). Though the tasks are relatively clearly identified from the start, the locations to visit in accomplishing them are not immediately obvious to the player, so exploration and back-tracking are frequently necessary.

Travel between locations is not ludified, with space scrolling in preset directions and increments displaying the same images on each pass. Coupled with the game's camera being fixed and giving a wide-angle view of the setting, the main playing experience is that of wandering through richly decorated locations. Though the same impression can be had while playing other point-and-click adventure games, because *Salammbô* maintains the specific look of its source, the roaming inherent to this type of gameplay becomes an approximation of reading the BD's sweeping illustrations.

Fassone argues that in adapting film, games engage in the "discretisation and abstraction of the narrative of the original" (2018, 113), and in *Salammbô* the same logic is evident in the treatment of the images. The BD's complex pages are broken down into individual vignettes, linked to create the diegetic geography. Given the main character's frequent isolation in the environment and the lack of time pressure exerted either narratively or through timed puzzles, the player is relatively free to explore it at leisure. The new spatial arrangement does not approximate the "Z" reading pattern of comics, but it was not necessarily the most useful cognitive path in Druillet, whose complex page compositions frequently deconstruct the standard grid format. While the geography prevents users from determining their own reading pattern, the navigation of sites on an average playthrough offers both variety and harmony of design, inviting contemplation. The act is not merely aesthetic, since, like in the BD, puzzles that draw the user deeper into the graphics allow the plot to be derived from the interpretation of images.

Playing *Salammbô* thus depends on the users successfully employing interpretative codes derived from their experience with games and BD in sequence. In this regard, the game follows trends that are evident in French digital comics of the 1990s, as analyzed by Julien Beaudry. As he shows, comics of that period began to be adapted into point-and-click adventure games, and most frequently the BD provided content for games, while form was generally sacrificed. In some cases, games based on comics were, however, designed so that they could "conserver un mode de narration visuelle proche de la bande dessinée. Ils intègrent des citations directes des albums et utilisent des codes graphiques propres à ce média (cases, bulles, récitatifs . . .)" ("keep a mode of visual narration close to comics. They integrate direct citations from the albums and use graphic codes specific to this medium [panels, speech balloons, captions . . .]") (2018, 78). Situated between these models, Édouard Lussan's *Opération Teddy Bear* (1996), functioned by "alterner des moments ludiques et des moments narratifs" ("alternating between playful moments and narrative moments"), yielding "un nouvel objet culturel, à mi-chemin entre la bande dessinée et le jeu vidéo" ("a new cultural object, halfway between comics and video games") (54). While *Salammbô*, too, occupies this space, the use it makes of its BD source, as a game, can also be read through a comparison with similar products that are much more closely aligned in their development and marketing with the video game side, such as Ubisoft's *XIII*, a French-produced title released the same year as *Salammbô* and based on the eponymous Belgian comic by Jean Van Hamme and William Vance, and a more recent Japanese title, Atlus' *Persona 5* (2016).

In *XIII*, the BD look is primarily achieved through the process of cel-shading characters and environments, in which three-dimensional models are rendered as though they were two-dimensional, and more particularly, using the conventions of comic book shading. Bold outlines around characters and sharp perspective on objects and architecture echo the impression of two-dimensional approximation of volumes. Onomatopoeias are also used, with diegetic noises such as gunshots and exclamations suggesting injuries displayed on screen in distinctive lettering during gameplay. But through this, *XIII* alludes to comics in general and not *XIII* in particular, the differences between the two being underlined by the game's palette. Though it achieves the look of a "comic book in action" through the exaggeration of the medium's most striking visual conventions, the game adaptation no longer resembles its BD source.

The game mimics most closely the look of a comic book in its menus (Fig. 2). There, a tight panel layout illustrated with various images (snapshots of upcoming actions, characters, and locations) serves as background to captions denoting different options. The illustrations are colored in and receive onomatopoeia when the user's pointer hovers over them. Though the game's reproduction of comic book layout is at its most traditional in the menus, its use of nonsequential illustrations troubles the interpretation. In this case, *XIII* relies on the user's perception of the panels as a structuring and delimiting device, rather than asking them to employ meaning-making strategies familiar from reading comics.

Despite *XIII*'s commitment to the comic book aesthetic, it demonstrates an unease with the fixity of the print medium. The opening sequence already announces the game's desire to replace it through other media. An open book with a traditional layout of panels is initially displayed to the player, but it is

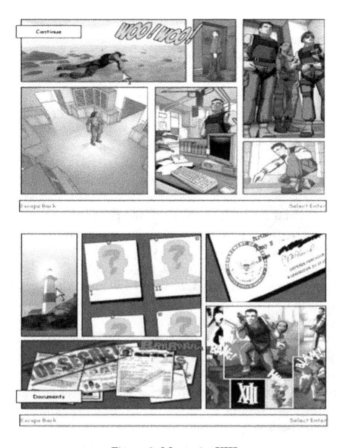

Figure 2: Menus in *XIII*

not meant to be read since it is not visible long enough, nor are there evident captions or speech bubbles to assist comprehension. The camera then sinks into it and goes on to jump between panels on the first and subsequent pages, playing brief animations. These sequences show what ensues from the illustrations, either filling in the gaps between displayed panels or going far beyond what was portrayed on the overview of the book. The camera movement thus appears to simulate reading the comic and to illustrate how meaning is made from separate images, but it also speeds up the process and settles it into the content of the animations.

It is also important to note that several of the sequences' bridging panels allude to other visual media, such as film or video. Artifacts such as film grain or the framing outline and recording indicator from a camera display are superimposed onto the animation, though onomatopoeias are also used to punctuate the main events. In combining these elements, the sequence foreshadows the change in medium and announces the game's aesthetic. At the same time, a concern with expediently "covering" the narrative territory occupied by the comic book is evident. It is evoked in the game's opening only so it can be replaced through other, more motile media. This creates the impression that intermediality is rejected even as it is illustrated—the comic book medium is reduced to an aesthetic divorced both from its own and game mechanics.

A different approach to replicating the comic book look in a video game is offered by *Persona 5*, which valorizes secondary aesthetic characteristics of comic books and also assigns them a game-specific function. A Japanese game, it highlights the traits of manga as a printed, paper medium in punctuating important transitions in gameplay. Graphic elements such as grayscale and halftone shading are deconstructed and decoupled from their original purpose—the game is in color, and shading is achieved differently by its programming—and related to a gameplaying feature specific to *Persona 5*'s genre, the Japanese role-playing game (JRPG).

The game narrative has the characters navigate between two distinct environments: a realistic setting (modern-day Tokyo), in which they are high school students, and a supernatural realm (the Metaverse), in which they possess superpowers and confront a wide variety of enemies, collectively identified as Shadows. Confronting the Shadows allows the characters to progress both geographically within dungeons, the structures to be traversed in order to reach the main villain of a given stage, and in terms of their resources and abilities.

The comic book elements are most evident in the Metaverse, during the characters' battles with the Shadows. There, the status bar displayed recalls manga through its representation of the player's party in high-contrast grayscale cartoon miniatures in fixed overlay. The medium's visual vocabulary is evident also in the way the impact of the attacks is conveyed through distinctive, fixed lettering and onomatopoeia. Rare dialogues juxtapose a two-dimensional rendering of the characters with the three-dimensional battle scene. Thick, irregular lines are used to separate the two, creating panel borders and defining speech bubbles. A further allusion to the look of manga is made through the use of visible, decorative halftone patterns (such as stars) in grayscale. These are noticeable, for example, following a successful "all-out attack," when characters are shown celebrating victory in a two-dimensional static image. Various versions of this shading method appear also in menus

Figure 3: Menu in *Persona 5* featuring decorative halftone patterns

(Fig. 3), and on the screen separating the characters' celebration of the conclusion of a battle and the series of slides informing the player what resources were acquired.

The function ascribed to the particularities of manga as a print medium evoked in marking the end of a battle is that of realizing a transition between two main types of gameplay activity: the traversal of the dungeon and the confrontation with enemies. In the first setting, the player is relatively free in his or her movements, while during battles the playable characters and the Shadows alternate attacks in a scripted fashion. The turn-based gameplay is structured so that the player does not control the characters' movement but selects attacks that are carried out on screen through preset animations. A staple of the JRPG, this transition was jarring in games such as those of the *Final Fantasy* series, where enemies would not be indicated on the map, and consequently the user would engage in random battles as he navigated the space. *Persona 5*'s framing of the dungeon-battle-dungeon transition through manga softens the transition. The variety of gameplay activity is conveyed as the turning of pages, encouraging the user to see the two types of actions in which he engages as continuous.

This comparison suggests that *Salammbô* strives for an integration of the two media in the player experience: It draws on the visual characteristics of its source, like *XIII*, and assimilates the distinctive elements of its medium into gameplay, like *Persona 5*. As adaptation projects, both *Salammbô* and

XIII engage with the question of both recalling their comic book source and functioning as a game, but they take divergent routes. While *XIII* prefers the gaming side and reduces its reuse of the comic book elements to utilitarian functions (menus and some transitions), *Salammbô*'s game mechanics can in fact be seen to emulate the experience of reading the BD.

Conclusion

Salammbô stands out from games such as *XIII* and *Persona 5* through its integration of the two media on which it relies, because it reproduces key aspects of the BD experience both through gameplay and graphically. The most visible allusions to the game's source, Druillet's book, appear in the transition screens, which borrow the layout of six distinctive spreads. In these screens, the flattening of the images into two dimensions recalls the BD illustrations more closely than the game's three-dimensional models. References to the BD thus mark important points in the game, in which progress is marked and game activities in which the user has engaged are related to the story.

Even as they stress the game's nature as an adaptation, the transition screens also attest to the differences between Cryo's approach to its source and that of Druillet. In the album, this layout is reserved for longer Flaubertian citations that bear the marks of Druillet's editing and are juxtaposed with his complex illustrations. An encapsulation of his method of adapting Flaubert, the pages show that in the BD the source text is contained and restrained. It powers the album, but it develops in different, unexpected directions, with expansion and flow being the key characteristics of its visual narrative. While Cryo, with the artist's collaboration, privileges graphics, as the reading of *Salammbô* predecessor *Dune* indicates, its emphasis is on fidelity to its source.

The game genre into which *Salammbô* was adapted entails visual puzzles and the navigation of space in a particular, pre-scripted manner. This type of movement imparted to the BD is more in keeping with the reading of a large-format album than with the three-dimensional movement required by *XIII*. There, though the look of a comic book in motion is achieved, the emphasis is on the motion. Transitions featuring comic book elements fulfill much of the same function as in *Salammbô*, but they also recall the particularities of its source, which are erased in *XIII*. If *Persona 5* assigns a game-specific function to the traits of manga as the printed, paper medium it reuses, it also decouples these from their original function. The decorative use of these elements is woven into the game's themes, further characterizing the unexpected heroic nature of the protagonists. While the manga elements look distinctive in the game, their mix in *Salammbô* creates less of a sense of an encounter between media. Gameplay and graphics allow the two to flow through each other, yielding a continuity of experience between game and BD.

Endnotes

1. In an interview, Druillet approximated that 70 percent of the text in the BD is Flaubert's (Barbier 2017, 20).

2. In Druillet's *Nosferatu* (1989), citations from Baudelaire used in speech bubbles are acknowledged in the illustrations as such.

3. In a similar vein, Barbier refers to the Flaubertian citations as jewels 2017, (9).

4. The 2018 Titan Comics English-language translation of the collected *Salammbô* bears the title *Lone Sloane Salammbô*, in keeping with *Lone Sloane: Delirius* and *Lone Sloane: Gail.*

5. For further details on Cryo's historical games see *Video Games Around the World*, edited by Mark JP Wolf (2015).

6. Cryo returned to the same subject matter in 2001, following the Sci-Fi channel's adaptation of the novel, with *Frank Herbert's Dune*, which was far less successful.

7. Representative reviews include those of Richard Corliss, writing for *Time* (July 29, 1985), who considered the film "inward and remote," Pauline Kael in *The New Yorker* (December 24, 1984), who found that it was "heavy on exposition," and presented in "scenes that are like illustrations," and Rita Kempley in *The Washington Post* (December 14, 1984), who observed that the adaptation "turns epic to myopic."

8. Thierry Groensteen observed that popular science fiction works such *Star Wars*, *Blade Runner*, and *Alien* would have been impossible without the magazine (2006, 86).

9. The character appears for the first time in 1966, in *Lone Sloane: Le Mystère des abîmes* (*The Mystery of The Abyss*), and in a total of fourteen albums to date.

10. The representation of characters in the game is more stylized by Druillet, and they are costumed in more overtly science fiction outfits, though the architecture remains similar to that in the BD.

11. Gonçalves's article also goes into greater detail of which episodes from the BD are kept in the game.

12. Unlike the illustrations, the decorated passages are signed by the BD letterer, Dominique Amat.

Works Cited

BARBIER, Marie. 2017. *Flaubert Druillet: une rencontre*. Paris: Marie Barbier éditions.

BARTHES, Roland. 1997. *Image—Music—Text*. Translated by Stephen Heath. New York: Hill & Wang.

BEAUDRY, Julien. 2018. *Cases Pixels*. Tours, France: PUFR.

BLANCHET, Alexis. 2015. "France." In *Video Games Around the World*, edited by Mark JP Wolf, 175–93. Cambridge, MA: MIT Press.

COMPAGNON, Antoine. 1979. *La Seconde main ou le travail de la citation*. Paris: Seuil.

DRUILLET, Philippe. 2010. *Salammbô l'intégrale*. Issy-les-Moulineaux, France: Glénat.

DRUILLET, Philippe, and David ALLIOT. 2014. *Delirium, autoportrait*. Paris: Les Arènes.

FASSONE, Riccardo. 2018. "Notoriously Bad: Early film-to-video game adaptations (1982–1994)." In *The Routledge Companion to Adaptation*, edited by Dennis Cutchins, et al., 106–16. London: Routledge.

FISCHER, Judith. 1995. "Image versus Text in the Illustrated Novels of William Thackeray." In *Victorian Literature and the Victorian Visual Imagination*, edited by Carol T. Christ and John O. Jordan, 60–87. Berkeley: University of California Press.

FLAUBERT, Gustave. 1927a. *Correspondance* III. Paris: Conrad.

———. 1927b. *Correspondance* IV. Paris: Conrad.

———. 2013. *Œuvres Complètes*. Paris: Gallimard.

GROENSTEEN, Thierry. 2006. *Un Objet culturel non identifié*. n.p.: Éditions de l'An 2.

HUTCHEON, Linda. 2006. *A Theory of Adaptation*. London: Routledge.

KUKKONEN, Karin. 2018. "The Fully Extended Mind." In *The Edinburgh Companion to Contemporary Narrative Theories*, edited by Zara Dinnen and Robyn Warhol, 56–66. Edinburgh: Edinburgh University Press.

LAGERWALL, Sonia. 2014. "Drawing the Written Woman: Philippe Druillet's Adaptation of Gustave Flaubert's *Salammbô*." *European Comic Art* 7 (2): 31–63.

LIPPITZ, Armin. 2017. "Lost in the Static? Comics in Video Games." In *Intermedia Games—Games Inter Media: Video Games and Intermediality*, edited by Michael Fuchs and Jeff Thoss, 115–32. New York: Bloomsbury Academic.

MOORE, Michael Ryan. 2010. "Adaptation and New Media." *Adaptation* 3 (2): 179–92.

NEEFS, Jacques. 1974. "*Salammbô*, textes critiques." *Littérature* 15: 52–64.

NEWELL, Kate. 2017. *Expanding Adaptation Networks: From Illustration to Novelization*. London: Palgrave Macmillan.

PIMENTA GONÇALVES, Luis. 2014. "*Salammbô*, les déambulations d'une œuvre entre littérature et jeu vidéo." *Mémoires du livre / Studies in Book Culture* 5 (2): n.p.

RADISICH, Paula. 1993. "Evolution and Salvation: The Iconic Origins of Druillet's Monstrous Combatants of the Night." In *Flights of Fancy: Armed Conflict in Science Fiction and Fantasy*, edited by George Slusser and Eric S Rabkin, 103–13. Athens: University of Georgia Press.

SAMINADAYAR-PERRIN, Corinne. 2011. "Salammbô et la querelle du 'roman archéologique,'" *Revue d'histoire littéraire de la France* 111: 605–20.

TOOKE, Adrienne. 2000. *Flaubert and the Pictorial Arts*. Oxford: Oxford University Press.

PART FIVE
Comics and Music

CHAPTER THIRTEEN:
Songs and Music of French Colonialism in the Maghreb through Comics
Mark McKinney

Song and Music as Relics and Icons

It is noteworthy that French cartoonist Jacques Tardi created the cover illustration of the volume *Quand on chantait les colonies: Colonisation et culture populaire de 1830 à nos jours* (*When We Sang the Colonies: Colonization and Popular Culture from 1830 to Today*), by historians Claude and Josette Liauzu (2002), and that this image provides a critique of orientalism and French colonialism in the Maghreb. It shows a gramophone with its horn amplifier sitting on top of a small table made of carved wood. Next to these objects appears another small table or stool where someone has placed a metal tray on which sit a hookah, a liquor bottle with a doser attached, a glass, and matches. All this is positioned in front of a wall painted in blue, white, and red (the colors of the French flag), and stained with blood, with a machine gun hanging from a nail. In the background, on the left, one notices a minaret and a palm tree rising above a hedge (Fig. 1).

Figure 1: A drawing by Jacques Tardi alludes to the violence of French colonialism and the French songs that celebrated it. ©Syllepse.

In the introduction to their study, Claude and Josette Liauzu observe that, despite its richness, song has generally been neglected by historians, including those who study colonialism.

Si l'écrit a été et demeure le document obligé de toute histoire, et de celle de la colonisation en particulier, si l'iconographie est devenue récemment indispensable, la chanson a été négligée jusqu'ici, malgré quelques titres récents. Pourtant, elle associe trois types de matériaux nécessaires à une histoire qui se veut totale: le texte, le son et l'image (celle des illustrations hier, des clips aujourd'hui).

La chanson peut donc contribuer à renouveler les études de la co-lonisation, qui sont restées par trop convenues, qui se sont limitées surtout à l'étude des idées, des doctrines, des débats idéologiques, des batailles et des combats politiques. En effet, elle fournit un éclairage irremplaçable des représentations, des mentalités populaires.

(If the written word has been and remains the obligatory document of any history, and that of colonization in particular, if iconography has recently become indispensable, song has been neglected until now, despite a few recent titles. However, it brings together three types of materials necessary to a history that aims for totality: text, sound, and image [that of illustrations yesterday, of clips today].

Song can thereby help renew studies of colonization, which have remained too conventional, which have mainly limited themselves to the study of ideas, doctrines, ideological debates, battles, and po-litical fights. Indeed, it sheds an irreplaceable light on popular repre-sentations and attitudes.)[1] (2002, 5)

This call to examine a multimedia form of popular culture is all the more convincing because Claude Liauzu, himself born in Casablanca in 1940, was a well-respected historian of colonialism and the Maghreb. For those who study comics, the most striking aspect of this quotation is that its terms apply almost word-for-word to this visual-textual art form, with the exception of the reference to sound, of course. Indeed, for a long time, and today still, comics have been a popular art form that has illustrated colonial expansion and retraction.[2] As such, they provide a rich and surprisingly little-exploited resource for the cultural critic or the historian desiring to study colonialism and its representations. Tardi himself gave a critical representation of colonialism in several of his comics, notably on the exploitation of colonized people as soldiers during the Great War, which makes him an appropriate choice to illustrate the cover of the Liauzus' study. And, in spite of the mute nature of their art, cartoonists often use its visual and textual resources to depict music and sound, as various theoreticians, such as Frédéric Pomier (1988, 58–64), Benoît Peeters (1998, 145–47), and Thierry Groensteen (1999, 65–67) have shown.[3]

Representing the Maghreb, and above all Algeria, provides one of the oldest links of colonial representation in comics and of French-language caricature, dating at least as far back as the conquest of Algeria starting in 1830 (Kunzle 1990; McKinney 2013). The cover illustration of Alain Ruscio's book, *Que la France était belle au temps des colonies . . . : Anthologie de chansons coloniales et exotiques françaises* (*How Beautiful France Was in the Time of the Colonies . . . : Anthology of French Colonial and Exotic Songs*) (2001), published the year before the Liauzus' study, recalls the beginnings of the modern colonial era and of the evolution of comics: It is an image that appeared on the sheet music of the lascivious military song "La Mouker" ("The *mouker*," i.e., Arab woman), also known under the name "Travadjar la mouker," created around 1850, the refrain to which remains one of the better known fragments of colonial song linked to North Africa.[4] The illustration (Fig. 2), split into two frames that together produce a mini-story, calls to mind the "images d'Epinal" ("Epinal pictures") that disseminated the French colonial epic story and were an ancestor of modern comics. Here, the story is about a French colonial soldier seducing a Maghrebi woman and thereby cuckolding a Maghrebi

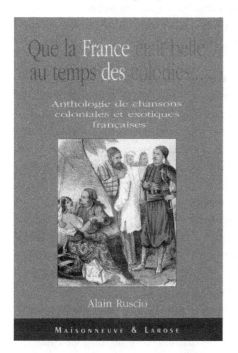

Figure 2: The image illustrating the sheet music for the colonial song "La mouker" stages a widespread colonial fantasy: the cuckolding of the Maghrebi by the French. ©Maisonneuve & Larose.

man. This situation is one of the most common colonial fantasies of French song (Ruscio 2001, 354; Liauzu and Liauzu 2002, 99), colonial caricature dating back to the conquest (Porterfield 1998, 138–41), and comics (Basfao 1990, 226–27).

Historically, therefore, comics, song, and music have transmitted colonial ideology and history to a large popular audience. To a lesser but growing degree, they also constitute a place where colonialism has been critiqued and contested. In my analysis of how song and music have been incorporated in comics (re)published since 1962—especially, but not exclusively, in texts published in France by French artists (of different backgrounds)—that represent French colonization of the Maghreb and particularly of Algeria, I propose to show here how divergent and contradictory memories are recreated and transmitted in popular culture. Even though my perspective here is mainly sociohistorical, I will also consider comics' formal aspects. Throughout this chapter, I will build on the analyses of French colonialism in song conducted by the Liauzus and Ruscio, as well as on the analyses of Algerian and French song in colonial Algeria developed by Nadya Bouzar-Kasbadji (*L'Émergence artistique*, "La Marseillaise").

Like many other visual and textual documents of the colonial period reproduced or cited in contemporary comics, colonial songs often function like fragments recovered from the past and enshrined in the present, like historical and cultural relics disappearing from a world that new forms of imperialism and resistance are refashioning in an accelerated manner. Here I borrow the term "relic" from Michel de Certeau and Luce Giard (1994, 266–68), who used it to describe the way in which immigrants and their offspring strive to preserve the fragments of a minority culture whose general framework and practices get weaker and disappear under the corrosive effects of assimilation. We shall see that the metonymic nature of comics (Miller 2007, 78) lends itself to this type of activity. One often finds the practice of enshrining relics of the (pre)colonial world in comics by French cartoonists of Algerian or *Pied-Noir* background and by cartoonists located in the Maghreb. Among the reasons for this activity, one can identify French and Maghrebi nationalist ideologies, as well as the extreme violence of colonization and liberation. The fact that cartoonists of diverse ethnic or national origins, and of different political perspectives, often work with the same songs and musical traditions, bears witness in part to a common cultural heritage, but with different inflections. In the rest of this chapter, I shall examine three groups of musical and cultural references in a comics corpus about the Maghreb: military music, patriotic songs, and other songs imbued with colonial nostalgia; folklore and orientalism in traditional music and dance; and Algerian-French *métissage* (cultural or ethnic mixing), cultural conflict, and song.[5] My analysis of these references owes much to the contrapuntal analysis of Edward Said in *Culture and Imperialism*, and to his earlier critique of orientalism (1994a).

Not Regretting Anything:
Colonial Nostalgia, Military Music, and Patriotic Songs

The best-known French military song about the conquest of the Maghreb can be found in *L'Ogre du Djebel* (*The Ogre of the Mountain*) (1986), drawn by Annie Goetzinger and scripted by Victor Mora, which takes place in Morocco. The arrival of a unit of the Foreign Legion is announced by "La Casquette du père Bugeaud" ("Father Bugeaud's Cap") (Fig. 3), which the legionaries sing (1986, 38).[6] For Liauzu and Liauzu, the immense popularity of this song is "un succès de propagande, ainsi qu'un témoignage de la présence que l'Algérie conquiert progressivement dans la culture populaire (française)" ("a propaganda success, as well as a testimony to the presence that Algeria gains progressively in [French] popular culture") (2002, 22; cf. Ruscio 2001, 50).[7]

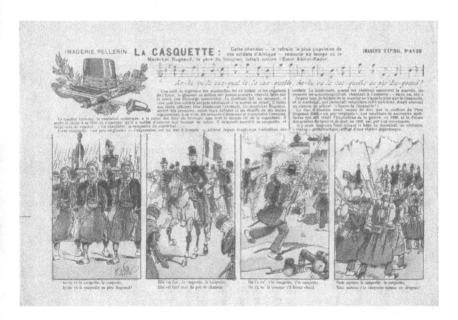

Figure 3: An *image d'Epinal* (Epinal image) celebrates the French conquest of Algeria through the military song "La Casquette du père Bugeaud" ("Father Bugeaud's Cap"). (Mark McKinney's personal collection.)

According to Bouzar-Kasbadji (1989, 243), this tune was sung in Algeria's French schools and in the French colonial Armée d'Afrique (African Army).[8] In the album, the collective nature of the song is indicated by the multiple tails attached to the speech balloons. Indeed, among the most prevalent musical genres in comics about French colonialism in the Maghreb, one finds the marching songs and other tunes of the colonial military units; they form an especially important part of the "Histoire de la Légion Etrangère" ("History of the Foreign Legion"), a four-volume series celebrating the Foreign Legion. Drawn by Philippe Glogowski, scripted by Marien Puisaye (Guy Lehideux) and published from 2002 to 2005 by the Éditions du Triomphe, a traditionalist Catholic publisher associated with the French Far Right, these albums include at the end of each volume an appendix gathering the lyrics of the war songs and marching chants of the Legion's different units, as well as other songs associated with them.

Several of them come from the conquest and colonization of the Maghreb: "Adieu, vieille Europe" ("Farewell, Old Europe") (Glogowski and Puisaye 2002, 46); "Sous le soleil brûlant d'Afrique" ("Under Africa's Burning Sun") (Glogowski and Puisaye 2003, 45); "Le Fanion de la Légion" ("The Legion's Fanion") (46); "En Algérie" ("In Algeria") (Glogowski and Puisaye 2004, 47); "Adieu, adieu (chant du 1e RE)" ("Farewell, Farewell [Song of the 1st Foreign Regiment]"); "Soldats de la Légion Etrangère (DLEM-2e REC)" ("Soldiers of the Foreign Legion [2nd Foreign Cavalry Regiment]"); and "C'est le '4' (chant du 4e RE)" ("It's the '4' [Song of the 4th Foreign Regiment]") (Glogowski and Puisaye 2005, 43–45).[9] We may recall that the Legion, the French colonial unit *par excellence*, was created by decree on March 9, 1831— that is, the year following the capture of Algiers (Liauzu and Liauzu 2002, 23).The Legion is probably the French military corps most often cited in comics whose theme is the French colonization of Algeria, and especially the Algerian War. In this series, the sepia-colored pages and the accompanying illustrations aim to inspire nostalgia and respect for the Legionaries and their exploits, no doubt achieved to the sound of those same songs. It is, however, somewhat surprising to find very little mention of these songs in the hagiographic tale of this series of comics, whose characters do not sing.

One finds an example of mute music in another hagiographic comic: *C'est nous les Africains . . . : L'Algérie de 1880 à 1920* (*We are the Africans . . . : Algeria from 1880 to 1920*), scripted by Evelyne Joyaux-Brédy and drawn by Pierre Joux (1998, 53), the fourth volume in a series of five—published by the Cercle Algérianiste (Algerianist Circle), a militant and conservative *Pied-Noir* association—that commemorates the French colonization of Algeria.

The French colony's patriotic contribution to the military effort of mainland France during the First World War is illustrated by two panels where colonial units are embarking to the rhythm of music played by a military orchestra. But the music itself is not represented by drawn musical notes, and we know neither the words nor the title. In contrast, the album's title comes from the refrain of one of the best-known songs associated with the colonization of the Maghreb, "Les Africains" ("The Africans"). However, the authors note on the title page that "Le chant des Africains auquel est emprunté ce titre a sans doute été créé en 1941 mais il nous a semblé correspondre à la réalité de 1914/1918" ("The song 'The Africans,' from which this title is borrowed, was probably created in 1941 but it seemed to us that it fit the reality of 1914/1918"). The cartoonists thereby shift the song from the Vichy period, when it was (re)written, to the First World War, to characterize the joint military effort of Algerians and colonists, in a multiethnic military force going to the defense of mainland France. The irony in this admission of anachronism is that "Les Africains" was already a rewriting of the "Marche des Marocains" ("March of the Moroccans"), written in 1914 to celebrate the sacrifice of Moroccan colonial troops in the French army during the Great War (Ruscio 2001, 190–91, 205–6, 219–21; cf. Bouzard 2000, 373–75). For Bouzar-Kasbadji, this song was degrading for the colonized:

> Pure création coloniale, le texte de "C'est nous les Africains qui arrivons de loin" exprime implicitement l'infantilisme présumé des troupes "indigènes" s'offrant sur l'autel de la Mère-Patrie: "venant des colonies . . . nous voulons porter haut et fier le beau drapeau de notre France . . . Pour la patrie, mourir au loin."

> (A purely colonial creation, the text of "We are the Africans Coming from Far Away" implicitly expresses the presumed infantilism of the "indigenous" troops sacrificing themselves on the altar of the motherland: "coming from the colonies . . . we want to carry high and proud the beautiful flag of our France . . . For the homeland, to die far away.") (1998, 243)

The use of the song's title in the title of the comic book *C'est nous les Africains . . . : L'Algérie de 1880 à 1920* is a quintessential colonialist gesture, because the (ex)colonizers thereby appropriate the identity of the colonized for themselves. But this choice also responds to a second ideological motivation:

Le patriotisme affiché par les pieds noirs au lendemain de la deuxième guerre [mondiale], qui masque mal leurs sympathies antérieures
envers Vichy, est à l'origine de la captation du Chant des Africains,
captation si réussie qu'on jurerait qu'il s'agit d'un hymne pied noir.
Cette marche a été composée en réalité par Félix Boyer—par ailleurs
auteur du léger Boire un petit coup—, et les paroles par Reyjade.
Envoyé par Vichy en Afrique en 1942, Félix Boyer rallie les gaullistes,
et son chant est adopté par les militaires des Forces Françaises Libres.

(The patriotism exhibited by the Pieds-Noirs at the end of the Second
World War, which poorly hides their former sympathies toward
Vichy, is responsible for the misappropriation of the Song of the
Africans, a misappropriation so successful that one could swear that
it is indeed a Pied-Noir hymn. This march was actually composed
by Félix Boyer—the author of the light song Boire un petit coup
[Having a little drink]—and with lyrics by Reyjade. Sent by Vichy to
Africa in 1942, Félix Boyer rallied the Gaullists, and his song was ad-
opted by the military personnel of the Free French Forces.) (Liauzu
and Liauzu 2002, 123–24; cf. Rioux 1992, 260)

Les Rivages amers: L'Algérie, 1920–1962 (*The Bitter Shores: Algeria,
1920–1962*) (Joyaux-Brédy and Joux 1994, 36–56), the following volume
in the series, confirms the authors' desire to evacuate the historical reality
described by the Liauzus—that is, the fact that the *Pieds-Noirs* had supported the Vichy regime.

My last three examples of military songs in comics are interesting from
both political and artistic perspectives. In *Algérie française!* (*French Algeria!*),
by Denis Mérezette and Dumenil, we again find a marching song, this time
serving as background to the torture of Ahmed, an Algerian who just ex-
ploded a bomb in a French hotel:

Sous les pins de la "BA"
Branle-bas de combat
La "Quatre" s'en va
Crâne rasé et gueule de bois
Cette fois c'est du vrai car le convoi démarre
Salut les filles, n'ayez pas le cafard
Sur la piste et les sentiers, l'œil aux aguets
Et les fellaghas ne pourront résister

Devant l'assaut de la "Quatre" au paquet[10]

(Under the pines of the rear army base
Getting ready for combat
The "Four" is going away
Shaved head and hungover
This time it's true, because the convoy sets off
Bye, girls, don't be blue
On the trail and the footpaths, eyes peeled
And the Arab bandits won't be able to resist
Faced with the forceful assault of the "Fourth") (1985, 35–37)

The narrative here alternates between a military parade ground and the nearby torture room. The speech balloons with lyrics and musical notes—indicating to us that the song is being sung—grow progressively bigger and invade the torture panels, while the images zoom in on the faces of the parading French soldiers and the tortured man. The multi-frame sequence (Groensteen 1999, 121–69) that occupies the top three-fourths of the page culminates when the torturers manage to break Ahmed's resistance. The swagger of the song might be confirmed by this (temporary) conclusion, if torture were a fair fight. The partial obscuring of the words of the Algerian's forced confession by the speech balloon, including the song's last lyrics, underlines the fact that torture constitutes an illegal and illegitimate form of combat that must be hidden. Indeed, in at least one account of torture during the Algerian War, one finds mention of the fact that French torturers would play popular music at high volume in order to mask the cries of their victims (Alleg 1986, 50). Here, although at least one of the authors (Mérezette) is of *Pied-Noir* background, the military song does not function as a relic (unlike the use of "Les Africains" in the album *C'est nous les Africains*), but serves instead as a critical device to expose the hidden violence of French Algeria, including that exercised by the occupying army and euphemistically called "the maintenance of order."

A related use of a military song and speech balloons can be found in *Une Éducation algérienne* (*An Algerian Education*) (1982), scripted by Guy Vidal and drawn by Alain Bignon, in another album that—with *Algérie française!*—was one of the first French comics about the Algerian War. Its splash page opens the story with the image of a column of soldiers singing as they return to the base:

Les cavaliers partent pour l'aventure
Ils s'en vont sur la terre d'Algérie
Sur les pas de leurs aînés
Et s'il le faut, ils donneront
Leur vie pour leur patrie bien-aimée[11]

(The cavalrymen are leaving for an adventure
They are going to the Algerian soil
In the footsteps of their elders
And if required, they will give
Their lives for their beloved fatherland) (1982, 3)

The speech balloon containing the song's lyrics and iconic musical notes blends into that of the soldier leading the group and marking the pace of their march ("HAM! DÉ!", etc. ["ONE! TWO!"])—thereby suggesting a simultaneity of sounds—even though the two differ in the size of the partially merged speech balloons, text orientation and arrangement (the lyrics are canted; the marching count rises and falls on the page), and typography. The marching song introduces a theme that runs through the whole story: the idea that the Algerian War forms the last chapter of France's imperial adventure. Indeed, in comics, French colonialism has often been depicted as a grand adventure for boys and men. However, two speech balloons emanating from the barracks satirically conjure up a contradictory idea, that the imperial adventure is no more than a farce: "A8. A toi, Albert," "Coulé! T'as gagné" ("A8. Your turn, Albert," "Sunk! You won"). One can thereby already trace an evolution on this page, from the romantic idea of mounted cavalry riding on horseback in a French-Algerian equivalent of the American Far West, to the mechanized "Armée blindée cavalerie" ("Armored Army Cavalry") announced by the sign at the base's entrance, to the game of Battleship on paper that Albert, a conscript, and his comrade are playing and which parodies a degraded heroic ideal. At this moment, the end of the war is nigh, and even though French soldiers are still dying, their death has lost its earlier meaning of supreme sacrifice for the fatherland, as proclaimed by the song. The main preoccupation of most French soldiers in the album is to relieve boredom and stick it out until the end of their compulsory service. This page and the following one, where we see it was indeed a game, satirize the French imperial epic narrative (Vidal and Bignon 1982, 3–4; cf. 49, panel 7).

In 1981, the year preceding the album publication of *L'Éducation algérienne*, Algerian cartoonist Mustapha Tenani published *De nos montagnes* (*From*

Our Mountains), the title of which comes from an Algerian patriotic song, "Min Djibelina" ("From Our Mountains"). This album provides an example of the nationalist comics about the Algerian War that Algerian state publishers released during the 1980s (cf. Slim 1968; McKinney 2008; Labter 2009). The song does not appear inside the album, but Henri Alleg cites one of its stanzas at the end of *La Question* (*The Question*), his account of the torture he endured at the hands of French paratroopers in Algeria during the war:

> De nos montagnes
> La voix des hommes libres s'est élevée:
> Elle clame l'indépendance
> De la patrie.
> Je te donne tout ce que j'aime,
> Je te donne ma vie,
> O mon pays . . . O mon pays

> (From our mountains
> Has risen the voice of free men
> It proclaims the independence
> Of the fatherland
> I give you everything I love
> I give you my life
> Oh my country . . . Oh my country) (1986, 111–12)

In *La Question*, jailed Algerian women sing this hymn while three Algerian men are being guillotined by the French. At this moment in the narrative, in contrast to the previous use of the song (paratroopers playing popular songs to cover the cries of the victims), its singing serves to strengthen the will of the condemned men going up the scaffold.[12]

Several songs appearing in comics about the Maghreb are not specifically colonial, but they often serve to reinforce a nostalgic or retro atmosphere. That is the case, for instance, for *O.A.S. Aïscha* (*Secret Army Organization Aïscha*) by Louis Joos and Yann Le Pennetier, where a 1963 song helps anchor the story in the time period and conclude the album (1990, 44). The verbal reaction to the song ("Coupe ça! . . . Y fait chier, Alain Barrière!" ["Turn it off! Alain Barrière pisses me off!"]) and the anticipated gesture (turning off the radio) end the story on an ironic note, because the reader understands the hidden meaning of that song for the main character, a French sailor who slept with a woman *harki*—an Algerian soldier in the French army—and probably fell in love with her. The final frame simultaneously suggests a nostalgia for the colonial past and its rejection. One finds in *Une Éducation algérienne* a similar way of producing and ironically undercutting nostalgia, when another French soldier protests because Albert keeps playing nostalgic songs by Charles Trenet, notably "Que reste-t-il de nos amours?" ("What is left of our loves?") (Vidal and Bignon 1982, 9).

One of the best-known historical examples of a French popular song that served in a colonial context can be found in two comics that commemorate French Algeria and the colonial army in a hagiographic manner: The French soldiers who participated in the failed military putsch of April 1961 in Algeria adopted "Je ne regrette rien" ("I don't regret anything") (Horne 1978, 460, 561), the famous song recorded by Edith Piaf in 1960. The third volume of the series "La Légion" and *Les Rivages amers* depict the Régiment Etranger de Parachutistes (Foreign Paratrooper Regiment) leaving its Zéralda base, before being disbanded for its role in the putsch. Whereas *La Légion: Histoire de la Légion étrangère, 1946-62: Diên Biên Phu* (*The Legion: History of the Foreign Legion, 1946-62: Diên Biên Phu*) (Glogowski and Puisaye 2004, 37; cf. 42) shows the soldiers singing in the departing trucks, the authors of *Rivages amers* (Joyaux-Brédy and Joux 1994, 70) choose instead from the book by the former OAS leader Pierre Sergent (with the same title, *Je ne regrette rien*) the vulgar and defiant image of paratroopers giving a *bras d'honneur* (shooting the finger) to the policemen and the soldiers tasked with guarding them. This hagiographic staging belongs to a sacred history of colonialism, which has its martyrs, its hymns, and its relics.

Folklore and Orientalism in Traditional Dance and Music

For European cartoonists, traditional Maghrebi music almost inevitably evokes the image of a belly dance to the music of folk instruments. Traditional culture and orientalist fantasies are both closely connected in such scenes, which can be found throughout modern comics about North Africa. In the first pages of *Carnets d'Orient* (*Sketchbooks from the Orient*), the inaugural volume of the eponymous series by Jacques Ferrandez (1994) and one of the best-known albums about French Algeria, the reader finds a bordello scene located in Algiers in 1832 (5) that Ferrandez constructed by mixing visual elements drawn from colonial and exotic imagery, but whose script and words were borrowed almost verbatim from the description given by Gustave Flaubert of his meeting with Kuchuk Hanem, an Egyptian prostitute and dancer.[13] In Flaubert's narrative, the woman performs a dance to the tune of two musicians. In *Carnets d'Orient*, the musicians and their grating music serve as a foil to the seductive prostitute, transformed by Ferrandez into an Algerian woman, but Hanem's striptease in Flaubert's account—the bee's dance—is replaced by a sequence of frames that fulfills the same function: The fragmented body of the prostitute is unveiled little by little on the page.

Similar imagery can be found in an album by two Belgian artists, whose story takes place in Morocco a century later: *La Kermesse ensablée* (*The Sanded-Up Fair*), scripted by Jan Bucquoy and drawn by Daniel Hulet (1990), the third volume of the series "Les Chemins de la gloire" ("Pathways to Glory"). These titles are ironic, because the story is about the downfall of a boxer who had to enlist in the Foreign Legion. One sees, back-to-back, a diptych of scenes: In the first, the boxer-legionary sleeps with a Moroccan woman, the inhabitant of a mountain village, who invited him in as thanks for having saved a child who had fallen into a crevice; the second one recounts a confrontation with Moroccan rebels who succeeded in trapping the legionaries in a desert canyon. A night scene shows the Moroccan warriors celebrating with a dancer in front of a bonfire: The woman does a striptease to taunt the legionaries, while the rebels sing and applaud her. Like the bordello sequence in Ferrandez, this passage stages orientalist kitsch, but with a Manichean split between the welcoming and dangerous North African women (Basfao 1990, 226–27). The colonial and sexist ideology of these scenes in Bucquoy and Hulet is not inflected in any way by their anarchist denigration of the French colonial army's hierarchy, nor by a scene in the next album, *La Valse à l'envers* (*The Backward Waltz*), that presents a homoerotic and orientalist version of the Maghrebi dance, this time by a North African man for his legionary lover and the latter's comrade (1990, 38).

The albums by Bucquoy and Hulet, published in the "Vécu" ("Lived") collection by Glénat, as well as Ferrandez's series belong to the genre analyzed by Pierre Fresnault-Deruelle (1979) in his article on the "effet d'histoire" ("history effect") in comics: In such narratives, some historical and cultural references—here including elements meant to represent authentic Maghrebi music, song, and dance during the colonial period—add some local color and thereby help create a reality and history effect in fictional stories. The paradox is that the same mimetic elements contribute strongly to an orientalist and mythologizing version of North African societies, and thereby recall a substantial number of colonial songs, including those featuring colonized women, mostly represented as sex toys of the French (Ruscio 2001, 350–99; Liauzu and Liauzu 2002, 98–111). A well-targeted parody can be found in *L'Empire* (*The Empire*), volume two (2007) of the brilliant "Petite histoire des colonies françaises" ("A Short History of the French Colonies") series scripted by Grégory Jarry and drawn by Otto T. (Thomas Dupuis). The volume's first chapter ends with a satire of Western perspectives on oriental music, song, and dance: The Dey of Algiers sings and does a disco dance with a belly dancer. In that album, the famous fly whisk incident—during which the Dey reportedly hit Pierre Deval, the French consul, and which became in the epic French colonial narrative the event that triggered the capture of Algiers, necessary to restore France's honor—becomes a potpourri of orientalist stereotypes: Behind the Dey, during his confrontation with Deval, are, among others, a man smoking a hookah, a belly dancer, and musicians playing drums, a Middle Eastern lute (*oud*), and a flute. In a later scene, we see a parody of the homoerotic dance of the legionaries that recalls the one in *Valse à l'envers*: In the desert, Abdelkader and his men encounter French soldiers sitting around one of their own, who, veiled, performs a belly dance for them. The ironic contrast between the tongue-in-cheek version of the past given by the narrator (Charles de Gaulle) in the recitative, and the actions of the characters, at times violent or ridiculous, drawn in stick-figure style, satirizes not only French colonial history but also the orientalist fantasies and the realist drawing style of the historical comics just discussed.

These examples suggest that today's adult comics often use North African music and dance as pretexts for colonial eroticism or pornography. Such scenes, however, have some kinship with French and Belgian comics for children that were published before 1962. The latter, even when devoid of any sexual allusions, often represent colonial conquests and colonization in a folksy and depoliticized mode. That is the case, for instance, in *Trésor de la vallée perdue* (*Treasure of the Lost Valley*), an episode of "Yann le Vaillant" ("Yann the Valiant"), scripted by Jacques Conoan and drawn by Noël Gloesner, which was published serially in the Catholic children's magazine *Cœurs vaillants* (*Valiant Hearts*) in 1952–1953 and republished in album form by the Éditions du Triomphe in 2004. Located mostly in the Atlas Mountains, the plot is typically colonialist: A community of Muslim Berbers, whose ancestors were Christian during Roman times, live in a lost city. The city is at war with a rival tribe for the control of water, a vital and rare resource in this semi-desert environment. With the help of modern French military technology, including walkie-talkies and a helicopter, the Catholic protagonists, led by Yann, manage to resolve the dispute by having someone open an old trunk that includes a manuscript left by Christian Berber ancestors. The document contains an evangelical message of fraternal love written in Latin. The last image shows us the two tribes, finally reconciled and having decided to share the water, playing a Berber song to celebrate the event: "les deux tribus, fraternellement réunies, célèbrent l'eau maternelle par un 'haïdous' d'allégresse" ("the two tribes, fraternally reunited, celebrate the maternal water with a joyful 'haidous'") (Conoan and Gloesner 2004, 36). Here, the colonial relationship is sealed by a form of *métissage*, the physical union of colonizer and colonized: In the course of the album, we learn that one of the French boys is in fact the son of a French mother but also a Berber father and that he is therefore a grandson of the Berber sheikh who reigns over the lost city (33).

A chaste yet gendered encounter between the Tuareg and French colonizers is expressed in musical terms in *Charles de Foucauld: Conquérant pacifique du Sahara* (*Charles de Foucauld: Peaceful Conqueror of the Sahara*), a colonialist Catholic hagiography drawn by the Belgian artist Jijé (Joseph Gillain) and serialized in *Spirou* magazine from April 9 to September 10, 1959—that is, in the midst of the Algerian War. (It too was later republished by the Éditions du Triomphe.) Shortly before the martyrdom of the Catholic priest, a Protestant French military doctor arrives at the Hoggar mission in order to vaccinate the Tuareg. Although the Catholic priest does not succeed in convincing Dassine—a majestic poetess and musician who plays the amzad, an indigenous instrument—to accept Western medicine, the doctor, himself an amateur musician, manages to seduce some of the tribe's members, including above all the matriarch, by playing the cello. The next day, Dassine agrees to be vaccinated by the doctor, thereby setting an example for her tribe. Jijé's narrative dissolves the colonial violence of the French occupation of the Algerian hinterland, replacing it with a peaceful and symbolic competition between Tuareg and Western music. The latter wins, allowing Western medicine brought by a Christian representative of the French army to triumph over indigenous Muslim resistance. This is an emblematic version of colonial ideology, of the European self-given, so-called civilizing mission, here portrayed as healing physical ailments of the heathen (cf. Douvry 1983, 31). In contrast, in the more recent "Le Chat du rabbin" ("The Rabbi's Cat") series by Joann Sfar, a French cartoonist who is also a musician, the musical competition theme plays a very different role: that of symbolizing the fundamental kinship between Muslims and Jews in colonial Algeria. When, in *Le Malka des lions* (*Malka of the Lions*) (2003a, 34–39), Rabbi Abraham Sfar leaves Algiers to pay his respects to the grave of his ancestor Messaoud Sfar, he meets his friend the sheikh Mohammed Sfar, an Arab musician who is a distant relative, because the two characters—one a Muslim and the other a Jew—share this common ancestor. Both dance, sing, and play music together, symbolizing a common North African origin and musical tradition.[14]

The representation of traditional North African music in works by French artists of Maghrebi background, such as Sfar, and by North African artists can be markedly different, suggesting, for example, precolonial cultural autonomy and authenticity in the latter, as in *L'Émir Ben Abdelkrim* (*The Emir Ben Abdelkrim*) by Mohammed Nadrani, where a young Berber shepherd playing the flute must flee when his village is attacked during the Rif War, in the 1920s (2008, 16–18). The text of the recitative and the musical notes of the bars winding gracefully across the sky in the first two panels of the page invite contemplation in synchrony with the idyllic pastoral scene (cf. Groensteen 1999, 65–67). This Edenic harmony is brutally destroyed by Spanish military planes that drop bombs on and machine-gun the defenseless Moroccan rural population. The author, who learned to draw while a political prisoner in Morocco (1977–1984), conceptualizes his album like a necessary revision of this episode of national history, which was long hidden by the French colonial power and the Moroccan regime that replaced it: "L'histoire du héros du Rif, dont je suis originaire, a été, pour des raisons politiques, occultée durant presque un siècle" ("The story of the hero of the Rif, where I am from, was for political reasons obscured for almost a century") (Nadrani 2009).

Similarly, in *La Rupture* (*The Breakup*), the second volume of *Les Contes du djinn: Hadj Moussa* (*Tales of the Genie: Hadj Moussa*), Farid Boudjellal and Leïla Leïz feature traditional Algerian music and dance in the narrative in a way that celebrates Algerian cultural authenticity during the colonial period: The ululations of Algerian women accompany traditional music during a wedding celebrated at the outset of the Great War (2008, 28-31) (Fig. 4).

Nejma successively wears six wedding dresses representing Algerian cultural and regional diversity (from Constantine, Chaouïa, Tlemcen, Algiers, Kabylia, Oran) as she dances for Moussa (Fig. 5). Their wedding comes after the breaking of the engagement between Moussa (also called Maurice), a young évolué (assimilated colonial subject), and Catherine, a French woman. The impossibility of the mixed couple, separated by the colonial prejudices of the French family, symbolizes the limits of Algerian assimilation into French colonial society, whereas the music, dance, and dresses at Moussa and Nejma's wedding celebrate Algerian identity instead. The manner in which Boudjellal and Leïz depict traditional music and song seems to be the antithesis of what we saw in the albums of Ferrandez, Bucquoy, and Hulet. *La Rupture* represents the pre-history of another series by Boudjellal, about the life of the Slimani family in France

Figure 4: Traditional music and ululation liven up an Algerian wedding celebrated in Constantine during the Great War. ©Soleil Productions and Farid
Boudjellal. Reproduced with the gracious permission of the author.

from the 1950s to the present. Seen from that perspective, the Hadj
Moussa albums function a little bit, after all, like Ferrandez's "Carnets
d'Orient," in their attempts to recover and preserve cultural relics of colonized Algeria, even though their treatment is significantly different.

Franc'Arab Song: *Métissage*, Cultural Conflict and Song

In *L'Exode* (*The Exodus*) (2003), the third volume of his "Le Chat du rabbin" series, Sfar uses Algerian music to illustrate intercultural mixing, in an
even more complex way than in the musical duo formed by Abraham and
Mohammed Sfar. When Abraham travels for the first time from Algiers to Paris
to meet his daughter's in-laws, we encounter his nephew, Raymond Rebibo,

Figure 5: A genie grants a wish to Moussa, allowing him to compliment
Nejma, his new wife, through thought on the six traditional dresses
that she wears during their wedding. The couple performs a virtual dance to
the sounds of traditional music.
©Soleil Productions and Farid Boudjellal. Reproduced with the gracious
permission of the author.

also known as El Rebibo because of his mastery of *maalouf* music. Together, in the garret shared by Raymond and his French Catholic girlfriend, the uncle and nephew play *maalouf* together. Sfar visually renders the haunting instrumental music as a winding pattern of notes and speed lines against the apartment walls lit by a pale-yellow Parisian sun streaming through the skylight. The notes, in groups of two and three, bent by Sfar's quivering drawing style, almost resemble Hebrew letters, and in one frame seem to emerge from two anthropomorphic kettles that appear to be smiling and are reminiscent of Edmond-François Calvo's comics or of *Fantasia*, the Disney animated cartoon.

To earn a living, Raymond works as a street musician, but in an unusual way, because he dresses as an Arab and sings a burlesque and erotic song for the Parisians waiting in line in front of the famous Théâtre du Grand Guignol (Sfar 2003b, 22–26). The angular contortions of Raymond's body when he dances while twirling the tassel of his red fez echo the macabre images of the posters advertising theater shows. When Abraham asks him "Mais pourquoi tu fais semblant d'être un Arabe?" ("But why do you pretend to be an Arab?"), Raymond explains: "Parce que pour faire le juif, il faut l'accent polonais, et je sais pas le faire. Oui, parce que juif du Maghreb, ça ne les intéresse pas trop, les gens, ça leur complique" ("Because to play the Jew, you need a Polish accent, and I can't do it. Yes, because a Jew from the Maghreb, that doesn't interest people that much, it complicates things for them") (26). The cartoonist thereby satirizes both colonial orientalism and the ignorance of the complexities of Jewish identities among the ethnic majority in mainland France. On the other hand, Sfar relegates another portion of Algerian musical history to a footnote, where he acknowledges having borrowed Raymond's words from a song titled "Arrouah, j't'y cire" ("Arrouah, I polish you up"), sung by Aïssa (25) and released on the compact disc *Algérie: Fantaisistes des années 1930* (*Algeria: Entertainers of the 1930s*).[15] Claude and Josette Liauzu suggest that one should not hasten to relegate songs that "relèvent d'un genre 'franc'arabe' dont la trivialité apparente ne doit pas cacher qu'il exprime les métissages culturels" ("belong to a 'Franc'Arab' genre whose apparent triviality should not conceal the fact that it expresses cultural mixings") to the category of "des chansons prolongeant le comique raciste" ("songs prolonging racist comedy") (2002, 154–55; cf. Bouzar-Kasbadji 1989, 245). However, the separation between such categories is perhaps not absolute, to the extent that different audiences could react differently to the same song. Aïssa's songs gathered in this compilation, and ones collected by Ruscio, mix colonial stereotypes about North African carpet sellers and shoe shiners with suggestive sexual language about French tourism to the Maghreb and Maghrebi migration to France

(Ruscio 2001, 417–18, 421–23).[16] One finds similar imagery on colonial post-cards redrawn by Ferrandez in his albums, sometimes with a critical inflection. Raymond ends up being hired to play the same type of music in a Parisian theater managed by Ventura, a character with a physical resemblance to the actor Lino Ventura (Sfar 2003b, 32–38). Raymond Rebibo, too, was clearly modeled after a famous person: Raymond Leyris, also known as Cheikh Leyris, a renowned master of *maalouf* music who was a Jew from Constantine and the father-in-law of the *Pied-Noir* singer Enrico Macias (né Gaston Ghrenassia). Leyris was assassinated on June 22, 1961, during the Algerian War (Liauzu and Liauzu 2002, 172–74; Stora 2004, 288, 305, 314–16).

About thirty years after the story of *L'Exode*, during the Algerian War, the song "Mustapha" represented Algerian-French *métissage*, according to Liauzu and Liauzu (2002, 154–55; cf. Rioux 1992, 261). Created by Bob Azzam, an Algerian Jew, and by Eddy Barclay, it was a hit in France in 1960. It appears in two of the most interesting comics about the war: *Une Éducation algérienne*, discussed earlier, and *Rue de la bombe* (*Bomb Street*). In the first, the cartoonists juxtapose in a satirical and tragic manner an Algerian's cry, who calls his mother because he is being tortured, with the lyrics of this song, full of sexual allusions ("Tu m'as allumé avec une allumette" ["You lit me up with a match"]) (Vidal and Bignon 1982, 11). Several frames show French conscripts slow dancing to "Mustapha," suggesting that a comment ostensibly referring to torture ("Pierrot les passe à la casserole" ["Pierrot is cooking them up"]) is in fact more ambiguous: It connotes both torture and pleasure (of food and sex), torture as a source of perverse pleasure, and perhaps torture by rape. The artists add another political and historical critique to the homoerotic theme when Albert, the album's antihero, alludes to the decadence of the Roman empire. At this moment, very close to the end of the war, he realizes that the French empire is declining, as did the Roman empire several centuries before. This ironic comparison reminds us that colonial ideology proclaimed the French to be the heirs of Roman imperialism in North Africa, as we saw in filigree in *Le Trésor de la vallée perdue*. The national and political crisis thereby created by the fall of French Algeria (after the French loss of Indochina) provoked a crisis of heterosexual masculinity, embodied by the French colonial soldier, who was for a long time a revered figure in comics and sometimes still is today, as in the series about "La Légion." *Une Éducation algérienne* clearly plays on the rupture that decolonization has produced in this traditionally heroic role.

In *Rue de la bombe*, published more than twenty years later, Ferrandez inserts a different verse from "Mustapha" in a scene located in the Algiers casbah, after the French army has broken the general strike during the battle of

Algiers in 1957.[17] Here, the lyrics' lightness ("Chéri je t'aime, chéri je t'adore" ["Darling I love you, darling I adore you"]) stands in ironic contrast with the violence of a "bleu de chauffe" ("blue boilersuit"), that is, an Algerian agent working for the secret services of the French army (Ferrandez 2004, 32). The fear expressed by the Algerian civilians in this scene suggests how much the war has made Algerian-French *métissage* unimaginable, a mixing that Liauzu and Liauzu see as the topic of, and condition of possibility for, "Mustapha" and other "franc'arabe" songs of popular music. The fact that these two comics only cite the French lyrics of the song, and not the Arabic ones, is interesting and probably reveals the limits of cultural mixing.

Conclusion: Postcolonial Maghrebi-French *Métissage* in Comics

One finds new perspectives in the work of Slim, the Algerian cartoonist, and of Boudjellal and Larbi Mechkour, two French artists of Algerian heritage, even when looking back at the colonial past. Slim, famous for the multilingual humor of his comics, uses French songs with (post)colonial connotations in "Le Coup de l'éventail" ("The fly whisk blow"), an unpublished album that recounts the capture of Algiers in a parodic and anachronistic mode. The Janissaries sing "Tiens, voilà du merguèze, voilà du merguèze" ("Here is some merguez, here is some merguez"), a play on the famous Legion's song, "Tiens voilà du boudin" ("Here is some blood sausage"), because they form "une sorte de Légion étrangère composée essentiellement de chrétiens convertis à l'islam depuis leur jeune âge" ("A kind of Foreign Legion comprised mostly of Christians converted to Islam at a young age") (ca. 2006, 2) (Fig. 6).

Figure 6: A parody of the Foreign Legion's song, sung by the Janissaries of the Dey of Algiers at the time of the capture of Algiers. ©Slim. Reproduced with the gracious permission of the author.

Figure 7: The anachronistic reprise of a *Pied-Noir* song:
During his departure into exile, after the capture of Algiers by the French, the
Dey of Algiers sings an Enrico Macias song.
©Slim. Reproduced with the gracious permission of the author.

Twice, Slim transforms songs of Enrico Macias: During the French preparations for the Algiers expedition in 1830, the carefree Algiers inhabitants sing, "Ah qu'elles sont jolies les filles de mon pays! Lay, lay, lay" ("Ah, they are so pretty, the girls of my country") (ca. 2006, 36); and when the Dey goes into exile, he sings, "J'ai quitté mon pays" ("I left my country") (41). This gesture could be interpreted as repatriating these songs of exile (Fig. 7).

In *Les Beurs* (*The Arabs*) by Mechkour and Boudjellal, the artists celebrate Maghrebi-French music and explore the possibilities and limits of cultural mixing in 1980s France. For example, fictitious musical groups—Jambon-Beur (Ham-Arab/Butter, prefiguring the title of a later album by Boudjellal) and "Cap'tain Mohamed et ses Mohamedettes" ("Cap'tain Mohamed and his Mohamedettes")—give a free concert. The artists gleefully mix rockabilly (which has become "Rock-Kabylie" ["Rock-Kabylia"]), back in fashion around this time thanks to the Stray Cats and other groups, with references to French pop and its African American origins (Claude François and the Clodettes; Ray Charles and the Raelettes, etc.). The lyrics celebrate

**Figure 8: Maghrebi-French musical mixing enters comics:
Rockabilly is transformed into "Rock-Kabylie" (Kabylia rock)
by young Maghrebi-French characters.
©Éditions Tartamudo. Reproduced with the gracious permission
of the authors and Éditions Tartamudo.**

the hedonistic consumption of drugs to overcome psychic discomfort, while subverting racist terminology with colonial origins: "Si t'as les boules, petit bougnoule, bourre ton sandouiche plein de haschich . . . Bourre ta chéchia plein de chicha . . . " ("If you are down, little Arab, stuff your sandwich full of hashish. . .Stuff your chechia full of shisha") (1985, n.p.) (Fig. 8).

But the concert, which ends in a fight between fascistic skinheads and Maghrebi-French young people (Fig. 9), does not make the latter want to go back the next day to the Couscous-Cassoulet concert in Belleville; they prefer the isolation of the Maghrebi café, with its games of dominoes. Elsewhere, the cartoonists allude to real Maghrebi-French artists of the time—including Karim Kacel and his hit "Banlieue" ("Suburb"), Rockin' Babouches, and Carte de Séjour (Residency Permit) with its song "Rhorhomanie" ("Arabmania," the lyrics of which, in Arabic and French, celebrate diverse cultural influences, from Oum Kelthoum to Jimmy Cliff, and from James Brown to Jimmy Hendrix)—and to the anti-racist initiative, Rock against Police.[18] Joyful ululations, as well as some songs they cite, give rhythm to this album. The book reminds us that it is no coincidence if the return to the colonial period in French-language European comics in the 1980s coincided with the cultural effervescence of the Beur movement.

Figure 9: Cap'tain Mohamed and his Mohamedettes start singing during a fight
between some Maghrebi-French and skinheads. Everything is finally interrupted by the collapse of the nearby squat. ©Éditions Tartamudo. Reproduced
with the gracious permission of the authors and Éditions Tartamudo.

Endnotes

1. All translations are mine.

2. Kunzle 1990; and McKinney 2001, 2011, and 2013. Heartfelt thanks to the comics' authors and publishers for their generous authorization to reproduce the illustrations in this chapter. I read an early version of this essay at the International *Bande
Dessinée* Society conference at Manchester Metropolitan University in July 2005. A
French version of my essay was published in *Etudes francophones* 24, no. 1-2 (2009):
70–95.

3. I am grateful to Pascal Lefèvre for the reference to Pomier.

4. Ruscio 2001, 8, 353–54, 357–59; cf. Bacri 1983, 127; Bouzard 2000, 394–95; and Michallat 2007, 317. Michel Simon, playing the role of père Jules, memorably sings part of its refrain for Dita Parlo in the role of Juliette in Jean Vigo's 1934 film *L'Atalante*.

5. I had to set aside many examples in other comics, for lack of space.

6. I give the handwritten page numbering by the artist when it exists; otherwise, I use the printed one, by the publisher.

7. Even though this song does not appear in the school curriculum anymore, one can see a lesson on the topic, from a 1955 textbook, on the website of the Ligue des Droits de l'Homme de Toulon (Toulon's Human Rights League), https://section-ldh-toulon.net/.

8. Bouzard (2000, 376) tells the legendary story behind the song, anchored in Bugeaud's fight against Abdelkader.

9. Several of these songs are reproduced in Bouzard 2000.

10. Cf. Bouzard 2000, 193–94 and http://www.rcp1.terre.defense.gouv.fr/index.php?css=wai.css&centre=coeur_regiment/organisation/2cie.html (accessed November 8, 2009).

11. Cf. "Les Commandos" ("The Commandos"), song of the "11th shock" unit of Paul Aussaresses, who defended his use of terror during the Algerian War, that starts with "Les commandos partent pour l'aventure" ("The commandos leave for adventure") (Bouzard 2000, 187–88).

12. Kateb Yacine cites it in a passage of *Nedjma* (1989, 227) that recounts the 1945 uprising and repression in Sétif (and Guelma). On the importance of the scout movement and of this song in the Algerian national movement, cf. Nadya Bouzar-Kasbadji 1989, 249.

13. Flaubert 1991, 281–88, cf. 70–77, 362–63, 366; 1996, 113–19; cf. Said 1994a, 6, 186–87, 207–8; McKinney 2001, 45–47; and McKinney 2013, 75.

14. Abraham and Mohammed meet again and play music together again in Sfar's fifth volume (*Jérusalem d'Afrique*).

15. The liner notes of this record say little about the artist: "Aïssa, autre comique de renom, figure également dans cette anthologie. Son style est plus populaire—voire plus facile—que les précédents. On peut même parler d'humour gras. Les titres parlent d'eux-mêmes: 'Qui veut des tapis,' ou encore 'Arrouah j't'y cire.'" ("Aissa, another renowned comic, is also featured in this anthology. His style is more popular—and more facile—than the preceding ones. One may even speak of crude humor. The titles speak for themselves: 'Who wants carpets' or 'Arrouah I shine you up').

16. About this milieu in Paris during the 1930s, see Blanchard, et al., 2000 (especially 104–5); and on Algerian music in Algeria during the same period, see Bouzar-Kasbadji 1988. I found no mention of Aïssa in these two works.

17. The use of the song therefore seems anachronistic.

18. The references to: Rockin Babouches are in "Beur Blanc Rouge" (1.1) and "Cap'tain Samir" (3.1, 4); Karim Kacel in "La Djinna" (2.7) and "Cap'tain Samir" (3.3); Rock Against Police in "Cap'tain Samir" (3.1); and "Rhorhomanie" in "Love Story Beur" (1.10). "Rhorhomanie" is included on the album *Ramsa* (a rerelease for the export market), with Piranha (PIR 6). On this musical milieu, see Moreira 1987, who explains that "rhorho" is "beur à Lyon; dérivé de rhouya, mon frère en arabe" ("*beur* in Lyon; derived from rhouya, my brother in Arabic") (15). A slightly revised version of the album *Les Beurs* is found in Mechkour and Boudjellal (*Black Blanc Beur*).

Works Cited

Comics:

Boudjellal, Farid (script), and Leïla Leïz (art). 2008. *Les Contes du djinn: Hadj Moussa*. Vol. 2: *La rupture*. Toulon, France: Soleil.

Bucquoy, Jan (script), and Daniel Hulet (art). 1990. *Les Chemins de la gloire*. Vol. 3: *La Kermesse ensablée*. Grenoble, France: Glénat.

Conoan, Jacques (script), and Noël Gloesner (art). 2004. *Le Trésor de la vallée perdue*. Paris: Éditions du Triomphe.

Ferrandez, Jacques. 1994. *Carnets d'Orient*. Vol. 1. Tournai, Belgium: Casterman. (Later published under the title *Djemilah*.)

———. 2004. *Carnets d'Orient*. Vol. 7: *Rue de la bombe*. Pref. Bruno Etienne. Tournai, Belgium: Casterman.

Glogowski, Philippe (art), and Marien Puisaye [Guy Lehideux] (script). 2002. *La Légion: Histoire de la Légion étrangère, 1831–1918*. Vol. 1: *Camerone*. Pref. Yann Péron. Paris: Éditions du Triomphe.

———. 2003. *La Légion: Histoire de la Légion étrangère, 1919–45*. Vol. 2: *Bir-Hakeim*. Pref. Pierre Messmer. Paris: Éditions du Triomphe.

———. 2004. *La Légion: Histoire de la Légion étrangère, 1946–62*. Vol. 3: *Diên Biên Phu*. Pref. Hélie de Saint-Marc. Paris: Éditions du Triomphe.

———. 2005. *La Légion: Histoire de la Légion étrangère, 1963 à demain*. Vol. 4: *Kolwezi*. Pref. Bruno Dary. Paris: Éditions du Triomphe.

Hulet, Daniel. 1994. *Les Chemins de la gloire*. Vol. 4: *La Valse à l'envers*. Grenoble, France: Glénat.

Jarry, Grégory (script), and Otto T. [Thomas Dupuis] (art). 2007. *Petite histoire des colonies françaises*. Vol. 2: *L'Empire*. Colors Guillaume Heurtault and Thomas Tudoux. Poitiers, France: FLBLB.

JIJÉ [Joseph Gillain]. 1994. "Charles de Foucauld: Conquérant pacifique du Sahara." In *Tout Jijé, 1958–1959,* 101–44. Paris: Dupuis.

JOOS, Louis, and Yann [LE PENNETIER]. 1990. *O.A.S. Aïscha.* Grenoble, France: Glénat.

JOYAUX-BRÉDY, Evelyne (script), and Pierre JOUX (art). *Les Rivages amers: L'Algérie, 1920–1962.* 1994. Aix-en-Provence, France: Cercle Algérianiste d'Aix-en-Provence.

———. 1998. *C'est nous les Africains . . . : L'Algérie de 1880 à 1920.* Aix-en-Provence, France: Cercle Algérianiste d'Aix-en-Provence.

MECHKOUR, Larbi (art), and Farid BOUDJELLAL (script). 1985. *Les Beurs.* Paris: Albin Michel.

———. 2004. *Black Blanc Beur: Les folles années de l'intégration.* Song lyrics André Igwal. Pref. Martine Lagardette. Cachan, France: Institut du Monde Arabe, Éditions Tartamudo.

MÉREZETTE, Denis, and DUMENIL. 1985. *Algérie française!* Brussels: Michel Deligne.

MORA, Victor (script), and Annie GOETZINGER (art). 1986. *Félina: L'ogre du djebel.* Paris: Dargaud.

NADRANI, Mohammed. 2008. *L'Émir: Ben Abdelkrim.* Casablanca: Alayam.

SFAR, Joann. 2003a. *Le Chat du rabbin.* Vol. 2: *Le Malka des lions.* Pref. Fellag. Colors Brigitte Findakly. Paris: Dargaud.

———. 2003b. *Le Chat du rabbin.* Vol. 3: *L'Exode.* Pref. Georges Moustaki. Colors Brigitte Findakly. Paris: Dargaud.

———. 2006. *Le Chat du rabbin.* Vol. 5: *Jérusalem d'Afrique.* Pref. Philippe Val. Colors Brigitte Findakly. Paris: Dargaud.

SLIM [Menouar Merabtène]. 1968. *Moustache et les Belgacem.* Algérie Actualité.

———. 1995. *Le Monde merveilleux des barbus.* Soleil.

———. ca. 2006. *Le Coup de l'éventail.* Unpublished manuscript. Courtesy of Slim.

TENANI, Mustapha. 1981. *De nos montagnes.* Alger: SNED.

VIDAL, Guy (script), and Alain BIGNON (art). 1982. *Une Éducation algérienne.* Colors Anne Delobel. Paris: Dargaud.

Other Sources:

ALLEG, Henri. 1986. *La Question.* Paris: Éditions de Minuit.

BACRI, Roland. 1983. *Trésor des racines pataouètes.* Illus. Charles Brouty. Paris: Belin.

BASFAO, Kacem. 1990. "Arrêt sur images: Les rapports franco-maghrébins au miroir de la bande dessinée." *Annuaire de l'Afrique du Nord* 29: 225–35.

BLANCHARD, Pascal, Eric DEROO, Driss EL YAZAMI, Pierre FOURNIÉ, and Gilles MANCERON. 2003. *Le Paris arabe: Deux siècles de présence des orientaux et des Maghrébins*. Paris: La Découverte.

BOUZAR-KASBADJI, Nadya. 1988. *L'Émergence artistique algérienne au XXᵉ siècle: Reflet de la presse coloniale et indigène, 1920–56*. Ben Aknoun, Alger: Office des publications universitaires; ENAL.

———. 1989. "La Marseillaise et ses dissonances en Algérie coloniale." *Revue du monde musulman et de la Méditerranée* 52 (1): 241–50. Accessed September 4, 2020. www.persee.fr/doc/ remmm_0997-1327_1989_num_52_1_2304?q=Bouzar-Kasbadji.

BOUZARD, Thierry. 2000. *Anthologie du chant militaire français*. Pref. Patrick-Marie Aubert. Paris: Grancher.

CERTEAU, Michel de. 1994. *La Prise de parole et autres écrits politiques*. Edited by Luce Giard. Paris: Seuil.

DOUVRY, Jean-François. 1983. "La Bande dessinée et la guerre d'Algérie." *Bulles-Dingues: Spécial nostalgie* no. 2 (October): 31–36.

FLAUBERT, Gustave. 1991. *Voyage en Egypte*. Edited by Pierre-Marc de Biasi. Paris: Bernard Grasset.

———. 1996. *Flaubert in Egypt: A Sensibility on Tour*. Translated and edited by Francis Steegmuller. New York: Penguin Books.

FRESNAULT-DERUELLE, Pierre. 1979. "L'Effet d'histoire." In *Histoire et bande dessinée: Actes du deuxième Colloque international éducation et bande dessinée, La Roque d'Antheron, 16–17 février 1979*, edited by Jean-Claude Faur, 98–104. La Roque, France: Objectif Promo-Durance; Colloque international Education et Bande dessinée.

GROENSTEEN, Thierry. 1999. *Système de la bande dessinée*. Paris: Presses Universitaires de France.

HORNE, Alistair. 1978. *A Savage War of Peace: Algeria 1954–1962*. New York: Viking Press.

KATEB, Yacine. 1989. *Nedjma*. Paris: Seuil.

KUNZLE, David. 1990. *The History of the Comic Strip: The Nineteenth Century*. Berkeley: University of California Press.

LABTER, Lazhari. 2009. *Panorama de la bande dessinée algérienne 1969–2009*. Alger: Lazhari Labter éditions.

LIAUZU, Claude, and Josette LIAUZU. 2002. *Quand on chantait les colonies: Colonisation et culture populaire de 1830 à nos jours*. Paris: Syllepse.

McKINNEY, Mark. 2001. "'Tout cela, je ne voulais pas le laisser perdre': colonial *lieux de mémoire* in the comic books of Jacques Ferrandez." *Modern and Contemporary France* 9 (1): 43–53.

————. 2008. "The Frontier and the Affrontier: French-Language Algerian Comics and Cartoons Confront the Nation." Translated by Ann Miller. *European Comic Art* 1 (2): 175–99.

————. 2011. *The Colonial Heritage of French Comics*. Liverpool: Liverpool University Press.

————. 2013. *Redrawing French Empire in Comics*. Columbus: The Ohio State University Press.

MICHALLAT, Wendy. 2007. "Modern Life is Still Rubbish: Houellebecq and the Refiguring of 'Reactionary' Retro." *Journal of European Studies* 37 (3): 313–31.

MILLER, Ann. 2007. *Reading* Bande Dessinée: *Critical Approaches to French-Language Comic Strip*. Bristol: Intellect.

MOREIRA, Paul. 1987. *Rock métis en France*. Paris: Souffles.

NADRANI, Mohammed. 2009. "Mohammed Nadrani, le dessin ou la folie . . . " Interview with Christophe Cassiau-Haurie. *Africultures*. January 2009. Accessed September 4, 2020. africultures.com/mohammed-nadrani-le-dessin-ou-la-folie-10218/.

PEETERS, Benoît. *Lire la bande dessinée*. Paris: Casterman, 1998. (2ⁿᵈ ed.)

POMIER, Frédéric. 1988. "Chronique d'un curieux mariage: Chanson et bande dessinée." *Les Cahiers de la bande dessinée* 83: 58–64.

PORTERFIELD, Todd. 1998. *The Allure of Empire: Art in the Service of French Imperialism, 1798–1836*. Princeton, NJ: Princeton University Press.

RIOUX, Lucien. 1992. "De 'Bambino' à 'Mustapha': Le fonds sonore de la guerre." In *La France en guerre d'Algérie: Novembre 1954–juillet 1962*, edited by Laurent Gervereau, Jean-Pierre Rioux, and Benjamin Stora, 256–61. Paris: Bibliothèque de documentation internationale contemporaine (BDIC).

RUSCIO, Alain. 2001. *Que la France était belle au temps des colonies . . . : Anthologie de chansons coloniales et exotiques françaises*. Paris: Maisonneuve & Larose.

SAID, Edward. 1994a [1978]. *Orientalism*. New York: Vintage Books.

————. 1994b. *Culture and Imperialism*. New York: Vintage Books.

STORA, Benjamin. 2004. "L'impossible neutralité des Juifs d'Algérie." In *La guerre d'Algérie 1954–2004, la fin de l'amnésie*, edited by Mohammed Harbi et Benjamin Stora, 87–316. Paris: Robert Laffont.

List of Figures

Chapter Five:

Figure 1: Michelangelo Antonioni, *L'amorosa menzogna* (1949) (screenshot of a publicity poster of the eponym photonovel starring Anna Vita and Sergio Raimondi, 2'31). Jan Baetens's private collection.

Figure 2: *Sogno* no. 9 (1947), the actor Sergio Raimondi as he appeared in "L'amorosa menzogna." Jan Baetens's private collection.

Figure 3: Front cover of *Regards* no. 352 (1952), special issue "Les Secrets de la presse du cœur" ("The Secrets of the Romance Magazines"). Jan Baetens's private collection.

Figure 4: Back cover of *Regards* no. 352 (1952), with a pell-mell of the most important "bad" women's magazines of the era. (One easily recognizes: *Rêves, Intimité, Madrigal, Confidences, Eve, Festival, Nous Deux, Boléro,* and *A tout coeur*). Jan Baetens's private collection.

Figure 5: "Catene" in *Bolero* no. 1 (1947). Jan Baetens's private collection.

Figure 6: "Âmes ensorcelées" ("Souls under Spell") in *Nous Deux* no. 1 (1947), which was actually a translation/adaptation of *Anime Incatenate*, a drawn novel published in the first issue of the Italian sister magazine *Grand Hôtel* in 1946. Jan Baetens's private collection.

Figure 7: "A l'aube de l'amour" ("The Dawn of Love"): Appearance of the first photonovel in *Nous Deux* no. 165 (1950). Jan Baetens's private collection.

Figure 8: The drawn novel installment on the opposite page. Jan Baetens's private collection.

Figure 9: Last page of the first photonovel installment, back cover of issue no. 165 of *Nous Deux* (1950). Jan Baetens's private collection.

Figure 10: Front cover of *Nous Deux* no. 166 (1950). Jan Baetens's private collection.

Figure 11: "Les Sept Gouttes d'or" ("The Seven Golden Drops") in *Nous Deux* no. 8 (1947). Jan Baetens's private collection.

Figure 12: Back cover, *Nous Deux* no. 8 (1947). Jan Baetens's private collection.

Figure 13: Advertisement for Axelle lipstick, *Nous Deux* no. 26 (1947). Jan Baetens's private collection.

Figure 14: "Anges dans la tourmente" ("Angels in Torment") (fragment of a panel) *Nous Deux* no. 26 (1947). Jan Baetens's private collection.

Figure 15: Publicity page in *Nous Deux* no. 25 (1947). Jan Baetens's private collection.

Figure 16: "45 years old: don't give up, enjoy life"; advertisement for beauty products for women, *Modes de Paris* no. 73 (1948). Jan Baetens's private collection.

Figure 17: Shampoo, haircut, eye lash, lipstick, etc., all in one image. Back cover of *Nous Deux* no. 13 (1947). Jan Baetens's private collection.

Figure 18: "Aux portes du ciel" ("At Heaven's Gate"), *Festival* no. 5 (1949). Jan Baetens's private collection.

Figure 19: Front cover of *Ève* no. 144 (1949). Jan Baetens's private collection.

Figure 20: "Ève vous guide et vous conseille" ("Eve guides and advises you"). Header of the letters to the editor section of *Ève* no. 144 (1949). Jan Baetens's private collection.

Collection. Cambridge, MA: H.C. Fung Library, Harvard University. Detail. Image reproduced with kind permission of Fotini Christia.

Figure 8: Mural of Imam Husayn and an anonymous war martyr, on Modarres Highway at the Resalat Street exit, Tehran. Photograph by Christiane Gruber. Image reproduced with kind permission of Christiane Gruber.

Figure 9: Michelangelo, *La Pietà*, 1499. St. Peter's Basilica, the Vatican. Photo by Stanislav Traykov, March 6, 2008. Reprinted under Fair Use.

Figure 10: 4.4 "Le Concours." *©Marjane Satrapi & L'Association, 2007.* Reprinted with kind permission of the publisher.

Figure 11: Reza Deghati, "Neda Masks," Paris, 25 July 2009. Idea and photograph: REZA/Webistan. Image reproduced with kind permission of Reza Deghati.

Figure 12: Payman and Sina, *Persepolis 2.0*, 27 June 2009, 10. Reprinted by Fair Use.

Chapter Nine:

Figure 1: Goblet, *Faire semblant c'est mentir*: Cécile explodes and accuses Nikita of lying. *©Dominique Goblet & L'Association, 2007.* Reprinted by kind permission of the author and publisher.

Figure 2: Marco's reflections on the redemptive power of poetry. *Le Combat ordinaire 4—Planter des clous* (30). *©DARGAUD 2008, by Larcenet (www.dargaud.com).* Reprinted by kind permission of the publisher.

Figure 3: Peter Blake, *Children Reading Comics* (1954). From the collection of Tullie House Museum, Carlisle, UK. *©SABAM Belgium 2019.* Reprinted with permission.

Chapter Ten:

Figure 1: Dominique Théate, untitled (2017), pencil on paper, 50 cm x 65 cm. Coll. La "S" Grand Atelier. Reprinted with kind permission of the publisher.

Figure 2 (a & b): Charlotte Salomon, *Leben? Oder Theater?* p. 19 (1940–1942), gouache on paper (including texts painted on tracing paper), 32.5 × 25 cm. Collection Jewish Historical Museum, Amsterdam *©Charlotte Salomon Foundation.* Reprinted with kind permission.

Figure 3: Wouter Coumou, untitled (c. 2000), felt pen on paper, 21 cm x 29.6 cm. Coll. Trink Hall Museum, Liège. Reprinted with kind permission of the Trink Hall Museum.

Figure 4: Katsutoshi Kuroda, untitled (2019), felt pen on paper, 30 cm x 40 cm. Coll. *Nishiawaji Kibou-no-*ye, Osaka. Reprinted with kind permission of the author.

Figure 5: Pakito Bolino, *Spermanga, ©L'Association, 2009.* Reprinted with kind permission of the publisher.

Figure 6: Jean-Christophe Menu, *Le Mickey maudit* (1987), reprinted in *Gnognottes, ©L'Association, 1999.* Reprinted with kind permission of the publisher.

Figure 7: Jean-Christophe Menu, *Le Mickey maudit* (1987), reprinted in *Gnognottes, ©L'Association, 1999.* Reprinted with kind permission of the publisher.

Figure 8: Olivier Josso Hamel, *Au Travail 1, ©L'Association, 2012.* Reprinted with kind permission of the publisher.

Figures 9 & 10: Nikita Fossoul and Dominique Goblet, *Chronographie,* ©*L'Association, 2010.* Reprinted with kind permission of the publisher.

Chapter Eleven:
Figure 1: The Brussels mural reproducing an iconic scene from *L'Affaire Tournesol.* Photo courtesy of Benoît Majerus.

Chapter Twelve:
Figure 1: Transition screen in *Salammbô.*
Figure 2: Menus in *XIII.*
Figure 3: Menu in *Persona 5* featuring decorative halftone patterns.

Chapter Thirteen:
Figure 1: A drawing by Jacques Tardi alludes to the violence of French colonialism and the French songs that celebrated it. ©*Syllepse.*
Figure 2: The image illustrating the sheet music for the colonial song "La mouker" stages a widespread colonial fantasy: the cuckolding of the Maghrebi by the French. ©*Maisonneuve & Larose.*
Figure 3: An *image d'Epinal* (Epinal image) celebrates the French conquest of Algeria through the military song "La Casquette du père Bugeaud" ("Father Bugeaud's Cap"). (Mark McKinney's personal collection.)
Figure 4: Traditional music and ululation liven up an Algerian wedding celebrated in Constantine during the Great War. ©*Soleil Productions and Farid Boudjellal.* Reproduced with the gracious permission of the author.
Figure 5: A genie grants a wish to Moussa, allowing him to compliment Nejma, his new wife, through thought on the six traditional dresses that she wears during their wedding. The couple performs a virtual dance to the sounds of traditional music. ©*Soleil Productions and Farid Boudjellal.* Reproduced with the gracious permission of the author.
Figure 6: A parody of the Foreign Legion's song, sung by the Janissaries of the Dey of Algiers at the time of the capture of Algiers. ©*Slim.* Reproduced with the gracious permission of the author.
Figure 7: The anachronistic reprise of a *Pied-Noir* song: During his departure into exile, after the capture of Algiers by the French, the Dey of Algiers sings an Enrico Macias song. ©*Slim.* Reproduced with the gracious permission of the author.
Figure 8: Franco-Maghrebi musical mixing enters comics: Rockabilly is transformed into "Rock-Kabylie" (Kabylia rock) by young Franco-Maghrebi characters. ©*Éditions Tartamudo.* Reproduced with the gracious permission of the authors and Éditions Tartamudo.
Figure 9: Cap'tain Mohamed and his Mohamedettes start singing during a fight between some Maghrebi-French and skinheads. Everything is finally interrupted by the collapse of the nearby squat. ©*Éditions Tartamudo.* Reproduced with the gracious permission of the authors and Éditions Tartamudo.

Contributors

MAAHEEN AHMED is an associate professor of comparative literature at Ghent University (Belgium). She is also the principal investigator of a European Research Council-funded project on children in comics. She has published on superheroes, autobiographical comics, the representation of war in comics and, more recently, children in comics. Her recent book publications include: *Openness of Comics: Generating Meaning within Flexible Structures* (University Press of Mississippi, 2016), *Comics Memory: Archives and Styles* (coedited with Benoît Crucifix, Palgrave, 2018), and *Monstrous Imaginaries: The Legacy of Romanticism in Comics* (University Press of Mississippi, 2019).

RENÉE ALTERGOTT is a PhD candidate in French and francophone literature at Princeton University. Her work focuses on sound studies, archives, and the history of sound recording in France and the former French Colonial Empire. Recent and forthcoming publications include articles on the tape recorder in Patrick Chamoiseau's early novels (*Women in French Studies,* Fall 2019) and on French representations of Charles Cros as the "true" inventor of the phonograph across media (*French Forum*).

LIVIO BELLOÏ is a research associate at the Belgian National Fund for Scientific Research (FNRS) and an associate professor in the Media, Culture and Communication Department of the University of Liège. His research focuses on early cinema, experimental cinema, contemporary comics, and text-image relationships. His book publications include: *Le Regard retourné. Aspects du cinéma des premiers temps* (Nota Bene/Méridiens-Klincksieck, 2001), *Film ist. La pensée visuelle selon Gustav Deutsch* (L'Âge d'Homme, 2013), *La Mécanique du détail. Approches transversales* (ENS Éditions, 2014, co-edited with Maud Hagelstein), *Boucle et répétition. Musique, littérature arts visuels* (Presses de l'Université de Liège, 2015, coedited with Michel Delville, Christophe Levaux, and Christophe Pirenne), *Pierre La Police. Une esthétique de la malfaçon* (coauthored with Fabrice Leroy, Serious Publishing, 2019), and *L'Image pour enjeu: Essais sur le cinéma expérimental contemporain* (Éditions Mimésis, 2021).

MICHELLE BUMATAY is an assistant professor of French at Florida State University specializing in African francophone and diasporic cultural production (literature, comics, film, art). Her research focuses primarily on *bandes dessinées* as a fraught yet crucial site of meaning-making in the

297

francophone world, and also investigates comics as journalism and documentary. She is the 2015 recipient of the Annual Lawrence R. Schehr Memorial Award. She has published articles on comics in journals such as *Contemporary French Civilization, European Comic Art, Research in African Literatures*, and *Alternative Francophone*. She has contributed chapters on migration to *Postcolonial Comics: Texts, Events, Identities* (eds. Pia Mukherji and Binita Mehta, Routledge, 2020) and *Immigrants and Comics: Graphic Spaces of Remembrance, Transaction, and Mimesis* (ed. Nhora Serrano, Routledge, 2021).

ERWIN DEJASSE is an art historian, teacher, and exhibition curator. In 2008, he cofounded ACME Comics Research Group. As a FNRS (Belgian National Fund for Scientific Research) post-doctoral researcher at the Université libre de Bruxelles (ULB), he is managing a program entitled *Art brut, Outsider Art and Alternative Comics: Influences and Artistic Dialogues between Two Cultural Fields in Dissent*. His other research projects deal with, among others, Argentinian comics, works published in the *Spirou* magazine, and alternative comics. His book *La Musique silencieuse de Muñoz et Sampayo* is soon to be published by Presses Universitaires François-Rabelais.

MAXENCE LECONTE is visiting assistant professor of French at Trinity University. His research examines the cultural discourses created by modernity and corporeality between the *Belle Époque* and the *Années Folles* in France. His work has been published in peer-reviewed journals such as *Roman 20-50, Etudes Francophones*, and *Sport in Society*. His latest article to date, "Philippe Aronson, Un trou dans le ciel (2016) ou la dualité réconciliée du boxeur de couleur noire" is published in a special issue of the comparative journal *Lendemains* (Tübingen: Narr Verlag).

MARK MCKINNEY is a professor of French at Miami University (Oxford, Ohio, USA). With Alec G. Hargreaves, he edited *Post-Colonial Cultures in France* (Routledge, 1997). He also edited *History and Politics in French-Language Comics and Graphic Novels* (University Press of Mississippi, 2008). He authored *The Colonial Heritage of French Comics* (Liverpool University Press, 2011), *Redrawing French Empire in Comics* (The Ohio State University Press, 2013), and *Postcolonialism and Migration in French Comics* (Leuven University Press, 2021). With Laurence Grove and Ann Miller, he cofounded the refereed journal *European Comic Art* and edited it with them for nine years (2008–2016). He has published numerous articles on postcolonialism in comics and prose fiction.

ANA OANCEA is an assistant professor of French at the University of Delaware. Her teaching and research interests include the literature and culture of the French nineteenth century, with a particular focus on early science fiction, naturalism, and decadence. Her work analyzes the reinterpretation and reuse of nineteenth-century sources in modern and contemporary works, with recent publications discussing the adaptation of French literary sources into other media (film, comic books, and video games) and their transposition in other cultures.

TAMARA TASEVSKA is a PhD candidate in French and francophone studies at Northwestern University, where she also serves as a Mellon fellow with the critical theory studies program. Her dissertation, "The Color-Image: Chromaticism and the Multiplicity of Worlds in Jean-Luc Godard and Claire Denis," examines the formal experimentations with color and chromatics in post-WWII French cinema, and the way in which these experimentations elaborate an aesthetic politics that resists dominant cultural forms.

FREDERIK TRUYEN is a professor at the Faculty of Arts, KU Leuven. He publishes on digitalization, photographic heritage, and e-learning. He is the head of CS Digital at KU Leuven, a unit that focuses on digitized cultural heritage and digital culture. He is experienced in data modeling and metadata development for image databases in the cultural-historical field. He is the president of Photoconsortium, an international membership organization for photographic archives. Truyen is treasurer of the Europeana Network Association and a member of DARIAH-VL.

CHARLOTTE WERBE is presently director of admissions at Polygence, an EdTech startup. She was assistant professor of French at Gettysburg from 2018–2020, after having received her PhD from Princeton University in 2018. Her research in testimony and visual media has appeared in numerous peer-reviewed publications, including *French Forum, The Journal of Holocaust Research,* and *Études Francophones.*